The Authorised Version of the English Bible, 1611 Volume

CAMBRIDGE ENGLISH CLASSICS

THE ENGLISH BIBLE

In five volumes

VOLUME IV

APOCRYPHA

CAMBRIDGE UNIVERSITY PRESS WAREHOUSE,
C. F. CLAY, MANAGER.
London: FETTER LANE, E.C.
Edinburgh: 100, PRINCES STREET.

Berlin: A. ASHER AND CO.
Leipzig: F. A. BROCKHAUS.
New York: G. P. PUTNAM'S SONS.
Bombay and Calcutta: MACMILLAN AND CO., LTD.

THE AUTHORISED VERSION OF THE ENGLISH BIBLE 1611

EDITED BY

WILLIAM ALDIS WRIGHT, M.A.

VICE-MASTER OF TRINITY COLLEGE, CAMBRIDGE

VOLUME IV

Cambridge
at the University Press
1909

Cambridge:
PRINTED BY JOHN CLAY, M.A.
AT THE UNIVERSITY PRESS.

VOLUME IV
APOCRYPHA

APO

¶ I. ES

CHAP. I.

1 Iosias his charge to the Priests and Leuites. 7 A great Passeouer is kept. 32 His death is much lamented: 34 His Successours. 53 The Temple, Citie, and people are destroyed. 56 The rest are caried vnto Babylon.

*2. King. 23. 22. 2. chro. 35. 1. AND Iosias helde the *Feast of the Passeouer in Ierusalem
vnto his Lord, and offered the Passeouer the fourteenth
day of the first moneth:
2 Hauing set the Priests according to their daily courses,
being arayed in long garments, in the Temple of the Lord.
3 And hee spake vnto the Leuites the holy ministers of
Israel, that they should hallow themselues vnto the Lord,
to set the holy Arke of the Lord, in the house that king
Solomon the sonne of Dauid had built:
4 And said, Ye shall no more beare the Arke vpon your
shoulders: now therefore serue the Lord your God, and
minister vnto his people Israel, and prepare you after your
families and kinreds.
5 According as Dauid the king of Israel prescribed, &
according to the magnificence of Solomon his sonne: &
standing in the Temple according to the seuerall dignitie
of the families of you the Leuites, who minister in the
presence of your brethren the children of Israel.
6 Offer the Passeouer in order, and make ready the sacrifices for your brethren, and keepe the Passeouer according
to the commaundement of the

CRYPHA.

DRAS.

Lord, which was giuen vnto Moyses.
7 And vnto the people that was found there, Iosias gaue
thirtie thousand lambes, and kids, and three thousand calues:
these things were giuen of the kings allowance, according
as hee promised to the people, to the Priestes, and to the
Leuites.
8 And Helkias, Zacharias, and ||Sielus the gouernours of ||*Or,*
the Temple, gaue to the Priests for the Passeouer, two *Iehiel.*
thousand and sixe hundred sheepe, and three hundreth calues.
9 And Iechonias, and Samaias, and Nathanael his brother,
and Assabias, and Ochiel, and Ioram captaines ouer thousands,
gaue to the Leuites for the Passeouer fiue thousand sheepe,
and ||seuen hundreth calues. ||*Fiue*
10 And when these things were done, the Priests and *hundred*
Leuites hauing the vnleauened bread, stood in very comely *calues,* 2. *chro.* 35.
order according to the kinreds, 9.
11 And according to the seuerall dignities of the fathers,
before the people, to offer to the Lord, as it is written in the
booke of Moyses: †And thus did they in the morning. †2. *Chron.*
12 And they rosted the Passeouer with fire, as appertaineth: 35. 12.
as for the sacrifices, they sodde them in brasse pots, and *And so of the bul-*
pannes ||with a good sauour. *lockes.*
13 And set them before all the people, and afterward they ||*With good*
prepared for themselues, and for the Priests their brethren *speed, or willingly,*
the sonnes of Aaron. 2. *chron.*
14 For the Priests offered the fat vntill night: and the 35. 13.
Leuites prepared for themselues, and the Priests their brethren
the sonnes of Aaron.
15 The holy Singers also, the sonnes of Asaph, were in
their order, according
to

*2. Chron. 35. 15. to the appointment of *Dauid, to wit, Asaph, Zacharias, and
of Dauid and Asaph. Ieduthun, who was *of the kings retinue.
16 Moreouer the porters were at euery gate: it was not
*2. Chro. 35. 15. the kings seer. lawfull for any to goe from his ordinary seruice: for their
brethren the Leuites prepared for them.
17 Thus were the things that belonged to the sacrifices of
the Lord accomplished in that day, that they might hold the
Passeouer,
18 And offer sacrifices vpon the altar of the Lord, according
to the commandement of king Iosias.
19 So the children of Israel which were present, held the
Passeouer at that time, and the feast of sweet bread seuen
dayes.
20 And such a Passeouer was not kept in Israel since the
time of the Prophet Samuel.
21 Yea all the kings of Israel held not such a Passeouer as
Iosias, and the Priests and the Leuites, & the Iewes held
with all Israel that were found dwelling at Ierusalem.
22 In the eighteenth yeere of the reigne of Iosias was this
Passeouer kept.
23 And the workes of Iosias were vpright before his Lord
with an heart full of godlinesse.
24 As for the things that came to passe in his time, they
were written in former times, concerning those that sinned,
‖*Or, were vngodly.* and ‖did wickedly against the Lord aboue all people and
‖*Or, sensibly.* kingdomes, and how they grieued him ‖exceedingly, so that
the words of the Lord rose vp against Israel.
*2. Chron. 35. 20. 25 *Now after all these acts of Iosias, it came to passe
that Pharao the king of Egypt came to raise warre at
Carchamis vpon Euphrates: and Iosias went out against
him.
26 But the king of Egypt sent to him saying, What haue I
to doe with thee, O king of Iudea?
27 I am not sent out from the Lord God against thee: for
my warre is vpon Euphrates, and now the Lord is with mee,
yea the Lord is with mee hasting me forward : Depart from
me and be not against the Lord.
28 Howbeit Iosias did not turne backe his chariot from
him, but vndertooke to fight with him, not regarding the
words of the Prophet Ieremie,

spoken by the mouth of the Lord:
29 But ioyned battell with him in the plaine of Magiddo,
and the princes came against king Iosias.
30 Then said the king vnto his seruants, carry me away
out of the battell for I am very weake: and immediately his
seruants tooke him away out of the battell.
31 Then gate he vp vpon his second chariot, and being
brought backe to Ierusalem, dyed, and was buried in his
fathers sepulchre.
32 And in all Iury they mourned for Iosias, yea Ieremie
the Prophet lamented for Iosias, and the cheefe men with
the women made lamentation for him vnto this day: and
this was giuen out for an ordinance to be done continually in
all the nation of Israel.
33 These things are written in the booke of the stories of
the kings of Iudah, and euery one of the acts that Iosias did,
and his glory, and his vnderstanding in the law of the Lord,
and the things that he had done before, and the things now
recited, are reported in the bookes of the Kings of Israel and
Iudea.
34 * And the people tooke Ioachaz the sonne of Iosias, and *2. King.
made him king in stead of Iosias his father, when hee was 23. 30.
twentie and three yeeres old. 2. chron. 36. 1.
35 And he reigned in Iudea and in Ierusalem three moneths:
and then the King of Egypt deposed him from reigning in
Ierusalem.
36 And he set a taxe vpon the land of an hundreth talents
of siluer, and one talent of gold.
37 The king of Egypt also made king Ioacim his brother
king of Iudea and Ierusalem.
38 And hee bound Ioacim and the nobles: but Zaraces his
brother he apprehended, and brought him out of Egypt.
39 Fiue and twentie yeere old was Ioacim † when he was †2. *Chro.*
made king in the land of Iudea and Ierusalem, and he did 36. 45.
euill before the Lord. *Iehoiakim, or*
40 Wherefore against him Nabuchodonosor the King of *Eliakim.*
Babylon came vp, and bound him with a chaine of brasse,
and carried him vnto Babylon.
41 Nabuchodonosor also tooke of the holy vessels of the
Lord, and carried them away, and set them in his owne
temple at Babylon.

42 But

42 But those things that are recorded of him, and of his vncleannes, and impietie, are written in the Chronicles of the kings.

43 And Ioacim his sonne reigned in his stead: he was made king being eighteene yeeres old,

44 And reigned but three moneths and ten dayes in Ierusalem, and did euill before the Lord.

45 So after a yere Nabuchodonosor sent, and caused him to be brought into Babylon with yͤ holy vessels of yͤ Lord,

46 And made Zedechias king of Iudea and Ierusalem, when he was one and twentie yeeres old, and he reigned eleuen yeeres:

47 And he did euill also in the sight of the Lord, & cared not for the words that were spoken vnto him, by the Prophet Ieremie from the mouth of the Lord.

48 And after that king Nabuchodonosor had made him to sweare by the Name of the Lord, he forswore himselfe, and rebelled, and hardening his necke, and his heart, hee transgressed the lawes of the Lord God of Israel.

49 The gouernours also of the people and of the priests did many things against the lawes, and passed al the pollutions of all nations, and defiled the Temple of the Lord which was sanctified in Ierusalem.

50 Neuerthelesse, the God of their fathers sent by his messenger to call them backe, because he spared them and his tabernacle also:

51 But they had his messengers in derision, and looke when the Lorde spake vnto them, they made a sport of his prophets,

52 So farre foorth that he being wroth with his people for their great vngodlinesse, commanded the kings of the Caldees to come vp against them.

53 Who slew their yong men with the sword, yea euen within the compasse of their holy Temple, & spared neither yong man nor maid, old man nor child among them, for hee deliuered all into their hands.

54 And they tooke all the holy vessels of the Lord, both great and small, with the vessels of the Ark of God, and the kings treasures, and caried them away into Babylon.

55 As for the house of the Lord they burnt it, brake downe

the walles of Ie-

rusalem, set fire vpon her towres.
56 And as for her glorious things, they neuer ceased til they
had consumed and brought them all to nought, and the people
that were not slaine with the sword, he caried vnto Babylon:
57 Who became seruants to him and his children, till the
Persians reigned, to fulfill the *word of the Lord spoken by * Ier. 25. 11 and 29. 10.
the mouth of Ieremie:
58 Vntill the land had enioyed her Sabbaths, the whole
time of her desolation shal she ||rest, vntill the full terme || *Or, Keepe Sabbath.*
of seuentie yeeres.

CHAP. II.

1 Cyrus is moued by God to build the Temple, 5 And giueth leaue to the Iewes to returne & contribute to it. 11 He deliuereth againe the vessels which had bin taken thence. 25 Artaxerxes forbiddeth the Iewes to build any more.

IN the first yeere of Cyrus king of the Persians, that the *2. Chron. 36. 22. ezra 1. 1, &c.
worde of the Lorde might bee accomplished, that hee
had promised by the mouth of Ieremie:
2 The Lord raised vp the spirit of Cyrus the king of the
Persians, and he made proclamation thorow al his kingdome,
and also by writing,
3 Saying, Thus saith Cyrus king of the Persians, The Lord
of Israel the most high Lord, hath made me king of the
whole world,
4 And commanded me to build him an house at Ierusalem
in Iurie.
5 If therefore there bee any of you that are of his people,
let the Lord, euen his Lord be with him, and let him goe vp
to Ierusalem that is in Iudea, and build the house of the Lord
of Israel: for ||he is the Lord that dwelleth in Ierusalem. || *Or, this.*
6 Whosoeuer then dwell in the places about, let them
helpe him, those I say that are his neighbours, with gold
and with siluer,
7 With gifts, with horses, and with cattell, and other
things, which haue bene set forth by vowe, for the Temple
of the Lord at Ierusalem.
8 ¶ Then the chiefe of the families of Iudea, and of the
tribes of Beniamin stood vp: the priests also and the Leuites,
and all they whose minde the Lord had moued to goe vp,
and to build an house for the Lord at Ierusalem,
9 And they that dwelt round about
them,

them, and helped them in all things with siluer and gold,

†Hebr. substance, Ezr. 1. 6.

with †horses and cattell, and with very free gifts of a great
number whose mindes were stirred vp thereto.
10 King Cyrus also brought foorth the holy vessels which
Nabuchodonosor had caried away from Ierusalem, and had
set vp in his temple of idoles.
11 Now when Cyrus king of the Persians had brought them
foorth, hee deliuered them to Mithridates his treasurer:

†Shash-bazar. Greek. the first part of the word is corruptly ioyned to the word going before, Ezra 1. 8.

12 And by him they were deliuered to †Sanabassar ye
gouernour of Iudea.
13 And this was the number of them, a thousand golden
cuppes, and a thousand of siluer, †censers of siluer twentie
nine, vials of gold thirtie, and of siluer †two thousand foure
hundred and ten, and a thousand other vessels.
14 So all the vessels of gold, and of siluer which were
caried away, were †fiue thousand, foure hundred, three-

†Hebr. kniues, Ezra 1. 9.

score and nine.
15 These were brought back by Sanabassar, together with

†Ezra. 1. 10. but foure hundred and ten.

them of the captiuity, from Babylon to Ierusalem.
16 *But in the time of Artaxerxes king of the Persians,
Belemus, and Mithridates, and Tabellius, and †Rathumus,
and Beeltethmus, and †Semellius the Secretarie, with others

†Ezra. 1. 11. but fiue thousand foure hundred.

that were in commission with them, dwelling in Samaria
and other places, wrote vnto him against them that dwelt in
Iudea and Ierusalem, these letters following.
17 To King Artaxerxes our lord, Thy seruants Rathumus

**Ezra 4. 6.*

the story writer, and Semellius the scribe, and the rest of

†Bahumus and the name which followeth, is but an epithete to the former, Ezra 4. 9.

their counsell, and the Iudges that are in Coelosyria and
Phenice.
18 Be it now knowen to the lord the king, that the Iewes
that are come vp from you to vs, being come into Ierusalem
(that rebellious and wicked citie,) doe build the market places,
and repaire the walles of it, and doe lay the foundation of
the Temple.
19 Now if this citie, and the walles thereof be made vp

†Shimshai, Ezra 4. 8.

againe, they will not onely refuse to giue tribute, but also
rebell against kings.
20 And forasmuch as the things pertaining to the Temple,
are now in hand, we thinke it meete not to neglect such a
matter,

21 But to speake vnto our lord the

king, to the intent that if it be thy pleasure, it may be
sought out in the bookes of thy fathers:
22 And thou shalt finde in the Chronicles, what is written
concerning these things, and shalt vnderstand that that citie
was rebellious, troubling both kings and cities:
23 And that the Iewes were rebellious, and raised alwayes
warres therin, for the which cause euen this citie was made
desolate.
24 Wherefore now wee doe declare vnto thee, (O lord the
king) that if this citie bee built againe, and the walles thereof
set vp anew, thou shalt from hencefoorth haue no passage
into Coelosyria and Phenice.
25 Then the King wrote backe againe to Rathumus the
storie-writer, to Beeltethmus, to Semellius the scribe, and to
the rest that were in commission, and dwellers in Samaria
and Syria, and Phenice, after this maner.
26 I haue read the Epistle which ye haue sent vnto mee:
therefore I commanded to make diligent search, and it hath
bene found, that that city was from the beginning practising
against Kings.
27 And the men therein were giuen to rebellion, and warre,
and that mightie Kings and fierce were in Ierusalem, who
reigned and exacted tributes in Coelosyria and Phenice.
28 Now therefore I haue commanded to hinder those men
from building the citie, and heed to be taken that there be
no more done in it,
29 And that those wicked workers proceed no further to
the annoyance of Kings.
30 Then king Artaxerxes his letters being read, Rathumus
and Semellius the scribe, and the rest that were in commission with them, remoouing in hast towards Ierusalem with a
troupe of horsemen, and a ||multitude of people in battell || *Or. a*
aray, began to hinder the builders, and the building of the *great*
Temple in Ierusalem ceased vntill the second yeere of the *number of*
reigne of Darius King of the Persians. *souldiers.*

CHAP. III.

4 Three striue to excell each other in wise speaches. 9 They referre
themselues to the iudgement of the King. 18 The first declareth
the strength of Wine.

Now

NOw when Darius reigned, hee made a great feast vnto all his Subiects and vnto all his houshold, and vnto all the princes of Media and Persia,

2 And to all the gouernours and captaines, and lieutenants that were vnder him, from India vnto Ethiopia, of an hundreth twenty and seuen prouinces.

3 And when they had eaten and drunken, and being satisfied were gone home, then Darius the king went into his bed-chamber, and slept, and soone after awaked.

4 Then three yong men that were of the guard, that kept the kings body, spake one to another:

5 Let euery one of vs speake a sentence: hee that shall ouercome, & whose sentence shall seeme wiser then the others, vnto him shall the king Darius giue great gifts, and great things in token of victory:

6 As to be clothed in purple, to drink in golde, and to sleepe vpon golde, and a chariot with bridles of golde, and an head-tyre of fine linen, and a chaine about his necke:

7 And hee shall sit next to Darius, because of his wisedome, and shalbe called, Darius his cousin.

8 And then euery one wrote his sentence, sealed it, and laide it vnder king Darius his pillow,

9 And sayd, that when the king is risen, some will giue him the writings, and of whose side the king, and the three princes of Persia shall iudge, that his sentence is the wisest, to him shall the victory be giuen as was appointed.

10 The first wrote: Wine is the strongest.

11 The second wrote: The King is strongest.

12 The third wrote; Women are strongest, but aboue all things trueth beareth away the victory.

13 ¶ Now when the king was risen vp, they tooke their writings, and deliuered them vnto him, and so hee read them.

14 And sending foorth, hee called all the Princes of Persia and Media, and the gouernours, and the captaines, and the lieutenants, and the chiefe officers,

15 And sate him downe in the ||royall seate of Iudgement, and the writings

|| *Or, counsell.*

were read before them:
16 And he said, Call the young men, and they shall declare
their owne sentences: so they were called, and came in.
17 And hee said vnto them, Declare vnto vs your minde,
concerning the writings. Then began the first, who had
spoken of the strength of wine;
18 And he said thus: O ye men, how exceeding strong is
wine! it causeth all men to erre that drinke it:
19 It maketh the minde of the king, and of the fatherlesse
childe to be all one; of the bondman and of the freeman, of
the poore man and of the rich:
20 It turneth also euery thought into iollitie and mirth, so
that a man remembreth neither sorow nor debt:
21 And it maketh euery heart rich, so that a man remembreth neither king nor gouernour; and it maketh to
speake all things by talents:
22 And when they are in their cups, they forget their loue
both to friends and brethren, and a litle after draw out
swords:
23 But when they are from the wine, they remember not
what they haue done.
24 O ye men, is not wine the strongest, that enforceth to
doe thus? And when hee had so spoken, hee helde his peace.

CHAP. IIII.

1 The second declareth the power of a King. 14 The third, the force
of women: 33 and of Trueth. 41 The third is iudged to be
wisest, 47 and obtaineth Letters of the King to build Ierusalem.
58 He praiseth God, and sheweth his brethren what he had done.

THen the second that had spoken of the strength of the
King, began to say;
2 O yee men, doe not men excel in strength, that ‖beare
rule ouer Sea and land, and all things in them?

‖ *Or, haue the command.*

3 But yet the King is more mighty: for hee is lord of all
these things, and hath dominion ouer them, and whatsoeuer
he commandeth them, they doe:
4 If hee bid them make warre the one against the other,
they doe it: if hee send them out against the enemies, they
goe, and breake downe mountaines, walles and towres.
5 They slay and are slaine, and transgresse not the Kings
commande-
ment:

ment: if they get the victory, they bring all to the King, as
well the spoile as all things else.
6 Likewise for those that are no souldiers, and haue not to
doe with warres, but vse husbandrie; when they haue reaped
againe, that which they had sowen, they bring it to the
King, and compell one another to pay tribute vnto the King.
7 And yet he is but one man; if hee commaund to kill,
they kill, if he command to spare, they spare.
8 If he command to smite, they smite; if he command to
make desolate, they make desolate; if hee command to build,
they build:
9 If he command to cut downe, they cut downe; if he
command to plant, they plant.
10 So all his people and his armies obey him; furthermore
he lieth downe, he eateth and drinketh, & taketh his rest.
||Or, can. 11 And these keepe (watch) round about him, neither ||may
any one depart, and doe his owne businesse, neither disobey
they him in any thing.
12 O yee men, how should not the King be mightiest,
when in such sort he is obeyed? and he held his tongue.
13 ¶ Then the third, who had spoken of women, and of
the truth (this was Zorobabel) beganne to speake.
14 O yee men, it is not the great King, nor the multitude
†Heb. is of force. of men, neither is it wine that †excelleth; who is it then
that ruleth them, or hath the lordship ouer them, are they
not women?
15 Women haue borne the King and all the people, that
beare rule by sea and land.
16 Euen of thē came they: & they nourished them vp that
planted the vineyards from whence the wine commeth.
17 These also make garments for men; these bring glory
vnto men, and without women cannot men be.
18 Yea and if men haue gathered together gold and siluer,
or any other goodly thing, doe they not loue a woman, which
is comely in fauour and beautie?
19 And letting all those things goe, doe they not gape, and
euen with open mouth fixe their eyes fast on her; and haue
not all men more desire vnto her, then vnto siluer or gold, or
any goodly thing whatsoeuer?

20 A man leaueth his owne father

that brought him vp, and his owne countrie, and cleaueth
vnto his wife.
21 He stickes not to spend his life with his wife, and
remembreth neither father, nor mother, nor countrey.
22 By this also you must know, that women haue dominion
ouer you: doe yee not labour and toyle, and giue and bring
all to the woman?
23 Yea a man taketh his sword, and goeth his way to rob,
and to steale, to saile vpon the sea, and vpon riuers,
24 And looketh vpon a lyon, and goeth in the darknesse,
and when he hath stolen, spoiled and robbed, he bringeth it
to his loue.
25 Wherefore a man loueth his wife better then father and
mother.
26 Yea many there be that haue ||run out of their wits for
women, and become seruants for their sakes:
27 Many also haue perished, haue erred, and sinned for women.
28 And now doe yee not belieue me? is not the King great
in his power? doe not all regions feare to touch him?
29 Yet did I see him and Apame the Kings concubine, the
daughter of the admirable Bartacus, sitting at the right hand
of the King,
30 And taking the crowne from the Kings head, and
setting it vpon her owne head; she also strooke the King
with her left hand.
31 And yet ||for all this, the King gaped and gazed vpon
her with open mouth: if she laughed vpon him, hee laughed
also: but if she tooke any displeasure at him, the King was
faine to flatter, that she might ||be reconciled to him againe.
32 O ye men, how can it be but women should be strong,
seeing they doe thus?
33 Then the king & the princes looked one vpon another:
so he began to speake of the trueth.
34 O ye men, are not women strong? great is the earth,
high is the heauen, swift is the Sunne in his course, for he
compasseth the heauens round about, and fetcheth his course
againe to his owne place in one day.
35 Is he not great that maketh these things? therefore great
is the truth, and stronger then all things.
36 All the earth ||calleth vpon the truth, & the heauen
blesseth it, all works shake and tremble at it, and with it is
no vnrighteous thing.

|| Or, growen desperate.

Ioseph. antiq. lib. 11. cap. 4. Rabsaces Themasius.

|| Or, heere at.

|| Or, be friends with him.

|| Or, praiseth the truth. Athanas.

37 Wine

37 Wine is wicked, the king is wicked, women are wicked,
all the children of men are wicked, and such are all their
wicked workes, and there is no trueth in them. In their
vnrighteousnes also they shall perish.
38 As for the trueth it endureth, and is alwayes strong, it
liueth and conquereth for euermore.
39 With her there is no accepting of persons, or rewards,
but she doeth the things that are iust, and refraineth from all
vniust and wicked things, and all men doe well like of her
workes.
40 Neither in her iudgement is any vnrighteousnesse, & she
is the strength, kingdome, power and maiestie of all ages.
Blessed be the God of trueth.
41 And with that he held his peace, and al the people then
shouted and said, Great is trueth, and mightie aboue all
things.
42 Then saide the king vnto him, Aske what thou wilt,
more then is appointed in the writing, and we wil giue it
thee, because thou art found wisest, and thou shalt sit next
me, and shalt bee called my cousin.
43 Then said hee vnto the king, Remember thy vow which
thou hast vowed to build Ierusalem in the day when thou
camest to the kingdome,
44 And to send away all the vessels that were taken away
out of Ierusalem, which Cyrus set apart, when hee vowed to
destroy Babylon, and to send them againe thither.
45 Thou also hast vowed to build vp the Temple, which
the Edomites burnt when Iudea was made desolate by the
Chaldees.
46 And now, O lord the king, this is that which I require,
and which I desire of thee, and this is the princely liberalitie
proceeding from thy selfe: I desire therefore that thou make
good the vow, the performance wherof with thine owne
mouth thou hast vowed to the king of heauen.
47 Then Darius the king stood vp and kissed him, and
wrote letters for him vnto all the treasurers and lieutenants,
and captaines and gouernours that they should safely conuey
on their way, both him, and all those that go vp with him to
build Ierusalem.
48 Hee wrote letters also vnto the lieutenants that were in
Coelosyria and Phenice, and vnto them in Libanus,

that they should bring Cedar wood from Libanus vnto
Ierusalem, and that they should build the city with him
49 Moreouer he wrote for all the Iewes that went out of
his realme vp into Iurie, concerning their freedome, that no
officer, no ruler, no lieutenant, nor ‖treasurer, should forcibly ‖*Or, steward.*
enter into their dores,
50 And that all the countrey which they hold, should be
free without tribute, & that the Edomites should giue ouer
the villages of the Iewes which then they held,
51 Yea that there should be yereely giuen twentie talents
to yͤ building of the Temple, vntill yͤ time that it were built,
52 And other tenne talents yeerely, to maintaine the burnt
offerings vpon the Altar euery day (as they had a commandement to offer seuenteene)
53 And that all they that went from Babylon to build the
citie, should haue free liberty as well they as their posteritie,
and all the priests that went away.
54 He wrote also concerning the charges, and the priests
vestments wherein they minister:
55 And likewise for the charges of the Leuites, to be
giuen them, vntill the day that the house were finished,
and Ierusalem builded vp.
56 And he commanded to giue to all that kept the city,
‖pensions and wages. ‖*Or, portions of land.*
57 He sent away also all the vessels frō Babylon that Cyrus had
set apart, and all that Cyrus had giuen in commandement, the
same charged hee also to be done, and sent vnto Ierusalem.
58 Now when this yong man was gone forth, he lifted vp
his face to heauen toward Ierusalem, and praised the king of
heauen,
59 And said, From thee commeth victory, from thee commeth wisedom, and thine is the glory, & I am thy seruant.
60 Blessed art thou who hast giuen me wisedom: for to
thee I giue thanks, O Lord of our fathers.
61 And so he tooke the letters, and went out, and came
vnto Babylon, and told it all his brethren.
62 And they praised the God of their fathers: because he
had giuen them freedome and libertie
63 To goe vp, and to build Ierusalem, and the Temple
which is called by his Name, and they feasted with instruments of musick, & gladnes seuen dayes.

CHAP.

CHAP. V.

4 The names and number of the Iewes that returned home. 50 The Altar is set vp in his place. 57 The foundation of the Temple is layd. 73 The worke is hindred for a time.

AFter this were the principall men of the families chosen
according to their tribes, to go vp with their wiues,
and sonnes, and daughters, with their men-seruants and maid-
seruants, and their cattel.
2 And Darius sent with them a thousand horsmen, til
they had brought them backe to Ierusalem safely, and with
musicall [instruments,] tabrets and flutes:
3 And all their brethren played, and hee made them goe
vp together with them.
4 And these are the names of the men which went vp,
according to their families, amongst their tribes, after their
seuerall heads.
5 The Priestes the sonnes of Phinees, the sonne of Aaron:
Iesus the sonne of Iosedec, the sonne of Saraias, and ||Ioachim
the sonne of Zorobabel, the sonne of Salathiel of the house
of Dauid, out of the kindred of Phares, of the tribe of Iuda;
6 [a]Who spake wise sentences before Darius the king of
Persia, in the second yeere of his reigne, in the moneth
Nisan, which is the first moneth.
7 And these are they of Iewrie that came vp from the
captiuitie, where they dwelt as strangers, whom Nabuchodonosor the king of Babylon had carried away vnto Babylon:
8 And they returned vnto Ierusalem, and to the other
parts of Iurie euery man to his owne city, who came
with Zorobabel, with Iesus, Nehemias, and [b]Zacharias, and
Reesaias, Enenius, Mardocheus, Beelsarus, [c]Aspharasus,
[d]Reelius, Roimus, and Baana their guides.
9 The number of them of the nation, and their gouernours:
sonnes of [e]Phoros two thousand an hundred seuentie and
two: the sonnes of [f]Saphat [g]foure hundred seuentie and
two;
10 The sonnes of Ares seuen hundred fiftie and sixe:
11 The sonnes of Phaath Moab, two thousand eight hundred
& twelue:
12 The sonnes of Elam, a thousand

||Ioachim and Zorobabel. This place is corrupt: For Ioachim was the sonne of Iosedech, Neh. 12. 10. and not Zorobabel, who was of the tribe of Iuda.

[a] *Zorobabel.*
[b] *Saraiah.*
[c] *Or Mispar.*
[d] *Or Reelaiah.*
[e] *Parosh, Ezra 2. 3. Nehem. 7. 9. where for breuity looke for the true numbers of the particulars following: for here they vary much, & the names much more.*
[f] *Shephatia.*
[g] *Or, three hundred seuentie two.*

two hundred fifty and foure: the sonnes of [h]Zathui, nine *[h]Zattu.*
hundred fourtie and fiue : the sonnes of [i]Corbe seuen hundred *[i]Zacchai.*
and fiue : the sonnes of Bani, sixe hundred fourtie and eight:
13 The sonnes of Bebai, sixe hundred twentie and three:
the sonnes of [k]Sadas, three thousand two hundred twentie *[k]Asgad.*
and two:
14 The sonnes of Adonican, sixe hundred sixtie and seuen:
the sonnes of [l]Bagoi, two thousand sixtie and sixe : the sonnes *[l]Bigui.*
of Adin, foure hundred fiftie and foure:
15 The sonnes of [m]Aterezias, ninetie and two: the sonnes *[m]Alerhezekia.*
of Ceilan and Azetas, threescore and seuen: the sonnes of
Azuran, foure hundred thirtie & two.
16 The sonnes of Ananias, an hundred and one: the sonnes
of Arom thirtie two, and the sonnes of [n]Bassa, three hundred *[n]Besai.*
twentie and three: the sonnes of Azephurith, an hundred
and two:
17 The sonnes of Meterus, three thousand and fiue: the
sonnes of [o]Bethlomon, an hundred twentie and three. *[o]Bethlehem.*
18 They of Netophah fiftie and fiue: they of Anathoth, an
hundred fiftie and eight: they of [p]Bethsamos, fourtie and two: *[p]Asmaueth.*
19 They of [q]Kiriathiarius, twentie and fiue: they of *[q]Kiriashiarim.*
Caphira and Beroth, seuen hundred fourtie and three: they of
Pyra, seuen hundred:
20 They of Chadias and Ammidioi, foure hundred twenty *[r]Rama.*
and two: they of [r]Cyrama, and [s]Gabdes, sixe hundred *[s]Gabah. [t]Michmas.*
twentie and one: *[u]Bethel.*
21 They of [t]Macalon, an hundred twentie and two: they *[x]Maghbis.*
of [u]Betolius fiftie and two : the sonnes of [x]Nephis, an hundred *[y]Lodhadid.*
fiftie and sixe. *[z]Senaah.*
22 The sonnes of [y]Calamolalus, and Onus, seuen hundred *[a]Iedaiah.*
twentie and fiue: the sonnes of Ierechus, two hundred fourtie *[b]Immar. [c]Pashur.*
and fiue: *[d]Harim.*
23 The sonnes of [z]Annaas, three thousand three hundred *[e]Or, 217. according to some copies.*
and thirtie:
24 The Priests, the sonnes of [a]Ieddu, the sonne of Iesus,
among the sonnes of Sanasib, nine hundred seuentie and *[f]Thus it is read, Ezra 2. 40. the sonnes of Ieshua, and Cadmeel, of the sonnes of Hodouiah.*
two: the sonnes of [b]Meruth, a thousand fiftie and two:
25 The sonnes of [c]Phassaron, a thousand fourtie and seuen:
the sonnes of [d]Carme [e]a thousand and seuenteene.
26 The Leuites: the sonnes of [f]Iessue, and Cadmiel, and
Banuas, and Sudias, seuentie and foure.

27 The

27 The holy singers: the sonnes of Asaph an hundred
twentie and eight.
28 The porters: the sonnes of [a]Salum, the sonnes of [b]Iatal,
the sonnes of Talmon, the sonnes of [c]Dacobi, the sonnes of
[d]Teta, the sonnes of [e]Sami, in all an hundred thirty and nine.
29 The seruants of the Temple: the sonnes of [f]Esau, the
sonnes of [g]Asipha, the sonnes of Tabaoth, the sonnes of
[h]Ceras: the sonnes of [i]Sud, the sonnes of [k]Phaleas, the
sonnes of Labana, the sonnes of [l]Graba:
30 The sonnes of [m]Acua, the sonnes of Vta, the sonnes of
[n]Cetab, the sons of Agaba, the sonnes of [o]Subai, the sonnes
of Anan, the sonnes of [p]Cathua, the sonnes of [q]Geddur:
31 The sonnes of [r]Airus, the sonnes of [s]Daisan, thė sonnes
of [t]Noeba, the sonnes of Chaseba, the sonnes of [u]Gazera, the
sonnes of [x]Azia, the sonnes of [y]Phinees, the sonnes of Azara,
the sonnes of [z]Bastai, the sonnes of [a]Asana, the sonnes of
[b]Meani, the sonnes of [c]Naphisi, the sonnes of [d]Acub, the
sons of [e]Asipha, the sonnes of [f]Assur, the sonnes of Pharacim,
the sons of [g]Basaloth.
32 The sonnes of [h]Meeda: the sons of Coutha, the sonnes
of [i]Charea, the sonnes of [k]Chareus, the sonnes of [l]Aserer,
the sonnes of [m]Thomoi, the sonnes of [n]Nasith, the sons of
Atipha.
33 The sons of the seruants of Solomon: the sonnes of
[o]Azaphion, the sonnes of [p]Pharira, the sonnes of [q]Ioeli, the
sonnes of [r]Lozon, the sonnes of [s]Isdael, the sonnes of
[t]Sapheth:
34 The sonnes of [u]Hagia, the sons of [x]Phacareth, the sonnes
of Sabie, the sonnes of Sarothie, the sonnes of Masias, the
sonnes of Gar, the sons of Addus, the sonnes of Suba, the
sonnes of Apherra, the sonnes of Barodis, the sonnes of Sabat,
the sonnes of Allom.
35 All the ministers of the Temple, and the sonnes of the
seruants of Solomon, were three hundred seuenty & two.
36 These came vp from Thermeleth, and Thelersas,
Charaathalar leading them and Aalar.
37 Neither could they shewe their families, nor their stock,
how they were of Israel: the sonnes of [y]Ladan, the sonnes
of [z]Ban, the sonnes of [a]Necodan, sixe hundred fiftie and two.
38 And of the Priests that vsurped the office of the Priesthood, and were

[a] *Shallum.* [b] *Ater.* [c] *Akkub.* [d] *Hatita.* [e] *Shobai.* [f] *Zich.* [g] *Hasupha.* [h] *Keros.* [i] *Siaha.* [k] *Padon.* [l] *Agabah.* [m] *Akkub.* [n] *Hagab.* [o] *Shamlai.* [p] *Giddes.* [q] *Gahar.* [r] *Reaiah.* [s] *Rezin.* [t] *Necodah.* [u] *Gazam.* [x] *Huzza.* [y] *Paseah.* [z] *Besai.* [a] *Asnah.* [b] *Neumin.* [c] *Nephusin.* [d] *Bakbuk.* [e] *Hacupa.* [f] *Harhur.* [g] *Bazluth.* [h] *Mehida.* [i] *Harsha.* [k] *Barcos.* [l] *Sisera.* [m] *Thamai.* [n] *Neziah.* [o] *Sophereth.* [p] *Peruda.* [q] *Iaalah.* [r] *Darcon.* [s] *Giddel.* [t] *Shephatiah* [u] *Hatti.* [x] *Phoceroth Hazzebaim, Ezra* 2. 25. [y] *Delaiah.* [z] *Tobiah.* [a] *Necodah.*

not found, the sonnes of [b]Obdia: the sonnes of [c]Accoz, the [b] *Hobaiah.*
sonnes of [d]Addus, who married Augia one of the daughters [c] *Cos.* [d] *Barzelai.*
of Berzelus, and was named after his name.
39 And when the description of the kinred of these men
was sought in the Register, and was not found, they were
remooued from executing the office of the Priesthood.
40 For vnto them said ||Nehemias, and Atharias, that they || *Nehemias, who also is Atharias, two of one. Nehe. 8. 9. and 10. 2. chap. 2. 63.*
should not be partakers of the holy things, till there arose vp
an high Priest, clothed with †Doctrine and Trueth. † *Heb. Vrim and Thummim.*
41 So of Israel from them of twelue yeeres olde and vpward,
they were all in number fourtie thousand, besides men
seruants and women seruants, two thousand three hundred
and sixtie.
42 Their ||men seruants and handmaids were seuen thousand || *See Nehe.* 7. 66.
three hundred fourtie and seuen: the singing men and singing
women, two hundred fortie and fiue.
43 Foure hundred thirtie and fiue camels, seuen thousand
thirtie and sixe horses, two hundred fourtie and fiue mules,
*fiue thousand fiue hundred twentie & fiue ||beasts vsed to * Ezra. 2. 67.
the yoke. || *Asses.*
44 And certaine of the chiefe of their families, when they
came to the Temple of God that is in Ierusalem, vowed to
set vp the house againe in his owne place according to their
abilitie:
45 And to giue into the holy treasurie of the workes, a
thousand pounds of golde, fiue thousand of siluer, and an
hundred priestly vestments.
46 And so dwelt the Priests, and the Leuites, and the people
in Ierusalem, and in the countrey: the Singers also, and the
Porters, and all Israel in their villages.
47 But when the seuenth moneth was at hand, and when
the children of Israel were euery man in his owne place,
they came all together with one consent into the open place
of the ||first gate, which is towards the East. || *Or, before the East gate.*
48 Then stood vp Iesus the sonne of Iosedec, and his brethren
the Priests, and Zorobabel the sonne of Salathiel, and his
brethren, and made ready the Altar of the God of Israel,
49 To offer burnt sacrifices vpon it, according as it is
expresly commanded in the booke of Moses the man of God.
50 And there were gathered vnto

them out of the other nations of the land, and they erected
the Altar vpon his owne place, because all the nations of the
land were at enmitie with them, and oppressed them, and
they offered sacrifices according to the time, and burnt
offerings to the Lord both morning, and euening.
51 Also they held the feast of Tabernacles, as it is commanded in the law, and *offered* sacrifices daily as was meet:

|| Or, daily sacrifice.

52 And after, that the ||continuall oblations, and the sac-
rifice of the Sabbaths, and of the new Moones, and of all holy
feasts.

† Grek. halowed.

53 And all they that †had made any vow to God, beganne
to offer sacrifices to God from the first day of the seuenth
moneth, although the Temple of the Lord was not yet
built.
54 And they gaue vnto the Masons and Carpenters, money,
meate and drinke with cheerefulnesse.
55 Vnto them of Sidon also and Tyre, they gaue carres that
they should bring Cedar trees from Libanus, which should bee
brought by flotes to the hauen of Ioppe, according as it was
commanded them by Cyrus King of the Persians.
56 And in the second yeere and second moneth, after his
comming to the Temple of God at Ierusalem, beganne
Zorobabel the sonne of Salathiel, and Iesus the sonne of
Iosedec, and their brethren and the priests, and the Leuites,
and all they that were come vnto Ierusalem out of the
captiuity:
57 And they layd the foundation of the house of God, in
the first day of the second moneth, in the second yeere after
they were come to Iury & Ierusalem.

|| See Ezra 3. 9.

58 ||And they appointed the Lenites from twenty yeeres old,
ouer the workes of the Lord. Then stood vp Iesus and his
sonnes, and brethren, and Cadmiel his brother, & the sonnes
of Madiabun, with the sonnes of Ioda the sonne of Eliadun,
with their sonnes and brethren, all Leuites, with one accord

|| Or, ouerseers or encouragers of them that wrought in the house of the Lord.

||seters forward of the businesse, labouring to aduance the
workes in the house of God. So the workmen built the
temple of the Lord.
59 And the Priests stood arayed in their vestiments with
musicall instruments, and trumpets, and the Leuites the
sonnes of Asaph had Cymbals,

60 Singing songs of thanksgiuing, and praising the Lord
||according as Dauid the king of Israel had ordained. || *Or, after the maner of Dauid king of Israel.*
61 And they sung *with* loud voices songs to the praise of
the Lord: because his mercy and glory is for euer in all
Israel.
62 And all the people sounded trumpets, and shouted with
a loud voyce, singing songs of thankesgiuing vnto the Lord
for the rearing vp of the house of the Lord.
63 *Also of the Priests and Leuites, and of the chiefe of * Ezra 3. 12 13.
their families the ancients who had seene the former house,
came to the building of this with weeping and great crying.
64 But many with trumpets and ioy shouted with loud voyce.
65 Insomuch that the trumpets might not be ||heard for the
weeping of the people: yet the multitude sounded mar- || *Or, discerned.*
ueilously, so that it was heard a farre off.
66 Wherefore when the enemies of the Tribe of Iuda and
Beniamin heard it, they came to know what that noise of
trumpets should meane.
67 And they perceiued, that they that were of the captiuity
did build the temple vnto the Lord God of Israel.
68 So they went to Zorobabel and Iesus, and to the chiefe
of the families, and said vnto them, We will build together
with you.
69 For we likewise, as you, doe obey your Lord, and doe
sacrifice vnto him from the dayes of ||Asbazareth the king of || Asar-haddon, *chap.* 4. 3.
the Assyrians who brought vs hither
70 Then Zorobabel and Iesus, and the chiefe of the families
of Israel said vnto them, It is not for vs and you to build
together an house vnto the Lord our God.
71 We our selues alone will build vnto the Lord of Israel,
according as Cyrus the King of the Persians hath commanded
vs.
72 But the heathen of the land lying heauy vpon the inhabitants of Iudea, and holding them straite, hindred their
building:
73 And by their secret plots, and popular perswasions, and
commotions, they hindred the finishing of the building, all
the time that king Cyrus liued, so they were hindered from || *Vntill the secondyeere of Darius. Ezra* 4. 5, 6, 7.
building for the space of ||two yeeres, vntill the reigne of
Darius.

CHAP.

CHAP. VI.

1 The Prophets stirre vp the people to build the Temple. 8 Darius is
solicited to hinder it. 27 But he doth further it by all meanes,
32 and threatneth those that shall hinder it.

NOw in the second yeere of the reigne of Darius,
|| *Or, Iddo.* Aggeus, and Zacharias the sonne of || Addo, the
prophets prophesied vnto the Iewes, in Iurie and Ierusalem
|| *Or, which was called on them.* in the Name of the Lord God of Israel ||which was vpon
them.
2 Then stood vp Zorobabel the sonne of Salathiel, and Iesus
the son of Iosedec, and beganne to build the house of the
Lord at Ierusalem, the prophets of the Lord being with
them, *and* helping them.
*Ezra. 5. 3. 3 *At the same time came vnto them ||Sisinnes the gouernor
|| *Or, Tatnai* of Syria, and Phenice, with || Sathrabuzanes, and his com-
|| *Or, Shetherboznai.* panions, and said vnto them,
7 By whose appointment doe you build this house, and this
roofe, and performe all the other things? and who are the
workemen that performe these things?
5 Neuerthelesse the Elders of the Iewes obtained fauour:
because the Lord had visited the captiuitie.
6 And they were not hindred from building vntil such
time as signification was giuen vnto Darius concerning
them, and an answere receiued.
7 The copie of the letters which Sisinnes gouernour of
Syria, and Phenice, and Sathrabuzanes with their companions
rulers in Syria and Phenice, wrote and sent vnto Darius, To
king Darius, greeting.
8 Let all things bee knowen vnto our lord the King, that
being come into the countrey of Iudea, and entred into the
citie of Ierusalem, we found in the citie of Ierusalem the
ancients of the Iewes that were of the captiuitie;
9 Building an house vnto the Lord, great, *and* newe, of
hewen and costly stones, and the timber already laid vpon
the walles.
10 And those workes are done with great speede, and the
worke goeth on prosperously in their handes, and with all
glory and diligence is it made.
11 Then asked wee these Elders, saying, By whose commaundement builde you this house, and lay the

foundations of these workes?
12 Therefore to the intent that wee might giue knowledge
vnto thee by writing, we demanded of them who were the
chiefe doers, and we required of them the names in writing
of their principall men.
13 So they gaue vs this answere: We are the seruants of
the Lord which made heauen and earth.
14 And as for this house, it was builded many yeeres agoe,
by a king of Israel great and strong, and was finished.
15 But when our fathers prouoked God vnto wrath, and
sinned against the Lord of Israel which is in heauen, hee
gaue them ouer into the power of Nabuchodonosor king of
Babylon of the Chaldees:
16 Who pulled downe the house and burnt it, and caried
away the people captiues vnto Babylon.
17 But in the first yeere that King Cyrus reigned ouer the
country of Babylon, Cyrus the king wrote to build vp this
house.
18 And the holy vessels of gold and of siluer, that Nabuchodonosor had caried away out of the house at Ierusalem,
and had set them in his owne temple, those Cyrus the
king brought forth againe out of the temple at Babylon, and
they were deliuered to ||Zorobabel and to Sanabassarus the
ruler,
19 With commaundement that hee should carrie away the
same vessels, and put them in the Temple at Ierusalem, and
that the Temple of ye Lord should be built in his place.
20 Then the same Sanabassarus being come hither, laid the
foundations of the house of the Lord at Ierusalem, and from
that time to this, being still a building, it is not yet fully
ended.

|| *Or, Zorobabel, which is also Sanabassar the ruler, so as Zorobabel seemeth to be added to the text, Ezra* 1. 8.

21 Now therefore if it seeme good vnto the king, let search
be made among the ||records of King Cyrus,
22 And if it be found, that the building of the house of the
Lord at Ierusalem hath bene done with the consent of King
Cyrus, and if our lord the king be so minded, let him signifie
vnto vs thereof.

|| *Or, roules.*

23 Then commanded king Darius to seeke among the
records at Babylon: and so at Ecbatana the palace which is
in the countrey of Media,

‖Or, place. there was found a ‖roule wherein these things were recorded.

24 In the first yeere of the reigne of Cyrus, king Cyrus commaunded that the house of the Lord at Ierusalem should bee built againe where they doe sacrifice with continuall fire.

25 Whose height shalbe sixtie cubits, and the breadth sixtie cubits, with three rowes of hewen stones, and one row of new wood of that countrey, and the expenses thereof to bee giuen out of the house of king Cyrus.

26 And that the holy vessels of the house of the Lord, both of gold and siluer that Nabuchodonosor tooke out of the house at Ierusalem, and brought to Babylon, should be restored to the house at Ierusalem, and bee set in the place where they were before.

27 And also he commanded that Sisinnes the gouernour of Syria and Phenice, and Sathrabuzanes, and their companions, and those which were appointed rulers in Syria, and Phenice should be carefull not to meddle with the place, but suffer Zorobabel the seruant of the Lord, and gouernour of Iudea, and the Elders of the Iewes, to build the house of the Lord in that place.

28 I haue commanded also to haue it built vp whole againe, and that they looke diligently to helpe those that be of the captiuitie of the Iewes, till the house of the Lord be finished.

29 And out of the tribute of Coelosyria, and Phenice, a portion carefully to be giuen these men, for the sacrifices of the Lord *that is*, to Zorobabel the gouernour, for bullocks, and rammes, and lambes;

30 And also corne, salt, wine and oile, and that continually euery yeere without further question, according as the Priests that be in Ierusalem shall signifie, to be daily spent:

‖Drinke offerings. 31 That ‖offrings may be made to the most high God, for the king and for his children, and that they may pray for their liues.

32 And he commanded, that whosoeuer should transgresse, yea, or make light of any thing afore spoken or written, out of his owne house should a tree be taken, and he thereon be hanged, and all his goods seized for the king.

33 The Lord therfore whose Name is there called vpon,

vtterly destroy eue-

ry king and nation, that stretcheth out his hand to hinder or
endammage that house of the Lord in Ierusalem.
34 I Darius the king haue ordeined, that according vnto
these things it be done with diligence.

CHAP. VII.

1 Sisinnes and others, helpe forward the building. 5 The Temple is finished, and dedicated. 10 The Passeouer is kept.

THen *Sisinnes the gouernour of Coelosyria, and *Ezra 6. 13.
Phenice, and Sathrabuzanes, with their companions,
following the commandements of king Darius,
2 Did very carefully ouersee the holy workes, assisting the
ancients of the Iewes, & gouernours of the Temple.
3 And so the holy workes prospered, when Aggeus, and
Zacharias the Prophets prophecied.
4 And they finished these things, by the commandement of
the Lord God of Israel, and with ||the consent of Cyrus, || *Or, the decree.*
Darius, and Artaxerxes, kings of Persia.
5 And thus was the holy house finished, in the †three and † *Hebr. the third day, Ezra* 6. 15.
twentieth day of the moneth Adar, in the sixt yeere of
Darius king of the Persians.
6 And the children of Israel: the Priests, and the Leuites,
and other that were of the captiuitie, that were added vnto
them, did according to the things written in the booke of
Moses.
7 And to the dedication of the Temple of the Lord, they
offered an hundred bullockes, two hundred rammes, foure
hundred lambes;
8 And twelue goats for the sinne of all Israel, according to
the number of ||the chiefe of the tribes of Israel. || *Or, tribes.*
9 The Priests also and the Leuites, stood arayed in their
vestments according to their †kinreds, in the seruices of the † *Hebr. diuisions, Esdr.* 6. 18.
Lord God of Israel, according to the booke of Moses: and
the porters at euery gate.
10 And the children of Israel ||that were of the captiuitie, || *Or, with those that, &c.*
held the Passeouer the fourteenth day of the first moueth,
after that the Priests and the Leuites were sanctified.
11 They that were of the captiuitie were not all sanctified
together: but the Leuites were all sanctified together,

12 And

12 And so they offered the Passeouer for all them of the
captiuitie, and for their brethren the Priestes, and for themselues.
13 And the children of Israel that came out of the captiuitie,
did eate, euen all they that had separated themselues from
the abominations of the people of the land, and sought the
Lord.
14 And they kept the feast of vnleauened bread seuen dayes,
making merry before the Lord,
|| Or, mind. 15 For that he had turned the ||counsell of the King of
Assyria towards them to strengthen their hands in the
workes of the Lord God of Israel.

CHAP. VIII.

1 Esdras bringeth the Kings Commission to build. 8 The copy of it. 28 He declareth the names and number of those that came with him: 61 And his iourney. 71 Hee lamenteth the sinnes of his people, 96 And sweareth the Priestes to put away their strange wiues.

AND after these things, when Artaxerxes the king of the
Persians reigned, came Esdras the sonne of Saraias, the
|| Azarias. sonne of ||Ezerias, the sonne of Helchiah, the sonne of Salum,
2 The sonne of Sadduc, the sonne of Achitob, the sonne of
|| Azarias. Amarias, the sonne of ||Ozias, the sonne of ||Memeroth, the
|| Meraioth. sonne of Zaraias, the sonne of ||Sauias, the sonne of Boccas,
|| Vzzi. Some copies want these three names. the sonne of Abisum, the sonne of Phinees, the sonne of
Eleasar, the sonne of Aaron the †chiefe Priest.
3 This Esdras went vp from Babylon, as a Scribe being
† Heb. was first, Ezra 7. 1. very ready in the Law of Moyses, that was giuen by the
God of Israel,
4 And the king did him honour: for he found grace in his
sight in all his requests.
5 There went vp with him also certaine of the children of
Israel, of the Priests, of the Leuites, of the holy Singers,
|| Nethinims. Porters, and ||Ministers of the Temple, vnto Ierusalem,
6 In †the seuenth yere of the reigne of king Artaxerxes, in
† See Ezra 7. 7, 8, 9. the fifth moneth, (this was the kings seuenth yeere) for they
went from Babylon in the first day of the first moneth, and
|| Or, successe came to Ierusalem, according to the ||prosperous

iourney which the Lord gaue them.
7 For Esdras had very great skill, so that he omitted nothing
of the Law and Commaundements of the Lord, but taught
all Israel the Ordinances and Iudgements.
8 Now the copy of the ||Commission which was written || *Or, decree.*
from Artaxerxes the King, and came to Esdras the priest and
reader of the Law of the Lord, is this that followeth.
9 King Artaxerxes vnto Esdras the Priest and reader of the
Law of the Lord, sendeth greeting.
10 Hauing determined to deale graciously, I haue giuen
order, that such of the nation of the Iewes, and of the Priests
and Leuites being within our Realme, as are willing and
desirous, should goe with thee vnto Ierusalem.
11 As many therefore as haue a minde thereunto, let them
depart with thee, as it hath seemed good both to me, & my
seuen friends the counsellors,
12 That they may looke vnto the affaires of Iudea and
Ierusalem, agreeably to that which is in the Law of the Lord.
13 And cary the gifts vnto the Lord of Israel to Ierusalem,
which I and my friends haue vowed, and all the golde and
siluer that in the countrey of Babylon can be ||found, to the || *Or, got.*
Lord in Ierusalem,
14 With that also which is giuen of the people, for the
Temple of the Lord their God at Ierusalem: and that siluer
and golde may be collected for bullocks, rammes and lambes,
and things thereunto appertaining,
15 To the end that they may offer sacrifices vnto the Lord,
vpon the Altar of the Lord their God, which is in Ierusalem.
16 And whatsoeuer thou and thy brethren will doe ||with || *With the rest of, Ezra* 7. 18.
the siluer and golde, that doe according to the will of thy
God.
17 And the holy vessels of the Lord which are giuen thee,
for the vse of the Temple of thy God which is in Ierusalem,
thou shalt set before thy God in Ierusalem.
18 And whatsoeuer thing else thou shalt remember for the
vse of the Temple of thy God, thou shalt giue it out of the
kings treasury.
19 And I, king Artaxerxes, haue also commaunded the
keepers of the

treasures in Syria and Phenice, that whatsoeuer Esdras the
priest, and the reader of the law of the most high God shall
send for, they should giue it him with speed,
20 To the summe of an hundred talents of siluer: likewise
also of wheat euen to an hundred ||cores, and an hundred
pieces of wine, and other things in abundance.

[|| *Or, measures or salt,* *Ezra* 7. 22.]

21 Let all things be performed after the law of God
diligently vnto the most high God, that wrath come not
vpon the kingdome of the King and his sonnes.
22 I command you also that yee require no taxe, nor any
other imposition of any of the Priests or Leuites, or holy
singers, or porters, or ministers of the temple, or of any that
haue doings in this temple, and that no man haue authority
to impose any thing vpon them.
23 And thou, Esdras, according to the wisedome of God,
ordaine iudges, and iustices, that they may iudge in all Syria
and Phenice, †all those that know the law of thy God, and
those that know it not thou shalt teach.

[† *Heb. of those that know Ezra* 7. 25.]

24 And *whosoeuer shal transgresse the law of thy God,
and of the king, shall be punished diligently, whether it be
by death or other punishment, by penalty of money, or by
imprisonment.

[* Ezra 7. 26.]

25 ¶ Then said Esdras the Scribe, Blessed be the onely
Lord God of my fathers, who hath put these things into the
heart of the king, to glorifie his house that is in Ierusalem;
26 And hath honoured mee in the sight of the king and his
counsellers, and all his friends and Nobles.
27 Therefore was I encouraged, by the helpe of the Lord
my God, and gathered together men of Israel to goe vp with
me:
28 And these are the chiefe according to their families and
seuerall dignities, that went vp with me from Babylon in the
reigne of king Artaxerxes.
29 Of the sonnes of Phinees, Gerson: of the sonnes of
Ithamar, ||Gamael: of the sonnes of Dauid; ||Lettus *the
sonne of Sechenias:
30 Of the sonnes of Pharez, Zacharias, and with him were
counted, an hundred and fifty men:
31 Of the sonnes of Pahath, Moab; Eliaonias, the sonne of
||Zaraias, and

[|| *Or, Daniel.* || *Or, Chattus.* * Ezra 8. 3. of the sons of Secheniah, of the sonnes of Parosh. || *Zerachaiah.*]

with him two hundred men:
32 Of the sonnes of ||Zathoe, Sechenias, the sonne of
Iezelus, and with him three hundred men; Of the sonnes of
Adin, Obeth the sonne of Ionathan, and with him †two
hundred and fifty men.
33 Of the sonnes of Elam, Iosias sonne of ||Gotholias, and
with him seuenty men:
34 Of the sonnes of Saphatias, ||Zaraias sonne of Michael,
and with him ||threescore and ten men:
35 Of the sonnes of Ioab, ||Abadias sonne of ||Iezelus, and
with him two hundred and ||twelue men:
36 Of the sonnes of Banid, ||Assalimoth sonne of Iosaphias,
and with him an hundred and threescore men:
37 Of the sonnes of Babi, Zacharias sonne of Bebai, and
with him twentie and eight men:
38 Of the sonnes of ||Astath, Iohannes *sonne of* ||Acatan,
and with him an hundred and ten men:
39 Of the sonnes of Adonicam the last, and these are the
names of them, Eliphalet, Ieuel, and ||Samaias and with
them ||seuenty men:
40 Of the sonnes of †Bago, Vthi, the sonne of Istalcurus,
and with him seuenty men:
41 And these I gathered together to the riuer, called
||Theras, where we pitched our tents three dayes, and then
I suruayed them.
42 But when I had found there, none of the priests and
Leuites,
43 Then sent I vnto Eleazar and ||Iduel, and ||Masman,
44 And Alnathan, and Mamaias, and ||Ioribas, and Nathan,
Eunatan, Zacharias, and Mosollamon principal men and
learned.
45 And I bad them that they should goe vnto Saddeus the
captaine, who was in the place of the treasury:
46 And commanded them that they should speake vnto
Daddeus, and to ||his brethren, and to the treasurers in that
place, to send vs such men as might execute the Priests office
in the house of the Lord.
47 And by the mighty hand of our Lord they brought vnto
vs skilful men of the sonnes of ||Moli, the sonne of Leui, the
sonne of Israel, ||Asebebia and his sonnes and his brethren,
who were eighteene.

48 And

||*Or, of the sonnes of Shecheniah the sonne of Iahaziel.*
†*Heb. fifty men.*
||*Or, Athaliah.*
||*Or, Zebadiah.*
||*Or, fourescore men.*
||*Or, Obadiah.*
||*Or, Iehiel.*
||*Or, eighteene men.*
||*Or, of the sonnes of Shelomith the sonne of Iosiphiah.*
||*Or, Azgad.*
||*Or, Catan.*
||*Or, Shemaia.*
||*Or, sixty men.*
||*Or, to the riuer called Ahaue. Ez.* 8. 11.
||*Or, he numbred the people and the priests: but found none of the sonnes of Leui.*
||*Or, Ariel.*
||*Or, Shemaiah.*
||*Or, Iarib.*
||*Or, these mens names with their generations are rightly distinguished Ezra* 8. 16.
||*Or, Iddo.*
||*Or, of*

||*Or, Casiphia.* ||*Or, the Nethinims at the place of Casiphia.* ||*Or, Machli.* ||*Sherebia Ezra* 8. 18. ||*Or, also Hashabia, and with him Ieshaiah of the sonnes of Merari with his brethren, Ezra* 8. 19.

48 And Asebia, and Annuus, and Osaias his brother of the sonnes of Channuneus, and their sonnes were twentie men.

49 And of the seruants of the Temple whom Dauid had ordeined, and the principall men, for the seruice of the Leuites (to wit) the seruants of the Temple, two hundred and twentie, the catalogue of whose names were shewed.

‖*Proclaimed.*

†*Heb. substance.*

50 And there I ‖vowed a fast vnto the yong men before our Lord, to desire of him a prosperous iourney, both for vs, and them that were with vs: for our children and for the †cattell:

51 For I was ashamed to aske the king footmen, & horsemen, and conduct for safegard against our aduersaries:

52 For wee had said vnto the king, that the power of the Lord our God, should be with them that seeke him, to support them in all wayes.

53 And againe wee besought our Lord, as touching these things, & found him fauourable vnto vs.

‖*Serenias and Hassibias.*

54 Then I separated twelue of the chiefe of the priests, ‖Esebrias, & Assanias, and ten men of their brethren with them.

55 And I weighed them the golde, and the siluer, and the holy vessels of the house of our Lord, which the king and his counsell, and the princes, and all Israel had giuen.

56 And when I had weighed it, I deliuered vnto them sixe hundred and fiftie talents of siluer, and siluer vessels of an hundred talents, and an hundred talents of gold,

†*Heb. two vessels, Ezr.* 8. 27.

57 And twentie golden vessels, and †twelue vessels of brasse, euen of fine brasse, glittering like gold.

58 And I said vnto them, Both you are holy vnto the Lord, and the vessels are holy, and the golde, and the siluer *is* a vowe vnto the Lord, the Lord of our fathers.

59 Watch ye, and keepe them till yee deliuer them to the chiefe of the priestes and Leuites, and to the principall men of the families of Israel in Ierusalem into the chambers of the house of our God.

60 So the priests and the Leuites who had receiued the siluer & the golde, and the vessels, brought them vnto Ierusalem into the Temple of the Lord.

61 And from the riuer Theras wee

departed the twelft day of the first moneth, and came to
Ierusalem by the mightie hand of our Lord, which was with
vs: and from the beginning of our ||iourney, the Lord ||*Dangers*
deliuered vs from euery enemy, and *so* wee came to Ierusalem. *in the way.*
62 And when wee had bene there three dayes, the golde
and siluer that was weighed, was deliuered in the house of
our Lord on the fourth day vnto ||Marmoth the priest, the ||*Or, vnto*
sonne of Iri. *Merimoth*
63 And with him was Eleazar the sonne of Phinees, and *the sonne of Vriah the*
with them were Iosabad the sonne of Iesu, and ||Moeth the *Priest.*
sonne of Sabban, Leuites: all was *deliuered them* by number ||*Noadiah*
and weight. *the sonne of Binnui.*
64 And all the weight of them was written vp the same
houre.
65 Moreouer they that were come out of the captiuitie
offered sacrifice vnto the Lord God of Israel, euen twelue
bullocks for all Israel, fourescore and sixteene rammes,
66 †Threescore and twelue lambes, goates for a peace †*Heb.* 77.
offering, twelue, all of them a sacrifice to the Lord. *lambes,* 12.
67 And they deliuered the kings commandements vnto the *hee goats for a sinne*
kings stewards, and to the gouernours of Coelosyria, and *offering,*
Phenice, and they honoured the people, and the Temple *Ezra* 8. 31.
of God.
68 Now when these things were done, the rulers came
vnto me, and said:
69 The nation of Israel, the princes, the priests, and Leuites
haue not put away from them the strange people of the *Ezra 9. 2.
land: nor the pollutions of the Gentiles, *to wit*, of the
Chanaanites, Hittites, Pheresites, Iebusites, and the Moabites,
Egyptians, and Edomites.
70 For both they, and their sonnes, haue maried with their
daughters, and the holy seed is mixed with the strange people
of the land, and from the beginning of this matter, the rulers
and the great men haue bene partakers of this iniquitie.
71 And assoone as I had heard these things, I rent my
clothes, and the holy garment, and pulled off the haire from
off my head, and beard, and sate me downe sad, and very
heauy.
72 So all they that were then mooued at the word of the
Lord God of Israel, assembled vnto me, whilest I
mour-

mourned for the iniquitie: but I sate still full of heauinesse,
vntill the euening sacrifice.
73 Then rising vp from the fast with my clothes and the
holy garment rent, and bowing my knees, and stretching
foorth my hands vnto the Lord:
74 I said, O Lord, I am confounded, and ashamed before
thy face;
75 For our sinnes †are multiplied aboue our heads, and our
ignorances haue reached vp vnto heauen.
76 For euer since the time of our fathers wee *haue bene* and
are in great sinne, euen vnto this day:
77 And for our sinnes and our fathers, we with our
brethren, and our kings, and our priests, were giuen vp
vnto the Kings of the earth, to the sword, and to captiuitie,
and for a pray with shame, vnto this day.
78 And now in some measure hath mercy bene shewed
vnto vs, from thee, O Lord, that there should be left vs a
roote, and a name, in the place of thy Sanctuary.
79 And to discouer vnto vs a light in the house of the Lord
our God, and to giue vs †foode in the time of our seruitude.
80 Yea, when we were in bondage, we were not forsaken
of our Lord; but he made vs gracious before the Kings of
Persia, so that they gaue vs food;
81 Yea, and honoured the Temple of our Lord, and raised
vp the desolate Sion, that they haue giuen vs a sure abiding
in Iurie, and Ierusalem.
82 And now, O Lord, what shall wee say hauing these
things? for wee haue transgressed thy Commaundements,
which thou gauest by the hand of thy seruants the Prophets,
saying,
83 That the land which ye enter into to possesse as an
heritage, is a land polluted with the pollutions of the
strangers of the land, and they haue filled it with their
vncleannesse.
84 Therefore now shal ye not ioyne your daughters vnto their
sonnes, neither shall ye take their daughters vnto your sonnes.
85 Moreouer you shall neuer seeke to haue peace with
them, that yee may be strong, and eate the good things of
the land, and that ye may leaue the inheritance of the land
vnto your children for euermore.
86 And all that is befallen, is done

† *Greeke. haue abounded.*

† *Hebr. life, Ezr. 9. 8.*

vnto vs for our wicked workes, and great sinnes: for thou,
O Lord, didst make our sinnes light:
87 And didst giue vnto vs such a roote: but we haue
turned backe againe to transgresse thy Law, and to mingle
our selues with the vncleannesse of the nations of the land.
88 ||Mightest not thou be angry with vs to destroy vs, till ||*Or, be not*
thou hadst left vs neither root, seed, nor name? *angry, &c.*
89 O Lord of Israel, thou art true: for we are left a root
this day.
90 Behold, now are we before thee in our iniquities, for
wee cannot stand any longer by reason of these things
before thee.
91 And as Esdras in his praier made his confession, weeping,
and lying flat vpon the ground before the Temple, there
gathered vnto him from Ierusalem, a very great multitude of
men, and women, & children: for there was great weeping
among the multitude.
92 Then Iechonias the sonne of Ieelus, one of the sonnes
of Israel called out and saide, O Esdras, wee haue sinned
against the Lord God, wee haue maried strange women of
the nations of the land, & now is all Israel ||aloft. ||*Or,*
93 Let vs make an oath to the Lord, that wee will put *exalted, Deut.* 28.
away all our wiues, which we haue taken of the heathen, 13. *&*
with their children, *Baruch.* 3.
94 Like as thou hast decreed, and as many as doe obey the
Law of the Lord.
95 Arise, and put in execution: for to thee doeth this
matter appertaine, and wee will bee with thee: doe valiantly.
96 So Esdras arose, and tooke an oath of the chiefe of the †*Hebr.*
Priestes, and Leuites of all †Israel, to do after these things, *and of*
and *so* they sware. *all Israel, Ezr.* 10. 5.

CHAP. IX.

3 Esdras assembleth all the people. 10 They promise to put away the strange wiues. 20 The names and number of them that did so. 40 The Law of Moses is read and declared before all the people. 49 They weepe, and are put in mind of the Feast day.

THen Esdras rising from the court of the Temple, went
to the chamber of Ioanan the sonne of Eliasib,

2 And

2 And remained there, and did eate no meate nor drinke
water, mourning for the great iniquities of the multitude.
3 And there was a proclamation in all Iury and Ierusalem,
to all them that were of the captiuitie, that they should be
gathered together at Ierusalem:
4 And that whosoeuer met not there within two or three
dayes according as the Elders that bare rule, appointed, their
cattell should be seized to the vse of the Temple, and him-
|| *Vtterly destroyed, Iosh.* 10. 8. selfe ||cast out from them that were of the captiuitie.
5 And in three dayes were all they of the tribe of Iuda and
Beniamin gathered together at Ierusalem the twentieth day
of the ninth moneth.
6 And all the multitude sate trembling in the broad court
of the Temple, because of the present foule weather.
7 So Esdras arose vp, and said vnto them, Ye haue transgressed the law in marrying strange wiues, thereby to increase
the sinnes of Israel.
8 And now by confessing giue glory vnto the Lord God of
our fathers,
9 And doe his will, and separate your selues from the heathen of the land, and from the strange women.
10 Then cryed the whole multitude, and sayd with a loude
voice; Like as thou hast spoken, so will we doe.
11 But forasmuch as the people are many, and it is foule
weather, so that wee cannot stand without, and this is not a
worke of a day or two, seeing our sinne in these things is
spread farre:
|| *Or, stand.* 12 Therefore let the rulers of the multitude ||stay, and let
all them of our habitations that haue strange wiues, come at
the time appointed,
13 And with them the Rulers and Iudges of euery place,
till we turne away the wrath of the Lord from vs, for this
matter.
14 Then Ionathan the sonne of Azael, and Ezechias the
sonne of Theocanus, accordingly tooke this matter vpon
them: and Mosollam, and Leuis, and Sabbatheus helped them.
15 And they that were of the capti utie, did according to
all these things.
16 And Esdras the Priest chose vnto him the principal men
of their families, all by name: and in the first day of the
tenth moneth, they sate together to examine the matter.

17 So their cause that helde strange wiues, was brought to
an ende in the first day of the first moneth.
18 And of the Priests that were come together, and had
strange wiues, there were found :
19 Of the sonnes of Iesus the sonne of Iosedec, and his
brethren, ||Matthelas, and Eleazar, and ||Ioribus, and ||Ioa-
danus.
20 And they gaue their hands to put away their wiues, &
to offer †rammes, to make reconcilement for their ||errors.
21 And of the sonnes of Emmer, Ananias, and Zabdeus,
and [a]Eanes, and [b]Sameius, and [c]Hierel, and [d]Azarias.
22 And of the sonnes of [e]Phaisur, Ellionas, Massias, Ismael,
and Nathanael, and [f]Ocidelus, and [g]Talsas.
23 And of the Leuites: Iosabad, and Semis, and [h]Colius
who was called [i]Calitas, and [k]Patheus, and Iudas, and
Ionas.
24 Of the holy Singers: [l]Eleazurus, Bacchurus.
25 Of the Porters: Sallumus, and [m]Tolbanes.
26 Of them of Israel, of the sonnes of [n]Phoros, [o]Hiermas,
and [p]Eddias, and Melchias, and [q]Maelus, and Eleazar, and
[r]Asibias, and Baanias.
27 Of the sonnes of Ela, Matthanias, Zacharias, and [s]Hieri-
elus, and Hieremoth, and [t]Aedias.
28 And of the sonnes of [u]Zamoth, [x]Eliadas, [y]Elisimus,
[z]Othonias, Iarimoth, and [a]Sabatus, and [b]Sardeus.
29 Of the sonnes of Bebai, Iohannes, and Ananias, and
[c]Iosabad, and [d]Amatheis.
30 Of the sonnes of [e]Many, [f]Olamus, [g]Mamuchus, [h]Iedeus,
Iasubus, [i]Iasael, and Hieremoth.
31 †And of the sonnes of Addi, Naathus, and Moosias,
Lacunus, and Naidus, and Mathanias, and Sesthel, Balunus,
and Manasseas.
32 And of the sonnes of Annas, Elionas, and Aseas, and
Milchias, and Sabbeus, and Simon Chosameus.
33 Aud of the sonnes of Asom, [k]Altaneus, and [l]Matthias,
and [m]Bannaia, Eliphalat, and Manasses, and Semei.
34 And of the sonnes of Maani, Ieremias, Momdis, Oma-
erus, Iuel, Mabdai, and Pelias, and Anos, Carabasion, and
Enasibus, & Mamnitanaimus, Eliasis, Bannus, Eliali, Samis,
Selenias, Nathanias: And of the sons
of

|| *Maasias.* || *Iarib.* || *Gedaliah.* † *Hebr. a ramme.* || *Or, purification.* [a] *Harim.* [b] *Maasiah.* [c] *Iehiel.* [d] *Vzziah.* [e] *Pashur.* [f] *Iosabad.* [g] *Elasah.* [h] *Kelaiah.* [i] *Kelitah.* [k] *Pethahiah.* [l] *Eliashib.* [m] *Telem.* [n] *Parosh.* [o] *Ramiah.* [p] *Iesaiah.* [q] *Miamin.* [r] *Malchuah.* [s] *Iehiel.* [t] *Abdi.* [u] *Zattu.* [x] *Elioenai.* [y] *Eliashib.* [z] *Mattaniah.* [a] *Sabad.* [b] *Aziza.* [c] *Zabbai.* [d] *Athlai.* [e] *Bani.* [f] *Meshullam* [g] *Malluch.* [h] *Adaiah.* [i] *Sheal.* † *Of the names in vers.* 31, 32, 34, 35, *See Ezr.* 10. 30, 31. 34, *&c.* [k] *Matenai.* [l] *Mattithiah* [m] *Zabad.*

of Ozora, Sesis, Esril, Azailus, Samatus, Zambis, Iosiphus,
35 And of the sonnes of Ethma, Mazitias, Zabadaias, Edes,
Iuel, Banaias.
36 All these had taken strange wiues, and they put them
away with their children.
37 And the priests, and Leuites, and they that were of
Israel dwelt in Ierusalem, and in the countrey, in the first
day of ye seuenth month: so the children of Israel were in
|| *Or, villa-ges.* their ||habitations.
*Nehe. 8. 1. 38 *And the whole multitude came together with one
accord, into the broad place of the holy porch toward the
East.
39 And they spake vnto Esdras the priest and reader, that
he would bring the law of Moses, that was giuen of the
Lord God of Israel.
40 So Esdras the chiefe priest, brought the law vnto the
whole multitude from man to woman, and to all the priests,
to heare the law in the first day of the seuenth moneth.
41 And hee read in the broad court before the holy porch
from morning vnto midday, before both men and women;
|| *Or, Hilkiah.* and all the multitude gaue heed vnto the law.
|| *Or, Maasiah.* 42 And Esdras the priest, and reader of the law stood vp,
vpon a pulpit of wood which was made *for that purpose.*
|| *Or, Pedaiah.* 43 And there stood vp by him Matathias, Sammus, Ananias,
|| *Or, Hashum.* Azarias, Vrias, ||Ezecias, ||Balasamus, vpon the right hand.
|| *See Nehem.* 8. 4. 44 And vpon his left hand stood ||Phaldaius, Misael, Mel-
chias, ||Lothasubus and ||Nabarias.

¶ II. ES

CHAP. II.

1 Esdras is commanded to reproue the people. 24 God threatneth to cast them off, 35 and to giue their houses to a people of more grace then they.

*Ezra 7. 1. THe second booke of the Prophet *Esdras the sonne of
|| *Or, Shallum.* Saraias, the sonne of Azarias, the sonne of Helchias,
the sonne of ||Sadamias, the

45 Then tooke Esdras the booke of the law before the
multitude: for he sate †honourably in the first place in the
sight of them all.
46 And when hee opened the law, they stood all streight
vp. So Esdras blessed the Lord God most high, the God of
hostes Almighty.
47 And all the people answered Amen, and lifting vp their
hands they fell to the ground, & worshipped the Lord.
48 Also Iesus, Anus, Sarabias, Adinus, Iacubus, Sabateus,
||Auteas, Maianeas, and Calitas, Azarias, and Ioazabdus, and
Ananias, Biatas, the Leuites taught the law of the Lord,
making them withall to vnderstand it.
49 ||Then spake Attharates vnto Esdras the chiefe priest,
and reader, and to the Leuites that taught the multitude,
euen to all, saying,
50 This day is holy vnto ẏ Lord; for they all wept when
they heard the law.
51 Goe then and eate the fat, and drinke the sweet, and
send part to ||them that haue nothing.
52 For this day is holy vnto the Lord, and be not sorrowfull; for the Lord will bring you to honour.
53 So the Leuites published all things to the people, saying:
This day is holy to the Lord, be not sorrowfull.
54 Then went they their way, euery one to eate and drinke,
& make mery, and to giue part to them that had nothing, and
to make great cheere,
55 Because they vnderstood the words wherein they were
instructed, and for ẏ which they had bin assembled.

† Heb. aboue them all.

|| Or, Hodiiah.

|| Then Nehemiah and Ezra the priest and Scribe, and the Leuites that instructed the people, said vnto all the people. Nehem. 8. 9

|| Or, the poore.

DRAS.

sonne of Sadoc, the sonne of Achitob,
2 The sonne of Achias, the sonne of Phinees, the sonne of
Heli, the sonne of Amarias, the sonne of Aziei, the sonne of
Marimoth, the sonne of Arna, the sonne of Ozias, the sonne
of Borith, the sonne of Abisei, the sonne of Phinees, the
sonne of Eleazar,
3 The sonne of Aaron, of the Tribe of Leui, which was
captiue in the land of the Medes, in the reigne of Artaxerxes
king of the Persians.

4 *And

*Isa. 58. 1. 4 *And the word of the Lord came vnto me, saying,
5 Goe thy way, and shew my people their sinfull deeds, and
their children their wickednes which they haue done against
me, that they may tell their childrens children,
6 Because the sinnes of their fathers are increased in them:
for they haue forgotten me, & haue offered vnto strange gods.
7 Am not I euen hee that brought them out of the land of
Egypt, from the house of bondage? but they haue prouoked
me vnto wrath, and despised my counsels.
8 Pull thou off then the haire of thy head, and cast all euill
vpon them, for they haue not beene obedient vnto my law,
but it is a rebellious people.
9 How long shall I forbeare them vnto whō I haue done so
much good?
*Exod. 14. 10 *Many kings haue I destroyed for their sakes, Pharao
28. with his seruants, and all his power haue I smitten downe.
*Num. 21. 11 All the nations haue I destroyed before them, *& in the
24. iosh. 8. East I haue scattered the people of two prouinces, euen of
12. Tyrus and Sidon, and haue slaine all their enemies.
12 Speake thou therefore vnto them saying, Thus saith the
Lord,
*Eod. 14. 13 *I led you through the Sea, and in the beginning gaue
29. you a large and safe ||passage, *I gaue you Moyses for a
|| *Or, street.* leader, and Aaron for a priest,
*Exo. 3.
10. and 4. 14 *I gaue you light in a pillar of fire, and great wonders
14. haue I done among you, yet haue you forgotten me, saith
*Exod. 13. the Lord.
21.
*Exod. 16. 15 Thus saith the Almightie Lord, The quailes *were as a
13. psal. token for you, I gaue you tents for your safegard, neuerthe-
104 40. lesse you murmured there,
16 And triumphed not in my name for the destruction of
your enemies, but euer to this day doe ye yet murmure.
17 Where are the benefits that I haue done for you? when
*Num. 14. you were hungry and thirstie in the wildernesse, *did you
3. not crie vnto me?
18 Saying, Why hast thou brought vs into this wildernesse
to kill vs? It had bin better for vs to haue serued the
Egyptians, then to die in this wildernesse.
19 Then had I pity vpon your mournings, and gaue you
*Wisd. 16. Manna to eat, *so
20.

ye did eate Angels bread.
20 *When ye were thirstie, did I not cleaue the rocke, and *Numb.
waters flowed out ||to your fill? for the heate I couered you 20 11.
with the leaues of the trees. wisd. 11 4. || Or, abundantly.
21 I diuided amongst you a fruitfull land, I cast out the
Canaanites, the Pherezites, and the Philistines before you:
*what shall I yet doe more for you, saith the Lord? *Isa. 5. 4.
22 Thus saith the Almighty Lord, when you were in the & exod. 15. 23
wildernes in the riuer of the ||Amorites, being athirst, and || Or, at the bitter waters, or waters of Marah.
blaspheming my Name,
23 I gaue you not fire for your blasphemies, but cast a tree
in the water, and made the riuer sweet.
24 What shall I doe vnto thee, O Iacob? thou *Iuda *Exo. 32. 8.
wouldest not obey me: I will turne me to other nations, and
vnto those will I giue my Name, that they may keepe my
Statutes.
25 Seeing yee haue forsaken mee, I will forsake you also:
when yee desire me to be gracious vnto you, I shall haue no
mercy vpon you.
26 *Whensoeuer you shall call vpon me, I will not heare *Isa. 1. 15.
you: for yee haue defiled your hands with blood, and your
feete are swift to commit manslaughter.
27 Yee haue not as it were forsaken me, but your owne
selues, saith the Lord.
28 Thus saith the Almighty Lord, Haue I not prayed you
as a father his sonnes, as a mother her daughters, and a nurse
her young babes,
29 That yee would be my people, ||and I shoud be your God, || Or, as I am your God
that ye would be my children, and I should be your father?
30 *I gathered you together, as a henne gathereth her *Mat. 23. 37.
chickens vnder her wings: but now, what shall I doe vnto
you? I will cast you out from my face.
31 *When you offer vnto me, I will turne my face from *Isa. 1. 13.
you: for your solemne feast dayes, your newe Moone, and
your circumcisions haue I forsaken.
32 I sent vnto you my seruants the Prophets, whom yee
haue taken and slaine, and torne their bodies in pieces, whose
blood I will require of your hands, saith the Lord.
33 Thus saith the Almighty Lord, Your house is desolate,
I will cast you
out,

out, as the wind doth stubble.
34 And your children shall not bee fruitful : for they haue
despised my Commandement, and done the thing that is euill
before me.
35 Your houses wil I giue to a people that shall come, which
not hauing heard of mee, yet shall beleeue mee, to whom I
haue shewed no signes, yet they shall doe that I haue commaunded them.
36 They haue seene no Prophets, yet they shall call their
sinnes to remembrance, and acknowledge them.
37 I take to witnesse the grace of the people to come,
whose little ones reioyce in gladnesse: and though they haue
not seene me with bodily eyes, yet in spirit they beleeue the
thing that I say.
38 And now brother, behold what glory : and see the people that commeth from the East.
39 Vnto whom I will giue for leaders, Abraham, Isaac, and
Iacob, Oseas, Amos, and Micheas, Ioel, Abdias, and Ionas,
40 Nahum, and Abacuc, Sophonias, Aggeus, Zacharie, and
Malachie, which is called also an *Angel of the Lord.

*Mala. 3. 1.

CHAP. II.

1 God complaineth of his people : 10 Yet Esdras is willed to comfort them. 34 Because they refused, the Gentiles are called. 43 Esdras seeth the Sonne of God, and those that are crowned by him.

THus saith the Lord, I brought this people out of bondage,
and I gaue them my Commaundements by my seruants
the prophets, whom they would not heare, but despised my
counsailes.
2 The mother that bare them, saith vnto them, Goe your
way ye children, for I am a widow, and forsaken.
3 I brought you vp with gladnesse, but with sorrow and
heauinesse haue I lost you : for yee haue sinned before the
Lord your God, and done that thing that is euil before him.
4 But what shall I now doe vnto you ? I am a widow and
forsaken : goe your way, O my children, and aske mercy of
the Lord.
5 As for mee, O father, I call vpon thee for a witnesse ouer
the mother of

these children, which would not keepe my Couenant,
6 That thou bring them to confusion, and their mother to
a spoile, that there may be no off spring of them.
7 Let them bee scattered abroad among the heathen, let their
names bee put out of the earth: for they haue despised my
||Couenant. ||*Sacrament or oath.*
8 Woe be vnto thee Assur, thou that hidest the vnrighteous
in thee, O thou wicked people, remember *what I did vnto *Gene. 19. 24.
Sodome and Gomorrhe.
9 Whose land lieth in clods of pitch and heapes of ashes:
euen so also wil I doe vnto them that heare me not, saith the
Almightie Lord.
10 Thus saith the Lord vnto Esdras, Tell my people that I
will giue them the kingdome of Hierusalem, which I would
haue giuen vnto Israel.
11 Their glory also wil I take vnto mee, and giue these the
euerlasting Tabernacles, which I had prepared for them.
12 They shall haue the tree of Life for an oyntment of
sweet sauour, they shall nether labour, nor be weary.
13 Goe and yee shall receiue: pray for few dayes vnto you,
that they may be shortned: the kingdome is already prepared
for you: Watch.
14 Take heauen and earth to witnesse; for I haue broken
the euill in pieces, and created the good; for I liue, saith the
Lord.
15 Mother, embrace thy children, and ||bring them vp with ||*Or, bring them vp with gladnesse as a doue: make their feet fast. For, &c.*
gladnesse, make their feet as fast as a pillar: for I haue chosen
thee, saith the Lord.
16 And those that be dead wil I raise vp againe from their
places, and bring them out of the graues: for I haue knowen
||my Name in Israel. ||*Or, thy name, O Israel.*
17 Feare not thou mother of the children: for I haue chosen
thee, saith the Lord.
18 For thy helpe I will send my seruants Esay and Ieremie,
after whose counsaile I haue sanctified and prepared for thee
twelue trees, laden with diuers fruits;
19 And as many fountaines flowing with milke and hony:
and seuen mightie mountaines, whereupon there grow roses
and lillies, whereby I will fill thy children with ioy.
20 Doe right to the widow, iudge
for

for the fatherlesse, giue to the poore, defend the orphane,
clothe the naked,
21 Heale the broken and the weake, laugh not a lame man
to scorne, defend the maimed, and let the blind man come
into the sight of my clearenesse.
22 Keepe the olde and yong within thy walles.
*Tob. 17. 18. 23 *Wheresoeuer thou findest the dead, †take them and bury
†*Signing bury them.* them, and I will giue thee the first place in my resurrection.
24 Abide still, O my people, and take thy rest, for thy
quietnesse shall come.
25 Nourish thy children, O thou good nource, stablish
their feete.
26 As for the seruants whom I haue giuen thee, there shall
not one of them perish ; for I will require them from among
thy number.
27 Be not weary, for when the day of trouble and heauinesse commeth, others shal weepe and be sorrowfull, but
thou shalt be merry, and haue abundance.
28 The heathen shall enuie thee, but they shall be able to
doe nothing against thee, sayth the Lord.
29 My hands shal couer thee, so that thy children shall not
see hell.
30 Be ioyfull, O thou mother, with thy children, for I will
deliuer thee, sayth the Lord.
31 Remember thy children that sleep, for I shall bring them
out of the sides of the earth, and shew mercy vnto them : for
I am mercifull, sayth the Lord Almightie.
‖*Or, preach.* 32 Embrace thy children vntill I come and ‖shew mercy vnto
them : for my welles runne ouer, and my grace shall not faile.
33 I Esdras receiued a charge of the Lord vpon the mount
Oreb, that I should goe vnto Israel ; but when I came vnto
them, they set me at nought, and despised the commandement of the Lord.
34 And therefore I say vnto you, O yee heathen, that heare
and vnderstand, Looke for your shepheard, hee shall giue you
euerlasting rest ; for he is nigh at hand, that shall come in
the end of the world.
35 Be ready to the reward of the kingdome, for the euerlasting light shal shine vpon you for euermore.
36 Flee the shadow of this world, receiue the ioyfulnesse of
your glory : I te-

stifie my Sauiour openly.
37 O receiue the gift that is giuen you, and be glad, giuing
thankes vnto him that hath called you to the heauenly kingdome.
38 Arise vp and stand, behold the number of those that be
sealed ‖in the feast of the Lord: ‖*Or, for.*
39 Which are departed from the shadow of the world, and
haue receiued glorious garments of the Lord.
40 Take thy number, O Sion, and †shut vp those of thine †*Lat. con-*
that are clothed in white, which haue fulfilled the Law of *clude.*
the Lord.
41 The number of thy children whom thou longedst for, is
fulfilled: beseech the power of the Lord, that thy people
which haue been called from the beginning, may be hallowed.
42 *I Esdras saw vpon the mount Sion a great people, *Reu. 7. 9.
whom I could not number, and they all praised the Lord
with songs.
43 And in the middest of them there was a young man of
a high stature, taller then all the rest, and vpon euery one of
their heads he set crownes, and was more exalted, which I
marueiled at greatly.
44 So I asked the Angel, and said, ‖Sir, what are these? ‖*Or, Lord.*
45 Hee answered, and said vnto me, These be they that
haue put off the mortall clothing, and put on the immortall,
and haue confessed the Name of God: now are they crowned,
and receiue palmes.
46 Then sayd I vnto the Angel, What yong person is it
that crowneth them, and giueth them palmes in their handes?
47 So hee answered, and said vnto me, It is the sonne of
God, whom they haue confessed in the world. Then began
I greatly to commend them, that stood so stiffely for the
Name of the Lord.
48 Then the Angel sayd vnto me, Goe thy way, and tell
my people what maner of things, and how great wonders of
the Lord thy God thou hast seene.

CHAP. III.

1 Esdras is troubled, 13 and acknowledgeth the sinnes of the people: 28 yet complaineth that the heathen were lords ouer them, being more wicked then they.

IN the thirtieth yeere after the ruine of the citie, I was
in Babylon, and lay troubled vpon my bed, and my
thoughts came vp ouer my heart.
2 For I saw the desolation of Sion, and the wealth of them
that dwelt at Babylon.
3 And my spirit was sore moued, so that I began to speake
words full of feare to the most High, and said,
4 O Lord, who bearest rule, thou spakest at the beginning,
when thou didst plant the earth (and that thy selfe alone) and
commandedst the people,
*Gen. 2. 7. 5 *And gauest a body vnto Adam without soule, which was
the workemanship of thine hands, & didst breathe into him
the breath of life, and he was made liuing before thee.
6 And thou leddest him into paradise, which thy right hand
had planted, before euer the earth came forward.
7 And vnto him thou gauest commandement to loue thy
way, which he transgressed, and immediatly thou appoint-
edst death in him, and in his generations, of whom came
nations, tribes, people, and kinreds out of number.
*Gen. 6. 8 *And euery people walked after their owne will, and did
12. wonderfull things before thee, and despised thy commandements.
*Gen. 7. 9 *And againe in processe of time thou broughtest the
10 flood vpon those that dwelt in the world, and destroyedst
them.
10 And it came to passe in euery of them, that as death
was to Adam, so was the flood to these.
*1. Pet. 3. 11 Neuerthelesse one of them thou leftest, namely *Noah
20. with his household, of whom came all righteous men.
12 And it happened, that when they that dwelt vpō the
earth began to multiply, and had gotten them many children,
and were a great people, they beganne againe to be more
vngodly then the first.
*Gen. 12. 13 Now when they liued so wickedly before thee, *thou
1 diddest choose thee a man from among them, whose name
*Gen. 17. was *Abraham.
5 14 Him thou louedst, and vnto him onely thou shewedst
thy will:
15 And madest an euerlasting couenant with him, promising him that thou wouldest neuer forsake his seede.

16 *And vnto him, thou gauest Isahac, and *vnto Isahac *Gen. 21.
also thou gauest Iacob and Esau. As for Iacob thou *didst 2, 3. *Gen. 25.
choose him to thee, and put by Esau: and so Iacob became 25, 26.
a great multitude. *Mal. 1. 2,
17 And it came to passe, that when thou leddest his seede 3
out of Egypt, *thou broughtest them vp to the mount *Rom. 9.
Sina. 13. exod. 19. 1. deut.
18 And bowing the heauens, thou didest set fast the earth, 4. 10.
mouedst the whole world, and madest the depth to tremble,
and troubledst the men of that age.
19 And thy glory went through foure gates, of fire, and of
earthquake, and of wind, and of cold, that thou mightest giue
the law vnto the seed of Iacob, ||and diligence vnto the gene- ||*And to all the generation of Israel, that they should keepe it with diligence.*
ration of Israel.
20 And yet tookest thou not away from them a wicked
heart, that thy law might bring forth fruite in them.
21 For the first Adam bearing a wicked heart transgressed,
and was ouercome; and so be all they that are borne of
him.
22 Thus infirmity was made permanent; and the law
(also) in the heart of the people with the malignity of the
roote, so that the good departed away, and the euill abode
still.
23 So the times passed away, and the yeeres were brought
to an end: *then diddest thou raise thee vp a seruant, called *1. Sam. 16. 13.
Dauid,
24 *Whom thou commandedst to build a citie vnto thy *2. Sam.
name, and to offer incense and oblations vnto thee therein. 5. 1. and 7. 5. 13.
25 When this was done many yeeres, then they that in-
habited the citie forsooke thee,
26 And in all things did euen as Adam, and all his generations had done, for they also had a wicked heart.
27 And so thou gauest the citie ouer into the hands of thine
enemies.
28 Are their deeds then any better that inhabite Babylon,
that they should therefore haue the dominion ouer Sion?
29 For when I came thither, and had seene impieties without number, then my soule saw many euill doers in this
thirtieth yeere, so that my heart failed me.
30 For I haue seene how thou sufferest

rest them sinning, and hast spared wicked doers: and hast destroyed thy people, and hast preserued thine enemies, and hast not signified it.

‖ *Or, I conceiue.*

31 ‖I doe not remember how this way may be left: Are they then of Babylon better then they of Sion?

32 Or is there any other people that knoweth thee besides Israel? or what generation hath so beleeued thy Couenants as Iacob?

33 And yet their reward appeareth not, and their labour hath no fruite: for I haue gone here and there through the heathen, and I see that they ‖flowe in wealth, and think not vpon thy commandements.

‖ *Or, abound*

34 Weigh thou therfore our wickednesse now in the ballance, and theirs also that dwell in the world: and so shall thy Name no where be found, but in Israel.

35 Or when was it that they which dwell vpon the earth, haue not sinned in thy sight? or what people hath so kept thy commandements?

36 Thou shalt find that Israel by name hath kept thy precepts: but not the heathen.

CHAP. IIII.

1 The Angel declareth the ignorance of Esdras in Gods iudgments, 13 and aduiseth him not to meddle with things aboue his reach. 23 Neuerthelesse Esdras asketh diuers questions, and receiueth answeres to them.

AND the Angel that was sent vnto me, whose name was Vriel, gaue mee an answere,

2 And said, Thy heart hath gone too farre in this world, and thinkest thou to comprehend the way of the most High?

3 Then said I, Yea my Lord: and he answered me and said, I am sent to shew thee three wayes, and to set forth three similitudes before thee.

4 Whereof if thou canst declare me one, I will shew thee also the way that thou desirest to see, & I shall shew thee from whence the wicked heart cōmeth.

5 And I said, Tel on my Lord. Then said he vnto me, Goe thy way, weigh me the weight of the fire, or measure me the blast of the wind, or call me againe the day that is past.

6 Then answered I and said, What man is able to doe that, that thou shoul-

dest aske such things of mee?
7 And he said vnto me, If I should aske thee how great
dwellings are in the midst of ẏ sea, or how many springs are
in the beginning of the deepe, or how many springs are aboue
the firmament, or which are the outgoings of Paradise:
8 Peraduenture thou wouldest say vnto me, I neuer went
downe into the deepe, nor as yet into hell, neither did I euer
climbe vp into heauen.
9 Neuerthelesse, now haue I asked thee but onely of the fire
and winde, and of the day where through thou hast passed,
and of things frō which thou canst not be separated, and yet
canst thou giue me uo answeere of them.
10 He said moreouer vnto me, Thine owne things, and such
as are growen vp with thee, canst thou not know.
11 How should thy vessel then bee able to comprehend the
way of the highest, and the world being now outwardly cor-
rupted, to vnderstand the ||corruption that is euident in my
sight?

|| *Or, incorruption.*

12 Then said I vnto him, It were better that we were not
at all, then that we should liue still in wickednesse, and to
suffer, and not to know wherefore.
13 He answered me and said, I went into a forest into a
plaine, and the *trees tooke counsell,
14 And said, Come, let vs goe and make warre against the
Sea, that it may depart away before vs, and that we may
make vs more woods.

* Iudg. 9. 8. 2. chron. 25 18.

15 The floods of the Sea also in like maner tooke counsell,
and said, Come, let vs goe vp and subdue the woods of the
plaine, that there also we may make vs another countrey.
16 The thought of the wood was in vaine, for the fire came
and consumed it.
17 The thought of the floods of the Sea came likewise to
nought, for the sand stood vp and stopped them.
18 If thou wert iudge now betwixt these two, whom wouldest thou begin to iustifie, or whom wouldest thou condemne?
19 I answered and said, Verily it is a foolish thought that
they both haue deuised: for the ||ground is giuen vnto the
wood, and the sea also hath his place to beare his ||floods.
20 Then answered he me and said, Thou hast giuen a right
iudgment, but why iudgest thou not thy selfe also?

|| *Or, the land.*
|| *Or, waues.*

|| *The land.* 21 For like as ||the ground is giuen vnto the wood, & the
* Isay 55. sea to his floods: euen so *they that dwell vpon the earth
8, 9 iohn may vnderstand nothing, but that which is vpon the earth:
3. 31. 1. cor. 2. and hee that dwelleth aboue the heauens, may onely vnder-
13. stand the things that are aboue the height of the heauens.
22 Then answered I, and said, I beseech thee, O Lord, let
me haue vnderstanding.
23 For it was not my minde to be curious of the high
things, but of such as passe by vs dayly, namely wherefore
Israel is giuen vp as a reproch to the heathen, and for what
cause the people whom thou hast loued, is giuen ouer vnto
vngodly nations, and why the Lawe of our forefathers is
brought to nought, and the written Couenants come to
|| *Or, no where.* ||none effect.
24 And wee passe away out of the world as grassehoppers,
and our life is astonishment and feare, and we are not worthy
to obtaine mercie.
25 What will he then doe vnto his Name, whereby we are
called? of these things haue I asked.
26 Then answered he me, and said, The more thou searchest, the more thou shalt marueile, for the world hasteth fast
to passe away,
27 And cannot comprehend the things that are promised to
the righteous in time to come: for this world is ful of vnrighteousnesse and infirmities.
28 But as concerning the things whereof thou askest me, I
wil tell thee; for the euil is sowen, but the destruction
thereof is not yet come.
29* If therefore that which is sowen, be not turned vpside
downe; and if the place where the euil is sowen passe not
away, then cannot it come that is sowen with good.
30 For the graine of euill seed hath bene sowen in the heart
of Adam from the beginning, and how much vngodlinesse
hath it brought vp vnto this time? and how much shall it yet
|| *Or, floore.* bring foorth vntill the ||time of threshing come.
31 Ponder now by thy selfe, how great fruit of wickednesse
the graine of euil seed hath brought forth.
32 And when the eares shall bee cut downe, which are
without number, how great a floore shall they fill?
33 Then I answered and said, How and when shall these
things come to

passe? wherefore are our yeeres few and euill?
34 And he answered me, saying, Do not thou hasten aboue
the most Highest: for thy haste is in vaine to be aboue him,
for thou hast much exceeded.
35 Did not the soules also of the righteous aske question of
these things in their chambers, saying, How long shall I hope
on this fashion? when commeth the fruit of the floore of our
reward?
36 And vnto these things ||Vriel the Archangel gaue them ||*Ieremiel*
answere, and said, Euen when the number of seedes is filled
in you: for he hath weighed the world in the ballance.
37 By measure hath hee measured the times, and by number
hath he numbred the times; and he doeth not mooue nor
stirre them, vntill the said measure be fulfilled.
38 Then answered I, and said, O Lord that bearest rule,
euen we all are full of impietie.
39 And for our sakes peraduenture it is that the floores of
the righteous are not filled, because of the sinnes of them that
dwell vpon the earth.
40 So he answered me, and said, Go thy way to a wman
with childe, and aske of her, when she hath fulfilled her nine
moneths, if her wombe may keepe the birth any longer within her?
41 Then said I, No Lord, that can she not. And he said
vnto mee, In the graue, the chambers of soules are like the
wombe of a woman:
42 For like as a woman that trauaileth, maketh haste to
escape the necessitie of the trauaile: euen so doe these places
haste to deliuer those things that are committed vnto them.
43 From the beginning looke what thou desirest to see, it
shalbe shewed thee.
44 Then answered I, and said, If I haue found fauour in
thy sight, and if it be possible, and if I be meet therefore,
45 Shew me then whether there be more to come then is
past, or more past then is to come.
46 What is past I know; but what is for to come I know not.
47 And he said vnto me, Stand vp vpon the right side, and
I shal expound the similitude vnto you.
48 So I stood and saw, and behold an hot burning ouen
passed by before mee: and it happened that when the
flame

flame was gone by, I looked, and behold, the smoke remained still.

49 After this there passed by before me a watrie cloude, and sent downe much raine with a storme, and when the stormie raine was past, the drops remained still.

50 Then said he vnto me, Consider with thy selfe: as the raine is more then the drops, and as the fire is greater then the smoke: but the drops and the smoke remaine behind: so the ||quantity which is past, did more exceede.

|| *Or, measure.*

51 Then I prayed, and sayd, May I liue, thinkest thou, vntill that time? ||or what shall happen in those dayes?

|| *Or, who shalbe manuscript?*

52 He answered me, and sayd, As for the tokens whereof thou askest me, I may tell thee of them in part; but as touching thy life, I am not sent to shew thee, for I doe not know it.

CHAP. V.

1 The signes of the times to come. 23 He asketh why God choosing but one people, did cast them off. 30 Hee is taught, that Gods Iudgements are vnsearchable: 46 and that God doeth not all at once.

|| *Shalbe found with great wealth*

NEuertheles as concerning the tokens, beholde, the dayes shall come that they which dwell vpon earth, ||shall bee taken in a great number, and the way of trueth shall be hidden, and the land shall be barren of faith.

* Mat. 24. 12

2 But *iniquitie shalbe increased aboue that which now thou seest, or that thou hast heard long agoe.

|| *Or, that thou treadest vpon and seest.*

3 And the land ||that thou seest now to haue roote, shalt thou see wasted suddenly.

4 But if the most high graunt thee to liue, thou shalt see after the third trumpet, that the Sunne shall suddenly shine againe in the night, and the Moone thrice in the day.

5 And blood shal drop out of wood, and the stone shall giue his voice, and the people shalbe troubled.

6 And enen he shal rule whom they looke not for that dwel vpon the earth, and the foules shall take their flight away together.

7 And the Sodomitish sea shall cast out fish, and make a noyse in the night, which many haue not knowen: but they shall all heare the voice thereof.

8 There shall be a confusion also in many places, and the
fire shalbe oft ||sent out againe, and the wilde beasts shall || *Or, slaked.*
change their places, and menstruous women shall bring foorth
monsters.
9 And salt waters shall be found in the sweete, and all
friends shall destroy one another: then shall wit hide it selfe,
and vnderstanding withdraw it selfe into his secret chamber,
10 And shall be sought of many, and yet not be found:
then shall vnrighteousnesse and incontinencie be multiplyed
vpon earth.
11 One land also shall aske another, and say, Is righteousnes
that maketh a man righteous, gone through thee? And it
shall say, No.
12 At the same time shall men hope, but nothing obtaine:
they shall labour, but their wayes shall not ||prosper. || *Or, be reiected.*
13 To shew thee such tokens I haue leaue: and if thou
wilt pray againe, and weepe as now, and fast seuen dayes,
thou shalt heare yet greater things.
14 Then I awaked, & an extreme fearefulnesse went through
all my body, and my minde was troubled, so that it fainted.
15 So the Angel that was come to talke with me, helde me,
comforted me, and set me vp vpon my feete.
16 And in the second night it came to passe, that Salathiel
the captaine of the people came vnto mee, saying, Where
hast thou beene? and why is thy countenance so heauie?
17 Knowest thou not that Israel is committed vnto thee, in
the land of their captiuitie?
18 Vp then, and eate bread, and forsake vs not as the shepheard that leaueth his flocke in the handes of cruell wolues.
19 Then sayd I vnto him, Goe thy waies from me, and
come not nigh me: And he heard what I said, and went
from me.
20 And so I fasted seuen dayes, monrning and weeping, like
as Vriel the Angel commanded me.
21 And after seuen dayes, so it was that the thoughts of my
heart were very grieuous vnto me againe.
22 And my soule recouered the spirit of vnderstanding, and
I began to talke with the most high againe,
23 And said, O Lord, that bearest rule of euery wood of
the earth, and of

all the trees thereof, thou hast chosen thee one onely vine.
24 And of all lands of the whole world thou hast chosen
thee one pit: and of all the flowers thereof, one Lillie.
25 And of all the depths of the Sea, thou hast filled thee
one riuer: and of all builded cities, thou hast hallowed Sion
vnto thy selfe.
26 And of all the foules that are created, thou hast named
thee one Doue: and of all the cattell that are made, thou
hast prouided thee one sheepe.
27 And among all the multitudes of peoples, thou hast
gotten thee one people: and vnto this people whom thou
louedst, thou gauest a law that is approued of all.
28 And now O Lord, why hast thou giuen this one people
|| *Or, ouer.* ouer vnto many? and ||vpon the one roote hast thou prepared
others, and why hast thou scattered thy onely one people
among many?
29 And they which did gainesay thy promises, and beleeued
not thy couenants, haue trodden them downe.
30 If thou didst so much hate thy people, yet shouldest thou
punish them with thine owne hands.
31 Now when I had spoken these words, the Angell that
came to me the night afore, was sent vnto me,
32 And said vnto me, Heare me, and I will instruct thee,
hearken to the thing that I say, & I shal tell thee more.
33 And I said, Speake on, my Lord: then said he vnto me,
thou art sore troubled in minde for Israels sake: louest thou
that people better then hee that made them?
34 And I said, No Lord, but of very griefe haue I spoken:
For my reines paine me euery houre, while I labour to comprehend the way of the most High, and to seeke out part of
his iudgement.
35 And he said vnto me, Thou canst not: and I said,
wherfore Lord? wherunto was I borne then? or why was
not my mothers wombe then my graue, that I might not
haue seene the trauell of Iacob, and the wearisome toyle of
the stocke of Israel?
36 And he said vnto me, Number me the things that are
not yet come, gather me together the droppes that are scattered abroad, make mee the flowres greene againe that are
withered.

37 Open me the places that are closed, and bring me forth
the winds that in them are shut vp, shew me the image of a
voyce: and then I will declare to thee the thing that thou
labourest to knowe.
38 And I said, O Lord, that bearest rule, who may know
these things, but hee that hath not his dwelling with men?
39 As for me, I am vnwise: how may I then speake of
these things whereof thou askest me?
40 Then said he vnto me, Like as thou canst doe none of
these things that I haue spoken of, euen so canst thou not
find out my iudgement, or in the end the loue that I haue
promised vnto my people.
41 And I said, behold, O Lord, yet art thou nigh vnto
them that be reserued till the end; and what shall they doe
that haue beene before me, or we (that be now) or they that
shall come after vs?
42 And he said vnto me, I wil liken my iudgement vnto a
ring: like as there is no slacknesse of the last, euen so there
is no swiftnesse of the first.
43 So I answered and said, Couldst thou not make those
that haue beene made, and be now, and that are for to come,
at once, that thou mightest shewe thy iudgement the sooner?
44 Then answered he me, and said, The creature may not
hast aboue the maker, neither may the world hold them at
once that shalbe created therin.
45 And I said, As thou hast said vnto thy seruant, that thou
which giuest life to all, hast giuen life at once to the creature
that thou hast created, and the creature bare it: euen so it
might now also beare them that now be present at once.
46 And he said vnto me, Aske the wombe of a woman, &
say vnto her, If thou bringest forth children, why doest thou it
not together, but one after another? pray her therefore to
bring forth tenne children at once.
47 And I said, She cannot: but must doe it by distance of
time.
48 Then said he vnto me, Euen so haue I giuen the wombe
of the earth to those that be sowen in it, in their times.
49 For like as a young child may not bring forth the things
that belong to the aged, euen so haue I disposed the world
which I created.

50 And

50 And I asked and said, Seeing thou hast now giuen me
the way, I will *proceed to* speak before thee: for our mother
of whom thou hast told me that she is yong, draweth now
nigh vnto age.
51 He answered me and said, Aske a woman that beareth
children, and shee shall tell thee.
52 Say vnto her, Wherefore are not they whome thou hast
now brought forth, like those that were before, but lesse of
stature?
53 And she shall answere thee, They that be borne in the
strength of youth, are of one fashion, and they that are borne
in the time of age (when the wombe faileth) are otherwise.
54 Consider thou therfore also, how that yee are lesse of
stature then those that were before you.
55 And so are they that come after you lesse then ye, as the
creatures which now begin to be old, and haue passed ouer
the strength of youth.
56 Then saide I, Lord, I beseech thee, if I haue found fauor
in thy sight, shew thy seruant by whom thou visitest thy
creature.

CHAP. VI.

1 Gods purpose is eternall. 8 The next world shall follow this immediatly. 13 What shall fall out at the last. 31 Hee is promised more knowledge, 38 and reckoneth vp the workes of the creation, 57 and complaineth that they haue no part in the world for whome it was made.

|| *Or, circle of the earth.*

AND he said vnto me, in the beginning when yͤ ||earth was
made, before the borders of the world stood, or euer the
windes blew,
2 Before it thundred and lightned, or euer the foundations
of Paradise were laide,
3 Before the faire flowers were seene, or euer the moueable
powers were established, before yͤ innumerable multitude of
Angels were gathered together,
4 Or euer the heights of the aire were lifted vp, before the
measures of the firmament were named, or euer the chimnies
in Sion were hot,
5 And ere the present yeeres were sought out, and or euer
the inuentions of them that now sinne were turned, before
they were sealed that haue gathered faith for a treasure:
6 Then did I consider these things,

and they all were made through mee alone, and through none
other: by mee also they shall be ended, & by none other.
7 Then answered I and said, What shall bee the parting
asunder of the times? or when shall be the ende of the first,
and the beginning of it that followeth?
8 And he said vnto me, From Abraham vnto Isaac, when
Iacob and Esau were borne of him, *Iacobs hand held ||first
the heele of Esau.
9 For Esau is the end of the world, and Iacob is the beginning of it that followeth.
10 The hand of man is betwixt the heele and the hand:
other question, Esdras, aske thou not.
11 ¶ I answered then and said, O Lord that bearest rule, if
I haue found fauour in thy sight,
12 I beseech thee, shew thy seruant the end of thy tokens,
whereof thou shewedst me part the last night.
13 So he answered and said vnto me, Stand vp vpon thy
feete, and heare a mightie sounding voyce.
14 And it shall be as it were a great ||motion, but the place
where thou standest, shall not be moued.
15 And therefore when it speaketh be not afraid: for the
word is of the end, and the foundation of the earth is vnderstood.
16 And why? because the speech of these things trembleth
and is mooued: for it knoweth that the ende of these things
must be changed.
17 And it happened that when I had heard it, I stood vp
vpon my feet, and hearkened, & behold, there was a voice
that spake, and the sound of it was like the sound of many
waters.
18 And it said, Behold, the dayes come, that I will begin to
draw nigh, and to visit them that dwell vpon the earth,
19 And will begin to make inquisition of them, what they
be that haue hurt vniustly with their vnrighteousnesse, and
when the affliction of Sion shalbe fulfilled.
20 And when the world that shal begin to vanish away shall
bee ||finished: then will I shew these tokens, the books shalbe
opened before the firmament, and they shall see all together.
21 And the children of a yeere olde shall speake with their
voyces, the wo-
men

*Gen. 25. 26.

|| Or, from the beginning.

|| Or, earthquake.

|| Or, sealed.

men with childe shall bring foorth vntimely children, of three
or foure moneths old: and they shall liue, and bee raised vp.
22 And suddenly shal the sowen places appeare vnsowen,
the full storehouses shall suddenly be found empty.
23 And the trumpet shall giue a sound, which when euery
man heareth they shalbe suddenly afraid.
24 At that time shall friendes fight one against another like
enemies, and the earth shall stand in feare with those that
dwell therein, the springs of the fountaines shall stand still,
and in three houres they shall not runne.
25 Whosoeuer remaineth from all these that I haue told
thee, shall escape, and see my saluation, and the ende of your
world.
26 And the men that are receiued, shall see it, who haue
not tasted death from their birth: and the heart of the inhabitants shalbe changed, and turned into another meaning.
27 For euil shalbe put out, and deceit shalbe quenched.
28 As for faith, it shall flourish, corruption shalbe ouercome,
& the trueth which hath bene so long without fruit, shalbe
declared.
29 And when hee talked with mee, behold, I looked by little
and little vpon him before whom I stood.
30 And these words said he vnto me, I am come to shew
thee the time of the night to come.
31 If thou wilt pray yet more, & fast seuen daies againe, I
|| *See cap. 13. vers. 52.* shal tel thee greater things ||by day, then I haue heard.
32 For thy voice is heard before the most High: for the
mighty hath seene thy righteous dealing, he hath seene also
thy chastitie, which thou hast had euer since thy youth.
33 And therefore hath he sent mee to shew thee al these
things, and to say vnto thee, Be of good comfort, & feare
not.
34 And hasten not with the times that are past, to thinke
vaine things, that thou mayest not hasten from the latter
times.
35 And it came to passe after this, that I wept againe, and
fasted seuen dayes in like maner, that I might fulfill the three
weekes which he told me.
36 And in the eight night was my heart vexed within mee
againe, and I began to speake before the most High.

37 For my spirit was greatly set on fire, and my soule was
in distresse.
38 And I said, O Lord, thou spakest from the beginning of
the creation, euen the first day, & saidest thus, *Let heauen *Gen. 1. 1.
and earth bee made: and thy word was a perfect worke.
39 And then was the spirit, and darkenesse, and silence were
on euery side; the sound of mans voice was not yet formed.
40 Then commandedst thou a faire light to come foorth of
thy treasures, that thy worke might appeare.
41 Vpon the second day thou madest the spirit of the firmament, and commandedst it to part asunder, and to make a
diuision betwixt the waters, that the one part might goe vp,
and the other remaine beneath.
42 Vpon the thirde day thou didst commaund that the
waters should bee gathered in the seuenth part of the earth:
sixe parts hast thou dried vp and kept them, to the intent that
of these some being planted of God and tilled, might serue thee.
43 For as soone as thy word went foorth, the worke was
made.
44 For immediatly there was great and innumerable fruit,
and many and diuers pleasures for the taste, & flowers of
vnchangeable colour, and odours of wonderfull smell: and
this was done the third day.
45 *Vpon the fourth day thou commandedst that the Sunne *Gen. 1.
should shine, and the Moone giue her light, and the starres 14.
should be in order,
46 And gauest them a charge to do *seruice vnto man, that Gen. 1. 15. deut. 4. 19.
was to be made.
47 Vpon the fift day, thou saydst vnto the seuenth part,
*where the waters were gathered, that it should bring foorth Gene. 1.
liuing creatures, foules and fishes: and so it came to passe. 20.
48 For the dumbe water, and without life, brought foorth
liuing things at the commandement of God, that al people
might praise thy wondrous works.
49 Then didst thou ordeine two liuing creatures, the one
thou calledst ||Enoch, and the other Leuiathan, ||*Behe-*
50 And didst separate the one from the other: for the *moth.*
seuenth part (namely where the water was gathered together)
might not hold them both.
51 Vnto Enoch thou gauest one part which was dried vp
the third day, that
he

he should dwel in the same part, wherein are a thousand
hilles.
52 But vnto Leuiathan thou gauest the seuenth part, namely
the moist, and hast kept him to be deuoured of whom thou
wilt, and when.
53 Vpon the sixt day thou gauest commaundement vnto the
earth, that before thee it should bring foorth beasts, cattell,
and creeping things:
54 And after these, Adam also whom thou madest lord of
all thy creatures, of him come wee all, and the people also
whom thou hast chosen.
55 All this haue I spoken before thee, O Lord, because thou
madest the world for our sakes.
56 As for the other people which also come of Adam, thou
hast said that they are nothing, but be like vnto spittle, and
hast likened the abundance of them vnto a drop that falleth
from a vessell.
57 And now, O Lord, behold, these heathen, which haue
euer been reputed as nothing, haue begun to be lordes ouer
vs, and to deuoure vs:
58 But wee thy people (whom thou hast called thy first
borne, thy onely begotten, and thy feruent louer) are giuen
into their hands.
59 If the world now be made for our sakes, why doe we
not possesse an inheritance with the world? how long shall
this endure?

CHAP. VII.

4 The way is narrow. 12 When it was made narrow. 28 All shall die and rise againe. 33 Christ shall sit in iudgement. 46 God hath not made Paradise in vaine, 62 & is merciful.

AND when I had made an ende of speaking these words,
there was sent vnto mee the Angel which had beene
sent vnto mee the nights afore.
2 And he said vnto me, Vp Esdras, and heare the wordes
that I am come to tell thee.
3 And I said, Speake on, my God. Then said he vnto me,
The Sea is set in a wide place, that it might be deepe and
great.
4 But put the case the entrance were narrow, and like a
riuer,
5 Who then could goe into the Sea to looke vpon it, and to
rule it? If hee

went not through the narrow, how could he come into the
broad?
6 There is also another thing. A city is builded, and set
vpon a broad field, and is full of all good things.
7 The entrance thereof is narrow, and is set in a ||dangerous || *Or, steepe*
place to fall, like as if there were a fire on the right hand, *place.*
and on the left a deepe water.
8 And one only path between them both, euen betweene
the fire and the water, *so small* that there could but one man
goe there at once.
9 If this city now were giuen vnto a man for an inheritance,
if he neuer shall passe the danger set before it, how shall he
receiue this inheritance?
10 And I said, It is so, Lord. Then said he vnto me, Euen
so also is Israels portion:
11 Because for their sakes I made the world: and when Adam
transgressed my Statutes, then was decreed that now is done.
12 Then were the entrances of this world made narrow,
full of sorrow and trauaile: they are but few and euill, full
of perils, and very painefull.
13 For the entrances of the ||elder world were wide and || *Or,*
sure, and brought immortall fruit. *greater*
14 If then they that liue, labour not to enter these strait
and vaine things, they can neuer receiue those that are laide
vp for them.
15 Now therefore why disquietest thou thy selfe, seeing
thou art but a corruptible man? and why art thou mooued,
whereas thou art but mortall?
16 Why hast thou not considered in thy minde this thing
that is to come, rather then that which is present?
17 Then answered I, and sayd, O Lord, that bearest rule,
thou hast ordained in thy *Law, that the righteous should *Deut. 8.
inherite these things, but that the vngodly should perish: 1.
18 Neuerthelesse, the righteous shal suffer strait things, and
hope for wide: for they that haue done wickedly, haue suffered
the strait things, and yet shall not see the wide.
19 And he said vnto me, There is no iudge aboue God, and
none that hath vnderstanding aboue the highest.
20 For there be many that perish in this life, because they
despise the Lawe of God that is set before them.
21 For God hath giuen strait com-
mande-

mandement to such as came, what they should doe to liue, euen as they came, and what they should obserue to auoid punishment.

22 Neuerthelesse they were not obedient vnto him, but spake against him, and imagined vaine things:

23 And deceiued themselues by their wicked deeds, and sayd of the most Hie, that he is not, and knew not his waies.

24 But his Law haue they despised, and denied his couenants; in his statutes haue they not beene faithfull, and haue not performed his workes.

25 And therfore Esdras, for the emptie, are emptie things, and for the ful, are the full things.

26 Behold, the time shall come, that these tokens which I haue told thee, shall come to passe, and the bride shall appeare, and she comming forth shall be seene, that now is withdrawen from the earth.

27 And whosoeuer is deliuered from the foresaid euils, shall see my wonders.

28 For my sonne Iesus shall be reuealed with those that be with him, and they that remaine shall reioyce within foure hundred yeeres.

29 After these yeeres shall my sonne Christ die, and all men that haue life.

30 And the world shall be turned into the old silence seuen dayes, like as in the ||former iudgements: so that no man shall remaine.

|| *Or, first beginning.*

31 And after seuen dayes, the world that yet awaketh not shall be raised vp, and that shall die, that is corrupt.

32 And the earth shall restore those that are asleepe in her, and so shall the dust those that dwell in silence, and the secret places shall deliuer those soules that were committed vnto them.

33 And the most high shall appeare vpon the seate of iudgement, and miserie shall passe away, and the long suffering shall haue an end.

34 But iudgement onely shall remaine, trueth shall stand, and faith shall waxe strong.

35 And the worke shall follow, and the reward shall be shewed, and the good deeds shall be of force, and wicked deeds shall beare no rule.

36 Then said I, *Abraham prayed first for the Sodomites, and *Moses for the fathers that sinned in the wildernesse:

*Gen. 18. 13.
*Exod. 32. 11.

37 And Iesus after him for Israel in the time of ||Achan, || Or, Archor.
38 And Samuel; and Dauid for the destruction: and *2. Sam. 24. 17.
*Solomon for them that should come to the sanctuary. *2. chro. 6. 14.
39 And *Helias for those that receiued raine, & for the
dead that hee might liue. *1. King. 17 21. and 18. 42. 45.
40 And *Ezechias for the people in the time of Sennacherib:
and many for many. *2. King. 19. 15.
41 Euen so now seeing corruption is growen vp, and wickednesse increased, and the righteous haue prayed for the vngodly:
wherefore shall it not be so now also?
42 He answered me and said, This present life is not the
end where much glory doth abide; therefore haue they prayed
for the weake.
43 But the day of doome shall be the end of this time, and
the beginning of the immortality for to come, wherein corruption is past.
44 Intemperancie is at an end, infidelity is cut off, righteousnesse is growen, and trueth is sprung vp.
45 Then shall no man be able to saue him that is destroyed,
nor to oppresse him that hath gotten the victory.
46 I answered then and said, This is my first and last saying;
that it had beene better not to haue giuen the earth vnto
Adam: or else when it was giuen him, to haue restrained
him from sinning.
47 For what profit is it for men now in this present time to
liue in heauinesse, and after death to looke for punishment?
48 O thou Adam, what hast thou done? for though it was
*thou that sinned, thou art not fallen alone, but we all that *Rom. 5. 18.
come of thee.
49 For what profit is it vnto vs, if there be promised vs an
immortall time, wheras we haue done the works that bring
death?
50 And that their is promised vs an euerlasting hope, whereas
our selues being most wicked are made vaine?
51 And that there are layd vp for vs dwellings of health and
safety, whereas we haue liued wickedly?
52 And that the glory of the most high is kept to defend
them which haue led ||a wary life, whereas we haue walked || Or, a chast life.
in the most wicked wayes of all?
53 And that there should be shewed

a

|| Or, fulnes. a paradise whose fruite endureth for euer, wherein is ||securitie
and medicine, sith we shall not enter into it?
54 For we haue walked in vnpleasant places.
55 And that the faces of them which haue vsed abstinence,
shall shine aboue the starres, whereas our faces shall bee
blacker then darkenesse?
56 For while we liued and committed iniquitie, we considered not that we should begin to suffer for it after death.
|| Or, intent. 57 Then answered he me and saide, This is the ||condition
of the battell, which man that is borne vpon the earth shall
fight,
58 That if he be ouercome, he shall suffer as thou hast said,
but if he get the victorie, he shall receiue the thing that I say.
59 For this is the life whereof Moses spake vnto the people
* Deut. 30. 19. while hee liued, saying, *Choose thee life that thou mayest
liue.
60 Neuerthelesse they beleeued not him, nor yet the prophets after him, no nor me which haue spoken vnto them,
61 That there should not be such heauinesse in their
destruction, as shall bee ioy ouer them that are perswaded to
saluation.
62 I answered then and saide, I know, Lord, that the most
Hie is called mercifull, in that he hath mercy vpon them,
which are not yet come into the world,
63 And vpon those also that turne to his Law,
* Rom. 2. 4. 64 And that *he is patient, and long suffereth those that
haue sinned, as his creatures,
65 And that he is bountifull, for hee is ready to giue where
it needeth,
66 And that is of great mercie, for he multiplieth more and
more mercies to them that are present, and that are past, &
also to them which are to come.
67 For if he shall not multiplie his mercies, the world would
not continue with them that inherit therein.
68 And he pardoneth; for if hee did not so of his goodnesse,
that they which haue committed iniquities might be eased of
them, the ten thousand part of men should not remaine liuing.
69 And being Iudge, if he should not forgiue them that are
|| Or, created. ||cured with his word, and put out the multitude of ||con-
|| Or, contempts. tentions,

70 There should bee very fewe left peraduenture in an
innumerable multitude.

CHAP. VIII.

1 Many created, but few saued. 6 Hee asketh why God destroyeth
his owne worke, 26 and prayeth God to looke vpon the people which
onely serue him. 41 God answereth that all seed commeth not to
God, 52 and that glory is prepared for him and such like.

AND he answered me, saying, The most High hath made
this world for many, but the world to come for fewe.
2 I will tell thee a similitude, Esdras, As when thou askest
the earth, it shall say vnto thee, that it giueth much mold
wherof earthen vessels are made, but litle dust that golde
commeth of: euen so is ẏ course of this present world.
3 *There be many created, but few shall be saued. *Mat. 20.
4 So answered I and said, Swallow then downe O my soule, 16.
vnderstanding, and deuoure wisedome.
5 For thou hast agreed to giue eare, and art willing to prophesie: for thou hast no longer space then onely to liue.
6 O Lord, if thou suffer not thy seruant that we may pray
before thee, and thou ||giue vs seed vnto our heart, and culture || *Or, to*
to our vnderstanding, that there may come fruit of it, howe *giue vs.*
shall each man liue that is corrupt, who beareth the place of
a man?
7 For thou art alone, and we all one workemanship of thine
hands, like as thou hast said.
8 For when the body is fashioned now in the mothers
wombe, and thou giuest it members, ||thy creature is preserued || *Or, how*
in fire & water, and nine months doeth thy workemanship *is the body*
endure thy creature which is created in her. *fashioned.*
9 But that which keepeth, and is kept, shall both be preserued: and when the time commeth, the wombe preserued,
deliuereth vp the things that grew in it.
10 For thou hast commanded out of the parts of the body,
that is to say, out of the breasts milke to be giuen, which is
the fruit of the breasts,
11 That the thing which is fashioned, may bee nourished for
a time, till thou disposest it to thy mercy.
12 Thou broughtest it vp with thy
righ-

righteousnesse, and nourturedst it in thy Law, and reformedst
it with thy iudgement.
13 And thou shalt mortifie it as thy creature, and quicken
it as thy worke.
14 If therefore thou shalt destroy him which with so great
*Iob 10. 8. psal. 139. 14. &c. *labour was fashioned, it is an easie thing to be ordeined by
thy Commaundement, that the thing which was made might
be preserued.
15 Now therefore, Lord, I will speake (touchiug man in
generall, thou knowest best) but touching thy people, for
whose sake I am sory,
16 And for thine inheritance, for whose cause I mourne,
and for Israel, for whom I am heauy, and for Iacob, for
whose sake I am troubled:
17 Therefore will I begin to pray before thee, for my selfe,
and for them: for I see the falles of vs that dwell in the land.
18 But I haue heard the swiftnesse of the Iudge which is to
come.
19 Therefore heare my voyce, and vnderstand my wordes,
and I shall speake before thee: this is the beginning of the
words of Esdras, before he was taken vp: and I said;
20 O Lord, Thou that dwellest in euerlastingnes, which
beholdest from aboue, things in the heauen, & in the aire,
21 Whose Throne is inestimable, whose glory may not be
comprehended, before whom the hosts of Angels stand with
trembling,
22 (Whose seruice is conuersant in wind and fire,) whose
word is true, and sayings constant, whose Commandement is
strong, and ordinance fearefull,
23 Whose looke drieth vp the depths, and indignation maketh
the mountaines to melt away, which the trueth witnesseth:
24 O heare the prayer of thy seruant, and giue eare to the
petition of thy creature.
25 For while I liue, I will speake, and so long as I haue
vnderstanding, I wil answere.
26 O looke not vpon the sinnes of thy people: but on them
which serue thee in trueth.
27 Regard not the wicked inuentions of the heathen: but
the desire of those that keepe thy Testimonies in afflictions.
28 Thinke not vpon those that

haue walked fainedly before thee: but remember them, which
according to thy will haue knowen thy feare.
29 Let it not bee thy will to destroy them, which haue
liued like beasts: but to looke vpon them that haue clearely
taught thy Law.
30 Take thou no indignation at them which are deemed
worse then beasts: but loue them that alway put their trust
in thy righteousnesse, and glory.
31 For we and our fathers ||doe languish of such dis- || *Are sicke.*
eases; but because of vs sinners, thou shalt be called mercifull.
32 For if thou ||hast a desire to haue mercy vpon vs, thou ||*Be wil-*
shalt bee called mercifull, to vs namely, that haue no workes *ling.*
of righteousnesse.
33 For the iust which haue many good workes layed
vp with thee, shall out of their owne deedes receiue reward.
34 For what is man that thou shouldest take displeasure at
him? or what is a corruptible generation, that thou shouldest
be so bitter toward it?
35 *For in trueth there is no man among them that be *1. King.
borne, but he hath dealt wickedly, and among the faithfull, 8. 46. and 2. chro. 6
there is none which hath not done amisse. 36.
36 For in this, O Lord, thy righteousnesse, and thy goodnesse shalbe declared, if thou be mercifull vnto them which
haue not the ||confidence of good workes. || *Or, sub-*
37 Then answered he mee, and said, Some things hast thou *stance.*
spoken aright, and according vnto thy words it shalbe.
38 For indeed I will not thinke on the disposition of them
which haue sinned before death, before iudgement, before
destruction.
39 But *I will reioyce ouer the disposition of the righteous, *Gen. 4. 4.
and I wil remember also their pilgrimage, and the saluation,
and the reward that they shall haue.
40 Like as I haue spoken now, so shall it come to passe.
41 For as the husbandmau soweth much seed vpon the
ground, and planteth many trees, and yet the thing that is
sowen good in his season, commeth not vp, neither doeth all
that is planted take root: euen so is it of them that are sowen
in the world, they shall not all be saued.

42 I answered then, and said, If I haue found grace, let me speake.

43 Like as the husbandmans seede perisheth, if it come not vp, and receiue not the raine in due season, or if there come too much raine and corrupt it:

44 Euen so perisheth man also which is formed with thy hands, and is called thine owne image, because thou art like vnto him, for whose sake thou hast made all things, and likened him vnto the husbandmans seede.

45 Be not wroth with vs, but spare thy people, and haue mercy vpon thine owne inheritance: for thou art mercifull vnto thy creature.

46 Then answered he me, and said, Things present are for the present; and things to come, for such as be to come.

47 For thou commest farre short, that thou shouldest be able to loue my creature more then I: but I haue oft times drawen nigh vnto thee, and vnto it, but neuer to the vnrighteous.

48 In this also thou art marueilous before the most high;

49 In that thou hast humbled thy selfe as it becommeth thee, and hast not iudged thy selfe worthy to be much glorified among the righteous.

50 For many great miseries shall be done to them, that in the latter time shal dwell in the world, because they haue walked in great pride.

51 But vnderstand thou for thy selfe, and seeke out the glory for such as be like thee.

52 For vnto you is Paradise opened, the tree of life is planted, the time to come is prepared, plenteousnesse is made ready, a citie is builded, and rest is allowed, yea perfect goodnesse and wisedome.

53 The root of euil is sealed vp from you, weakenesse and the moth is hidde from you, and corruption is fled into ||hell to be forgotten.

||*Or, graue.*

54 Sorrows are passed, & in the end is shewed the treasure of immortalitie.

55 And therefore aske thou no more questions concerning the multitude of them that perish.

56 For when they had taken liberty, they despised the most High, thought scorne of his Lawe, and forsooke his wayes.

57 Moreouer, they haue troden downe his righteous,

58 And *said in their heart, that there

*Psal. 14. 1. and 53. 1.

is no God, yea and that knowing they must die.
59 For as the things aforesaid shall receiue you, so thirst
and paine are prepared for them; for it was not his will that
men should come to nought.
60 But they which be created, haue defiled the Name of
him that made them, and were vnthankefull vnto him which
prepared life for them.
61 And therefore is my iudgement now at hand.
62 These things haue I not shewed vnto all men, but vnto
thee, and a fewe like thee. Then answered I, and said,
63 Behold, O Lord, now hast thou shewed me the multitude of the wonders which thou wilt begin to doe in the last
times: but at what time, thou hast not shewed me.

CHAP. IX.

7 Who shall be saued, and who not. 19 All the world is now corrupted: 22 Yet God doeth saue a few. 33 Hee complaineth that those perish which keepe Gods Law: 38 and seeth a woman lamenting in a field.

HEe answered me then, and sayde, Measure thou the
time diligently in it selfe: and when thou seest part
of the signes past, which I haue tolde thee before,
2 Then shalt thou vnderstand, that it is the very same
time, wherein the highest will begin to visite the world
which he made.
3 Therefore when there shall bee seene *earthquakes and *Mat. 24.
vprores of the people in the world: 7
4 Then shalt thou wel vnderstand, that the most high
spake of those things from the dayes that were before thee,
euen from the beginning.
5 For like as all that is made in the world hath a beginning,
and an ende, and the end is manifest:
6 Euen so the times also of the highest, haue plaine be-
ginnings in wonders and powerfull workes, and endings in
effects and signes.
7 And euery one that shalbe saued, and shalbe able to escape
by his works, and by faith, whereby ye haue beleeued,
8 Shall be preserued from the sayd perils, and shall see my
saluation, in my land, and within my borders: for I haue
sanctified them for me, from the beginning.
Mmmm 9 Then

‖Or, they shall maruell.

9 Then shall they ‖be in pitifull case which now haue
abused my wayes: and they that haue cast them away des-
spitefully, shall dwell in torments.
10 For such, as in their life haue receiued benefits, & haue
not knowen me:
11 And they that haue loathed my law, while they had
yet liberty, and when as yet place of repentance was open
vnto them, vnderstood not, but despised it:
12 The same must know it after death by paine.
13 And therefore be thou not curious, how the vngodly shalbe
punished and when: but enquire how the righteous shall be
saued, whose the world is, and for whom the world is created.
14 Then answered I, and said,
15 I haue said before, and now doe speake, and will speake
it also heereafter: that there be many moe of them which
perish, then of them which shall be saued,
16 Like as a waue is greater then a droppe.
17 And he answered me, saying: like as the field is, so is
also the seed: as the flowres be, such are the colours also:
such as the workeman is, such also is the worke: and as the
husbandman is himselfe, so is his husbandry also: for it was
the time of the world.

‖And now because the time of the world was come, when I was preparing the world &c.

‖But when the world was made, both now and then, the maners of euery one created were corrupted by a neuer failing haruest, and a law vnsearchable.

‖Or, graine.

‖Or, graine.

18 ‖And now when I prepared the world, which was not
yet made, euen for them to dwell in that now liue, no man
spake against me.
19 For then euery one obeyed, ‖but now the maners of
them which are created in this world that is made, are
corrupted by a perpetuall seed, & by a law which is vnsearchable, rid themselues.
20 So I considered the world, and behold there was perill,
because of the deuices that were come into it.
21 And I saw and spared it greatly, and haue kept me a
‖grape of the cluster, and a plant of a great people.
22 Let the multitude perish then, which was borne in
vaine, and let my ‖grape be kept and my plant: for with
great labour haue I made it perfect.
23 Neuerthelesse if thou wilt cease yet seuen dayes moe
(but thou shalt not fast in them.)
24 But goe into a field of flowres, where no house is builded,
and eate only the flowres of the field, Tast no flesh, drinke
no wine, but eate flowres onely.
25 And pray vnto the Highest conti-

nually, then wil I come and talke with thee.
26 So I went my way into the field which is called
Ardath, like as he commanded me, and there I sate
amongst the flowres, and did eate of the herbes of the
field, and the meate of the same satisfied me.
27 After seuen dayes I sate vpon the grasse, and my heart
was vexed within me, like as before.
28 And I opened my mouth, and beganne to talke before
the most High and said,
29 O Lord, thou that shewest thy selfe vnto vs, thou wast
*shewed vnto our fathers in the wildernesse, in a place where *Exod. 19.
no man ||treadeth, in a barren place when they came out of 9. and 24.
Egypt. 3. deut. 4. 12.
30 And thou spakest, saying, Heare me, O Israel, and || *Or, commeth.*
marke my words, thou seed of Iacob.
31 For behold I sow my law in you, and it shall bring
fruite in you, and yee shall be honoured in it for euer.
32 But our fathers which receiued the law, kept it not, and
obserued not thy ordinances, and though the fruite of thy law
did not perish, neither could it, for it was thine:
33 Yet they that receiued it, perished, because they kept
not the thing that was sowen in them.
34 And loe, it is a custome when the ground hath receiued
seed, or the Sea a ship, or any vessel, meate or drinke, that,
that being perished wherein it was sowen, or cast into,
35 That thing also which was sowen or cast therein, or
receiued, doth perish, and remaineth not with vs: but with
vs it hath not happened so.
36 For we that haue receiued the law perish by sinne, and
our heart also which receiued it.
37 Notwithstanding the law perisheth not, but remaineth
in his force.
38 And when I spake these things in my heart, I looked
backe with mine eyes, & vpon the right side I saw a woman,
and behold, she mourned, & wept with a loud voyce, and was
much grieued in heart, and her clothes were rent, and she
had ashes vpon her head.
39 Then let I my thoughts goe that I was in, and turned
me vnto her,
40 And said vnto her, Wherefore weepest thou? why art
thou so grieued in thy minde?

41 And

41 And she said vnto me, Sir, let me alone, that I may bewaile my selfe, and adde vnto my sorow, for I am sore vexed in my minde, and brought very low.
42 And I said vnto her, What aileth thee? Tell me.
43 She said vnto me, I thy seruant haue bene barren, and had no childe, though I had an husband thirty yeres.
44 And those thirtie yeeres I did nothing else day and night, and euery houre, but make my prayer to ye highest.
45 After thirtie yeeres, God heard me thine handmaid, looked vpon my misery, considered my trouble, and gaue me a sonne: and I was very glad of him, so was my husband also, and all my neighbours, and we gaue great honour vnto the Almightie.
46 And I nourished him with great trauaile.
47 So when he grew vp, and came to the time that he should haue a wife, I made a feast.

CHAP. X.

1 Hee comforteth the woman in the field. 17 She vanisheth away, and a citie appeareth in her place. 40 The Angel declareth these visions in the field.

AND it so came to passe, that when my sonne was entred into his wedding chamber, he fell downe and died.

2 Then we all ouerthrew the lights, and all my ||neighbours rose vp to comfort me, so I tooke my rest vnto the second day at night.

||Or countrey men citizens.

3 And it came to passe when they had all left off to comfort me, to the end I might be quiet: then rose I vp by night and fled, and came hither into this field, as thou seest.
4 And I doe now purpose not to returne into the citie, but here to stay, and neither to eate nor drinke, but continually to mourne, & to fast vntil I die.
5 Then left I the ||meditations wherein I was, and spake to her in anger, saying,

||Or, speeches.

6 Thou foolish woman aboue all other, seest thou not our mourning, and what happeneth vnto vs?
7 How that Sion our mother is full of all heauinesse, and much humbled, mourning very sore?
8 And now seeing we all mourne, and are sad, for we are all in heauinesse,

art thou grieued for one sonne?
9 For aske the earth, and she shall tell thee, that it is she,
which ought to mourne, for the fall of so many that grow
vpon her.
10 For out of her came all at the first, and out of her shal
all others come: and behold they walke almost all into de-
struction, and a multitude of them is vtterly ||rooted out.
11 Who then should make more mourning, then she that
hath lost so great a multitude, and not thou which art sory
but for one?
12 But if thou sayest vnto me, My lamentation is not like
the earths, because I haue lost the fruit of my womb, which
I brought foorth with paines, and bare with sorrowes.
13 ||But the earth *not so:* for the multitude present in it,
according to the course of the earth, is gone, as it came.
14 Then say I vnto thee, Like as thou hast brought foorth
with labour: euen so the earth also hath giuen her fruit,
namely man, euer sithence the beginning, vnto him that
made her.
15 Now therefore keepe thy sorrow to thy selfe, and beare
with a good courage that which hath befallen thee.
16 For if thou shalt acknowledge the determination of God
to be iust, thou shalt both receiue thy sonne in time, and
shalt be commended amongst women.
17 Goe thy way then into the citie, to thine husband.
18 And she said vnto me, That will I not doe: I will not
goe into the city, but here will I die.
19 So I proceeded to speake further vnto her, and said,
20 Doe not so, but bee counselled by me: for how many
are the aduersities of Sion? Bee comforted in regard of the
sorow of Ierusalem.
21 For thou seest that our Sanctuary is laid waste, our Altar
broken downe, our Temple destroyed.
22 Our Psaltery is laid on ẏͤ ground, our song is put to
silence, our reioycing is at an end, the light of our candlesticke is put out, the Arke of our Couenant is spoiled, our
holy things are defiled, and the Name that is called vpon us,
is almost prophaned: our children are put to shame, our
priests are burnt, our Leuites are gone into captiuitie, our
virgines are defiled, and our wiues rauished, our righteous
men caried away,

|| *Or, abolished.*

|| *But the earth after the maner of the earth: whereinto the present multitude is gone againe, as it came out.*

our litle ones destroyed, our yong men are brought in
bondage, and our strong men are become weake.
23 And which is the greatest of all, the seale of Sion hath
now lost her honour: for she is deliuered into the hands of
them that hate vs.
24 And therefore shake off thy great heauinesse, and put
away the multitude of sorrowes, that the mighty may be
mercifull vnto thee againe, and the highest shal giue thee
rest, and ease from thy labour.
25 And it came to passe while I was talking with her,
behold her face vpon a sudden shined exceedingly, & her
countenance glistered, so that I was afraid of her, and mused
what it might be.
26 And behold suddenly, she made a great cry very fearful:
so that the earth shooke at the noise of the woman.
27 And I looked, and beholde, the woman appeared vnto
me no more, but there was a city builded, and a large place
shewed it selfe from the foundations: then was I afraid, and
cried with a lowd voice, and said,
28 Where is *Vriel the Angel, who came vnto mee at the
first? for hee hath caused me to fall into many ||traunces, and
mine end is turned into corruption, and my prayer to rebuke.
29 And as I was speaking these wordes, behold, he came
vnto me, and looked vpon me.
30 And loe, I lay as one that had bene dead, & mine
vnderstanding was taken from me, and he tooke me by
the right hand, and comforted mee, and set me vpon my
feet, and said vnto me,
31 What aileth thee? and why art thou so disquieted, and
why is thine vnderstanding troubled, & the thoughts of thine
heart?
32 And I said, because thou hast forsaken me, and yet I did
according to thy *words, and I went into the field, and loe
I haue seene, and yet see, that I am not able to expresse.
33 And hee said vnto me, Stand vp manfully, and I wil
aduise thee.
34 Then said I, Speake on, my lord in me, onely forsake
me not, lest I die frustrate of my hope.
35 For I haue seene, that I knew not, and heare that I do
not know.
36 Or, is my sense deceiued, or my soule in a dreame?
37 Now therfore, I beseech thee, that

*Chap. 4. 1.
||*Or, into the multitude in a traunce.*
*Chap. 5. 20.

thou wilt shew thy seruant of this ||visiō. ||*Or, traunce.*
38 He answered me then, & said, Heare me, and I shall
enforme thee, and tell thee wherefore thou art afraid: for the
highest will reueile many secret things vnto thee.
39 Hee hath seene that thy ||way is right: for that thou ||*Or, purpose.*
sorrowest continually for thy people, and makest great
lamentation for Sion.
40 This therefore is the meaning of the vision which thou
lately sawest.
41 Thou sawest a woman mourning, and thou beganst to
comfort her:
42 But now seest thou the likenesse of the woman no
more, but there appeared vnto thee a city builded.
43 And whereas she told thee of the death of her sonne,
this is the ||solution. ||*Or, Interpretation.*
44 This woman whom thou sawest, is Sion: and whereas
she said vnto thee (euen she whom thou seest as a city builded.)
45 Whereas *I say*, she said vnto thee, that she hath bene
thirty yeres barren: those are the thirty yeeres wherein
there was no offering made in her.
46 But after thirtie yeeres, Solomon builded the city, &
offered offrings: and then bare the barren a sonne.
47 And whereas she told thee that shee nourished him with
labour: that was the dwelling in Hierusalem.
48 But whereas she said vnto thee, That my sonne comming
into his marriage chamber, happened to haue a fall, and died,
this was the destruction that came to Hierusalem.
49 And behold, thou sawest her likenesse, and because she
mourned for her sonne, thou beganst to comfort her, and of these
things which haue chaunced, these are to be opened vnto thee.
50 For now the most High seeth, that thou art grieued
vnfainedly, & sufferest from thy whole heart for her, so
hath he shewed thee the brightnes of her glory, and the
comelinesse of her beautie.
51 And therfore I bad thee remaine in ỹ field, where no
house was builded.
52 For I knew that the Highest would shew this vnto thee.
53 Therefore I commanded thee to goe into the field, where
no foundation of any building was.
54 For in the place wherein the Highest beginneth to shew
his city, ther can no mans building be able to stand.
55 And therfore feare not, let not thy
heart

heart be afrighted, but goe thy way in, and see the beautie
and greatnesse of the building, as much as thine eyes be able
to see:
56 And then shalt thou heare as much as thine eares may
comprehend.
57 For thou art blessed aboue many other, and art ||called
with the highest, and so are but few.
58 But to morrow at night thou shalt remaine here.
59 And so shall the highest shew thee visions of the ||high
things, which the most high will do vnto them, that dwel
vpon earth in the last dayes. So I slept that night and
another, like as he commanded me.

|| *Or, art called to be with, &c.*

|| *Or, last things.*

CHAP. XI.

1 Hee seeth in his dreame an Eagle comming out of the Sea: 37 And a Lion out of a wood talking to the Eagle.

THen saw I a dreame, and beholde, there came vp from
the Sea an Eagle, which had twelue feathered wings,
& three heads.
2 And I saw, and behold, she spred her wings ouer all the
earth, and all the windes of the ayre blewe on her, and were
gathered together.
3 And I beheld, and out of her feathers there grewe other
contrary feathers, and they became little feathers, and small.
4 But her heads were at rest: the head in the middest was
greater then the other, yet rested †it with the residue.
5 Moreouer I beheld, and loe, the Eagle flew with her
feathers, and reigned vpon earth, and ouer them that dwelt
therein.
6 And I saw that all things vnder heauen were subiect vnto
her, and no man spake against her, no not one creature vpon
earth.
7 And I beheld, and loe, the Eagle rose vpon her talents,
and spake to her feathers, saying,
8 Watch not all at once, sleepe euery one in his own place,
& watch by course.
9 But let the heads be preserued for the last.
10 And I beheld, and loe, the voice went not out of her
heads, but from the middest of her body.
11 And I numbred her contrary feathers, and behold, there
were eight of them.

† *Lat. shee.*

12 And I looked, and behold, on the right side there arose
one feather, and reigned ouer all the earth.
13 And so it was, that when it reigned, the ende of it came,
and the place thereof appeared no more: so the next following
stood vp and reigned, and had a great time.
14 And it happened, that when it reigned, the end of it
came also, like as the first, so that it appeared no more.
15 Then came there a voice vnto it, and sayd,
16 Heare, thou that hast borne rule ouer the earth so long:
this I say vnto thee, before thou beginnest to appeare no
more.
17 There shall none after thee attaine vnto thy time, neither
vnto the halfe thereof.
18 Then arose the third, and reigned as the other before:
and appeared no more also.
19 So went it with all the residue one after another, as that
euery one reigned, and then appeared no more.
20 Then I beheld, & loe, in processe of time, the feathers
that folowed, stood vp vpon the right side, that they might
rule also, and some of them ruled, but within a while they
appeared no more:
21 For some of them were set vp, but ruled not.
22 After this I looked, and behold, the twelue feathers
appeared no more, nor the two little feathers:
23 And there was no more vpon the Eagles body, but three
heads that rested, and sixe little wings.
24 Then saw I also that two little feathers diuided themselues from the sixe, and remained vnder the head, that
was vpon the right side: for the foure continued in their
place.
25 And I beheld, & loe, the feathers that were vnder the
wing, thought to set vp themselues, and to haue the rule.
26 And I beheld, & loe, there was one set vp, but shortly
it appeared no more.
27 And the second was sooner away then the first.
28 And I beheld, and loe, the two that remained, thought
also in themselues to reigne.
29 And when they so thought, behold, there awaked one
of the heads that were at rest, namely it that was in the
middest, for that was greater then the two other heads.

30 And then I saw, that the two other heads were ioyned
with it.
31 And behold, the head was turned with them that were
with it, and did eate vp the two feathers vnder the wing that
would haue reigned.
32 But this head put the whole earth in feare, and bare
rule in it ouer all those that dwelt vpon the earth, with
much oppression, and it had the gouernance of the world
more then all the wings that had beene.
33 And after this I beheld, and loe the head that was in the
midst, suddenly appeared no more, like as the wings.
34 But there remained the two heads, which also in like
sort ruled vpon the earth, and ouer those that dwelt therein.
35 And I beheld, and loe, the head vpon the right side,
deuoured it, that was vpon the left side.
36 Then I heard a voyce, which said vnto me, Looke before
thee, and consider the thing that thou seest.
37 And I beheld, and loe, as it were a roaring Lyon, chased
out of the wood: and I saw that hee sent out a mans voyce
vnto the Eagle, and said,
38 Heare thou, I will talke with thee, and the highest shall
say vnto thee,
39 Art not thou it that remainest of the foure beasts, whom
I made to raigne in my world, that the end of their times
might come through them?
40 And the fourth came and ouercame all the beasts that
were past, and had power ouer the world with great fearefulnesse, and ouer the whole compasse of the earth with
much wicked oppression, and so long time dwelt he vpon
the earth with deceit.
41 For the earth hast thou not iudged with trueth.
42 For thou hast afflicted the meeke, thou hast hurt the
peaceable, thou hast loued lyers, and destroyed the dwellings
of them that brought forth fruite, and hast cast downe the
walles of such, as did thee no harme.
43 Therefore is thy wrongfull dealing come vp vnto the
Highest, and thy pride vnto the Mighty.
44 The Highest also hath looked vpon the proud times, and
behold, they are ended, and his abominations are fulfilled.
45 And therefore appeare no more thou Eagle, nor thy
horrible wings, nor

thy wicked feathers, nor thy malitious heads, nor thy hurtfull clawes, nor all thy vaine body:

46 That all the earth may be refreshed, and may returne, being deliuered from thy violence, and that she may hope for the iudgement, and mercy of him that made her.

CHAP. XII.

3 The Eagle which hee saw, is destroyed. 10 The vision is interpreted. 37 He is bid to write his visions, 39 and to fast, that he may see more. 46 He doth comfort those, that were grieued for his absence.

ANd it came to passe whiles the Lyon spake these words vnto the Eagle, I saw:

2 And behold, the head that remained, and the foure wings appeared no more, and the two went vnto it, and set themselues vp to raigne, and their kingdome was small and full of vprore.

3 And I saw, and behold, they appeared no more, and the whole body of the Eagle was burnt, so that the earth was in great feare: then awaked I out of the trouble and traunce of my minde, and from great feare, and said vnto my spirit,

4 Loe, this hast thou done vnto me, in that thou searchest out the wayes of the Highest.

5 Loe, yet am I weary in my mind, and very weake in my spirit: and litle strength is there in me; for the great feare, wherewith I was affrighted this night.

6 Therefore wil I now beseech the Highest, that hee will comfort me vnto the end.

7 And I said, Lord, that bearest rule, If I haue found grace before thy sight, and if I am iustified with thee, before many others, and if my prayer indeed be come vp before thy face,

8 Comfort me then, and shew me thy seruant the interpretation, and plaine difference of this fearefull vision, that thou maist perfectly comfort my soule.

9 For thou hast iudged me worthy, to shew me the last times.

10 And he said vnto me, This is the interpretation of the vision.

11 The Eagle whom thou sawest come vp from the sea, is the kingdome which

*Daniel 7. 7. which was seene, in the *vision of thy brother Daniel.
12 But it was not expounded vnto him, therefore now I declare it vnto thee.
13 Behold, the dayes will come, that there shall rise vp a kingdome vpon earth, and it shall be feared aboue all the kingdomes that were before it.
14 In the same shall twelue kings reigne, one after another.
15 Whereof the second shall begin to reigne, and shall haue more time then any of the twelue.
16 And this doe the twelue wings signifie which thou sawest.
17 As for the voice which thou heardest speake, and that thou sawest not to goe out from the heads, but from the mids of the body thereof, this is the interpretation:
18 That after the time of that kingdome, there shall arise great striuings, and it shall stand in perill of falling: neuerthelesse it shall not then fall, but shal be restored againe to his beginning.
19 And whereas thou sawest the eight small vnder feathers sticking to her wings, this is the interpretation:
20 That in him there shal arise eight kings, whose time shall bee but small, and their yeeres swift.
21 And two of them shall perish: the middle time approching, foure shall bee kept vntill their end begin to approch: but two shall be kept vnto the end.
22 And whereas thou sawest three heads resting, this is the interpretation
23 In his last dayes shall the most High raise vp three kingdomes, and renew many things therein, and they shal haue the dominion of the earth,
24 And of those that dwell therein with much oppression, aboue all those that were before them: therefore are they called the heads of the Eagle.
25 For these are they that shal accomplish his wickednesse, and that shall finish his last end.
26 And whereas thou sawest that the great head appeared no more, it signifieth that one of them shall die vpon his bed, and yet with paine.
27 For the two that remaine, shall be slaine with the sword.
28 For the sword of the one shall deuoure the other: but at the last shall he fall through the sword himselfe.

29 And whereas thou sawest two

feathers vnder the wings passing ouer the head, that is on
the right side:
30 It signifieth that these are they whom the Highest hath
kept vnto their end: this is the small kingdom and full of
trouble, as thou sawest.
31 And the Lyon whom thou sawest rising vp out of the
wood, and roaring, and speaking to the Eagle, and rebuking
her for her vnrighteousnesse, with all the words which thou
hast heard,
32 This is the Anointed which the Highest hath kept for
them, and for their wickednesse vnto the end: he shall
reprooue them, and shall vpbraid them with their crueltie.
33 For hee shall set them before him aliue in iudgement,
and shall rebuke them and correct them.
34 For the rest of my people shall he deliuer with mercie,
those that haue bin preserued vpon my borders, and he shal
make them ioyfull vntill the comming of the day of iudgement, whereof I haue spoken vnto thee from the beginning.
35 This is the dreame that thou sawest, and these are the
interpretations.
36 Thou onely hast bene meete to know this secret of the
Highest.
37 Therefore write all these things that thou hast seene,
in a booke, and hide them.
38 And teach them to the wise of the people, whose hearts
thou knowest may comprehend, & keepe these seerets.
39 But wait thou here thy selfe yet seuen dayes moe, that
it may be shewed thee whatsoeuer it pleaseth the Highest to
declare vnto thee: And with that he went his way.
40 And it came to passe when all the people saw that the
seuen dayes were past, and I not come againe into the citie,
they gathered them all together, from the least vnto the
greatest, and came vnto me, and said,
41 What haue we offended thee? and what euill haue we
done against thee, that thou forsakest vs, and sittest here in
this place?
42 For of all the ||prophets thou only art left vs, as a cluster || *Or,*
of the vintage, and as a candle in a darke place, and as a *people.*
hauen or ship preserued from the tempest:
43 Are not the euils which are come to vs, sufficient?
44 If thou shalt forsake vs, how
much

much better had it bene for vs, if we also had bene burnt in
the midst of Sion.
45 For we are not better then they that died there. And
they wept with a loud voice: then answered I them, and said,
46 Be of good comfort, O Israel, and be not heauy thou
house of Iacob.
47 For the Highest hath you in remembrance, and the
mighty hath not forgotten you in temptation.
48 As for mee, I haue not forsaken you, neither am I
departed from you: but am come into this place, to pray
for the desolation of Sion, and that I might seeke mercy
for the low estate of your Sanctuary.
49 And now goe your way home euery man, and after
these dayes will I come vnto you.
50 So the people went their way into the city, like as I
commanded them:
51 But I remained still in the field seuen dayes, as the Angel
commanded me, and did eate onely in those dayes, of the
flowers of the fielde, and had my meat of the herbes.

CHAP. XIII.

1 Hee seeth in his dreame a man comming out of the sea. 25 The declaration of his dreame. 54 He is praised, and promised to see more.

AND it came to passe after seuen dayes, I dreamed a dreame
by night.
2 And ||loe, there arose a winde from the sea that it mooued
all the waues thereof.
3 And I beheld, and loe, that man waxed strong with the
||thousands of heauen: and when he turned his countenance
to looke, all the things trembled that were seene vnder him.
4 And whensoeuer the voyce went out of his mouth, all
they burnt, that heard his voyce, like as the earth faileth
when it feeleth the fire.
5 And after this I beheld, and loe, there was gathered together
a multitude of men out of number, from the foure windes
of the heauen, to subdue the man that came out of the sea.
6 But I beheld, and loe, hee had graued himselfe a great
mountaine, and flew vp vpon it.
7 But I would haue seene the region, or place, whereout
the hill was grauen, and I could not.

8 And after this I beheld, and loe,

||*A certaine man as the winde. Iunius.*

||*Clouds.*

all they which were gathered together to subdue him, were
sore afraid, and yet durst fight.
9 And loe, as hee saw the violence of the multitude that
came, hee neither lift vp his hand, nor held sword, nor any
instrument of warre.
10 But onely I saw that he sent out of his mouth, as it had
bene a blast of fire, and out of his lippes a flaming breath,
and out of his tongue he cast out sparkes and tempests,
11 And they were all mixt together; the blast of fire, the
flaming breath, and the great tempest, and fel with violence
vpon the multitude, which was prepared to fight, and burnt
them vp euery one, so that vpon a sudden, of an innumerable
multitude, nothing was to be perceiued, but onely dust and
smell of smoke: whē I saw this, I was afraid.
12 Afterward saw I the same man come downe from the
mountaine, and call vnto him an other peaceable multitude.
13 And there came much people vnto him, whereof some
were glad, some were sory, some of them were bound, and
other some brought of ||them that were offred: then was I
sicke through great feare, and I awaked and said,
14 Thou hast shewed thy seruant wonders from the beginning, and hast counted me worthy that thou shouldest
receiue my prayer:
15 Shew mee now yet the interpretation of this dreame.
16 For as I conceiue in mine vnderstanding, woe vnto them
that shall be left in those dayes; and much more woe vnto
them that are not left behinde.
17 For they that were not left, were in heauinesse.
18 Now vnderstand I the things that are layde vp in the
latter dayes, which shall happen vnto them, and to those
that are left behinde.
19 Therefore are they come into great perils, and many
necessities, like as these dreames declare.
20 Yet is it easier for him that is in danger, to come into
||these things, then to passe away as a cloud out of the world,
and not to see the things that happen in the last dayes. And
he answered vnto me, and said,
21 The interpretation of the vision shal I shew thee, and
I wil open vnto thee, the thing that thou hast required.

22 Where-

|| *Iunius. Of the things that were offered.*

|| *Or, this day.*

22 Wheras thou hast spoken of them that are left behinde,
this is the interpretation.
23 He that shall endure the perill in that time, hath kept
himselfe: they that be fallen into danger, are such as haue
workes, and faith towards the Almightie.
24 Know this therefore, that they which be left behinde,
are more blessed then they that be dead.
25 This is the meaning of the vision: Whereas thou sawest
a man comming vp from the middest of the Sea:
26 The same is hee whom God the highest hath kept a
great season, which by his owne selfe shall deliuer his
creature: and hee shall order them that are left behinde.
27 And whereas thou sawest, that out of his mouth there
came as a blast of winde, and fire, and storme:
28 And that he helde neither sword, nor any instrument of
warre, but that the rushing in of him destroyed the whole
multitude that came to subdue him, this is the interpretation.
29 Behold, the dayes come, when the most high wil begin
to deliuer them that are vpon the earth.
30 And he shall come to the astonishment of them that
dwell on the earth.
31 And one shall vndertake to fight against another, one
city against another, one place against another, *one people
against another, and one realme against another.

* Mat. 24. 7.

32 And the time shalbe, when these things shall come to
passe, and the signes shall happen which I shewed thee
before, and then shall my sonne be declared, whom thou
sawest as a man ascending.
33 And when all the people heare his voice, euery man
shall in their owne land, leaue the battaile they haue one
against another.
34 And an innumerable multitude shalbe gathered together,
as thou sawest them willing to come, and to ouercome him
by fighting.
35 But hee shall stand vpon the top of the mount Sion.
36 And Sion shall come and shall be shewed to all men,
being prepared and builded, like as thou sawest the hill
grauen without hands.
37 And this my sonne shall rebuke the wicked inuentions
of those nations,

which for their wicked life are fallen into the tempest,
38 And shall lay before them their euill thoughts, and the
torments wherwith they shall begin to be tormented, which
are like vnto a flame: and hee shall destroy them without
labour, by the law which is like vnto fire.
39 And whereas thou sawest that hee gathered another
peaceable multitude vnto him;
40 Those are the ten tribes, which were caried away
prisoners out of their owne land, in the time of Osea the
king, whom *Salmanasar the king of Assyria ledde away *2. Kings
captiue, and hee caried them ouer the waters, and so came 17. 3.
they into another land.
41 But they tooke this counsaile amongst themselues, that
they would leaue the multitude of the heathen, and goe
foorth into a further countrey, where neuer mankind dwelt,
42 That they might there keepe their statutes, which they
neuer kept in their owne land.
43 And they entred into Euphrates by the narrow passages
of the Riuer.
44 For the most high then shewed *signes for them, and *Exod. 14.
held still the flood, till they were passed ouer. 21. iosh. 3. 15, 16.
45 For through that countrey there was a great way to
goe; namely, of a yeere and a halfe: and the same region is
called ||Arsareth. || *Or, Ara-*
46 Then dwelt they there vntill the latter time; and now *rath.*
when they shall begin to come,
47 The highest shall stay the springs of the streame againe,
that they may go through: therefore sawest thou the multitude with peace.
48 But those that be left behinde of thy people, are they
that are found within my borders.
49 Now when hee destroyeth the multitude of the nations that
are gathered together, he shal defend his people that remaine.
50 And then shall hee shewe them great wonders.
51 Then said I, O Lord, that bearest rule, shew me this:
Wherefore haue I seene the man comming vp from the
midst of the Sea?
52 And he said vnto me, Like as thou canst neither seeke
out, nor know the things that are in the deepe of the sea:
euen so can no man vpon earth see my
sonne,

sonne, or those that be with him, but in the day time.
53 This is the interpretation of the dreame which thou
sawest, and whereby thou onely art here lightened.
54 For thou hast forsaken thine owne way, and applied thy
diligence vnto my law, and sought it.
55 Thy life hast thou ordered in wisdome, and hast called
vnderstanding thy mother.
56 And therefore haue I shewed thee the treasures of the
Highest: After other three dayes, I will speake other things
vnto thee, and declare vnto thee mightie and wonderous
things.
57 Then went I forth into the field giuing praise and
thanks greatly vnto the most High, because of his wonders
which he did in time,
58 And because hee gouerneth the same, and such things
as fall in their seasons, and there I sate three dayes.

CHAP. XIIII.

1 A voice out of a bush calleth Esdras, 10 and telleth him that the world waxeth old. 22 He desireth, because the Law was burnt, to write all againe, 24 and is bid to get swift writers. 39 Hee and they are filled with vnderstanding: 45 but hee is charged not to publish all that is written.

AND it came to passe, vpon the third day I sate vnder an
oke, and behold, there came a voyce out of a bush ouer
against me, and said, Esdras, Esdras.
2 And I said, Here am I Lord, and I stood vp vpon my feet.
*Exod. 3. 3 Then said he vnto me, *In the bush I did manifestly
2, 8. reueale my selfe vnto Moses, and talked with him, when
my people serued in Egypt.
4 And I sent him, and led my people out of Egypt, and
brought him vp to the mount of Sinai, where I held him by
me, a long season,
5 And told him many wonderous things, and shewed him
the secrets of the times, and the end, and commanded him,
saying,
6 These wordes shalt thou declare, and these shalt thou
hide.
7 And now I say vnto thee,
8 That thou lay vp in thy heart the signes that I haue
shewed, and the dreames that thou hast seene, and the

interpretations which thou hast heard:
9 For thou shalt be taken away from all, and from henceforth thou shalt remaine with my sonne, and with such as
be like thee, vntill the times be ended.
10 For the world hath lost his youth, and the times begin
to waxe old.
11 For the world is diuided into twelue parts, and the ten
parts of it are gone already, and halfe of a tenth part.
12 And there remaineth that which is after the halfe of
the tenth part.
13 Now therefore set thine house in order, and reproue thy
people, comfort such of them as be in trouble, and now
renounce corruption.
14 Let go frō thee mortall thoughts, cast away the burdens
of man, put off now the weake nature,
15 And set aside the thoughts that are most heauy vnto
thee, and haste thee to flie from these times.
16 For *yet greater euils then those which thou hast seene *Mat. 24. 7
happen, shall bee done hereafter.
17 For looke how much the world shall be weaker through
age: so much the more shall euils increase vpon them that
dwell therein.
18 For the trueth is fled farre away, and leasing is hard at hand:
For now hasteth the vision to come, which thou hast seene.
19 Then answered I before thee, and said,
20 Behold, Lord, I will go as thou hast commanded me, and
reprooue the people which are present, but they that shall be
borne afterward, who shall admonish them? thus the world is
set in darkenes, and they that dwell therein, are without light.
21 For thy law is burnt, therefore no man knoweth the
things that are done of thee, or the works that shal begin.
22 But if I haue found grace before thee, send the holy
Ghost into me, and I shall write all that hath bene done in
the world, since the beginning, which were written in thy
Lawe, that men may find thy path, and that they which
will liue in the latter dayes, may liue.
23 And he answered me, saying, Goe thy way, gather the
people together, and say vnto them, that they seeke thee not
for fourtie dayes.
24 But looke thou prepare thee many ||boxe trees, and take || *Or, boxe tables to write on, See ver. 44.*
with thee Sarea, Dabria, Selemia, ||Ecanus and || *Or, Banus.*
Asiel,

Asiel, these fiue which are ready to write swiftly.
25 And come hither, and I shall light a candle of vnderstanding in thine heart, which shall not be put out, till the
things be performed which thou shalt beginne to write.
26 And when thou hast done, some things shalt thou
publish, and some things shalt thou shew secretly to the
wise: to morrowe this houre shalt thou beginne to write.
27 Then went I foorth as he commanded, and gathered all
the people together, and said,
28 Heare these words, O Israel.
*Gene. 47. 29 *Our fathers at the beginning were strangers in Egypt,
4. from whence they were deliuered:
*Act. 7. 30 *And receiued the law of life which they kept not,
53. which ye also haue transgressed after them.
31 Then was the land, euen the land of Sion, parted among
you by lot, but your fathers, and yee your selues haue done
vnrighteousnesse, and haue not kept the wayes which the
Highest commanded you.
32 And for as much as he is a righteous iudge, hee tooke
from you in time, the thing that he had giuen you.
33 And now are you heere, and your brethren amongst
you.
34 Therefore if so be that you will subdue your owne
vnderstanding, and reforme your hearts, yee shall be kept
aliue, and after death yee shall obtaine mercy.
35 For after death, shall the iudgement come, when we
shall liue againe: and then shall the names of the righteous
be manifest, and the workes of the vngodly shall be declared.
36 Let no man therefore come vnto me now, nor seeke
after me these fourty dayes.
37 So I tooke the fiue men as hee commanded me, and we
went into the field, and remained there.
38 And the next day behold a voyce called mee saying,
*Ezek. 3. Esdras, *open thy mouth and drinke that I giue thee to
2. drinke.
39 Then opened I my mouth, and behold, he reached me
a full cup, which was full as it were with water, but the
colour of it was like fire.
40 And I tooke it, and dranke: and when I had drunke of
it, my heart vt-

tered vnderstanding: and wisedome grew in my brest, for
my spirit strengthened my memory.
41 And my mouth was opened and shut no more.
42 The highest gaue vnderstanding vnto the fiue men, and
they wrote the wonderfull visions of the night, that were
told, which they knew not: And they sate fourty dayes, and
they wrote in the day, and at night they ate bread.
43 As for me I spake in the day, and held not my tongue
by night:
44 In fourty dayes they wrote ||two hundred and foure || *Or,* 904.
bookes.
45 And it came to passe when the fourty dayes were
fulfilled, that the Highest spake, saying, The first that thou
hast written, publish openly, that the worthy and vnworthy
may read it.
46 But keepe the seuenty last, that thou mayest deliuer
them onely to such as be wise, among the people.
47 For in them is the spring of vnderstanding, the fountains
of wisedome, and the ||streame of knowledge. || *Or, the light of knowledge.*
48 And I did so.

CHAP. XV.

1 This prophecie is certaine. 5 God will take vengeance vpon the wicked, 12 Vpon Egypt, 28 An horrible vision. 43 Babylon and Asia are threatned.

BEhold, speake thou in the eares of my people the words
of prophesie, which I will put in thy mouth, saith the
Lord.
2 And cause them to be written in paper: for they are
faithfull and true.
3 Feare not the imaginations against thee, let not the in-
credulity of them trouble thee, that speake against thee.
4 For all the vnfaithfull shall die in their vnfaithfulnesse.
5 Behold, saith the Lord, I will bring plagues vpon the
world; the sword, famine, death, and destruction.
6 For wickednesse hath exceedingly polluted the whole
earth, and their hurtfull workes are fulfilled.
7 Therefore saith the Lord,
8 I will hold my tongue no more as touching their wickednesse, which they prophanely commit, neither wil I suffer
them in those things, in which they wickedly exercise them- * Reuel. 6. 10. and 19. 2.
selues: behold, the *innocent & righteous blood
cryeth

cryeth vnto me, and the soules of the iust complaine continually.
9 And therefore saith the Lord, I wil surely auenge them,
and receiue vnto me, all the innocent blood from among them.
10 Beholde, my people is ledde as a flocke to the slaughter:
I wil not suffer them now to dwel in the land of Egypt.
11 But I will bring them with a mighty hand, and a
stretched out arme, and smite Egypt with plagues as before,
and wil destroy al the land thereof.
12 Egypt shal mourne, and the foundation of it shall bee
smitten with the plague and punishment, that God shall
bring vpon it.
13 They that till the ground shall mourne: for their seedes
shall faile, through the blasting, and haile, and with a fearefull
constellation.
14 Woe to the world, and them that dwell therein.
15 For the sword and their destruction draweth nigh, and
one people shall stand vp to fight against another, and swords
in their hands.
16 For there shalbe sedition among men, and inuading one
another, they shal not regard their kings, nor princes, and
the course of their actions shall stand in their power.
17 A man shall desire to goe into a citie, and shall not
be able.
18 For because of their pride, the cities shalbe troubled,
the houses shalbe destroyed, and men shalbe afraid.
19 A man shall haue no pitie vpon his neighbour, but shall
destroy their houses with the sword, and spoile their goods,
because of the lacke of bread, and for great tribulation.
20 Behold, saith God, I will call together all the Kings of
the earth to reuerence me, which are from the rising of the
Sunne, from the South, from the East, and Libanus: to
turne themselues one against another, and repay the things
that they haue done to them.
21 Like as they doe yet this day vnto my chosen, so will I
doe also and recompense in their bosome, Thus saith the
Lord God;
22 My right hand shall not spare the sinners, and my
sword shal not cease ouer them, that shed innocent blood
vpon earth.
23 The fire is gone foorth from his wrath, and hath
consumed the founda-

tions of the earth, and the sinners like the straw that is
kindled.
24 Wo to them that sinne and keepe not my cōmandements, saith the Lord.
25 I will not spare them: goe your way ye children from
the power, defile not my Sanctuary:
26 For the Lord knoweth all them that sinne against him,
and therefore deliuereth he them vnto death and destruction.
27 For now are the plagues come vpon the whole earth,
and ye shall remaine in them, for God shal not deliuer you,
because ye haue sinned against him.
28 Behold an horrible vision, and the appearance thereof
from the East.
29 Where the nations of the dragons of Arabia shall come
out with many charets, and the multitude of them shalbe
caried as the winde vpon earth, that all they which heare
them, may feare and tremble.
30 Also the Carmanians raging in wrath, shall go forth as
the wilde bores of the wood, and with great power shall
they come, and ioyne battell with them, and shall waste a
portion of the land of the Assyrians.
31 And then shall the dragons haue the vpper hand,
remembring their nature, and if they shall turne themselues,
conspiring together in great power to persecute them,
32 Then these shalbe troubled, and keepe silence through
their power, and shall flee.
33 And from the land of the Assyrians, shall the enemy
besiege them, and consume some of them, and in their host
shall be feare, and dread and strife ||among their kings. || *Or, against.*
34 Behold clouds from the East, and from the North, vnto
the South, and they are very horrible to looke vpon; full of
wrath and storme.
35 They shall smite one vpon another, & they shall smite
downe a great multitude of starres vpon the earth, euen their
owne starre; and blood shalbe from the sword vnto the belly.
36 And doung of men vnto the camels ||hough. || *Or, Pasterne, or litter.*
37 And there shalbe great fearefulnesse and trembling vpon
earth: and they that see the wrath, shall be afraid, and
trembling shall come vpon them.
38 And then shall there come great stormes, from the
South, and from the
North,

North, & another part from the West.

39 And strong winds shal arise from the East, and shall open it, and the cloud which hee raised vp in wrath, and the starre stirred to cause feare toward the East and West winde, shalbe destroyed.

40 The great and mightie cloudes shall be lifted vp full of wrath, and the starre, that they may make all the earth afraid, and them that dwel therein, and they shall powre out ouer euery high and eminent place, an horrible starre.

41 Fire and haile, and fleeing swords, and many waters, that all fields may be full, and all riuers with the abundance of great waters.

42 And they shal breake downe the cities, and walls, mountaines and hils, trees of the wood, and grasse of the medowes, and their corne.

|| Or, destroy.

43 And they shal goe stedfastly vnto Babylon, and ||make her afraid.

44 They shall come to her, and besiege her, the starre and all wrath shall they powre out vpon her, then shall the dust and smoke goe vp vnto the heauen: and all they that be about her, shall bewaile her.

45 And they that remaine vnder her, shall doe seruice vnto them that haue put her in feare.

|| Or, like vnto Babylon.

46 And thou Asia that art ||partaker of the hope of Babylon, and art the glory of her person:

47 Woe be vnto thee thou wretch, because thou hast made thy selfe like vnto her, and hast deckt thy daughters in whoredome, that they might please and glory in thy louers, which haue alway desired to commit whordome with thee.

48 Thou hast followed her, that is hated in all her works and inuentions: therefore sayth God,

49 I will send plagues vpon thee: widowhood, pouertie, famine, sword, and pestilence, to waste thy houses with destruction and death.

50 And the glory of thy power shall be dried vp as floure, when the heate shall arise that is sent ouer thee.

51 Thou shalt bee weakened as a poore woman with stripes, and as one chastised with woundes, so that the mightie and louers shall not be able to receiue thee.

52 Would I with iealousie haue so proceeded against thee, saith the Lord,

53 If thou haddest not alway slaine my chosen, exalting

the stroke of thine

hands, & saying ouer their †dead, when thou wast drunken, †*Lat. death.*
54 Set foorth the beauty of thy countenance.

55 The reward of thy whoredome shall be in thy bosome, therefore shalt thou receiue recompense.

56 Like as thou hast done vnto my chosen, sayth the Lord; euen so shall God doe vnto thee, and shall deliuer thee into mischiefe.

57 Thy children shall die of hunger, and thou shalt fall through the sword: thy cities shalbe broken downe, and all thine shall perish with the sword in the field.

58 They that be in the mountaines shall die of hunger, and eate their owne flesh, and drinke their owne blood, for very hunger of bread, & thirst of water.

59 Thou, as vnhappy, shalt come through the Sea, and receiue plagues againe.

60 And in the passage, they shall rush on the idle citie, and shall destroy some portion of thy land, and consume part of thy glory, and shall returne to Babylon that was destroyed.

61 And thou shalt be cast downe by them, as stubble, and they shall be vnto thee as fire,

62 And shall consume thee and thy cities, thy land and thy mountaines, all thy woods and thy fruitfull trees shall they burne vp with fire.

63 Thy children shall they cary away captiue, and looke what thou hast, they shall spoile it, and ||marre the beauty of thy face. || *Or, blemish.*

CHAP. XVI.

1 Babylon and other places are threatned with plagues that cannot be auoided: 23 and with desolation. 40 The seruants of the Lorde must looke for troubles: 51 and not hide their sinnes, 74 but leaue them, and they shall be deliuered.

WOe be vnto thee, Babylon and Asia, woe be vnto thee Egypt and Syria.

2 Gird vp your selues with clothes of sacke and haire, bewaile your children, and be sory, for your destruction is at hand.

3 A sword is sent vpon you, and who may turne it backe?

4 A fire is sent among you, and who may quench it?

5 Plagues are sent vnto you, and

what is he that may driue them away?
6 May any man driue away a hungry Lion in the wood?
or may any one quench the fire in stubble, when it hath
begun to burne?
7 May one turne againe the arrow that is shot of a strong
archer?
8 The mightie Lord sendeth the plagues, and who is hee
that can driue them away?
9 A fire shall goe foorth from his wrath: & who is he that
may quench it?
10 He shall cast lightnings, and who shall not feare? he
shall thunder, and who shall not be afraid?
11 The Lord shall threaten, and who shall not be vtterly
beaten to powder at his presence?
12 The earth quaketh and the foundations thereof, the sea
ariseth vp with waues from the deepe, and the waues of it
are troubled, and the fishes thereof also before the Lord, and
before the glorie of his power.
13 For strong is his right hand that bendeth the bow, his
arrowes that hee shooteth are sharpe, and shall not misse
when they begin to bee shot into the ends of the world.
14 Behold, the plagues are sent, and shall not returne
againe, vntill they come vpon the earth.
15 The fire is kindled, and shall not be put out, till it
consume the foundation of the earth.
16 Like as an arrow which is shot of a mightie archer
returneth not backward: euen so the plagues that shall be
sent vpon earth, shall not returne againe.
17 Woe is me, woe is me, who will deliuer me in those dayes?
18 The beginning of sorrowes, and great mournings, the
beginning of famine, and great death: the beginning of
warres, and the powers shall stand in feare, the beginning of
euils, what shall I doe when these euils shal come?
19 Behold, famine, and plague, tribulation and anguish, are
sent as scourges for amendment.
20 But for all these things they shall not turne from their
wickednes, nor be alway mindfull of the scourges.
21 Behold, victuals shall be so good cheape vpon earth, that
they shal think themselues to be in good case, and euen then
shall ||euils growe vpon earth, sword, famine, and great
confusion.

|| *Or, plagues*

22 For many of them that dwell vpon earth, shall perish of
famine, and the other that escape the hunger, shall the sword
destroy.
23 And the dead shall be cast out as doung, and there
shalbe no man to comfort them, for the earth shall be wasted,
and the cities shall be cast downe.
24 There shall be no man left to till the earth, and to sow it.
25 The trees shall giue fruite, and who shall gather them?
26 The grapes shall ripe, and who shall treade them? for
all places shall be desolate of men.
27 So that one man shall desire to see another, and to heare
his voyce.
28 For of a citie there shalbe ten left, and two of the field
which shall hide themselues in the thicke groues, and in the
clefts of rockes.
29 As in an orchard of oliues, vpon euery tree there are
left three or foure oliues:
30 Or, when as a vineyard is gathered, there are left some
clusters of them that diligently seek through yͤ vineyard:
31 Euen so in those dayes there shalbe three or foure left
by them that search their houses with the sword.
32 And the earth shall be laid waste, and the fields therof
shal waxe old, and her wayes and all her paths shall grow
full of thornes, because no man shal trauaile therethrough.
33 The virgins shall mourne hauing no bridegromes, yͤ
women shal mourne hauing no husbands, their daughters
shall mourne hauing no helpers.
34 In the warres shall their bridegromes bee destroyed, and
their husbands shall perish of famine.
35 Heare now these things, and vnderstand them, ye
seruants of the Lord.
36 Behold the word of the Lord, receiue it, beleeue not
the gods of whom the Lord spake.
37 Behold, the plagues draw nigh, and are not slacke.
38 As when a woman with childe in the ninth month
bringeth forth her son, within two or three houres of her
birth great paines compasse her wombe, which paines, when
the child commeth forth, they slacke not a moment,
39 Euen so shall not the plagues bee slacke to come vpon
the earth, and the world shall mourne, and sorrowes shal
come vpon it on euery side.

40 O my

40 O my people, Heare my word: make you ready to the
battell, and in those euils, be euen as pilgrimes vpon the earth.
41 He that selleth let him be as hee that fleeth away: and
he that buyeth, as one that will loose.
42 He that occupieth merchandize, as he that had no
profit by it: and he that buildeth, as hee that shall not dwell
therein.
43 He that soweth, as if he should not reape: so also he that
planteth the vineyard, as he that shal not gather the grapes.
44 They that marry, as they that shall get no children: and
they that marrie not, as the widowers.
45 And therefore they that labour, labour in vaine.
46 For strangers shall reape their fruits, and spoile their
goods, ouerthrowe their houses; and take their children
captiues, for in captiuity and famine shall they get children.
47 And they that occupy their merchandize with robbery,
the more they decke their citties, their houses, their possessions
and their owne persons:
48 The more will I be angry with them for their sinne,
saith the Lord.
49 Like as an whore enuieth a right honest and vertuous
woman:
50 So shall righteousnesse hate iniquity, when she decketh
her selfe, and shall accuse her, to her face, when he commeth
that shall defend him that diligently searcheth out euery sinne
vpon earth.
51 And therfore be yee not like therunto, nor to the workes
thereof.
52 For yet a little iniquitie shall be taken away out of the
earth, and righteousnesse shall reigne among you.
53 Let not the sinner say that he hath not sinned: for God
shall burne coales of fire vpon his head, which saith before
the Lord God and his glory, I haue not sinned.
*Luke 16. 54 Behold, the Lord knoweth all the workes of men, *their
15. imaginations, their thoughts, and their hearts:
*Gene. 1. 55 Which spake but the word, let the earth be made, *and
1. it was made: let the heauen be made, and it was created.
56 In his word were the starres made, and he knoweth the
*Psal. 146. *number of them.
4. 57 He searcheth the deepe, and the

treasures thereof, he hath measured the Sea, and what it
containeth.
58 He hath shut the Sea in the midst of the waters, and
with his word hath he hanged the earth vpon the waters.
59 He spreadeth out the heauens like a vault, vpon the
waters hath he founded it.
60 In the desart hath hee made springs of water, and pooles
vpon the tops of the mountaines, that the floods might powre
downe from the high rockes to water the earth.
61 He made man, and put his heart in the midst of the
body, and gaue him breath, life, and vnderstanding.
62 Yea and the spirit of Almighty God, which made all
things, and searcheth out all hidden things in the secrets of
the earth.
63 Surely he knoweth your inuentions, and what you
thinke in your hearts, euen them that sinne, and would hide
their sinne.
64 Therefore hath the Lord exactly searched out all your
workes, and he will put you all to shame.
65 And when your sinnes are brought foorth yee shalbe
ashamed before men, and your owne sinnes shall be your
accusers in that day.
66 What will yee doe? or how will yee hide your sinnes
before God and his Angels?
67 Behold, God himselfe is the iudge, feare him: leaue off
from your sinnes, and forget your iniquities to medle no
more with them for euer, so shall God lead you forth, and
deliuer you from all trouble.
68 For behold, the burning wrath of a great multitude is
kindled ouer you, and they shall take away certaine of you,
and feede you ||being idle with things offered vnto idoles.
69 And they that consent vnto them shall be had in
derision, and in reproch, and troden vnder foote.
70 For there shall be in euery place, and in the next cities
a great insurrection vpon those that feare the Lord.
71 They shall be like mad men, sparing none, but still
spoiling and destroying those that feare the Lord.
72 For they shal waste and take away their goods, and cast
them out of their houses.
73 Then shall they be knowen who

|| *Or, being vnable to resist.*

are my chosen, and they shall be tried, as the gold in the fire:

74 Heare, O yee my beloued, saith the Lord: behold, the dayes of trouble are at hand, but I will deliuer you from the same.

75 Be yee not afraid, neither doubt, for God is your guide,
76 And the guide of them who keepe my commaundements, and precepts, saith the Lord God; Let not your

¶ TO

CHAP. I.

1 Tobit his stocke, and deuotion in his youth, 9 His marriage, 10 And captiuitie, 13 His preferment, 16 Almes and charitie in burying the dead, 19 For which he is accused and flieth, 22 And after returneth to Niniue.

|| *Or, acts.*

THE Booke of the ||wordes of Tobit, sonne of Tobiel, the son of Ananiel, the sonne of Aduel, the sonne of Gabael, of the seed of Asael, of the Tribe of Nephthali,

2 Who in the time of Enemessar king of the Assyrians,
was led captiue out of *Thisbe which is at the right hand
of that citie, which is called ||properly Nephthali in Galile
aboue Aser.

*2. King. 17. 3. || *Or, Kedes of Nephthali in Galile, Iudg.* 4 6.

3 I Tobit haue walked all the dayes of my life in the way of trueth, and iustice, and I did many almes deeds to my brethren, and my nation, who came with me to Nineue into the land of the Assyrians.

4 And when I was in mine owne countrey, in the land of Israel, being but yong, all the tribe of Nephthali my father, fell from the house of Ierusalem, which was chosen out of all the tribes of Israel, that all the tribes should sacrifice *there* where the Temple of the habitation of the most High was consecrated, and built for all ages.

5 Now all the tribes which toge-

sinnes weigh you downe, and let not your iniquities lift vp
themselues.
77 Woe bee vnto them that are bound with their sinnes,
and couered with their iniquities: like as a field is couered
ouer with bushes, and the path thereof couered with thornes,
that no man may trauell through.
78 It is ||left vndressed, and is cast into the fire, to bee || *Or, shut out.*
consumed therewith.

BIT.

ther reuolted, and the house of my father Nephthali sacrificed
vnto the *heifer Baal. *1. King. 12. 30. *Or, to the power of Baal, or the god Baal.*
6 But I alone went often to Ierusalem at the Feasts, as it
was ordeined vnto al the people of Israel by an euerlasting
decree, *hauing the first fruits, and tenths of encrease, with *Exod. 22. 29. deu. 12. 6.
that which was first shorne, and them gaue I at the Altar to
the Priestes the children of Aaron.
7 The first tenth part of al increase, I gaue to the sonnes
of ||Aaron, who ministred at Ierusalem: another tenth part I || *Or, Leui.*
sold away, and went, and spent it euery yeere at Ierusalem.
8 And the third, I gaue vnto them to whom it was meet,
as Debora my fathers mother had commanded mee, because
I was left an orphane by my father.
9 Furthermore when I was come to the age of a man, I
married Anna of mine *owne kinred, and of her I begate *Num. 36. 7.
Tobias.
10 And when we were caried away captiues to Nineue, all
my brethren, and those that were of my kinred, did eate of
the *bread of the Gentiles. *Gene. 43. 32.
11 But I kept †my selfe from eating; † *Greek. my soule.*
12 Because I remembred God with all my heart.
13 And the most High gaue me grace, and fauour before
Enemessar, so that I was his †purueyour. † *Greek. byer.*
14 And I went into Media, and left in trust with Gabael,
the brother of Gabrias ||at Rages a citie of Media, ten talents || *Or, in the land or countrey of Media.*
of siluer.

15 Now

15 Now when Enemessar was dead, Sennacherib his sonne
reigned in his stead, †whose estate was troubled, that I could
not goe into Media.

† *Gr. the wayes of whom were vnsetled.*

16 And in the time of Enemessar, I gaue many almes to
my brethren, and gaue my bread to the hungry,
17 And my clothes to the naked: and if I saw any of my
nation dead, or cast ‖about the walles of Nineue, I buried
him.

‖ *Or, behind the walles.*

18 And if the king Sennacherib had slaine any, when hee
was come, *and fledde from Iudea, I buried them priuily,
(for in his wrath hee killed many) but the bodies were not
found, when they were sought for of the king.
19 And when one of the Nineuites went, and complained
of me to the king that I buried them, and hid my selfe:
vnderstanding that I was sought for to be put to death, I
withdrew my selfe for feare.

*2. Kin. 19. 35, 36. isai. 37. 36, 37. ecclus. 48. 18, 22. 1. macc. 7. 41. 2. mac. 8. 19.

20 Then all my goods were forcibly taken away, neither
was there any thing left me, besides my wife Anna, and my
sonne Tobias.
21 And there passed not fiue and fiftie dayes before two of
his sonnes *killed him, and they fled into the mountaines of
Ararath, and ‖Sarchedonus his sonne reigned in his stead,
who appointed ouer his fathers accounts, and ouer all his
affaires, Achiacharus my brother Anaels sonne.

*2. King. 19. 37. 2. chr. 32. 21.
‖ *Or, Esar-Haddon.*

22 And Achiacharus entreating for me, I returned to
Nineue: now Achiacharus was Cup-bearer, and keeper of
the Signet, and Steward, and ouerseer of the accounts: and
‖Sarchedonus appointed him next vnto him: and hee was my
brothers sonne.

‖ *Or, Esar-Haddon.*

CHAP. II.

1 Tobit leaueth his meate to bury the dead, 10 and becommeth blinde. 11 His wife taketh in worke to get her liuing. 14 Her husband and she fall out about a kidde.

NOw when I was come home againe, and my wife Anna
was restored vnto me, with my sonne Tobias, in the
feast of Pentecost, which is the holy Feast of the seuen
weekes, there was a good dinner prepared me, in the which
I sate down to eate.
2 And when I saw abundance of

meate, I sayd to my sonne, Goe and bring what poore man
soeuer thou shalt finde out of our brethren, who is mindfull
of the Lord, and loe, I tarie for thee.
3 But he came againe and said, Father, one of our nation
is strangled, and is cast out in the market place.
4 Then before I had tasted of any meate, I start vp and
tooke him vp into a roume, vntill the going downe of the
Sunne.
5 Then I returned and washed my selfe, and ate my meate
in heauinesse,
6 Remembring that prophesie *of Amos, as hee said; Your
feasts shall be turned into mourning, and all your mirth into
lamentation.
7 Therefore I wept: and after the going downe of the
Sunne, I went and made a graue, and buried him.
8 But my neighbours mocked me, and said, This man is
not yet afraide to be put to death for this matter, * who fledde
away, and yet loe, he burieth the dead againe.
9 The same night also I returned from the buriall, and slept
by the wall of my court yard, being polluted, and my face
was vncouered:
10 And I knewe not that there were ||Sparrowes in the wall,
and mine eyes being open, the Sparrowes muted warme doung
into mine eyes, and a ||whitenesse came in mine eyes, and I
went to the Physicians, but they helped me not: moreouer
Achiacharus did nourish mee, vntill I went into Elymais.
11 And my wife Anna ||did take womens workes to doe.
12 And when shee had sent ||them home to the owners,
they payd her wages, and gaue her also besides a kid.
13 And when it was in mine house, and beganne to crie, I
said vnto her, From whence is this kidde? is it not stollen?
render it to the owners, *for it is not lawfull to eate any
thing that is stollen.
14 *But shee replyed vpon me, It was giuen for a gift more
then the wages: Howbeit I did not beleeue her, but bade her
render it to the owners: and I was abashed at her. But she
replyed vpon me, Where are thine almes, and thy righteous
deedes? ||behold, thou and all thy workes are knowen.

*Amos 8. 10.

*Cha. 1. 19.

|| Or, *Swallowes.*

|| Or, *white filmes.*

|| Or, *was hired to spinne in the womens rooms.*

|| Or, *her worke.*

*Deu. 22. 1.

*Iob 2. 9.

|| Or, *loe all things are knowen to thee.*

CHAP. III.

1 Tobit grieued with his wiues taunts, prayeth. 11 Sara reproched
by her fathers maides, prayeth also. 17 An Angel is sent to helpe
them both.

THen I being grieued, did weepe, and in my sorrowe
prayed, saying,

2 O Lord, thou art iust and all thy workes, and all thy
wayes are mercie and trueth, and thou iudgest truely & iustly
for euer.

3 Remember me, and looke on me, punish me not for my
sinnes and ignorances, and *the sinnes of* my fathers, who haue
sinned before thee.

4 For they obeyed not thy commandements, wherefore thou
*Deut. 28. 15, 37. hast deliuered vs *for a spoile, and vnto captiuitie, and vnto
death, and for a prouerbe of reproch to all the nations among
whom we are dispersed.

5 And now thy iudgments are many and true: Deale with
me according to my sinnes, and my fathers: because we haue
not kept thy commandements, neither haue walked in trueth
before thee.

6 Now therefore deale with me as seemeth best vnto thee,
and command my spirit to be taken from me, that I may be
|| *Or, dismissed, or deliuered.* ||dissolued, and become earth: for it is profitable for me to
die, rather then to liue, because I haue heard false reproches,
and haue much sorow: command therfore that I may now
be deliuered out of this distresse, and goe into the euerlasting
place: turne not thy face away from me.

7 It came to passe the same day, that in Ecbatane a citie
of Media, Sara the daughter of Raguel, was also reproched by
her fathers maides,

8 Because that she had bin maried to seuen husbands, whom
Asmodeus the euill spirit had killed, before they had lien with
her. Doest thou not knowe, said they, that thou hast strangled
thine husbands? thou hast had already seuen husbands, neither
wast thou named after any of them.

9 Wherefore doest thou beate vs for them? If they be dead,
goe thy wayes after them, let vs neuer see of thee either sonne
or daughter.

10 When she heard these things, she was very sorowful, so
that she thought to haue strangled her selfe, and she said,

I am the onely daughter of my father, and if I doe this, it
shall bee a reproch vnto him, and I shall bring his old age with
sorow vnto the graue.
11 Then she prayed toward the window, & said, Blessed
art thou, O Lord my God, and thine holy and glorious Name
is blessed, and honourable for euer, let al thy works praise
thee for euer.
12 And now, O Lord, I set mine eyes and my face toward
thee,
13 And say, take me out of the earth, that I may heare no
more the reproch.
14 Thou knowest, Lord, that I am pure from all sinne with
man,
15 And that I neuer polluted my name, nor the name of
my father in the land of my captiuitie : I am the onely daughter
of my father, neither hath he any child to bee his heire, neither
any ||neere kinseman, nor any sonne of his aliue, to whome I || *Or, brother*
may keepe my selfe for a wife : my seuen husbands are already
dead, and why should I liue ? but if it please not thee that I
should die, command some regard to be had of me, and pitie
taken of me, that I heare no more reproch.
16 So the prayers of them both were heard before the
Maiesty of the great God.
17 And Raphael was sent to heale them both, that is, to
scale away the whitenesse of Tobits eyes, and to giue Sara
the daughter of Raguel, for a wife to Tobias the sonne of
Tobit, and to bind Asmodeus the euill spirit, because she
belongeth to Tobias by right of inheritance. The selfe same
time came Tobit home, and entred into his house, and Sara,
the daughter of Raguel came downe from her vpper chamber.

CHAP. IIII.

3 Tobit giueth instructions to his sonne Tobias, 20 and telleth him of money left with Gabael in Media.

IN that day Tobit remembred the money, which he had
committed to Gabael in Rages of Media,
2 And said with himselfe, I haue wished for death, wherefore doe I not call for my sonne Tobias, that I may signifie
to him *of the money* before I die.
3 And when he had called him, he said; My sonne, when * Exod. 20.
I am dead, bury me, and despise not thy mother, *but 12. ecclus.
honour 7. 27.

honour her all the dayes of thy life, and doe that which shall please her, and greiue her not.

4 Remember, my sonne, that shee saw many dangers for thee, *when thou wast* in her wombe, and when shee is dead, bury her by me in one graue.

5 My sonne, be mindfull of the Lord our God all thy dayes, and let not thy will be set to sinne, or to transgresse his Commandements: doe vprightly all thy life long, and follow not the wayes of vnrighteousnesse.

6 For if thou deale truely, thy doings shall prosperously succeed to thee, and to all them that liue iustly.

*Prou. 3. 9. eccle. 4. 1. and 14. 13. luke 14. 13.

7 *Giue almes of thy substance, and when thou giuest almes, let not thine eye be enuious, neither turne thy face from any poore, and the face of God shall not be turned away from thee.

*Ecclu. 35. 10.

8 If thou hast abundance, *giue almes accordingly: if thou haue but a litle, be not afraid to giue according to that litle.

9 For thou layest vp a good treasure for thy selfe against the day of necessitie.

*Ecclu. 29. 13.

10 *Because that almes doth deliuer from death, and suffereth not to come into darknesse.

11 For almes is a good gift vnto all that giue it, in the sight of the most High.

*1. Thess. 4. 3.

12 Beware of all *whoredome, my sonne, and chiefely take a wife of the seed of thy fathers, and take not a strange woman to wife, which is not of thy fathers tribe: for we are the children of the Prophets, Noe, Abraham, Isaak, and Iacob: remember, my sonne, that our fathers from the beginning, euen that they all maried wiues of their owne kinred, and were blessed in their children, and their seede shall inherite the land.

13 Now therefore my sonne, loue thy brethren, and despise not in thy heart thy brethren, the sonnes and daughters of thy people, in not taking a wife of them: for in pride is destruction and much trouble, and in lewdnesse is decay, and great want: for lewdnesse is the mother of famine.

*Leuit. 19. 13. deut. 24. 14. 15.

14 Let not the *wages of any man, which hath wrought for thee, tary with thee, but giue him it out of hand: for if thou serue God he will also repay thee: be circumspect, my sonne, in all things thou doest, and be wise in all thy conuersation.

15 *Doe that to no man which thou hatest: drinke not *Matth. 7.
wine to make thee drunken; neither let drunkennesse goe 12. luc. 6.
with thee in thy iourney. 31.
16 *Giue of thy bread to the hungry, and of thy garments *Luc. 14.
to them that are naked, *and according to thine abundance 13. *Matth. 6.
giue almes, and let not thine eye be enuious, when thou 1
giuest almes.
17 Powre out thy bread on the buriall of the iust, but giue
nothing to the wicked.
18 Aske counsell of all that are wise, and despise not any
counsell that is profitable.
19 Blesse the Lord thy God alway, and desire of him that
thy wayes may be directed, and that all thy pathes, and
counsels may prosper: for euery nation hath not counsell,
but the Lord himselfe giueth all good things, and hee humbleth whom he will, as he will; now therefore my sonne,
remember my commandements, neither let them be put out
of thy minde.
20 And now I signifie this to thee, that I committed tenne
talents to Gabael the sonne of Gabrias at Rages in Media.
21 And feare not my sonne, that we are made poore, for
thou hast much wealth, if thou feare God, and depart from
all sinne, and doe that which is pleasing in his sight.

CHAP. V.

4 Yong Tobias seeketh a guide into Media. 6 The Angel will goe with him, 12 and saith he is his kinseman. 16 Tobias and the Angel depart together. 17 But his mother is grieued for her sonnes departing.

TObias then answered and said, Father, I will doe all
things, which thou hast commanded me.
2 But how can I receiue the money, seeing, I know him
not?
3 Then he gaue him the handwriting, and said vnto him,
Seeke thee a man which may goe with thee whiles I yet liue,
and I will giue him wages, and goe, and receiue the money.
4 Therefore when he went to seeke a man, he found
Raphael that was an Angell.
5 But he knew not; and he said vnto him, Canst thou goe
with me to Rages? & knowest thou those places well?
6 To

6 To whom the Angel said, I will goe with thee, and I know the way well: for I haue lodged with our brother Gabael.
7 Then Tobias said vnto him, Tary for me till I tell my father.
8 Then he said vnto him, Goe and tary not; so he went in, and said to his father; Behold, I haue found one, which wil goe with me. Then he said, Call him vnto me, that I may know of what tribe he is, and whether hee be a trustie man to goe with thee.
9 So he called him, and he came in, and they saluted one another.
10 Then Tobit said vnto him, Brother, shew me of what tribe and family thou art.
11 To whom hee said, Doest thou seeke for a tribe or family, or an hired man to goe with thy sonne? Then Tobit said vnto him, I would know, brother, thy kinred, and name.
12 Then he said, I am Azarias, the sonne of Ananias the great, and of thy brethren.
13 Then Tobit said, Thou art welcome brother, be not now angry with mee, because I haue enquired to know thy tribe, and thy family, for thou art my brother, of an honest & good stocke: for I know Ananias, and Ionathas sonnes of that great Samaias: as we went together to Ierusalem to worship, and offered the first borne, and the tenths of the fruits, and they were not seduced with the errour of our brethren: my brother, thou art of a good stocke.
14 But tell me, what wages shall I giue thee? *wilt thou* a drachme a day? and things necessary as to my owne sonne?
15 Yea moreouer, if ye returne safe, I will adde some thing to the wages.
16 So they were well pleased. Then said he to Tobias; Prepare thy selfe for the iourney, and God send you a good iourney. And when his sonne had prepared all things for the iourney, his father said; Goe thou with this man, and God which dwelleth in heauen prosper your iourney, & the Angel of God keepe you company. So they went foorth both, and the yong mans dogge with them.
17 But Anna his mother wept, and said to Tobit, Why hast thou sent away our sonne? is hee not the staffe of our hand, in going in and out before vs?

18 Be not greedy (to adde) money to money: but let it bee
‖as refuse in respect of our childe.
19 ‖For that which the Lord hath giuen vs to liue with,
doeth suffice vs.
20 Then said Tobit to her, Take no care my sister, he shal
returne in safety, and thine eyes shall see him.
21 For the good Angel will keepe him company, and his
iourney shall be prosperous, and he shall returne safe.
22 Then she made an end of weeping.

‖ *Let not money be added, but be the off scouring of our sonne.*

‖ *Or, so long as God hath granted vs to liue, this is sufficient.*

CHAP. VI.

4 The Angel biddeth Tobias to take the liuer, heart and gall out of a fish, 10 And to marry Sara the daughter of Raguel; 16 And teacheth how to driue the wicked spirit away.

AND as they went on their iourney, they came in the
euening to the riuer Tigris, & they lodged there.
2 And when the yong man went downe to wash himselfe, a
fish leaped out of the riuer, and would haue deuoured him.
3 Then the Angel said vnto him, Take the fish; and the
yong man layd hold of the fish, and ‖drew it to land.
4 To whom the Angel said, Open the fish, and take the
heart, and the liuer and the gall, and put them vp safely.
5 So the yong man did as the Angel commaunded him,
and when they had rosted the fish, they did eate it: then
they both went on their way, till they drew neere to
Ecbatane.
6 Then the yong man saide to the Angel; Brother Azarias,
to what vse is the heart, and the liuer, and the gall of the
fish?
7 And he said vnto him, Touching the heart and the liuer,
if a deuil, or an euil spirit trouble any, we must make a smoke
thereof before the man or the woman, and the party shalbe
no more vexed.
8 As for the gall *it is good* to anoint a man that hath whitenesse in his eyes, and he shalbe healed.
9 And when they were come neere to Rages;
10 The Angel said to the yong man, Brother, to day wee
shall lodge with Raguel, who is thy cousin; hee also hath
one onely daughter, named Sara, I wil speake for her, that
she may be giuen thee for a wife.

‖ *Cast it vp on the land.*

11 For

|| *Or, inheritance.*
*Num. 27. 8. & 36. 8.

11 For to thee doth the ||*right of her appertaine, seeing
thou onely art of her kinred.
12 And the maide is faire and wise, now therefore heare
me, & I wil speake to her father, and when wee returne
from Rages, we will celebrate the mariage: for I know that
Raguel cannot marry her to another according to the Law of
Moses, but he shalbe guiltie of death, because the right of
inheritance doeth rather appertaine to thee, then to any
other.
13 Then the yong man answered the Angel, I haue heard,
brother Azarias, that this maide hath beene giuen to seuen
men, who all died in the marriage chamber:
14 And now I am the onely sonne of my father, and I am
afraid, lest if I goe in vnto her, I die, as the other before; for
a wicked spirit loueth her, which hurteth no body, but those
which come vnto her; wherefore I also feare, lest I die, and
bring my fathers and my mothers life (because of me) to the
graue with sorrow, for they haue no other sonne to bury
them.
15 Then the Angel said vnto him, Doest thou not remember
the precepts, which thy father gaue thee, that thou shouldest
marrie a wife of thine owne kinred? wherefore heare me, O
my brother, for she shall be giuen thee to wife, and make
thou no reckoning of the euil spirit, for this same night shall
shee be giuen thee in mariage.
16 And when thou shalt come into the mariage chamber,
thou shalt take the ||ashes of perfume, and shalt lay vpon
them, some of the heart, and liuer of the fish, and shalt make
a smoke with it.

|| *Or, imbers.*

17 And the deuill shall smell it, and flee away, and neuer
come againe any more: but when thou shalt come to her,
rise vp both of you, and pray to God, which is mercifnll,
who will haue pity on you, and saue you: feare not, for shee
is appointed vnto thee from the beginning; and thou shalt
preserue her, and shee shall goe with thee. Moreouer I
suppose that shee shall beare thee children. Now when
Tobias had heard these things, he loued her, and his heart
was ||effectually ioyned to her.

|| *Or, vehemently.*

CHAP. VII.

11 Raguel telleth Tobias what had happened to his daughter: 12 and giueth her in marriage

vnto him. 17 She is conueyed to her chamber, and weepeth. 18 Her mother cōforteth her.

ANd when they were come to Ecbatane, they came to the house of Raguel; and Sara met them: and after that they had saluted one another, shee brought them into the house.

2 Then sayd Raguel to Edna his wife, How like is this yong man to Tobit my cousin?

3 And Raguel asked them, From whence are you, brethren? To whom they said, We are of the sonnes of Nephthali, which are captiues in Nineue.

4 Then hee said to them, Doe yee know Tobit our kinseman? And they said, We know him. Then said hee, Is he in good health?

5 And they said, Hee is both aliue, and in good health: And Tobias sayd, He is my father.

6 Then Raguel leaped vp, and kissed him, and wept,

7 And blessed him, and said vnto him, Thou art the sonne of an honest and good man: but when he had heard that Tobit was blinde, he was sorowfull, and wept.

8 And likewise Edna his wife, and Sara his daughter wept. Moreouer, they entertained them cheerefully, and after that they had killed a ‖ramme of the flocke, they set store of meat on the table. Then said Tobias to Raphael, Brother Azarias, speak of those things, of which thou diddest talke in the way, and let this businesse be dispatched.

‖ *A sucking ramme or lambe. Iunius.*

9 So he communicated the matter with Raguel, and Raguel said to Tobias, Eate and drink, and make merry:

10 For it is meet that thou shouldest marry my daughter: neuerthelesse I will declare vnto thee the trueth.

11 I haue giuen my daughter in mariage to seuen men, who died that night they came in vnto her: neuerthelesse for the present be merry: But Tobias said, I will eate nothing here, till we agree and sweare one to another.

12 Raguel said, Then take her from hencefoorth according to the ‖manner, for thou art her cousin, and she is thine, and the mercifull God giue you good successe in all things.

‖ *Or, Law.*

13 Then he called his daughter Sara, and she came to her father, and hee tooke her by the hand, and gaue her to be

*Num. 36. 6 be wife to Tobias, saying, Behold, take her after *the Law
of Moses, and leade her away to thy father: And he blessed
them,

14 And called Edna his wife, & tooke paper, and did write
an instrument *of couenants*, and sealed it.

15 Then they began to eate.

16 After Raguel called his wife Edna, and said vnto her,
Sister, prepare another chamber, & bring her in thither.

17 Which when she had done as hee had bidden her, she
|| Or, licked. brought her thither, and she wept, & she ||receiued the teares
of her daughter, and said vnto her,

18 Be of good comfort, my daughter, the Lord of heauen
and earth giue thee ioy for this thy sorow: be of good comfort, my daughter.

CHAP. VIII.

3 Tobias driueth the wicked spirit away, as hee was taught. 4 He and his wife rise vp to pray. 10 Raguel thought he was dead: 15 But finding him aliue, praiseth God, 12 and maketh a wedding feast.

AND when they had supped, they brought Tobias in vnto
her.

2 And as he went, he remembred the wordes of Raphael,
|| Or, imbers and tooke the ||ashes of the perfumes, and put the heart, and
the liuer of the fish thereupon, and made a smoke *therewith*.

3 The which smell, when the euill spirit had smelled, hee
fled into the outmost parts of Egypt, and the Angel bound
him.

4 And after that they were both shut in together, Tobias
rose out of the bed and said, Sister, arise, and let vs pray,
that God would haue pitie on vs.

5 Then began Tobias to say, Blessed art thou, O God of
our fathers, and blessed is thy holy and glorious Name for
euer, let the heauens blesse thee, and all thy creatures.

*Gen. 2.7, 18, 22. 6 Thou madest Adam, and gauest him *Eue his wife for
an helper & stay: of them came mankind: thou hast said, It
is not good that man should bee alone, let vs make vnto him
an aide like to himselfe.

7 And now, O Lord, I take not this my sister for lust, but
vprightly: therefore mercifully ordeine, that wee may become
aged together.

8 And she said with him, Amen.

9 So they slept both that night, and Raguel arose, and went
& made a graue
10 Saying, *I feare* lest he be dead.
11 But when Raguel was come into his house,
12 He said vnto his wife Edna, Send one of the maids, and
let her see, whether he be aliue: if *he be* not, that we may
bury him, and no man know it.
13 So the maid opened the doore and went in, and found
them both asleepe,
14 And came forth, and told them, that he was aliue.
15 Then Raguel praised God, and said, O God, thou art
worthy to be praised with all pure and holy praise: therefore
let thy Saints praise thee with all thy creatures, and let all
thine Angels and thine elect praise thee for euer.
16 Thou art to be praised, for thou hast made mee ioyfull,
and that is not come to me, which I suspected: but thou hast
dealt with vs according to thy great mercie.
17 Thou art to be praised, because thou hast had mercie of
two, that were the onely begotten children of their fathers,
grant them mercy, O Lord, and finish their life in health,
with ioy and mercie.
18 Then Raguel bade his seruants to fill the graue.
19 And hee kept the wedding feast fourteene dayes.
20 For before the dayes of the mariage were finished,
Raguel had said vnto him by an othe, that he should not
depart, till the fourteene dayes of the mariage were expired,
21 And then he should take the halfe of his goods, and goe
in safetie to his father, and should haue the rest when I and
my wife be dead.

CHAP. IX.

1 Tobias sendeth the Angel vnto Gabael for the money. 6 The Angel bringeth it, and Gabael to the wedding.

THen Tobias called Raphael, and said vnto him,
2 Brother Azarias, Take with thee a seruant, and two
camels, and go to Rages of Media to Gabael, & bring me the
money, & bring him to the wedding.
3 For Raguel hath sworne that I shall not depart.
4 But my father counteth the dayes, and if I tarie long, he
will be very sorie.

5 So

5 So Raphael went out and lodged with Gabael, and gaue
him the handwriting, who brought forth bags, which were
sealed vp, and gaue them to him.
6 And earely in the morning they went forth both together,
and came to the wedding, and ||Tobias blessed his wife.

|| Or, Gabael blessed Tobias and his wife. Iunius.

CHAP. X.

1 Tobit and his wife long for their sonne. 7 She will not be comforted by her husband. 10 Raguel sendeth Tobias and his wife away, with halfe their goods, 12 and blesseth them.

NOwe Tobit his father counted euery day, and when the
dayes of the iourney were expired, and they came
not:
2 Then Tobit said, Are they detained? or is Gabael dead?
and there is no man to giue him the money?
3 Therefore he was very sory.
4 Then his wife said to him, My sonne is dead, seeing hee
stayeth long, and she beganne to bewaile him, and said,
5 *Now I care for nothing*, my sonne, *since I haue let thee goe*,
the light of mine eyes.
6 To whom Tobit said, Hold thy peace, take no care; for
he is safe.
7 But she said, Hold thy peace, and deceiue me not: my
sonne is dead, and she went out euery day into the way
which they went, and did eate no meat on the day time, and
ceased not whole nights, to bewaile her sonne Tobias, vntill
the foureteene dayes of the wedding were expired, which
Raguel had sworne, that he should spend there: Then
Tobias said to Raguel, Let me goe, for my father, and my
mother look no more to see me.
8 But his father in law said vnto him, Tary with me, and
I will send to thy father, and they shall declare vnto him,
how things goe with thee.
9 But Tobias said, No: but let me goe to my father.
10 Then Raguel arose and gaue him Sara his wife, and halfe
his goods, seruants, & cattell, and money.
11 And hee blessed them, and sent them away, saying, The
God of heauen giue you a prosperous iourney, my children.

12 And he said to his daughter, Honour thy father and thy
mother in law, which are now thy parents, that I may heare
good report of thee: and hee kissed her. Edna also said to
Tobias, The Lord of heauen restore thee, my deare brother,
and grant that I may see thy children of my daughter Sara
before I die, that I may reioyce before the Lord: behold, I
commit my daughter vnto thee ||of speciall trust, wherefore || *Or, to be*
doe not entreate her euill. *safely kept.*

CHAP. XI.

6 Tobits mother spieth her sonne comming. 10 His father meeteth him at the doore, and recouereth his sight. 14 Hee praiseth God, 17 And welcommeth his daughter in Lawe.

AFter these things Tobias went his way, praising God that
he had giuen him a prosperous iourney, and blessed
Raguel, and Edna his wife, and went on his way till they
drew neere vnto Nineue.
2 Then Raphael said to Tobias, Thou knowest brother,
how thou didst leaue thy father.
3 Let vs haste before thy wife, and prepare the house.
4 And take in thine hand the gall of the fish: so they went
their way, and the dog went after them.
5 Now Anna sate looking about towards the way for her
sonne.
6 And when she espied him comming, she said to his father,
Behold, thy sonne commeth, and the man that went with
him.
7 Then said Raphael, I know, Tobias, that thy father will
open his eyes.
8 Therefore annoint thou his eies with the gall, and being
pricked therewith he shall rub, and the whitenesse shall fall
away, and he shall see thee.
9 Then Anna ran forth, and fell vpon the necke of her
sonne, and said vnto him, seeing I haue seene thee my sonne,
from henceforth, I am content to die, and they wept both.
10 Tobit also went forth toward the doore, and stumbled:
but his sonne ran vnto him,
11 And tooke hold of his father, and he strake of the gall on
his fathers eyes, saying, Be of good hope, my father.

12 And

12 And when his eyes beganne to smart, he rubbed them.
13 And the whitenesse pilled away from the corners of his
eyes, and when he saw his sonne, he fell vpon his necke.
14 And he wept, and said, Blessed art thou, O God, and
blessed is thy Name for euer, and blessed are all thine holy
Angels:
15 For thou hast scourged, and hast taken pitie on me: for
behold, I see my sonne Tobias. And his sonne went in
reioycing, and told his father the great things that had happened to him in Media.
16 Then Tobit went out to meete his daughter in law at
the gate of Niniue, reioycing and praysing God: and they
which saw him goe, marueiled because he had receiued his
sight.
17 But Tobit gaue thankes before them: because God had
mercy on him. And when hee came neere to Sara his
daughter in Law, hee blessed her, saying, Thou art welcome
daughter: God be blessed which hath brought thee vnto vs,
and blessed be thy father and thy mother; And there was ioy
amongst all his brethren which were at Nineue.
18 And Achiacharus, ||and Nasbas his brothers sonne came.
19 And Tobias wedding was kept seuen dayes with great
ioy.

|| *Iunius, who is also called Nasbas.*

CHAP. XII.

5 Tobit offereth halfe to the Angel for his paines; 6 But he calleth them both aside, and exhorteth them, 15 and telleth them that he was an Angel, 21 and was seene no more.

THen Tobit called his son Tobias, and said vnto him,
My sonne, see that the man haue his wages, which
went with thee, and thou must giue him more.
2 And Tobias said vnto him, O father, it is no harme to
me to giue him halfe of those things which I haue brought.
3 For he hath brought me againe to thee in safety, and
made whole my wife, and brought mee the money, and likewise healed thee.
4 Then the old man said: It is due vnto him.
5 So he called the Angell, and he said vnto him, Take halfe
of all that yee haue brought, and goe away in safety.
6 Then he tooke them both apart,

and sayd vnto them, Blesse God, praise him, and magnifie
him, and praise him for the things which he hath done vnto
you in the sight of all that liue. It is good to praise God and
exalt his name, & ||honorably to shew forth the works of || *Or, with honour.*
God, therfore be not slacke to praise him.
7 It is good to keepe close the secret of a King, but it is
honorable to reueale the works of God: do that which is
good, and no euill shall touch you.
8 Praier is good with fasting, and almes and righteousnesse:
a little with righteousnes is better then much with vnrighteousnesse: it is better to giue almes then to lay vp gold.
9 For almes doth deliuer from death, and shall purge away
all sinne. Those that exercise almes, and righteousnesse,
shall be filled with life.
10 But they that sinne are enemies to their owne life.
11 Surely I will keep close nothing from you. For I said,
it was good to keepe close the secret of a King, but that it
was honorable to reueale the works of God.
12 Now therefore, when thou didst pray, and Sara thy
daughter in Law, I did bring the remembrance of your
prayers before the holy one, and when thou didst bury the
dead, I was with thee likewise.
13 And when thou didst not delay to rise vp, and leaue thy
dinner †to go and couer the dead, thy good deede was not † *Greek. to go and bury.*
hidde from me: but I was with thee.
14 And now God hath sent mee to heale thee, & Sara thy
daughter in law.
15 I am Raphael one of the seuen holy Angels, which
present the prayers of the Saints, and which go in and out
before the glory of the Holy one.
16 Then they were both troubled, and fel vpon their faces:
for they feared.
17 But he said vnto them, feare not, for it shall go well with
you, praise God therefore.
18 For not of any fauour of mine, but by the will of our
God I came, wherefore praise him for euer.
19 *All these daies I did appeare vnto you, but I did neither *Gen. 18. 8. 19. 3. Iudg. 13. 16.
eat nor drinke, but you did see a vision.
20 Now therefore giue God thanks: for I go vp to him ẏ
sent me, but write all things which are done, in a booke.
21 And when they rose, they saw him no more.

22 Then

22 Then they confessed the great and wonderfull workes
of God, and how the Angel of the Lord had appeared vnto
them.

CHAP. XIII.

The thankesgiuing vnto God, which Tobit wrote.

THen Tobit wrote a prayer of reioycing, and said, Blessed
be God that liueth for euer, and blessed be his kingdome:
*Deut. 32. 39. 1. sam. 2. 6. wisd. 16. 13.
2 * For he doeth scourge, and hath mercy: hee leadeth downe
to hell, and bringeth vp againe: neither is there any that can
auoid his hand.
3 Confesse him before the Gentiles, ye children of Israel:
for he hath scattered vs among them.
4 There declare his greatnesse, and extoll him before all the
liuing, for he is our Lord, and he is the God our father for
euer:
5 And he wil scourge vs for our iniquities, and will haue
mercy againe, and will gather vs out of all nations, among
whom he hath scattered vs.
6 If you turne to him with your whole heart, and with
your whole minde, and deale vprightly before him, then will
hee turne vnto you, and will not hide his face from you:
Therefore see what he will doe with you, and confesse him
with your whole mouth, and praise the Lord of might, and
extoll the euerlasting King: in the land of my captiuitie doe
I praise him, and declare his might and maiesty to a sinnefull
nation: O yee sinners turne, and doe iustice before him:
who can tell if he will accept you, and haue mercy on you?
7 I wil extoll my God, and my soule shal praise the King
of heauen, and shal reioyce in his greatnesse.
8 Let all men speake, and let all praise him for his righteousnesse.
|| *Or, he will lay a scourge vpon the workes of thy children.*
9 O Ierusalem the holy Citie, ||he will scourge thee for thy
childrens workes, and will haue mercy againe on the sonnes
of the righteous.
|| *Or, to make.*
10 Giue praise to the Lord, for hee is good: and praise the
euerlasting King; that his Tabernacle may bee builded in
thee againe with ioy: and ||let him make ioyfull there in
thee, those that are captiues, and loue in thee for euer those
that are miserable.

12 Many nations shall come from

farre to the Name of the Lord God, with gifts in their
hands, euen giftes to the King of heauen: all generations
shall praise thee with great ioy.
12 Cursed are all they which hate thee, and blessed shall all
be, which loue thee for euer.
13 Reioyce & be glad for the children of the iust: for they
shall be gathered together, & shall blesse the Lord of the iust.
14 O blessed are they which loue thee, for they shall reioyce
in thy ||peace: blessed are they which haue been sorowfull || *Or, pro-*
for all thy scourges, for they shal reioyce for thee, when they *speritie.*
haue seene all thy glory, and shalbe glad for euer.
15 Let my soule blesse God the great King.
16 For Ierusalem shall be built vp with Saphires, and
Emerauds, and precious stone: thy walles and towres, and
battlements with pure golde.
17 And the streets of Ierusalem shal be paued with Berill,
and Carbuncle, and stones of Ophir.
18 And all her streets shall say, Halleluiah, and they shall
praise him, saying, Blessed be God which hath extolled it for
euer.

CHAP. XIIII.

3 Tobit giueth instructions to his sonne, 8 Specially to leaue Nineue. 11 Hee and his wife die, and are buried. 12 Tobias remoueth to Ecbatane, 14 and there died, after hee had heard of the destruction of Nineue.

SO Tobit made an ende of praising God.
2 And he was eight and fifty yeeres olde when hee lost
his sight, which was restored to him after eight yeeres, and
he gaue almes, and he ||increased in the feare of the Lord || *Or, did*
God, and praised him. *more and*
3 And when he was very aged, hee called his sonne, and *more feare.*
the sixe sons of his sonne, and said to him, My sonne, take
thy children; for behold, I am aged, and am ready to depart
out of this life.
4 Goe into Media, my sonne, for I surely beleeue those things
which Ionas the Prophet spake of Nineue, that it shall be ouerthrowen, and that for a time peace shal rather be in Media,
and that our brethren shall lie scattered in the earth from that
good land, and Ierusalem shall be desolate, and the house of
God in it shalbe burned, and shall be desolate for a time:

*Ezra 3. 8. and 6. 14. 5 *And that againe God will haue mercie on them, and
bring them againe into the land where they shall build a
Temple, but not like to the first, vntill the time of that age
be fulfilled, and afterward they shall returne from all places
of their captiuitie, and build vp Ierusalem gloriously, and the
|| For euer *is not in the Rom. copie.* house of God shall be built in it ||for euer, with a glorious
building, as the prophets haue spoken thereof.
6 And all nations shall turne, and feare the Lord God truely,
and shall burie their idoles.
7 So shall all nations praise the Lord, and his people shal
confesse God, and the Lord shall exalt his people, and all
those which loue the Lord God in trueth and iustice, shall
reioyce, shewing mercie to our brethren.
8 And now, my sonne, depart out of Nineue, because that
those things which the Prophet Ionas spake, shall surely come
to passe.
9 But keepe thou the Law and the Commandements, and
shew thy selfe mercifull and iust, that it may goe well with
thee.
10 And burie me decently, and thy mother with me, but
tarie no longer at Nineue. Remember, my sonne, how
Aman handled Achiacharus ẏ brought him vp, how out of
light he brought

CHAP. I.

2 Arphaxad doeth fortifie Ecbatane. 5 Nabuchodonosor maketh warre against him, 7 and craueth aide. 12 Hee threatneth those that would not aide him, 15 and killeth Arphaxad, 16 and returneth to Nineue.

IN the twelfth yeere of ẏ reigne of Nabuchodonosor, who reigned in Nineue the great citie, (in the dayes of Arphaxad, which reigned ouer the Medes in Ecbatane, him into darkenes, and how he rewarded him againe: yet Ahiacharus was ||saued, but the other had his reward, for hee went downe into darkenesse. ||Manasses gaue almes, and escaped the snares of death ||which they had set for him: but Aman fell into the snare and perished.

|| *Or, preserued.*
|| *Iunius readeth Nitsban.*
|| *Rom. which he had set.*

11 Wherefore now, my sonne, consider what almes doeth, and how righteousnesse doth deliuer. When he had said these things, he gaue vp the ghost in the bed, being an hundred, and eight and fiftie yeeres old, and ||he buried him honourably.

|| *Or, they.*

12 And when Anna his mother was dead, he buried her with his father: but Tobias departed with his wife and children to Ecbatane, to Raguel his father in law:

13 Where hee became old with honour, and hee buried his father and mother in lawe honourably, and hee ||inherited their substance, and his father Tobits.

|| *Or, possessed.*

14 And he died at Ecbatane in Media, being an hundred and seuen and twentie yeeres old.

15 But before he died, he heard of the destruction of Nineue, which was taken by Nabuchodonosor & Assuerus: and before his death hee reioyced ouer Nineue.

DETH.

2 And built in Ecbatane walles round about of stones hewen, three cubites broad, and sixe cubites long, and made the height of the wall seuenty cubites, and the breadth thereof fiftie cubites:

3 And set the towers thereof vpon the gates of it, an hundred cubites *high*, and the breadth thereof in the foundation threescore cubites.

4 And he made the gates thereof, euen gates that were raised to the height of seuentie cubites, & the breadth of them was fourtie cubites, for the going foorth of his mightie armies, and for the setting in aray of his footmen.)

5 Euen in those dayes, king Nabuchodo-

chodonosor made warre with king Arphaxad in the great
plaine, which is the plaine in the borders of Ragau.
6 And there came vnto him, all they that dwelt in the hill
countrey, and all that dwelt by Euphrates, and Tigris, and
Hydaspes, and the plaine of Arioch the king of the Elimeans,
and very many nations of the sonnes of Chelod, assembled
themselues to the battell.
7 Then Nabuchodonosor king of the Assyrians, sent vnto
all that dwelt in Persia, and to all that dwelt Westward,
and to those that dwelt in Cilicia, and Damascus and Libanus,
and Antilibanus, and to all that dwelt vpon the Sea
coast,
8 And to those amongst the nations that were of Carmel,
and Galaad, and the higher Galile, and the great plaine of
Esdrelon,
9 And to all that were in Samaria, and the cities thereof:
and beyond Iordan vnto Ierusalem, and Betane, and Chellus,
and Kades, and the riuer of Egypt, and Taphnes, and
Ramesse, and all the land of Gesem,
10 Vntill you come beyond Tanis, and Memphis, and to
all the inhabitants of Egypt, vntill you come to the borders
of Ethiopia.
11 But all the inhabitants of the land made light of the
commandement of Nabuchodonosor king of the Assyrians,
neither went they with him to the battell: for they were
not afraid of him: yea he was before them as one man, and
they sent away his Ambassadours from them without effect,
and with disgrace.
12 Therefore Nabuchodonosor was very angry with all this
countrey, and sware by his throne and kingdome, that hee
would surely be auenged vpon all those coasts of Cilicia, and
Damascus, and Syria, and that he would slay with the sword
all the inhabitants of the land of Moab, and the children of
Ammon, and all Iudea, and all that were in Egypt, till you
come to the borders of the two Seas.
13 Then he marched in battell aray with his power against
king Arphaxad in the seuenteenth yeere, and he preuailed in
his battell: for he ouerthrew all the power of Arphaxad, and
all his horsemen and all his chariots,
14 And became Lord of his cities,

and came vnto Ecbatane, and tooke the towers, and spoiled the streetes thereof, and turned the beauty thereof into shame.

15 Hee tooke also Arphaxad in the mountaines of Ragau, and smote him through with his dartes, and destroyed him vtterly that day.

16 So he returned afterward to Nineue, both he and all his company of sundry nations: being a very great multitude of men of warre, and there he tooke his ease and banketted, both he and his armie an hundred and twenty dayes.

CHAP. II.

4 Olofernes is appointed generall, 11 and charged to spare none, that will not yeeld. 15 His armie and prouision, 23 the places which he wonne and wasted, as he went.

AND in the eighteenth yeere, the two and twentieth day of the first month, there was talke in the house of Nabuchodonosor king of the Assyrians, that he should as he said auenge himselfe on all the earth.

2 So he called vnto him all his officers, and all his nobles,
and communicated with them his secret counsell, *and con- *1. Sam.
cluded the afflicting of the whole earth out of his owne 20 7. and 25. 17.
mouth.

3 Then they decreed to destroy all flesh that did not obey the commaundement of his mouth.

4 And when he had ended his counsell, Nabuchodonosor
king of the Assyrians called Olofernes the chiefe captaine of † *Gre. second man.*
his army, which was †next vnto him, and said vnto him,

5 Thus saith the great king, the Lord of the whole earth:
behold, thou shalt goe forth from my presence, and take with
thee men that trust in their owne strength, of footemen an
hundred and twenty thousand, and the number of horses with
their riders twelue thousand.

6 And thou shalt goe against all the West countrey, because
they disobeyed my commandement.

7 And thou shalt declare vnto them that they prepare for
me ||earth and water: for I will goe forth in my wrath
against them, and will couer the whole face of the earth with
the feete of mine armie, and I will giue them for a spoile
vnto them.

|| *Or, after the maner of the kings of Persia, to whom earth and water was wont to be giuen to acknowledge that they were Lords of land and sea. Herodotus.*

8 So that their slaine shall fill their vallies, and brookes, and
the riuer shall be filled with their dead, til it ouerflow.
9 And I will lead them captiues to the vtmost parts of all
the earth.
10 Thou therefore shalt goe foorth, and take before hand
for me all their coasts, and if they will yeeld themselues vnto
thee, thou shalt reserue them for me till the day of their
punishment.
11 But concerning them that rebell, let not thine eye spare
them: but put them to the slaughter, and spoile them wheresoeuer thou goest.
12 For as I liue, and by the power of my kingdome, whatsoeuer I haue spoken, that will I doe by mine hand.
13 And take thou heede that thou transgresse none of the
Commaundements of thy Lord, but accomplish them fully,
as I haue commaunded thee, and deferre not to doe them.
14 Then Olofernes went foorth from the presence of his
Lord, and called all the gouernours and Captaines, and the
officers of the army of Assur.
15 And he mustered the chosen men for the battell, as his
Lord had commaunded him, vnto an hundred and twenty
thousand, & twelue thousand archers on Horsebacke.
16 And he ranged them as a great army is ordered for the
warre.
17 And he tooke Camels, and Asses for their cariages a very
great number, and sheepe, and Oxen, & Goates without
number, for their prouision,
18 And plenty of vittaile for euery man of the army, and
very much gold, and siluer, out of the Kings house.
19 Then he went foorth and all his power to go before
King Nabuchodonosor in the voyage, and to couer al the face
of the earth Westward with their charets, and horsemen, and
their chosen footmen.
20 A great multitude also of sundry countries came with
them, like locusts, and like the sand of the earth: for the
multitude was without number.
21 And they went foorth of Nineue, three dayes iourney toward the plaine of Bectileth, and pitched from Bectileth neere
the mountaine, which is at the left hand of the vpper Cilicia.
22 Then he tooke all his armie, his footmen, and horsemen
and chariots, and went from thence into the hill countrey,

23 And destroyed Phud, and Lud: and spoiled all the
children of Rasses, and the children of Ismael, which were
toward the wildernesse at the South of the land of the Chellians.
24 Then he went ouer Euphrates, and went through
Mesopotamia, and destroyed all the high cities that were
vpon the riuer Arbonai, till you come to the sea.
25 And hee tooke the borders of Cilicia, and killed all that
resisted him, and came to the borders of Iapheth, which were
toward the South, ouer against Arabia.
26 He compassed also all the children of Madian, and burnt
vp their tabernacles, and spoiled their sheepcoats.
27 Then hee went downe into the plaine of Damascus in
the time of wheat-haruest, and burnt vp all their fieldes, and
destroyed their flockes, and heards, also he spoiled their cities,
and vtterly wasted their countreys, and smote all their yong
men with the edge of the sword.
28 Therefore the feare and dread of him, fell vpon all the
inhabitants of the sea coastes, which were in Sidon and Tyrus,
and them that dwelt in Sur, and Ocina, and all that dwelt
in Iemnaan, and they that dwelt in Azotus, and Aschalon
feared him greatly.

CHAP. III.

1 They of the Sea-coasts entreat for peace. 7 Olofernes is receiued
there: 8 Yet he destroyeth their gods, that they might worship onely
Nabuchodonosor. 9 He commeth neere to Iudea.

SO they sent Embassadours vnto him, to treat of peace,
saying,
2 Behold, we the seruants of Nabuchodonosor the great king
lie before thee; vse vs as shall be good in thy sight.
3 Behold, our houses, and all our places, and all our fieldes
of wheat, and flockes, and heards, and all the lodges of our
tents, lie before thy face: vse them as it pleaseth thee.
4 Behold, euen our cities and the inhabitants thereof are thy
seruants, come and deale with them, as seemeth good vnto
thee.
5 So the men came to Holofernes, & declared vnto him
after this maner.

6 Then came hee downe toward the

the Sea coast, both hee and his armie, and set garisons in the
high cities, and tooke out of them chosen men for aide.
7 So they and all the countrey round about, receiued them
with garlands, with dances, and with timbrels.
8 Yet hee did cast downe their frontiers, and cut downe
their groues: for hee had decreed to destroy all the gods
of the land, that all nations should worship Nabuchodonosor
onely, and that all tongues and tribes should call vpon him
as God.
9 Also he came ouer against ||Esdraelon neere vnto ||Iudea,
ouer against the †great strait of Iudea.
10 And hee pitched betweene Geba, and Scythopolis, and
there hee taried a whole moneth, that he might gather
together all the cariages of his armie.

|| Or, Esdrelom.
|| Or, Dotæa, Dothan. Iunius. Genes. 37. 17.
† Gr. great saw.

CHAP. IIII.

4 The Iewes are afraid of Holofernes, 5 and fortifie the hilles. 6 They of Bethulia take charge of the passages, 9 All Israel fall to fasting and prayer.

NOw the children of Israel that dwelt in Iudea, heard all that Holofernes the chiefe captaine of Nabuchodonosor king of the Assyrians had done to the nations, and after what manner hee had spoiled all their Temples, and brought them to nought.
2 Therefore they were exceedingly afraid of him, and were
troubled for Ierusalem, and for the Temple of the Lord their
God.
3 For they were newly returned from the captiuitie, and all
the people ||of Iudea were lately gathered together: and the
vessels, and the Altar, and the house, were sanctified after
the profanation.
4 Therefore they sent into all the coasts of Samaria, and the
villages, and to Bethoron, and Belmen, and Iericho, and to
Choba, and Esora, and to the valley of Salem,
5 And possessed themselues beforehand of all the tops of the
high mountaines, and fortified the villages that were in them,
and laid vp victuals for the prouision of warre: for their
fieldes were of late reaped.
6 Also Ioacim the hie Priest which was in those daies in
Ierusalem, wrote

|| Or, out of Iudea.

to them that dwelt in Bethulia, and Betomestham which is
ouer against ||Esdraelon toward the ||open countrey neere to || *Or, Es-*
Dothaim, *drelom.*
7 Charging them to keepe the passages of the hill countrey: || *Or, plaine.*
for by them there was an entrance into Iudea, and it was
easie to stoppe them that would come vp, because the passage
was strait ||for two men at the most. || *Or, two*
8 And the children of Israel did as Ioacim the hie Priest had *against all.*
commanded them, with the ||ancients of all the people of || *Or, gouer-*
Israel, which dwelt at Ierusalē. *nours.*
9 Then euery man of Israel cryed to God with great
feruencie, and with great vehemency did they humble their
soules:
10 Both they and their wiues, and their children, and their
cattell, and euery stranger and hireling, and their seruants
bought with money, put sackecloth vpon their loynes.
11 Thus euery man and woman, and the little children, &
the inhabitants of Ierusalem fell before the temple, and cast
ashes vpon their heads, and spread out their sackcloth before
the face of the Lord: also they put sackecloth about the Altar,
12 And cryed to the God of Israel all with one consent
earnestly, that hee would not giue their children for a pray,
and their wiues for a spoile, and the cities of their inheritance
to destruction, and the Sanctuary to profanation and reproch,
& for the nations to reioyce at.
13 So God heard their prayers, and looked vpon their afflictions: for the people fasted many dayes in all Iudea, and
Ierusalem, before the Sanctuary of the Lord Almighty.
14 And Ioacim the high Priest, and all the Priestes that
stood before the Lord, and they which ministred vnto the
Lord, had their loines girt with sackecloth, and offered the
daily burnt offerings, with the vowes and free gifts of the
people,
15 And had ashes on their miters, and cried vnto the Lord
with all their power, that hee would looke vpon all the house
of Israel graciously.

CHAP. V.

5 Achior telleth Holofernes what the Iewes are, 8 and what their God had done for them: 21 and aduiseth not to meddle with them. 22 All that heard him, were offended at him.

THen was it declared to Holofernes the chief captaine of
the armie of Assur that the children of Israel had
prepared for warre, and had shut vp the passages of the hill
† *Gre. all* countrey, and had fortified † all the tops of the high hilles,
the toppe. and had laide impediments in the champion countreys.
2 Wherewith he was very angry, and called all the princes
of Moab, and the captaines of Ammon, and all the gouernours of the Sea coast.
3 And he said vnto them, Tell mee now, ye sonnes of
Canaan, who this people is that dwelleth in the hill countrey?
and what are the cities that they inhabite? and what is the
multitude of their armie? and wherein is their power and
strength, and what king is set ouer them, or captaine of their
armie?
4 And why haue they determined not to come and meet
me, more then all the inhabitants of the West?
*Chap. 11. 5 *Then said Achior, the captaine of all the sonnes of
7, 9. Ammon: Let my lord now heare a word from the mouth of
thy seruant, and I will declare vnto thee the trueth, concerning this people which dwelleth neere thee, and inhabiteth
the hill countreys: and there shall no lie come out of the
mouth of thy seruant.
6 This people are descended of the Caldeans,
*Gen. 11. 7 *And they soiourned heretofore in Mesopotamia, because
31. they would not follow the gods of their fathers, which were
in the land of Caldea.
|| *Or, went* 8 For they || left the way of their ancestours, and worshipped
out of. the God of heauen, the God whom they knew: so they cast
them out from the face of their gods, and they fled into
Mesopotamia, and soiourned there many dayes.
*Gen. 12. 9 Then *their God commaunded them to depart from the
1 place where they soiourned, and to goe into the land of
Chanaan, where they dwelt, and were increased with gold
and siluer, and with very much cattell.
10 But when a famine couered all the land of Chanaan,
they went downe into Egypt, and soiourned there, while they
were nourished, and became there a great multitude, so that
one could not number their nation.
11 Therefore the king of Egypt rose vp against them, and
dealt subtilly with

them, and brought them low, with labouring in bricke, & *Exod. 1.
made them slaues. 8.
12 Then they cried vnto their God, and he smote all the
land of Egypt with incurable plagues, so the *Egyptians cast *Exod. 12.
them out of their sight. 31, 33.
13 And *God dried the red Sea before them: *Exod. 14.
14 And *brought them to mount †Sina, and Cades Barne, 21. *Exod. 19.
and cast forth all that dwelt in the wildernesse. 1
15 So they dwelt in the land of the Amorites, and they †*Greek.*
destroyed by their strength all them of Esebon, and passing *into the way of the*
ouer Iordan they possessed all the hill countrey. *wildernes*
16 *And they cast forth before them, the Chanaanite, the *of Sina.*
Pheresite, the Iebusite, and the Sychemite, and all the Ger- *Iosh. 12. 8
gesites, and they dwelt in that countrey many dayes.
17 And whilest they sinned not before their God, they
prospered, because the God that hateth iniquitie, was with
them.
18 But *when they departed from the way which he *Iudg. 2.
appointed them, they were destroyed in many battels very 11 and 3. 8.
sore, *and were led captiues into a land that was not theirs, *2. Kings
and the Temple of their God was cast to the ground, and 25. 1, 11.
their cities were taken by the enemies.
19 But *nowe are they returned to their God, and are come *Ezra 1. 1,
vp from the places, where they were scattered, and haue 3.
possessed Ierusalem, where their Sanctuary is, and ||are seated ||*Or, haue*
in the hill countrey, for it was desolate. *their dwellings.*
20 Now therefore, my lord and gouernour, if there be any
errour in this people, & they sinne against their God, let vs
consider that this shal be their ruine, and let vs goe vp, and
we shal ouercome them.
21 But if there be no iniquitie in their nation, let my
lord now passe by, lest their Lord defend them, and their
God be for them, and wee become a reproch before all the
world.
22 And when Achior had finished these sayings, all the
people standing round about the tent, murmured, and the
chiefe men of Holofernes, and all that dwelt by the Sea side,
and in Moab, spake that he should kill him.
23 For, *say they*, we will not be afraid of the face of the
children of Israel, for loe, it is a people that haue no strength,
nor

† *Gre. against a mighty armie.*

nor power †for a strong battell.
24 Now therefore, Lord Holofernes, we will goe vp, and
they shall be a pray, to be deuoured of all thine armie.

CHAP. VI.

3 Holofernes despiseth God. 7 He threatneth Achior and sendeth him away. 14 The Bethulians receiue and heare him. 18 They fall to prayer, and comfort Achior.

AND when the tumult of men that were about the councell was ceased, Holofernes the chiefe captaine of the armie of Assur, said vnto Achior and all the Moabites, before all the company of other nations,
2 And who art thou Achior and the hirelings of Ephraim,
that thou hast prophesied amongst vs as to day, and hast said,
that we should not make warre with the people of Israel,
because their God will defend them? and who is God but
Nabuchodonosor?
3 He will send his power, and will destroy them from the
face of the earth, and their God shall not deliuer them: but
we his seruants will destroy them as one man, for they are
not able to sustaine the power of our horses.
4 For with them we will tread them vnder foote, and their
mountains shall be drunken with their blood, and their fields
shall be fiilled with their dead bodies, and their footesteps
shall not be able to stand before vs, for they shal vtterly
perish, saith king Nabuchodonosor Lord of all the earth; for
hee said, none of my words shall be in vaine.
5 And thou Achior, an hireling of Ammon, which hast
spoken these words in the day of thine iniquity, shalt see my
face no more, from this day vntill I take vengeance of this
nation that came out of Egypt.
6 And then shall the sword of mine armie, and the multitude
of them that serue me, passe through thy sides, and thou
shalt fal among their slaine, when I returne.
7 Now therefore my seruants shall bring thee backe into
the hill countrey, and shall set thee in one of the cities of the
passages.
8 And thou shalt not perish till thou be destroyed with
them.
9 And if thou perswade thy selfe in thy minde, that they
shall not be taken,

let not thy countenance fall: I haue spoken it, and none of
my words shall be in vaine.
10 Then Holofernes commanded his seruants that waited
in his tent, to take Achior and bring him to Bethulia, and
deliuer him into the hands of the children of Israel.
11 So his seruants tooke him, and brought him out of the
campe into the plaine, and they went from the midst of the
plaine into the hill countrey, and came vnto the fountaines
that were vnder Bethulia.
12 And when the men of the citie saw them, they tooke
vp their weapons, and went out of the citie to the toppe of
the hill, and euery man that vsed a sling from comming vp
by casting of stones against them.
13 Neuerthelesse hauing gotten priuily vnder the hill, they
bound Achior and cast him downe, and left him at the foote
of the hill, and returned to their Lord.
14 But the Israelites descended from their citie, and came
vnto him, and loosed him, and brought him into Bethulia,
and presented him to the gouernours of the citie,
15 Which were in those dayes Ozias the sonne of Micha
of the tribe of Simeon, and Chabris the sonne of Gothoniel,
and Charmis the sonne of Melchiel.
16 And they called together all the ancients of the citie,
and all their youth ranne together, and their women to the
assembly, and they set Achior in the midst of all their people.
Then Ozias asked him of that which was done.
17 And he answered and declared vnto them the words
of the counsell of Holofernes, and all the words that he
had spoken in the midst of the princes of Assur, and whatsoeuer Holofernes had spoken proudly against the house of
Israel.
18 Then the people fell downe, and worshipped God, and
cryed vnto God, saying,
19 O Lord God of heauen, behold their pride, and pity the
low estate of our nation, and looke vpon the face of those
that are sanctified vnto thee this day.
20 Then they comforted Achior and praised him greatly.
21 And Ozias tooke him out of the assembly vnto his house,
and made a
feast

feast to the Elders, & they called on the God of Israel all
that night for helpe.

CHAP. VII.

1 Holofernes besiegeth Bethulia, 7 and stoppeth the water from them.
22 They faint and murmure against the gouernours, 30 Who promise to yeeld within fiue dayes.

THe next day Holofernes commanded all his army, and
all his people which were come to take his part, that
they should remooue their campe against Bethulia, to take
aforehand the ascents of the hill countrey, and to make warre
against the children of Israel.
2 Then their strong men remoued their campes in that day,
and the armie of the men of warre was, an hundred and
seuenty thousand footmen, and twelue thousand horsemen,
beside the baggage, & other men that were afoot amongst
them, a very great multitude.
3 And they camped in the valley neere vnto Bethulia, by
the fountaine, and they spred themselues in breadth ouer
‖Dothaim, euen to Belmaim, and in length from Bethulia
vnto †Cyamon which is ouer against Esdraelon.
4 Now the children of Israel, when they saw the multitude
of them, were greatly troubled, and said euery one to his
neighbour: Now will these men licke vp the face of the
earth; for neither the high mountaines, nor the valleys, nor
the hils, are able to beare their waight.
5 Then euery man tooke vp his weapons of warre, and
when they had kindled fires vpon their towers, they remained
and watched all that night.
6 But in the second day Holofernes brought foorth all his
horsemen, in the sight of the children of Israel which were
in Bethulia,
7 And viewed the passages vp to the city, and came to the
fountaine of their waters, and tooke them, and set garrisons
of men of warre ouer them, and he himselfe remooued
towards his people.
8 Then came vnto him all the chiefe of the children of
Esau, and al the gouernours of the people of Moab, and the
captaines of the sea coast, and said,
9 Let our lord now heare a word, that there be not an
ouerthrow in thine armie.

‖ From Dothaim. Iunius.
† Greek. beane field.

10 For this people of the children of Israel do not trust in
their speares, but in the height of the mountaines wherein
they dwell, because it is not easie to come vp to the tops of
their mountains.
11 Now therefore my lord, fight not against them in battell
aray, and there shall not so much as one man of thy people
perish.
12 Remaine in thy campe, and keepe all the men of thine
army, and let thy seruants get into their hands the fountaine
of water which issueth foorth of the foot of the mountaine.
13 For all the inhabitants of Bethulia haue their water
thence: so shall thirst kil them, & they shall giue vp their
citie, and we and our people shal goe vp to the tops of the
mountaines that are neere, and will campe vpon them, to
watch that none goe out of the city.
14 So they and their wiues, and their children shalbe consumed with famine, and before the sword come against them,
they shall be ouerthrowen in the streets where they dwel.
15 Thus shalt thou render them an euil reward: because
they rebelled and met not thy person peaceably.
16 And these words pleased Holofernes, and al his seruants,
and he appointed to doe as they had spoken.
17 So the campe of the children of Ammon departed, and
with them fiue thousand of the Assyrians, and they pitched
in the valley, and tooke the waters, and the fountaines of the
waters of the children of Israel.
18 Then the children of Esau went vp, with the children
of Ammon, and camped in the hil countrey ouer against
Dotha-em: and they sent some of them toward the South,
& toward the East ouer against Ekrebel, which is neere vnto
Chusi, that is vpon the brooke Mochmur, and the rest of the
army of the Assyrians camped in the plaine, and couered the
face of the whole land, and their tents and cariages were
pitched to a very great multitude.
19 Then the children of Israel cried vnto the Lord their
God, because their heart failed, for all their enemies had
compassed them round about, & there was no way to escape
out from among them.
20 Thus all the company of Assur remained about them,
both their footmen, charets and horsemen, foure and
thirtie

thirtie dayes, so that all their vessels of water failed all the
inhabitants of Bethulia.
|| Or, pits. 21 And the ||cisternes were emptied, and they had not
water to drinke their fill, for one day; for they gaue them
drinke by measure.
22 Therefore their young children were out of heart, and
their women and yong men fainted for thirst, and fell downe
in the streetes of the city, and by the passages of the gates,
and there was no longer any strength in them.
23 Then all the people assembled to Ozias, and to the chiefe
of the city, both young men, and women, and children, and
cryed with a loude voice, and saide before all the Elders;
*Exo. 5. 24 God *be Iudge betweene vs and you: for you haue
21. done vs great iniury in that you haue not required peace
of the children of Assur.
25 For now we haue no helper: but God hath sold vs into
their hands, that wee should be throwen downe before them
with thirst, and great destruction.
26 Now therefore call them vnto you, and deliuer the whole
citie for a spoile to the people of Olofernes, and to all his
armie.
27 For it is better for vs to be made a spoile vnto them,
then to die for thirst: for wee will be his seruants, that our
soules may liue, and not see the death of our infants before
our eyes, nor our wiues nor our children to die.
28 We take to witnesse against you, the heauen and the
earth, and our God, and Lord of our fathers, which punisheth
vs according to our sinnes, and the sinnes of our fathers, that
|| Or, lest he ||hee doe not according as we haue said this day.
doe: mea- 29 Then there was great weeping with one consent in the
ning, Olofernes. middest of the assembly, and they cryed vnto the Lord God
with a loude voice.
30 Then said Ozias to them, Brethren, be of good courage,
let vs yet endure fiue dayes, in the which space the Lord our
God may turne his mercy toward vs, for he will not forsake
vs vtterly.
31 And if these dayes passe, and there come no helpe vnto
vs, I wil doe according to your word.
32 And he dispersed the people euery one to their owne
charge, and they went vnto the walles and towres of their
citie, and sent the women and

children into their houses, and they were very low brought
in the city.

CHAP. VIII.

1 The state and behauiour of Iudeth a widow. 12 She blameth the gouernors for their promise to yeeld: 17 and aduiseth them to trust in God. 28 They excuse their promise. 32 She promiseth to doe something for them.

NOw at that time Iudeth heard thereof, which was the
daughter of Merari the sonne of Ox, the sonne of
Ioseph, the sonne of Oziel, the sonne of Elcia, the sonne
of Ananias, the sonne of Gedeon, the sonne of Raphaim,
the son of Acitho, the sonne of Eliu, the sonne of Eliab,
the sonne of Nathanael, the sonne of ||Samael, the sonne *|| Or, Samaliel.*
of Salasadai, the son of Israel.
2 And Manasses was her husband of her tribe and kinred,
who died in the barley haruest.
3 For as hee stood ouerseeing them that bound sheaues in
the field, the heat came vpon his head, and hee fell on his
bed, and died in the city of Bethulia, and they buried him
with his fathers, in the field betweene Dothaim and Balamo.
4 So Iudeth was a widow in her house three yeeres, and
foure moneths.
5 And she made her a tent vpon the top of her house, and
put on sackecloth on her loynes, and ware her widowes apparell.
6 And she fasted all the dayes of her widowhood, saue the
eues of the Sabbath, and the Sabbaths, and the eues of the
newe Moones, and the newe Moones, and the Feasts, and
solemne dayes of the house of Israel.
7 Shee was also of a goodly countenance, and very beautifull to behold: and her husband Manasses had left her golde
and siluer, and men seruants and maide seruants, and cattell,
and lands, ||and she remained vpon them. *|| Or, and she kept them.*
8 And there was none that gaue her an ill worde; for shee
feared God greatly.
9 Now when shee heard the euill wordes of the people
against the gouernor, that they fainted for lacke of water
(for Iudeth had heard all the wordes that Ozias had spoken
vnto them, and that he had *sworne to deliuer the citie vnto * Cha. 7. 26.
the Assyrians after fiue dayes)
10 Then shee sent her waiting woman that had the
gouernment of all
things

things that she had, to call Ozias, and Chabris, and Charmis,
the ancients of the citie.
11 And they came vnto her, and she said vnto them, Heare
me now, O yee gouernours of the inhabitants of Bethulia:
for your wordes that you haue spoken before the people this
day are not right, touching this othe which ye made, and
pronounced betweene God and you, and haue promised to
deliuer the citie to our enemies, vnlesse within these daies
the Lord turne to helpe you.
12 And now who are you, that haue tempted God this day,
& stand in stead of God amongst the children of men?
13 And now trie the Lord Almighty, but you shall neuer
know any thing.
14 For you cannot find the depth of the heart of man,
neither can ye perceiue the things that he thinketh: then
how can you search out God, that hath made all these things,
and knowe his minde, or comprehend his purpose? Nay my
brethren, prouoke not the Lord our God to anger.
15 For if he will not helpe vs within these few dayes, he
hath power to defend vs when he will, euen euery day, or to
destroy vs before our enemies.
|| *Or, ingage.* * Numb. 23 19.
16 Doe not ||binde the counsels of the Lord our God, for
*God is not as man, that he may be threatned, neither is he
as the sonne of man that he should bee wauering.
17 Therefore let vs waite for saluation of him, and call
vpon him to helpe vs, and he will heare our voyce if it
please him.
18 For there arose none in our age, neither is there any
now in these daies, neither tribe, nor familie, nor ||people, || *Or, towne.*
nor city among vs, which worship gods made with hands,
as hath bene aforetime.
* Iudg. 2. 11 and 4. 1. and 6. 1.
19 For the which cause our fathers *were giuen to the
sword, & for a spoile, and had a great fall before our enemies.
20 But we know none other god: therefore we trust that
he will not despise vs, nor any of our nation.
21 For if we be taken so, all Iudea shall lie waste, and our
Sanctuarie shal be spoiled, and he will require the prophanation thereof, at our mouth.
|| *Or, feare.*
22 And the ||slaughter of our brethren, and the captiuitie
of the countrey, and the desolation of our inheritance, will
he turne vpon our heads among the

Gentiles, wheresoeuer we shall bee in bondage, and we shall
be an offence and a reproch to all them that possesse vs.
23 For our seruitude shall not be directed to fauour: but
the Lord our God shall turne it to dishonour.
24 Now therefore, O brethren, let vs shew an example to
our brethren, because their hearts depend vpon vs, and the
Sanctuary, and the house, and the Altar rest vpon vs.
25 Moreouer, let vs giue thankes to the Lord our God,
which trieth vs, euen as he did our fathers.
26 Remember what things he did to *Abraham, and how he *Gen. 22.
tried Isaac, and what happened to *Iacob in Mesopotamia of 1 *Gen. 28.
Syria, when he kept the sheepe of Laban his mothers brother. 7
27 For, hee hath not tried vs in the fire as he did them,
for the examination of their hearts, neither hath hee taken
vengeance on vs: but the Lord doeth scourge them that
come neere vnto him to admonish them.
28 Then said Ozias to her, All that thou hast spoken, hast
thou spoken with a good heart, and there is none that may
gainesay thy words.
29 For this is not the first day wherin thy wisedome is
manifested, but from the beginning of thy dayes all thy
people haue knowen thy vnderstanding, because the disposition of thine heart is good.
30 But the people were very thirsty, and compelled vs to
doe vnto them as we haue spoken, and to bring an othe vpon
our selues, which wee will not breake.
31 Therefore now pray thou for vs, because thou art a godly
woman, and the Lord will send vs raine to fill our cisternes,
and we shall faint no more.
32 Then said Iudeth vnto them, Heare me, and I wil doe
a thing, which shall goe throughout all generations, to the
children of our nation.
33 You shall stand this night in the gate, and I will goe
foorth with my waiting woman: and within the dayes that
you haue promised to deliuer the citie to our enemies, the
Lord will visit Israel by mine hand.
34 But inquire not you of mine act: for I will not declare
it vnto you, til the things be finished that I doe.
35 Then said Ozias and the princes vnto her, Goe in
peace, and the Lord
God

God be before thee, to take vengeance on our enemies.
36 So they returned from the tent, and went to their wards.

CHAP. IX.

1 Iudeth humbleth herselfe, 2 and prayeth God to prosper her purpose against the enemies of his sanctuarie.

THen Iudeth fell vpon her face, and put ashes vpon her
head, and vncouered the sackcloth wherewith she was
clothed, and about the time, that the incense of that euening
was offered in Ierusalem, in the house of the Lord, Iudeth
cryed with a loud voyce, and said,
*Gen. 34. 2, 23. 2 O Lord God of my father *Simeon, to whom thou gauest
a sword to take vengeance of the strangers, who loosened the
girdle of a maide to defile her, and discouered the thigh to
her shame, and polluted her virginity to her reproch, (for
thou saidst it shall not be so, and yet they did so.)
3 Wherefore thou gauest their rulers to be slaine, so that
they died their bed in blood, being deceiued, and smotest
the seruants with their Lords, and the Lords vpon their
thrones:
4 And hast giuen their wiues for a pray, and their daughters
to bee captiues, and all their spoiles to be diuided amongst
thy deere children: which were mooued with thy zeale, and
abhorred the pollution of their blood, and called vpon thee
for aide: O God, O my God, heare me also a widow.
5 For thou hast wrought not onely those things, but also
the things which fell out before, and which ensewed after,
thou hast thought vpon the things which are now, and which
are to come.
6 Yea what things thou didst determine were redy at hand,
and said, loe we are heere; for all thy wayes are prepared,
and thy iudgements are in thy foreknowledge.
7 For behold, the Assyrians are multiplyed in their power:
they are exalted with horse and man: they glory in the
strength of their footemen: they trust in shield and speare,
and bow, and sling, and know not that thou art the Lord
that breakest the battels: the Lord is thy name.
8 Throw downe their strength in thy power, and bring
downe their

force in thy wrath; for they haue purposed to defile thy
Sanctuary, and to pollute the Tabernacle, where thy glorious
name resteth, and to cast downe with sword the horne of
thy altar.
9 Behold their pride, and send thy wrath vpon their heads:
giue into mine hand which am a widow, the power that I
haue conceiued.
10 *Smite by the deceit of my lips the seruant with the *Iudg. 4.
prince, and the prince with the seruant: breake downe their 21. & 5. 26.
statelinesse by the hand of a woman.
11 *For thy power standeth not in multitude, nor thy might *Iudg. 7.
in strong men, for thou art a God of the afflicted, an helper 2. 2. chro.
of the oppressed, an vpholder of the weake, a protector of the 14. 11. and
forelorne, a sauiour of them that are without hope. 16. 8. & 20. 6.
12 I pray thee, I pray thee, O God of my father, and God
of the inheritance of Israel, Lord of the heauens, and earth,
creator of the waters, king of euery creature: heare thou my
prayer:
13 And make my speech and deceit to be their wound &
stripe, who haue purposed cruell things against thy couenant,
and thy hallowed house, and against the top of Sion, and
against the house of the possession of thy children.
14 And make euery nation and tribe to acknowledge that
thou art the God of all power and might, and that there is
none other that protecteth the people of Israel but thou.

CHAP. X.

3 Iudeth doth set forth herselfe. 10 She and her maide goe forth into the campe. 17 The watch take and conduct her to Olofernes.

NOw after that she had ceased to cry vnto the God of
Israel, and had made an end of all these words,
2 She rose where she had fallen downe, and called her
maide, and went downe into the house, in the which she
abode in the Sabbath dayes and in her feast dayes,
3 And pulled off the sackcloth which she had on, and put
off the garments of her widowhood, and washed her body
all ouer with water, and annointed herselfe with precious
ointment, and braided the haire of her head, and put on †a †*Gre.*
tire vpon it, and put on her garments of gladnesse, wherewith *miter.*
she was clad during the life of Manasses her husband.
4 And she tooke sandals vpon her
feete,

feete, and put about her, her bracelets and her chaines, and
her rings, and her earerings, and all her ornaments, and
decked her selfe brauely to allure the eyes of all men that
should see her.

5 Then she gaue her mayd a bottle of wine, and a cruse
of oyle, and filled a bagge with parched corne, and lumpes
|| *Wrapped, or packed.* of figs, and with fine bread, so she ||folded all these things
together, and layd them vpon her.

6 Thus they went forth to the gate of the citie of Bethulia,
and found standiug there Ozias, and the ancients of the city
Chabris, and Charmis.

7 And when they saw her, that her countenance was altered,
and her apparel was changed, they wondered at her beautie
very greatly, and said vnto her,

8 The God, the God of our fathers giue thee fauour, and
accomplish thine enterprises to the glory of the children
of Israel, and to the exaltation of Ierusalem: then they
worshipped God.

9 And she said vnto them, Command the gates of the city to
be opened vnto me, that I may goe forth to accomplish the
things, whereof you haue spoken with me; so they commanded the yong men to open vnto her, as shee had spoken.

10 And when they had done so, Iudeth went out, she and
her mayd with her, and the men of the citie looked after her,
vntill shee was gone downe the mountaine, and till she had
passed the valley, and could see her no more.

11 Thus they went straight foorth in the valley: and the
first watch of the Assyrians met her;

12 And tooke her, and asked her, Of what people art thou?
and whence cōmest thou? and whither goest thou? And
she said, I am a woman of the Hebrewes, and am fled from
them: for they shalbe giuen you to be consumed:

13 And I am comming before Olofernes the chiefe captaine
of your army, to declare words of trueth, and I will shew him
a way, whereby he shall goe, and winne all the hil countrey,
without loosing the body or life of any one of his men.

14 Now when the men heard her wordes, and beheld her
countenance, they wondered greatly at her beautie, and said
vnto her;

15 Thou hast saued thy life, in that thou hast hasted to
come downe to the

presence of our lord: now therfore come to his tent, and
some of vs shall conduct thee, vntill they haue deliuered
thee to his hands.
16 And when thou standest before him, bee not afraid in
thine heart: but shew vnto him according to thy word, and
he will intreat thee well.
17 Then they chose out of them an hundred men, to
||accompany her and her mayd, and they brought her to
the tent of Olofernes.
18 Then was there a concourse throughout all the campe:
for her comming was noised among the tents, and they came
about her, as she stood without the tent of Olofernes, till
they told him of her.
19 And they wondered at her beautie, and admired the
children of Israel because of her, and euery one said to his
neighbour; Who would despise this people, that haue among
them such women, surely it is not good that one man of
them be left, who being let goe, might deceiue the whole
earth.
20 And they that lay neere Olofernes, went out, and all his
seruants, and they brought her into the tent.
21 Now Olofernes rested vpon his bed vnder a canopie
which was wouen with purple, and gold, and emeraudes,
and precious stones.
22 So they shewed him of her, and he came out before his
tent, with siluer lampes going before him.
23 And when Iudeth was come before him and his seruants,
they all marueiled at the beautie of her countenance; and
she fel downe vpon her face, and did reuerence vnto him;
and his seruants tooke her vp.

|| Or, and they prepared a chariot for her.

CHAP. XI.

3 Olofernes asketh Iudeth the cause of her comming. 6 She telleth him how, and when hee may preuaile. 20 Hee is much pleased with her wisedome and beautie.

THen said Olofernes vnto her, Woman, bee of good
comfort, feare not in thine heart: for I neuer hurt
any, that was willing to serue Nabuchodonosor the king
of all the earth.
2 Now therefore if thy people that dwelleth in the mountaines, had not set light by me, I would not haue lifted vp
my

my speare against them: but they haue done these things to
themselues.

3 But now tell me wherefore thou art fled from them, and
art come vnto vs: for thou art come for safeguard, be of
good comfort, thou shalt liue this night, and hereafter.

4 For none shall hurt thee, but intreat thee well, as they
doe the seruants of king Nabuchodonosor my lord.

5 Then Iudeth said vnto him, Receiue the words of thy
seruant, and suffer thine handmaid to speake in thy presence,
and I will declare no lie to my lord this night.

6 And if thou wilt follow the words of thine handmaid,
God will bring the thing perfectly to passe by thee, and my
lord shall not faile of his purposes,

7 As Nabuchodonosor king of all the earth liueth, and as
his power liueth, who hath sent thee for the vpholding of
euery liuing thing: for not only men shall serue him by
thee, but also the beasts of the field, and the cattell, and
the foules of the aire shall liue by thy power, vnder
Nabuchodonosor and all his house.

8 For wee haue heard of thy wisedome, and thy policies,
and it is reported in all the earth, that thou onely art
|| *Or, in fauour.* ||excellent in all the kingdome, and mightie in knowledge,
and wonderfull in feates of warre.

9 Now as concerning the matter which Achior did speake
in thy counsell, we haue heard his words; for the men of
|| *Or, gate him.* Bethulia ||saued him, and hee declared vnto them all that hee
had spoken vnto thee.

10 Therefore, O lord and gouernor, reiect not his word,
but lay it vp in thine heart, for it is true, for our nation
shall not be punished, neither can the sword preuaile against
them, except they sinne against their God.

11 And now, that my lord be not defeated, and frustrate of
his purpose, euen death is now fallen vpon them, and their
sinne hath ouertaken them, wherewith they will prouoke
their God to anger, whensoeuer they shall doe that which
is not fit to be done.

12 For their victuals faile them, and all their water is scant,
and they haue determined to lay hands vpon their cattell, and
purposed to consume all those things, that God hath forbidden
them to eate by his Lawes,

13 And are resolued to spend the first fruits of the corne,
& the tenths of wine and oyle, which they had sanctified,
and reserued for the Priests that serue in Ierusalem, before
the face of our God, the which things it is not lawfull for
any of the people so much as to touch with their hands.
14 For they haue sent some to Ierusalem, because they also
that dwel there haue done the like, to bring them a license
from the Senate.
15 Now when they shall bring them word, they will forthwith doe it, and they shall be giuen thee to be destroyed the
same day.
16 Wherefore I thine handmaide knowing all this, am
fledde from their presence, & God hath sent me to worke
things with thee, whereat all the earth shalbe astonished,
and whosoeuer shall heare it.
17 For thy seruant is religious, and serueth the God of
heauen day & night: now therefore, my lord, I will remaine
with thee, and thy seruant will goe out by night into the
valley, and I will pray vnto God, and he wil tel me when
they haue committed their sinnes.
18 And I will come, and shew it vnto thee: then thou
shalt goe forth with all thine army, and there shall be none
of them that shall resist thee.
19 And I will leade thee through the midst of Iudea, vntill
thou come before Ierusalem, and I will set thy throne in the
midst thereof, and thou shalt driue them as sheep that haue
no shepheard, and a dogge shall not so much as ‖open his
mouth at thee: for ‖these things were tolde mee, according
to my foreknowledge, and they were declared vnto me, and
I am sent to tell thee.
20 Then her wordes pleased Olofernes, and all his seruants,
and they marueiled at her wisedome, and said,
21 There is not such a woman from one end of the earth to
the other, both for beautie of face, and wisedome of wordes.
22 Likewise Olofernes said vnto her, God hath done well to
send thee before the people, that strength might be in our
hands, and destruction vpon them that lightly regard my lord:
23 And now thou art both beautifull in thy countenance,
and wittie in thy wordes; surely if thou doe as thou hast
spoken, thy God shall be my God,

‖ *Or, barke.*

‖ *Or, these things haue I spoken.*

Pppp and

and thou shalt dwel in the house of king Nabuchodonosor,
and shalt be renowmed through the whole earth.

CHAP. XII.

2 Iudeth will not eate of Olofernes meate. 7 She taried three dayes in
the campe, and euerie night went forth to pray. 13 Bagoas doth
moue her to be merry with Olofernes, 20 who for ioy of her companie
drunke much.

THen hee commaunded to bring her in, where his plate
was set, and bad that they should prepare for her of his
owne meats, and that she should drinke of his owne wine.
*Gen. 43. 2 And Iudeth said, *I will not eat thereof, lest there bee an
32. dan. 1. offence: but prouision shall be made for mee of the things
8 tob. 1. 11. that I haue brought.
3 Then Olofernes said vnto her, If thy prouision should
faile, howe should we giue thee the like? for there be none
with vs of thy nation.
4 Then said Iudeth vnto him, As thy soule liueth, my lord,
thine handemaid shall not spend those things that I haue,
before the Lord worke by mine hand, the things yͭ he hath
determined.
5 Then the seruants of Olofernes brought her into the
tent, and shee slept til midnight, and she arose when it was
towards the morning watch,
6 And sent to Olofernes, saying, Let my lord now command, that thine handmaid may goe forth vnto prayer.
7 Then Olofernes commaunded his guard that they should
not stay her: thus she abode in the camp three dayes, and
went out in the night into the valley of Bethulia, and washed
her selfe in a fountaine of water by the campe.
8 And when she came out, shee besought the Lord God of
Israel to direct her way, to the raising vp of the children of
her people.
9 So she came in cleane, and remained in the tent, vntill
shee did eate her meat at euening.
10 And in the fourth day Olofernes made a feast to his
owne seruants only, and called none of the officers to the
banquet.
11 Then said he to Bagoas the Eunuch, who had charge
ouer all that he had: Goe now, and perswade this Ebrewe
woman which is with thee,

that she come vnto vs, and eate and drinke with vs.
12 For loe, it will be a shame for our person, if we shall let
such a woman go, not hauing had her company: for if we
draw her not vnto vs, she will laugh vs to scorne.
13 Then went Bagoas from the presence of Olofernes, and
came to her, and he said, Let not this faire damosell feare to
come to my lord, and to bee honoured in his presence, and
drink wine, and be merry with vs, and be made this day as
one of the daughters of the Assyrians, which serue in the
house of Nabuchodonosor.
14 Then said Iudeth vnto him, Who am I now, that I should
gainesay my lord? surely whatsoeuer pleaseth him, I will doe
speedily, and it shall bee my ioy vnto the day of my death.
15 So she arose, and decked her selfe with her apparell,
and all her womans attire, and her maid went and laid soft
skinnes on the ground for her, ouer against Olofernes, which
she had receiued of Bagoas for her daily vse, that she might
sit, and eate vpon them.
16 Now when Iudeth came in, and sate downe, Olofernes
his heart was rauished with her, and his minde was moued,
and he desired greatly her company, for hee waited a time to
deceiue her, from the day that he had seene her.
17 Then said Olofernes vnto her, Drinke now, and be
merry with vs.
18 So Iudeth saide, I will drinke now my lord, because my
life is magnified in me this day, more then all the dayes since
I was borne.
19 Then she tooke and ate and dranke before him what
her maide had prepared.
20 And Olofernes tooke great delight in her, & dranke
much more wine, then he had drunke at any time in one
day, since he was borne.

CHAP. XIII.

2 Iudeth is left alone with Olofernes in his tent. 4 She prayeth God to giue her strength 8 She cut off his head while hee slept. 10 And returned with it to Bethulia: 17 They saw it, and commend her.

NOw when the euening was come, his seruants made haste to depart, and Bagoas shut his tent without, and dismissed the waiters

waiters from the presence of his lord, and they went to their beds: for they were all weary, because the feast had bene long.

2 And Iudeth was left alone in the tent, and Olofernes lying
* Ecclesi. along vpon his bed, for hee was filled with *wine.
31. 20. 25. 3 Now Iudeth had commanded her maide to stand without her bedchamber, and to waite for her comming forth as she did daily: for she said, she would goe forth to her prayers, and she spake to Bagoas, according to the same purpose.

4 So all went forth, and none was left in the bedchamber, neither little, nor great. Then Iudeth standing by his bed, said in her heart: O Lord God of all power, looke at this present vpon the workes of mine hands for the exaltation of Ierusalem.

5 For now is the time to helpe thine inheritance, and to execute mine enterprises, to the destruction of the enemies, which are risen against vs.

6 Then she came to the pillar of the bed, which was at Olofernes head, and tooke downe his fauchin from thence,

7 And approched to his bed, and tooke hold of the haire of his head, and said, Strengthen mee, O Lord God of Israel, this day.

8 And she smote twise vpon his necke with all her might, and she tooke away his head from him,

9 And tumbled his body downe from the bed, and pulled downe the canopy from the pillars, and anon after she went forth, and gaue Olofernes his head to her maide.

10 And she put it in her bag of meate, so they twaine went together according to their custome vnto prayer, and when they passed the campe, they compassed the valley, and went vp the mountaine of Bethulia, and came to the gates thereof.

11 Then said Iudeth a farre off to the watchmen at the gate, Open, open now the gate: God, euen our God is with vs, to shew his power yet in Ierusalem, and his forces against the enemie, as he hath euen done this day.

12 Now when the men of her citie heard her voyce, they made haste to goe downe to the gate of their citie, and they called the Elders of the citie.

13 And then they ranne altogether

both small and great, for it was strange vnto them that she
was come: so they opened the gate, and receiued them, and
made a fire for a light, and stood round about them.
14 Then she said to them with a loud voyce, Praise, praise
God, praise God, (I say) for hee hath not taken away his
mercy from the house of Israel, but hath destroyed our
enemies by mine hands this night.
15 So she tooke the head out of the bag, and shewed it,
and said vnto them, Behold the head of Olofernes the chiefe
captaine of the armie of Assur, and behold the canopy wherein
he did lie in his drunkennesse, and the Lord hath smitten
him by the hand of a woman.
16 As the Lord liueth, who hath kept me in my way that
I went, my countenance hath deceiued him to his destruction, and yet hath hee not committed sinne with mee, to
defile and shame mee.
17 Then all the people were wonderfully astonished, and
bowed themselues, and worshipped God, and said with one
accord: Blessed be thou, O our God, which hast this day
brought to nought the enemies of thy people.
18 Then said Ozias vnto her, O daughter, blessed art thou
of the most high God, aboue all the women vpon the earth,
and blessed be the Lord God, which hath created the heauens,
and the earth, which hath directed thee to the cutting off of
the head of the chiefe of our enemies.
19 For this thy confidence shall not depart from the heart
of men, which remember the power of God for euer.
20 And God turne these things to thee for a perpetuall
praise, to visite thee in good things, because thou hast not
spared thy life for ẏ affliction of our nation, but hast re-
uenged our ruine, walking a straight way before our God:
and all the people said, So be it, so be it.

CHAP. XIIII.

8 Achior heareth Iudeth shewe what she had done, and is circumcised, 11 the head of Olofernes is hanged vp, 15 hee is found dead, and much lamented.

THen saide Iudeth vnto them, Heare me now, my
brethren, & take this *head, and hang it vpon the *2. Mac. 15. 35.
highest place of your walles.

2 And so soone as the morning shall appeare, and the
Sunne shal come forth vpon the earth, take you euery one
his weapons, and goe forth euery valiant man out of the city,
& set you a captaine ouer them, as though you would goe
downe into the field toward the watch of the Assyrians, but
goe not downe.
3 Then they shal take their armour, and shal goe into their
campe, and raise vp the captaines of the armie of Assur, and
they shall runne to the tent of Olofernes, but shall not finde
him, then feare shall fall vpon them, and they shall flee before
your face.
4 So you, and all that inhabite the coast of Israel, shall
pursue them, and ouerthrow them as they goe.
5 But before you doe these things, call me Achior the
Ammonite, that hee may see and know him that despised
the house of Israel, and that sent him to vs as it were to his
death.
6 Then they called Achior out of the house of Ozias, and
when hee was come, and saw the head of Olofernes in a
mans hand, in the assembly of the people, he fell downe on
his face, and his spirit failed.
7 But when they had recouered him, hee fell at Iudeths
feete, and reuerenced her, and said: Blessed art thou in all
the tabernacle of Iuda, and in all nations, which hearing thy
name shall be astonished.
8 Now therefore tell mee all the things that thou hast done
in these dayes: Then Iudeth declared vnto him in the midst
of the people, all that shee had done from the day that shee
went foorth, vntill that houre she spake vnto them.
9 And when shee had left off speaking, the people shouted
with a lowd voice, & made a ioyful noise in their citie.
10 And when Achior had seene all that the God of Israel
had done, hee beleeued in God greatly, and circumcised the
foreskinne of his flesh, and was ioyned vnto the house of
Israel vnto this day.
11 And assoone as the morning arose, they hanged the
head of Olofernes vpon the wall, and euery man took his
weapons, and they went foorth by bandes vnto the ||straits
of the mountaine.
12 But when the Assyrians sawe them, they sent to their
leaders, which

|| *Or, ascents.*

came to their Captaines, and tribunes, and to euery one of
their rulers.
13 So they came to Olofernes tent, and said to him that
had the charge of all his things, Waken now our lord: for
the slaues haue beene bold to come downe against vs to
battell, that they may be vtterly destroyed.
14 Then went in Bagoas, and knocked at the doore of the
tent: for he thought that he had slept with Iudeth.
15 But because none answered, he opened it, and went into
the bedchamber, and found him cast vpon the floore dead,
& his head was taken from him.
16 ‖Therefore he cried with a lowd voice, with weeping, ‖ *Then.*
and sighing, and a mighty cry, and rent his garments.
17 After, hee went into the tent, where Iudeth lodged, and
when hee found her not, he leaped out to the people, and
cried;
18 These slaues haue dealt treacherously, one woman of
the Hebrewes hath brought shame vpon the house of king
Nabuchodonosor: for behold, Olofernes lieth vpon the
ground without a head.
19 When the captaines of the Assyrians armie heard these
words, they rent their coats, and their minds were wonderfully troubled, and there was a cry, and a very great noise
throughout the campe.

CHAP. XV.

1 The Assyrians are chased and slaine. 8 The high Priest commeth to see Iudeth. 11 The stuffe of Olofernes is giuen to Iudeth. 13 The women crowne her with a garland.

AND when they that were in the tents heard, they were
astonished at the thing that was done.
2 And feare and trembling fell vpon them, so that there
was no man that durst abide in the sight of his neighbour,
but rushing out altogether, they fled into euery way of the
plaine, and of the hill countrey.
3 They also that had camped in the mountaines, round about
Bethulia, fled away. Then the children of Israel euery one
that was a warriour among them, rushed out vpon them.
4 Then sent Ozias to Bethomasthem, and to Bebai, and
Chobai, and Cola, and to all the coasts of Israel, such as
should tell the things that were
done,

done, and that all should rush forth vpon their enemies to
destroy them.
5 Now when the children of Israel heard it, they all fell
vpon them with one consent, and slewe them vnto Choba:
likewise also they that came from Ierusalem, and from all
the hill country, for men had told them what things were
done in the campe of their enemies, and they that were in
Galaad and in Galile ||chased them with a great slaughter,
vntill they were past Damascus, and the borders thereof.

|| *Or, ouercame.*

6 And the residue that dwelt at Bethulia, fell vpon the
campe of Assur, and spoiled them, & were greatly enriched.
7 And the children of Israel that returned from the slaughter,
had that which remained, and the villages, and the cities that
were in the mountaines, and in the plaine, gate many spoiles:
for the multitude was very great.
8 Then Ioacim the high Priest, and the Ancients of the
children of Israel that dwelt in Ierusalem, came to behold
the good things that God had shewed to Israel, and to see
Iudeth, and to salute her.
9 And when they came vnto her, they blessed her with
one accord, and said vnto her, Thou art the exaltation of
Ierusalem: thou art the great glory of Israel: thou art the
great reioycing of our nation.
10 Thou hast done all these things by thine hand: thou
hast done much good to Israel, and God is pleased therewith:
blessed bee thou of the Almightie Lord for euermore: and
all the people said, So be it.
11 And the people spoiled the campe, the space of thirty
dayes, and they gaue vnto Iudeth Olofernes his tent, and all
his plate, and beds, and vessels, and all his stuffe: and she
tooke it, and laide it on her mule, and made ready her carts,
and laid them thereon.
12 Then all the women of Israel ran together to see her,
and blessed her, and made a dance among them for her: and
shee tooke branches in her hand, & gaue also to the women
that were with her.
13 And they put a garland of oliue vpon her, and her maid
that was with her, and shee went before the people in the
dance, leading all the women: and all the men of Israel
followed in their armor with garlands, and with songs in
their mouthes.

CHAP. XVI.

1 The song of Iudeth. 19 She dedicateth the stuffe of Olofernes.
23 Shee died at Bethulia a widow of great honour. 24 All Israel
did lament her death.

THen Iudeth began to sing this thankesgiuing in all Israel,
and all the people sang after her ||this song of praise. || *Or, this*
2 And Iudeth said, Begin vnto my God with timbrels, sing *praising.*
vnto my Lord with cymbals: tune vnto him a ||newe Psalme: || *Or,*
exalt him, & cal vpon his name. *Psalme*
3 For God breaketh the battels: for amongst the campes in *and praise.*
the midst of the people hee hath deliuered me out of the
hands of them that persecuted me.
4 Assur came out of the mountains from the North, he
came with ten thousands of his army, the *multitude wherof *Chap. 2.
stopped the torrents, and their horsemen haue couered the 11, 15.
hilles.
5 He bragged that he would burne vp my borders, and kill
my young men with the sword, and dash the sucking children
against the ground, and make mine infants as a pray, and my
virgins as a spoile.
6 But the Almighty Lord hath disappointed them by the
hand of a woman.
7 For the mighty one did not fall by the yong men,
neither did the sonnes of the Titans smite him, nor high
gyants set vpon him: but Iudeth the daughter of Merari
weakned him with the beautie of her countenance.
8 For she put off the garment of her widowhood, for the
exaltation of those that were oppressed in Israel, and anointed
her face with oyntment, & bound her haire in a †tyre, and †*Gr. or*
tooke a linnen garment to deceiue him. *miter.*
9 Her sandals rauished his eyes, her beautie tooke his minde
prisoner, and the fauchin passed through his necke.
10 The Persians quaked at her boldnesse, and the Medes
were ||daunted at her hardinesse. || *Or, con-*
11 Then my afflicted shouted for ioy, and my weake ones *founded.*
cryed aloude; but ||they were astonished: these lifted vp their || *The Assy-*
voices, but they were ouerthrowen. *rians.*
12 The sonnes of the damosels haue pierced them through,
and wounded them as fugitiues children: they perished by
the battell of the Lord.

|| Or, a song of praise.

13 I will sing vnto the Lord a ||new song, O Lord thou art
great and glorious, wonderful in strength & inuincible.
14 Let all creatures serue thee: for thou spakest, and they
were made, thou didst send forth thy spirit, and it created
them, and there is none that can resist thy voyce.
15 For the mountaines shall be mooued from their foundations with the waters, the rockes shall melt as waxe at thy
presence: yet thou art mercifull to them that feare thee.
16 For all sacrifice is too little for a sweete sauour vnto
thee, and all the fat is not sufficient, for thy burnt offering:
but he that feareth the Lord is great at all times.
17 Woe to the nations that rise vp against my kinred: the
Lord almighty will take vengeance of them in the day of
iudgement in putting fire & wormes in their flesh, and they
shall feele them and weepe for euer.
18 Now assoone as they entred into Ierusalem, they worshipped the Lord, and assoone as the people were purified,
they offered their burnt offerings, and their free offerings, and
their gifts.
19 Iudeth also dedicated all the stuffe of Olofernes, which
the people had giuen her, and gaue the canopy which she

¶ The rest of the Chapters

Esther, which are found

nor in

Part of the tenth Chapter

5 Mardocheus remembreth and expoundeth his dreame, of the riuer and the two dragons.

THen Mardocheus saide, God hath done these things.
5 For I remember a dreame, which I sawe concerning
these matters, and nothing thereof hath failed.
6 A little fountaine became a riuer, and there was light, &
the Sunne, and

had taken out of his bed chamber, for a gift vnto the Lord.
20 So the people continued feasting in Ierusalem before
the Sanctuarie, for the space of three moneths, and Iudeth
remained with them.
21 After this time, euery one returned to his owne inheritance, and Iudeth went to Bethulia, and remained in her
owne possession, and was in her time honourable in all the
countrey.
22 And many desired her, but none knew her all the dayes
of her life, after that Manasses her husband was dead, and
was gathered to his people.
23 But she encreased more and more in honour, and waxed
olde in her husbands house, being an hundred and fiue yeeres
olde, and made her maide free, so shee died in Bethulia: and
they buried her in the ||caue of her husband Manasses. || *Or, sepul-chre.*
24 And the house of Israel lamented her *seauen dayes, *Gen. 50. 10.
and before shee dyed, she did distribute her goods to all them
that are neerest of kinred to Manasses her husband: and to
them that were the neerest of her kinred.
25 And there was none that made the children of Israel
any more afraide, in the dayes of Iudeth, nor a long time
after her death.

of the Booke of

neither in the Hebrew,

the Calde.

after the Greeke.

much water: this riuer is Esther, whō the King married
and made Queene.
7 And the two Dragons are I, and Aman.
8 And the nations were those that were assembled, to
destroy the name of the Iewes.
9 And my nation is this Israel, which cryed to God and
were saued: for the Lord hath saued his people, and the
Lord hath deliuered vs from all those euils, and God hath
wrought signes, and great wonders, which haue not bin done
among the Gentiles.

10 There-

10 Therefore hath hee made two lots, one for the people of God, and another for all the Gentiles.
11 And these two lots came at the houre, and time, and day of iudgement before God amongst all nations.
12 So God remembred his people, and iustified his inheritance.
13 Therefore those dayes shall be vnto them in the moneth Adar, the foureteenth and fifteenth day of the same moneth, with an assembly, and ioy, and with gladnesse, before God, according to the generations for euer among his people.

CHAP. XI.

2 The stocke and qualitie of Mardocheus. 6 He dreameth of two dragons comming forth to fight, 10 and of a little fountaine, which became a great water.

IN the fourth yeere of the raigne of Ptolomeus, and Cleopatra, Dositheus, who said hee was a priest and Leuite, and Ptolomeus his sonne brought this Epistle of Phurim, which they said was the same, and that Lysimachus the sonne of Ptolomeus, that was in Ierusalem, had interpreted it.
2 In the second yeere of the raigne of Artaxerxes the great: in the first day of the moneth Nisan, Mardocheus the sonne of Iairus, the sonne of Semei, the sonne of Cisai of the tribe of Beniamin, had a dreame.
3 Who was a Iew and dwelt in the citie of Susa, a great man, being a seruitour in the kings court.
4 He was also one of the captiues, which Nabuchodonosor the king of Babylon caried from Ierusalem, with Iechonias king of Iudea; and this was his dreame.
5 Behold a noise of a tumult with thunder, and earthquakes, and vproare in the land.
6 And behold, two great dragons came forth ready to fight, and their crie was great.
7 And at their cry all nations were prepared to battel, that they might fight against the righteous people.
8 And loe a day of darknesse and obscurity: tribulation, and anguish, affliction, and great vproare vpon the earth.
9 And the whole righteous nation

was troubled, fearing their owne euils, and were ready to perish.
10 Then they cryed vnto God, and vpon their cry, as it were from a little fountaine, was made a great flood, euen much water.
11 The light and the Sunne rose vp, and the lowly were exalted, and deuoured the glorious.
12 Now when Mardocheus, who had seene this dreame, and what God had determined to doe, was awake: he bare this dreame in minde, and vntill night by all meanes was desirous to know it.

CHAP. XII.

2 The conspiracie of the two Eunuchs is discouered by Mardocheus, 5 for which he is entertained by the king and rewarded.

AND Mardocheus tooke his rest in the court with Gabatha, and Tharra, the two Eunuches of the king, and keepers of the palace.
2 *And he heard their deuices, and searched out their purposes, and learned that they were about to lay hands vpon Artaxerxes the king, and so he certified the king of them.

*Ester 2. 21. and 6. 2.

3 Then the king examined the two Eunuches, and after that they had confessed it, they were strangled.
4 And the king made a record of these things, and Mardocheus also wrote thereof.
5 So the king commaunded Mardocheus to serue in the court, and for this he rewarded him.
6 Howbeit Aman the sonne of Amadathus the Agagite, who was in great honour with the king, sought to molest Mardocheus and his people, because of the two Eunuches of the king.

CHAP. XIII.

1 The copie of the kings letters to destroy the Iewes. 8 The prayer of Mardocheus for them.

THE copy of the letters was this. The great king Artaxerxes, writeth these things to the princes, and gouernours that are vnder him from India vnto Ethiopia, in an hundred and seuen and twentie prouinces.

Ios. antiq. lib. 11. cap. 6

2 After that I became Lord ouer many nations, and had dominion ouer
the

the whole world, not lifted vp with presumption of my
authoritie, but carying my selfe alway with equitie and
mildenesse, I purposed to settle my subiects continually in a
|| *Or, milde.* quiet life, and making my kingdome ||peaceable, and open for
passage to the vtmost coastes, to renue peace which is desired
of all men.

3 Now when I asked my counsellers how this might bee
brought to passe, Aman that excelled in wisedome among vs,
and was approoued for his constant good will, and stedfast
fidelitie, and had the honour of the second place in the
kingdome,

4 Declared vnto vs, that in all nations throughout the
world, there was scattered a certaine malitious people, that
had Lawes contrary to all nations, and continually despised
the commandements of Kings, so as the vniting of our king-
|| *Or, be setled.* domes honourably intended by vs, cannot ||goe forward.

5 Seeing then we vnderstand that this people alone is continually in opposition vnto all men, differing in the strange
maner of their Lawes, and euill affected to our state, working
all the mischiefe they can, that our kingdome may not be
firmely stablished:

6 Therefore haue we commanded that al they that are
signified in writing vnto you by Aman (who is ordained ouer
|| *Or, second from vs.* the affaires, and is ||next vnto vs) shall all with their wiues
and children bee vtterly destroyed, by the sword of their
enemies, without all mercie and pitie, the fourteenth day of
the twelfth moneth Adar of this present yeere:

7 That they, who of old, and now also are malitious, may
in one day with violence goe into the graue, and so euer
hereafter, cause our affaires to be well settled, and without
trouble.

8 Then Mardocheus thought vpon all the works of the
Lord, and made his prayer vnto him,

9 Saying, O Lord, Lord, the king Almightie: for the
whole world is in thy power; and if thou hast appointed to
saue Israel, there is no man that can gainesay thee.

10 For thou hast made heauen and earth, and all the
wonderous things vnder the heauen.

11 Thou art Lord of all things, and there is no man that
can resist thee, which art the Lord.

12 Thou knowest all things, and

thou knowest Lord, that it was neither in contempt nor
pride, nor for any desire of glory, that I did not bow downe
to proud Aman.
13 For I could haue bene content with good will for the
saluation of Israel, to kisse the soles of his feet.
14 But I did this, that I might not preferre the glory of
man aboue the glory of God: neither will I worship any but
thee, O God, neither wil I doe it in pride.
15 And now, O Lord God, and King, spare thy people:
for their eyes are vpon vs, to bring vs to nought, yea they
desire to destroy the inheritance that hath beene thine from
the beginning.
16 Despise not the portion which thou hast deliuered out of
Egypt for thine owne selfe:
17 Heare my prayer, and be mercifull vnto thine inheritance: turne our sorrow into ioy, that wee may liue, O Lord,
and praise thy Name: and ||destroy not the mouthes of them || *Or, shut or stop not.*
that praise thee, O Lord.
18 All Israel in like maner cried most †earnestly vnto the † *Greeke mightily.*
Lord, because their death was before their eyes.

CHAP. XIIII.

1 The prayer of Queene Esther, for herselfe, and her people.

QVeene Esther also being in feare of death, resorted vnto
the Lord,
2 And layd away her glorious apparel, and put on the
garments of anguish, & mourning: and in stead of pretious
oyntments, she couered her head with ashes, & doung, and
she humbled her body greatly, and all the places of her ioy
she filled with her torne haire.
3 And shee prayed vnto the Lord God of Israel, saying, O
my Lord, thou onely art our king: helpe me desolate
woman, which haue no helper but thee:
4 *For my danger is in mine hand. *1. Sam.
5 From my youth vp I haue heard in the tribe of my 28. 21.
family, that thou, O Lord, tookest Israel from among all iob 13. 14. psa. 119
people, and our fathers from all their predecessours, for a 109.
perpetuall inheritance, and thou hast performed whatsoeuer
thou didst promise them.

6 And

6 And now we haue sinned before thee: therefore hast thou
giuen vs into the hands of our enemies,
7 Because wee worshipped their gods: O Lord, thou art
righteous.
8 Neuertheles it satisfieth them not, that we are in bitter
captiuitie, but they haue striken hands with their idols,
9 That they will abolish the thing, that thou with thy
mouth hast ordained, and destroy thine inheritance, and stop
the mouth of them that praise thee, and quench the glory of
thy house, and of thine Altar,
10 And open the mouthes of the heathen to set foorth the
praises of the †Idoles, and to magnifie a fleshly king for euer.
11 O Lord, giue not thy scepter vnto them that †be
nothing, and let them not laugh at our fall, but turne their
deuice vpon themselues, and make him an example that hath
begunne this against vs.
12 Remember, O Lord, make thy selfe knowen in time of
our affliction, and giue mee boldnesse, O King of the
‖nations, and Lord of all power.
13 Giue me eloquent speech in my mouth before the lyon:
turne his heart to hate him that fighteth against vs, that
there may be an end of him, and of all that are like minded
to him:
14 But deliuer vs with thine hand, and helpe me that am
desolate, & which haue no other helper but thee.
15 Thou knowest all things, O Lord, thou knowest that I
hate the glory of the vnrighteous, and abhorre the bed of the
vncircumcised, and of †all the heathen.
16 Thou knowest my necessitie: for I abhorre the signe of
my †high estate, which is vpon mine head, in the dayes
wherein I shewe my selfe, and that I abhorre it as a
menstruous ragge, and that I weare it not when I am
†priuate by my selfe.
17 And that thine handmaid hath not eaten at Amans
table, and that I haue not greatly esteemed the Kings feast,
nor drunke the wine of the drinke offerings:
18 Neither had thine handmaid any ioy, since the day †that
I was brought hither to this present, but in thee, O Lord
God of Abraham.
19 O thou mightie God aboue all, heare the voice of the
forlorne, and deli-

† *Gr. vaine things.*
† *Gr. be not*
‖ *Or, gods.*
† *Gr. euery stranger.*
† *Gr. pride.*
† *Gr. quiet, or priuate.*
† *Gr. of my change.*

uer vs out of the handes of the mischieuous, and deliuer me
out of my feare.

CHAP. XV.

6 Esther commeth into the Kings presence. 7 Hee looketh angerly, and she fainteth. 8 The king doth take her vp, and comfort her.

AND vpon the third day when shee had ended her prayer,
she laide away her mourning garments, and put on her
glorious apparell.
2 And being gloriously adorned, after she had called vpon
God, who is the beholder, and Sauiour of all things, she
tooke two maids with her.
3 And vpon the one shee leaned as carying her selfe
‖daintily.
4 And the other followed bearing vp her traine.
5 And she was ‖ruddy through the perfection of her
beautie, and her countenance was cheerefull, and very ‖ami-
able: but her heart was in anguish for feare.
6 Then hauing passed through all the doores, shee stood
before the King, who sate vpon his royall throne, and was
clothed with all his robes of maiestie, all glittering with golde
and precious stones, and he was very dreadfull.
7 Then lifting vp his countenance that shone with maiestie,
he looked very fiercely vpon her: and the Queene fell downe
and was pale, and fainted, and bowed her selfe vpon the head
of the maide that went ‖before her.
8 Then God changed the spirit of the king into mildnesse,
who in a †feare leaped from his throne, and tooke her in his
armes till she came to her selfe againe, and comforted her
with louing words, and sayd vnto her:
9 Esther, what is the matter? I am thy brother, be of good
cheere.
10 Thou shalt not die, though our cōmandement be
‖generall: come neere.
11 And so he held vp his golden scepter, and laid it vpon
her necke,
12 And embraced her, & said, Speake vnto me.
13 Then said shee vnto him, I saw thee, my lord, as an Angel
of God, and my heart was troubled for feare of thy maiestie.
14 For wonderfull art thou, lord, and thy countenance is
full of grace.

‖ *Or, delicately.*

‖ *Or, rose coloured.*

‖ *Or, as amiable or smiling.*

‖ *Or, with her, or by her.*

† *Gr. in an agonie.*

‖ *Or, as well thine as mine.*

15 And

|| Or, she fell in a swoone.

15 And as she was speaking, ||she fell downe for faintnesse.
16 Theu the king was troubled, and all his seruants comforted her.

CHAP. XVI.

1 The Letter of Artaxerxes, 10 wherein hee taxeth Aman, 17 and reuoketh the decree procured by Aman to destroy the Iewes, 22 and commandeth the day of their deliuerance to be kept holy.

Ioseph. Ant. lib. 11. c. 6.
|| Or, well affected to our State.
† Gr. their benefactors.

THe great king Artaxerxes vnto the princes and gouernours of an hundreth and seuen and twenty prouinces, from India vnto Ethiopia, and vnto all ||our faithfull Subiects, greeting.
2 Many, the more often they are honoured with the great bountie of their †gracious princes, the more proud they are waxen,
3 And endeauour to hurt not our Subiects onely, but not being able to beare abundance, doe take in hand to practise also against those that doe them good:
4 And take not only thankfulnesse away from among men, but also lifted vp with the glorious words of ||lewde persons ||that were neuer good, they thinke to escape the iustice of God, that seeth all things, and hateth euill.
5 Often times also faire speech of ||those that are put in trust to manage their friends affaires, hath caused many that are in authority to be partakers of innocent blood, and hath enwrapped them in remedilesse calamities:
6 Beguiling with the falshood and deceit of their lewd disposition, the innocencie and goodnesse of princes.
7 Now yee may see this as we haue declared, not so much by ancient histories, as yee may, if ye search what hath beene wickedly done of late through the pestilent behauiour of them that are vnworthily placed in authoritie.
8 And we must take care for the time to come, that our kingdome may bee quiet and peaceable for all men,
9 Both by changing our purposes, and alwayes iudging things that are euident, with more equall proceeding.
10 For Aman a Macedonian the son of Amadatha, being indeed a stranger from the Persian blood, and far distant

|| Or, needie.
|| Or, that neuer tasted prosperitie.
|| Or, of our friends put in trust to manage the affaires.

from our goodnesse, and as a stranger receiued of vs:
11 Had so farre forth obtained the fauour that wee shew
toward euery nation, as that he was called our father, and
was continually honoured of all men, as the next person vnto
the king.
12 But he not bearing his great dignitie, went about to
depriue vs of our kingdome and life:
13 Hauing by manifold and cunning deceits sought of vs
the destruction as well of Mardocheus, who saued our life,
and continually procured our good, as also of blamelesse
Esther partaker of our kingdome, with their whole nation.
14 For by these meanes he thought, finding vs destitute of
friends, to haue translated the kingdome of the Persians to
the Macedonians.
15 But wee finde that the Iewes, whom this wicked wretch
hath deliuered to vtter destruction, are no euill doers, but
liue by most iust lawes:
16 And that they be children of the most high and most
mighty liuing God, who hath ‖ordered the kingdome both ‖ *Or, prospered.*
vnto vs, and to our progenitors in the most excellent maner.
17 Wherefore ye shall doe well not to put in execution the
Letters sent vnto you by Aman the sonne of Amadatha.
18 For hee that was the worker of these things, is hanged
at the gates of Susa with all his family: God, who ruleth all
things, speedily rendring vengeance to him according to his
deserts.
19 Therefore ye shall publish the copy of this Letter in all
places, that the Iewes may freely liue after their owne lawes.
20 And ye shall aide them, that euen the same day, being
the thirteenth day of the twelfth moneth Adar, they may be
auenged on them, who in the time of their affliction shall set
vpon them.
21 For Almightie God hath turned to ioy vnto them the
day, wherein the chosen people should haue perished.
22 You shall therefore among your solemne feasts keepe it
an high day with all feasting,
23 That both now and hereafter there may be safetie to vs,
and the well affected Persians: but to those which doe conspire against vs, a memoriall of destruction.

24 There-

24 Therefore euery citie and countrey whatsoeuer, which shall not doe according to these things, shall bee destroyed without mercy, with fire

¶ The Wisedome

CHAP. I.

2 To whom God sheweth himselfe, 4 and Wisedome herselfe. 6 An euill speaker can not lie hid. 12 We procure our owne destruction: 13 for God created not death.

*1. King. 3. 3. esay. 56. 1 13. 4.

LOue *righteousnesse, yee that be iudges of the earth: thinke of the Lord with a good (heart) and in simplicitie of heart seeke him.

*Deut. 4. 29. 2. chro.

2 For hee will bee found of them that tempt him not: and sheweth himselfe vnto such as doe not *distrust him.

|| Or, *maketh manifest.*

3 For froward thoughts separate from God: and his power when it is tryed, ||reprooueth the vnwise.

4 For into a malitious soule wisedome shall not enter: nor dwell in the body that is subiect vnto sinne.

*Iere. 4. 22.

|| Or, *is rebuked, or sheweth it selfe.*

5 *For the holy spirit of discipline will flie deceit, & remoue from thoughts that are without vnderstanding: and will not ||abide when vnrighteousnesse commeth in.

*Gal. 5. 22.

|| Or, *lippes.*

|| Or, *vpholdeth.*

6 For wisedome is a *louing spirit: and will not acquite a blasphemour of his ||words: for God is witnesse of his reines, and a true beholder of his heart, and a hearer of his tongue.

7 For the spirit of the Lord filleth the world: and that which ||containeth all things hath knowledge of the voice.

8 Therefore he that speaketh vnrighteous things, cannot be hid: neither shal vengeance, when it punisheth. passe by him.

|| Or, *reprouing.*

9 For inquisition shall be made into the counsels of the vngodly: and the sound of his words, shall come vnto the Lord, for the ||manifestation of his wicked deedes.

10 For the eare of iealousie heareth al things: and the noise of murmurings is not hid.

and sword, and shall be made not onely vnpassable for men,
but also most hatefull to wilde beasts and foules for euer.

# of Solomon.

11 Therefore beware of murmuring, which is vnprofitable,
and refraine your tongue from backbiting: for there is no
word so secret that shall goe for nought: and the mouth
that ||belieth, slayeth the soule. || *Or, slandereth.*
12 Seeke not death in the errour of your life: and pull not
vpon your selues *destruction, with the workes of your *Deut. 4. 23.
hands.
13 For God made not death: neither hath he pleasure in
the destruction of the liuing.
14 For he created all things, that they might haue their
being: and the generations of the world were healthfull: and
there is no poyson of destruction in them: nor the kingdome
of death vpon the earth.
15 For righteousnesse is immortall.
16 But vngodly men with their workes, and words called
it to them: for when they thought to haue it their friend,
they consumed to nought, and made a couenant with it,
because they are worthy to take part with it.

CHAP. II.

1 The wicked thinke this life short, 5 and of no other after this. 6 Therefore they will take their pleasure in this, 10 and conspire against the iust. 21 What that is which doth blind them.

FOr the *vngodly* said, reasoning with themselues, but not
aright: *Our life is short and tedious, *and in the death *Iob. 7. 1.
of a man there is no remedie: neither was there any man *Math. 22. 23.
knowen to haue returned from the graue. 1. cor. 15 32.
2 For wee are borne at all aduenture: & we shalbe heereafter as though we had neuer bene: for the breath in our
nostrils is as smoke, and a litle sparke in the mouing of our
heart.

3 Which

3 Which being extinguished, our body shall be turned into
|| *Or, moist.* ashes, and our spirit shall vanish as the ||soft aire:
4 And our name shalbe forgotten in time, and no man
shall haue our works in remembrance, and our life shall
passe away as the trace of a cloud: and shall be dispersed as
a mist that is driuen away with the beames of the Sunne,
|| *Or, op-* and ||ouercome with the heat thereof.
pressed. * 1. Chr. 5 *For our time is a very shadow that passeth away: and
29. 15. after our end there is no returning: for ||it is fast sealed, so
|| *Or, he.* that no man commeth againe.
*Isa. 22. 6 Come on therefore, let vs enioy the good things *that
13. and 56. are present: and let vs ||speedily vse the *creatures like as in
12. || *Or, ear-* youth.
nestly. 7 Let vs fill our selues with costly wine, and ointments:
* 1. Cor. and let no flower of the Spring passe by vs.
15. 32. 8 Let vs crowne our selues with Rose buds, before they be
withered.
|| *Or,* 9 Let none of vs goe without his part of our ||voluptuous-
iolitie. nesse: let vs leaue tokens of our ioyfulnesse in euery place:
for this is our portion, and our lot is this.
10 Let vs oppresse the poore righteous man, let vs not spare
the widow, nor reuerence the ancient gray haires of the aged.
11 Let our strength bee the Lawe of iustice: for that which
is feeble is found to be nothing worth.
12 Therefore let vs lye in wait for the righteous: because
he is not for our turne, and he is cleane contrary to our
doings: he vpbraideth vs with our offending the Law, and
obiecteth to our infamy the transgressings of our education.
13 Hee professeth to haue the knowledge of God: and hee
calleth himselfe the childe of the Lord.
*Iohn 7. 7. 14 Hee was made to *reprooue our thoughts.
ephes. 5. 15 Hee is grieuous vnto vs euen to beholde: *for his life is
13, 14. *Isai. 53. not like other mens, his waies are of another fashion.
3. 16 We are esteemed of him as ||counterfeits: he abstaineth
|| *Or, false* from our wayes as from filthinesse: he pronounceth the end
coine. of the iust to be blessed, and maketh his boast that God is
his father.
*Psal. 22. 17 Let vs see if his wordes be true: and let vs proue what
8, 9. matth. 27. shall happen in the end of him.
43. 18 For if the iust man be the *sonne

of God, he will helpe him, and deliuer him from the hand
of his enemies.
19 Let vs *examine him with despitefulnesse and torrture, *Iere. 11.
that we may know his meekenesse, and prooue his patience. 19.
20 Let vs condemne him with a shamefull death: for by
his owne saying, he shall be respected.
21 Such things they did imagine, and were deceiued: for
their owne wickednesse hath blinded them.
22 As for the mysteries of God, they knew them not: †*Greeke,*
neither hoped they for the wages of righteousnesse: nor *preferred*
†discerned a reward for blamelesse soules. *or esteemed the reward.*
23 For God created man to bee immortall, and made him *Gen. 1.
to be an *image of his owne eternitie. 26. 27. and
24 *Neuerthelesse through enuie of the deuill came death 5. 1. eccle. 17. 3.
into the world: and they that doe holde of his side doe *Gen. 3.
finde it. 12.

CHAP. III.

1 The godly are happie in their death, 5 and in their troubles; 10 The wicked are not, nor their children: 15 But they that are pure, are happie, though they haue no children: 16 For the adulterer and his seed shall perish.

BVt *the soules of the righteous are in the hand of God, *Deut. 33.
and there shall no torment touch them. 3.
2 *In the sight of the vnwise they seemed to die: and their *Chap. 5.
departure is taken for misery, 4.
3 And their going from vs to be vtter destruction: but they *Rom. 8.
are in peace. 24. 1. cor.
4 For though they bee punished in the sight of men: yet 5. 1. 1. pet. 1. 13.
is their *hope full of immortalitie. ‖ *Or, bene-*
5 And hauing bene a little chastised, they shalbe greatly *fited.*
‖rewarded: for God *proued them, and found them ‖worthy *Exod. 16. 4. deut. 8.
for himselfe. 2.
6 As gold in the furnace hath hee tried them, and receiued ‖ *Or, meet.*
them as a burnt offering. *Matth. 13. 43.
7 And in the time of their *visitation, they shall shine and *Matt. 19.
runne to and fro, like sparkes among the stubble. 28. 1. cor.
8 They *shall iudge the nations, and haue dominion ouer 6. 2. ‖ *Or, and*
the people, and their Lord shall raigne for euer. *such as be*
9 They that put their trust in him, shall vnderstand the *faithfull*
trueth: ‖and such as be faithfull in loue, shall abide with *shall remaine with*
him: for grace & mercy is to his saints, *him in*
and *loue.*

and he hath care for his elect.
*Mat. 25. 41. 10 But the *vngodly shalbe punished according to their
owne imaginations, which haue neglected the righteous, and
forsaken the Lord.
11 For who so despiseth wisedome, and nurture, he is
miserable, and their hope is vaine, their labours vnfruitfull,
and their works vnprofitable.
|| *Or, light, or vnchaste.* 12 Their wiues are ||foolish, and their children wicked.
13 Their of-spring is cursed: wherefore blessed is the barren
that is vndefiled, which hath not knowen the sinfull bed: she
*Esai. 56. 5. *shall haue fruit in the visitation of soules.
14 And *blessed is* the Eunuch which with his hands hath
wrought no iniquitie: nor imagined wicked things against
*Esai. 56. 4, 5. God: for vnto him shall be giuen the *†speciall gift of faith,
† *Gre. the chosen, or amongst the people.* and an inheritance in the Temple of the Lord more acceptable to his minde.
15 For glorious is the fruit of good labours: and the root of
wisedom shall neuer fall away.
|| *Or, be partakers of holy things.* 16 As for the children of adulterers, they shall not ||come to
their perfection, and the seed of an vnrighteous bed shal be
rooted out.
17 For though they liue long, yet shall they bee nothing
regarded: and their last age shall be without honour.
|| *Or, hearing* 18 Or if they die quickly, they haue no hope, neither com-
fort in the day of ||triall.
19 For horrible is the end of the vnrighteous generation.

CHAP. IIII.

1 The chaste man shall be crowned. 3 Bastard slips shall not thriue. 6 They shall witnesse against their parents. 7 The iust die yong, and are happie. 19 The miserable ende of the wicked.

BEtter it is to haue no children, and to haue vertue: for
|| *Or, approued.* the memoriall thereof is immortal: because it is ||knowen
with God and with men.
2 When it is present, men take example at it, and when it
is gone they desire it: it weareth a crown, and triumpheth
for euer, hauing gotten the victorie, striuing for vndefiled
rewards.
3 But the multiplying brood of the vngodly shall not thriue,
nor take deepe rooting from bastard slips, nor lay any fast
foundation.

4 For though they flourish in branches for a time: *yet *Mat. 7.
standing not fast, they shall be shaken with the winde: and 19.
through the force of windes they shall be rooted out.
5 The vnperfect branches shall bee broken off, their fruit
vnprofitable, not ripe to eate: yea meet for nothing.
6 For children begotten of vnlawfull †beds, are witnesses of † *Gre. sleeps.*
wickednes against their parents in their triall.
7 But though the righteous be preuented with death: yet
shal he be in rest.
8 For honourable age is not that which standeth in length
of time, nor that is measured by number of yeeres.
9 But wisedome is the gray haire vnto men, & an vnspotted
life is old age.
10 *He pleased God, and was beloued of him: so that liuing *Gen. 5. 24
amongst sinners, he was translated. heb. 11. 5.
11 Yea, speedily was he taken away, lest that wickednes
should alter his vnderstanding, or deceit beguile his soule.
12 For the bewitching of naughtines doth obscure things
that are honest: and the wandring of concupiscence, doth
†vndermine the simple mind. † *Gre. peruert.*
13 He being made ||perfect in a short time, fulfilled a long || *Or, sanctified or consummated.*
time.
14 For his soule pleased the Lord: therefore hasted he *to*
take him away, from among the wicked.
15 This the people saw, and vnderstood it not: neither
laid they vp this in their mindes, That his grace and mercie
is with his Saints, and that he hath respect vnto his chosen.
16 Thus the righteous that is dead, shall condemne the
vngodly, which are liuing, and youth that is soone perfected,
the many yeeres and old age of the vnrighteous.
17 For they shall see the end of the wise, & shall not
vnderstand what God in his counsell hath decreed of him,
and to what end the Lord hath set him in safetie.
18 They shal see him and despise him, but God shall laugh
them to scorne, and they shal hereafter be a vile carkeis, and
a reproch among the dead for euermore.
19 For he shall rend them, and cast them downe headlong,
that they shalbe speechles: and he shal shake them from the
foundation: aud they shall bee vtterly laid waste, and be in
sorow: and their memoriall shall perish.
20 And ||when they cast vp the ac- || *Or, to the casting vp of the account.*

counts of their sinnes, they shall come with feare: and their
owne iniquities shall conuince them to their face.

CHAP. V.

1 The wicked shal wonder at the godly, 4 and confesse their errour,
5 and the vanitie of their liues. 15 God will reward the Iust, 17
and warre against the wicked.

THen shal the righteous man stand in great boldnesse,
before the face of such as haue afflicted him, and made
no account of his labours.

2 When they see it, they shalbe troubled with terrible feare,
& shall be amazed at the strangenesse of his saluation, so farre
beyond all that they looked for.

3 And they repenting, and groning for anguish of spirit,
shall say within themselues, This was he whom wee had
|| *Or, parable* sometimes in derision, and a ||prouerbe of reproch.
* Chap. 3. 2 4 *We fooles accounted his life madnes, and his end to be
without honour.

5 How is hee numbred among the children of God, and his
lot is among the Saints?

6 Therefore haue wee erred from the way of trueth, and
the light of righteousnesse hath not shined vnto vs, and the
Sunne of righteousnesse rose not vpon vs.

|| *Or, filled our selues, or surfeited.* 7 We ||wearied our selues in the way of wickednesse, and
destruction: yea, we haue gone through deserts, where there
lay no way: but as for the way of the Lord, we haue not
knowen it.

8 What hath pride profited vs? or what good hath riches
with *our* vaunting brought vs?

* 1. Chron. 29. 15. and 2. 5. 9 All those things are *passed away like a shadow, and as
a Poste that hasted by.

10 And as a ship that passeth ouer the waues of the water,
which when it is gone by, the trace thereof cannot bee found:
neither the path way of the keele in the waues.

* Pro. 30. 19 || *Or, flyeth.* 11 *Or as when a bird ||hath flowen thorow the aire, there
is no token of her way to be found, but the light aire being
beaten with the stroke of her wings, and parted with the
violent noise and motion of them, is passed thorow, and
therin afterwards no signe where she went, is to be found.

12 Or like as when an arrow is shot at a marke, it parteth
the aire, which im-

mediatly commeth together againe: so that a man cannot
know where it went thorow:
13 Euen so we in like maner, assoone as we were borne,
began to draw to our end, and had no signe of vertue to
shew: but were consumed in our owne wickednesse.
14 *For the hope of the vngodly is like †dust that is blowen
away with ẏ wind, like a thinne froth that is driuen away
with ẏ storme: like as the ||smoke which is *dispersed here
and there with a tempest, and passeth away as the remembrance of a guest that tarieth but a day.
15 But ẏ righteous liue for euermore, their reward also is
with the Lord, and the care of them is with the most High.
16 Therfore shall they receiue a glorious ||kingdome, &
a beautiful crowne from the Lords hande: for with his right
hand shall he couer them, and with his arme shall he protect
them.
17 He shall take to him his ielousie for cōplete armour, &
make the creature his weapon for the reuenge of his enemies.
18 He shal put on *righteousnesse as a brestplate, and true
iudgement in stead of an helmet.
19 He shall take ||holinesse for an inuincible shield.
20 His seuere wrath shall he sharpen for a sword, and the
world shall fight with him against the vnwise.
21 Then shal the right-aiming thunder bolts goe abroad,
and from the cloudes, as from a well-drawen bow, shall they
flie to the marke.
22 And hailestones full of wrath shal be cast *as* out of
a stonebow, and the water of the Sea shall rage against them,
& the floods shall cruelly drowne them.
23 Yea a mightie wind shall stand vp against them, & like
a storme shall blow them away: thus iniquity shal lay wast
the whole earth, and ill dealing shall ouerthrow the thrones
of the mightie.

*Iob 8. 9.
†*Gre. thistle downe.*
|| *Or, chaffe.*
Psal. 2. 4. & 103. 14. pro. 10. 25. and 11. 7. iam. 1. 10, 11.
|| *Or, palace, vnlesse the word be taken vnproperly, as 2. Mac. 2. 17.*
*Esa. 59. 17
|| *Or, equity.*

CHAP. VI.

1 Kings must giue eare. 3 They haue their power from God, 5 Who will not spare them. 12 Wisedome is soone found. 21 Princes must seeke for it: 24 For a wise Prince is the stay of his people.

HEare therefore, O yee kings, and vnderstand, learne yee
that be iudges of the ends of the earth.
2 Giue eare you that rule the people,
and

and glory in the multitude of nations.

*Rom. 13. 1, 2.

3 For *power is giuen you of the Lord, & soueraigntie from the Highest, who shall try your workes, and search out your counsels.

4 Because being Ministers of his kingdome, you haue not iudged aright, nor kept the law, nor walked after the counsell of God,

5 Horribly and speedily shall he come vpon you: for a sharpe iudgement shall be to them that be in high places.

6 For mercy will soone pardon the meanest: but mighty men shall be mightily tormented.

*2. Chro. 19. 17. deut. 10. 17. iob. 34. 19. ecclesi. 35. 12. 16. act. 10. 24. rom. 2. 11. gal. 2. 6. ephe. 6. 9 col. 3. 25. 1. pet. 1. 17.

7 For he which is Lord ouer all, shall feare no *mans person: neither shall he stand in awe of any mans greatnesse: for he hath made the small and great, and careth for all alike.

8 But a sore triall shall come vpon the mighty.

9 Vnto you therefore, *O kings*, doe I speake, that yee may learne wisedome, and not fall away.

|| *Or, iustified.*

|| *Or, a defence.*

10 For they that keepe holinesse holily, shall be ||iudged holy: and they that haue learned such things, shall find ||what to answere.

11 Wherefore set your affection vpon my words, desire them, and yee shall be instructed.

12 Wisedome is glorious and neuer fadeth away: yea she is easily seene of them that loue her, and found of such as seeke her.

13 She preuenteth them that desire her, in making herselfe first knowen vnto them.

14 Whoso seeketh her earely, shall haue no great trauaile: for he shall find her sitting at his doores.

15 To thinke therefore vpon her is perfection of wisedome: and who so watcheth for her, shall quickly be without care.

16 For she goeth about seeking such as are worthy of her, sheweth herselfe fauourably vnto them in the wayes, and meeteth them in euery thought.

|| *Or, nurture*

17 For the very true beginning of her, is the desire of ||discipline, and the care of discipline is loue:

18 And loue is the keeping of her lawes; and the giuing heed vnto her lawes, is the assurance of incorruption.

19 And incorruption maketh vs neere vnto God.

20 Therefore the desire of wisedome

bringeth to a kingdome.
21 If your delight be then in thrones and scepters, O ye
kings of the people, honour wisedome that yee may raigne
for euermore.
22 As for wisedome what she is, and how she came vp,
I will tell you, and will not hide mysteries from you: but
will seeke her out from the beginning of her natiuity, & bring
the knowledge of her into light, and will not passe ouer the
trueth.
23 Neither will I goe with consuming enuy: for such a
man shall haue no fellowship with wisedome.
24 But the multitnde of the wise is the welfare of the world:
and a wise king is the vpholding of the people.
25 Receiue therefore instruction thorough my words, and it
shall doe you good.

CHAP. VII.

1 All men haue their beginning and end alike. 6 He preferred wisedome before all things else. 8 God gaue him all the knowledge, which he had. 22 The praise of wisedome.

I My selfe also am a mortall man, like to all, and the
ofspring of him that was first made of the earth,
2 And in my mothers wombe was fashioned to be flesh
in the time of tenne moneths *being compacted in blood, of *Iob. 10.
the seed of man, and the pleasure that came with sleepe. 12.
3 And when I was borne, I drew in the common aire, and
fell vpon the earth which is of like nature, and the first voice
which I vttered, was crying as all others doe.
4 I was nursed in swadling clothes, and that with cares.
5 For there is no king that had any other beginning of
birth.
6 *For all men haue one entrance vnto life, and the like *Iob. 1.
going out. 21. 1. Timo.
7 Wherefore I prayed, and vnderstanding was giuen mee: 6. 7
I called *vpon God*, and the spirit of wisedome came to me.
8 I preferred her before scepters, and thrones, and esteemed
riches nothing in comparison of her.
9 Neither compared I vnto her any †precious stone, because †*Gre. stone of in-*
all gold in respect of her is as a little sand, and siluer shalbe *estimable*
counted as clay before her. *price.*
10 I loued her aboue health and

Qqqq 2 beautie,

beautie, and chose to haue her in stead of light: for the light
that commeth from her neuer goeth out.

*1. King. 3. 13. matt. 6. 33.

11 All *good things together came to me with her, and
innumerable riches in her hands.
12 And I reioyced in *them* all, because wisedome goeth
before them: and I knew not that shee was the mother of
them.

†*Greeke, without guile.* †*Gr. without enuie.* ||*Or, enter friendship with God.* ||*Or, God grant.* ||*Or, are to be spoken of.*

13 I learned †diligently, and doe communicate *her* †liber-
ally: I doe not hide her riches.
14 For shee is a treasure vnto men that neuer faileth: which
they that vse, ||become the friends of God: being commended
for the gifts that come from learning.
15 God hath ||granted me to speake as I would, and to con-
ceiue as is meet for the things ||that are giuen mee: because
it is hee that leadeth vnto wisedome, and directeth the wise.
16 For in his hand are both we and our wordes: all wisedome also and knowledge of workemanship.
17 For hee hath giuen mee certaine knowledge of the
things that are, namely to know how the world was made,
& the operation of the elements:
18 The beginning, ending, and midst of the times: the
alterations of the turning *of the Sunne*, and the change of
seasons:
19 The circuits of yeres, and the positions of starres:
20 The natures of liuing creatures, and the furies of wilde
beasts: the violence of windes, and the reasonings of men:
the diuersities of plants, and the vertues of rootes:
21 And all such things as are either secret or manifest:
them I know.

†*Greeke, onely begotten.*

22 For wisedome which is the worker of all things, taught
mee: for in her is an vnderstanding spirit, holy, †one onely,
manifold, subtile, liuely, cleare, vndefiled, plaine, not subiect
to hurt, louing the thing that is good, quicke, which cãnot be
letted, ready to do good:
23 Kinde to man, stedfast, sure, free from care, hauing all
power, ouerseeing all things, and going through all vnderstanding, pure, and most subtile spirits.
24 For wisedome is more moouing then any motion: she
passeth and goeth through all things by reason of her pure-
nesse.

25 For she is the ||breath of the power of God, and a pure || *Or, vapour.*
||influence flowing from the glory of the Almighty: therefore || *Or, streame.*
can no vndefiled thing fall into her.
26 For shee is the * brightnesse of the euerlasting light: the * Hebr. 1.
vnspotted mirrour of the power of God, and the Image of his 3.
goodnesse.
27 And being but one she can doe all things: and remayn-
ing in her selfe, she ||maketh all things new: and in all ages || *Or, createth.*
entring into holy soules, shę maketh them friends of God, &
Prophets.
28 For God loueth none but him, that dwelleth with wisedome.
29 For she is more beautiful then the Sunne, and aboue all
the order of starres; being compared with the light, she is
found before it.
30 For after this commeth night: but vice shall not preuaile against wisdome.

CHAP. VIII.

2 He is in loue with wisedome: 4 For he that hath it, hath euery good thing. 21 It cannot be had, but from God.

W*Isdome* reacheth from one ende to another mightily:
and ||sweetly doeth she order all things. || *Or, profitably.*
2 I loued her and sought *her* out, from my youth I dedesired
||to make her my spouse, and I was a louer of her beautie. || *Or, to marry her to my selfe.*
3 In that she is conuersant with God, she magnifieth her
nobilitie: yea, the Lord of all things himselfe loued her.
4 For she is ||priuy to the mysteries of the knowledge of || *Or, teacher.*
God, and a ||louer of his workes. || *Or, chuser.*
5 If riches be a possession to be desired in this life: what is
richer then wisedome that worketh all things?
6 And if *prudence worke; who of all that are, is a more * Exod. 31.
cunning workeman then she? 48.
7 And if a man loue righteousnesse, her labours are vertues:
for she teacheth temperance and prudence: iustice and forti-
tude, which are such things as men can haue nothing more
profitable in their life.
8 If a man desire much experience: she knoweth things of
old, and coniectureth *aright* what is to come: shee knoweth
the subtilties of speaches, and can expound darke sentences:
she

she foreseeth signes and wonders, and the euents of seasons
and times.
9 Therefore I purposed to take her to me to liue with mee,
†*Gr. will.* knowing that shee †would be a counsellour of good things,
and a comfort in cares & griefe.
10 For her sake I shall haue estimation among the multitude, and honour with the Elders, though I be yong.
11 I shall be found of a quicke conceit in iudgement, and
shall be admired in the sight of great men.
*Iob 29. 8, 9, 10, 11. 12 *When I hold my tongue they shal bide my leisure, and
when I speake they shall giue good eare vnto me: if I talke
much, they shall lay their handes vpon their mouth.
13 Moreouer, by the meanes of her, I shall obtaine immortalitie, and leaue behind me an euerlasting memoriall to them
that come after me.
||*Or, gouerne.* 14 I shall ||set the people in order, and the nations shalbe
subiect vnto me.
15 Horrible tyrants shall be afraide when they doe but
||*Or, appeare.* heare of me, I shall be ||found good among the multitude,
and valiant in warre.
||*Or, being entred into mine house.* 16 ||After I am come into mine house, I will repose my
selfe with her: for her conuersation hath no bitternes, and to
liue with her, hath no sorrow, but mirth and ioy.
17 Now when I considered these things in my selfe, and
*Prou. 7. 3. *pondered them in mine heart, how that to be allyed vnto
wisedome, is immortalitie,
18 And great pleasure it is to haue her friendship, and in
the workes of her hands are infinite riches, and in the exercise of conference with her, prudence: and in talking with
||*Or, fame.* ||*Or, marry her.* her a ||good report: I went about seeking how to ||take her
to me.
19 For I was a wittie child, and had a good spirit.
20 Yea rather being good, I came into a body vndefiled.
21 Neuerthelesse when I perceiued that I could not otherwise obtaine her, except God gaue her me (and that was
||*Or, went.* a point of wisdome also to know whose gift she was) I ||prayed
vnto the Lord, and besought him, and with my whole heart
I said:

CHAP. IX.

1 A prayer vnto God for his wisdome, 6 without which the best man is nothing worth, 13 neither can he tell how to please God.

O God of my fathers, and Lord of mercy, who hast made
all things with thy word,
2 And ordained man through thy wisedome, that he
should haue *dominion ouer the creatures, which thou hast *Gen. 1.
made, 28.
3 And order the world according to equitie and righteousnesse, and execute iudgement with an vpright heart:
4 Giue *me wisedome that sitteth by thy Throne, and *1. Kin. 3.
reiect me not from among thy children: 5.
5 For I *thy seruant and sonne of thine handmaide, am *Psal. 116.
a feeble person, and of a short time, and too young for the 16.
vnderstanding of iudgement and lawes.
6 For though a man be neuer so perfect among the children
of men, yet if thy wisedome be not with him, hee shall be
nothing regarded.
7 Thou hast chosen me to be a king of thy people, and *1. Chron.
a Iudge of thy sons and daughters: 28. 5. 2.
chro. 1. 9.
8 Thou hast commaunded me to build a Temple vpon thy
holy mount, and an Altar in the city wherein thou dwellest,
a resemblance of the holy Tabernacle which thou hast prepared from the beginning:
9 And *wisedome was with thee: which knoweth thy *Pro. 8.
workes, and was present when thou madest the world, and 22. ioh. 1.
knew what was acceptable in thy sight, and right in thy 2, 3, 10.
Commaundements.
10 O send her out of thy holy heauens, and from the
Throne of thy glory, that being present shee may labour with
mee, that I may know what is pleasing vnto thee.
11 For she knoweth and vnderstandeth all things, and shee
shall leade me soberly in my doings, and preserue me ||in her || *Or, by her*
power. *power or*
glory.
12 So shall my workes be acceptable, and then shall I iudge
thy people righteously, and be worthy to sit in my fathers
seate.
13 For what man is hee that can know the counsell of God? *Isai 40.
or who can thinke what the will of the Lord is? 13.
rom. 11.
14 For the thoughts of mortall men are ||miserable, and our 34.
deuices are but vncertaine. 1. cor. 2.
16.
15 For the corruptible body presseth downe the soule, and || *Or, feare-*
the earthy taber- *full.*
nacle

nacle weigheth downe the minde that museth vpon many things.

16 And hardly doe we gesse aright at things that are vpon
earth, and with labour doe wee find the things that are
† Gre. at hand. †before vs: but the things that are in heauen, who hath
searched out?

17 And thy counsell who hath knowen, except thou giue
wisedome, and send thy holy spirit from aboue?

18 For so the wayes of them which liued on the earth were
reformed, and men were taught the things that are pleasing
vnto thee, and were saued through wisedome.

CHAP. X.

1 What wisedome did for Adam, 4 Noe, 5 Abraham, 6 Lot, and against the fiue cities, 10 for Iacob, 13 Ioseph, 16 Moses, 17 and the Israelites.

SHe preserued the first formed father of the world that
was created alone, and brought him out of his fall,
*Gen. 2. 20. 2 And *gaue him power to rule all things.
*Gen. 4. 8. 3 *But when the vnrighteous went away from her in his
anger, he perished also in the fury wherwith he murdered his
brother.
*Gen. 7. 21 4 For whose cause the *earth being drowned with the flood,
Wisedome againe preserued it, & directed the course of the
righteous, in a piece of wood, of small value.
*Gen. 11. 9 5 Moreouer, *the nations in their wicked conspiracie being
confounded, she found out the righteous, and preserued him
|| Or, in. blamelesse vnto God, and kept him strong ||against his tender
compassion towards his sonne.
*Gen. 22. 10. gen. 19. 16. 6 *When the vngodly perished, shee deliuered the righteous
man, who fled from the fire which fell downe vpon the †fiue
† Gre. Pentapolis. cities.

7 Of whose wickednesse euen to this day the waste land
that smoketh, is a testimonie, and plants bearing fruite that
neuer come to ripenesse: and a standing pillar of salt *is* a
monument of an vnbeleeuing soule.

8 For regarding not wisedome, they gate not only this hurt,
that they knew not the things which were good: but also
left behind them to the world a memoriall of their foolishnes:
so that in

the things wherein they offended, they could not so much as
be hid.
9 But Wisedome deliuered from paine those that attended
vpon her.
10 When the righteous fled from his brothers wrath, she
guided him in right paths: shewed him the kingdome of
God: and gaue him knowledge of holy things, made him
rich in his trauailes, and multiplied *the fruit of* his labours.
11 In the couetousnesse of such as oppressed him, she stood
by him, and made him rich.
12 She defended him from his enemies, and kept him safe
from those that lay in wait, and in a sore conflict she gaue
him the victory, that he might knowe that godlinesse is
stronger then all.
13 *When the righteous was solde, she forsooke him not, *Gen. 37.
but deliuered him from sinne: she went downe with him 38. & 39. 7. acts 7. 10.
into the pit,
14 And left him not in bonds till she brought him the
scepter of the kingdom and ||power against those that oppres- || *Or, the*
sed him: as for them that had accused him, she shewed them *power of them that*
to be liers, and gaue them perpetuall glory. *ruled ouer him.*
15 *She deliuered the ||righteous people, and blamelesse *Exo. 1.
seed from the nation that oppressed them. 10. and 12.
16 She entred into the soule of the seruant of the Lord, and 42.
*withstood dreadfull kings in wonders and signes, || *Or, holy.*
17 Rendred to the righteous a reward of their labours, *Exod. 5. 1
guided them in a marueilous way, and was vnto them for
a couer by day, and a light ||of starres in the night season: || *Or, flame.*
18 *Brought them through the red sea, and led them thorow *Exod. 14.
much water. 21, 22.
19 But she drowned their enemies, and cast them vp out of psal. 78. 13.
the bottome of the deepe.
20 Therefore the righteous spoiled the vngodly, & *praised *Exo. 15.
thy holy Name, O Lord, and magnified with one accord 1.
thine hand that fought for them.
21 For wisedome opened the mouth of the dumbe, and
made the tongues of them that cannot speake, eloquent.

CHAP. XI.

5 The Egyptians were punished, and the Israelites reserued in the same thing. 15 They were plagued by the same things, wherein they sinned. 20 God could haue destroyed them otherwise, 23 but he is mercifull to all.

She

SHe prospered their works in the hand of the holy
Prophet.
*Exod. 16. 2 *They went thorough the wildernesse that was not in-
1. exod. 17. habited, and pitched tents in places where there lay no
10, 11. way.
3 They stood against their enemies, and were auenged of
their aduersaries.
4 When they were thirsty they called vpon thee, and water
was giuen them out of the flinty rocke, and their thirst was
quenched out of the hard stone.
5 For by what things their enemies were punished, by the
same they in their neede were benefited.
6 For in stead of a fountaine of a perpetuall running riuer,
troubled with foule blood,
7 For a manifest reproofe of that commandement, whereby
the infants were slaine, thou gauest vnto them abundance of
water by a meanes which they hoped not for,
*Exod. 7. 8 Declaring by that thirst then, *how thou hadst punished
20. their aduersaries.
9 For when they were tryed, albeit but in mercy chastised,
they knew how the vngodly were iudged in wrath and
tormented thirsting in another maner then the Iust.
10 For these thou didst admonish, and trie as a father: but
the other as a seuere king thou didst condemne and punish.
11 Whether they were absent, or present, they were vexed
alike.
12 For a double griefe came vpon them, and a groaning for
the remembrance of things past.
13 For when they heard by their owne punishments the
Or, per- other to be benefited, they ||had some feeling of the Lord.
ceiued. 14 For whom they reiected with scorne when hee was long
before throwen out at the casting forth *of the infants*, him in
the end, when they saw what came to passe, they admired,
15 But for the foolish deuises of their wickednesse, wherewith being deceiued, they worshipped serpents voyd of reason,
and vile beasts: thou didst send a multitude of vnreasonable
beasts vpon them for vengeance,
16 That they might knowe that wherewithall a man sinneth,
by the

same also shall he be punished.
17 For thy Almighty hand that made the world of matter
without forme, wanted not meanes to send among them a
multitude of Beares, or fierce Lyons,
18 Or vnknowen wild beasts full of rage newly created,
breathing out either a fiery vapour, or filthy sents of scattered
smoake, or shooting horrible sparkles out of their eyes:
19 Whereof not onely the harme might dispatch them at
once: but also the terrible sight vtterly destroy them.
20 Yea and without these might they haue fallen downe
with one blast, being persecuted of vengeance, and scattered
abroad thorough the breath of thy power, but thou hast
ordered all things in measure, and number, and weight.
21 For thou canst shew thy great strength at all times when
thou wilt, and who may withstand the power of thine arme?
22 For the whole world before thee is as a litle ||graine of *|| Or, little waight.*
the ballance, yea as a drop of the morning dew that falleth
downe vpon the earth.
23 But thou hast mercy vpon all: for thou canst doe all
things, and winkest at the sinnes of men: because they should
amend.
24 For thou louest all the things that are, and abhorrest
nothing which thou hast made: for neuer wouldest thou
haue made any thing, if thou hadst hated it.
25 And how could any thing haue endured if it had not
beene thy will? or beene preserued, if not called by thee?
26 But thou sparest all: for they are thine, O Lord, thou
louer of soules.

CHAP. XII.

2 God did not destroy those of Canaan all at once. 12 If he had done so, who could controll him? 19 but by sparing them hee taught vs, 27 they were punished with their Gods.

FOr thine vncorruptible spirit is in all things.
2 Therefore chastnest thou them by little, and little,
that offend, and warnest them by putting them in remembrance, wherin they haue offended, that leauing their wickednesse they may beleeue on thee O Lord.
3 For it was thy will to destroy by
the

|| Or, the handes of our fathers, both those ||old inhabitants of thy
ancient. holy land,
4 Whom thou hatedst for doing most odious workes of
|| Or, sor- ||witchcrafts, and wicked sacrifices;
ceries. 5 And also those mercilesse murderers of children, &
deuourers of mans flesh, and the feasts of blood;
6 With their Priests out of the midst of their idolatrous
crew, and the parents that killed with their owne hands,
soules destitute of helpe:
7 That the land which thou esteemedst aboue all other,
|| Or, new might receiue a worthy ||colonie of Gods children.
inhabit- 8 Neuerthelesse, euen those thou sparedst as men, and didst
ance.
* Exod. 33. send *waspes forerunners of thine hoste, to destroy them by
2. little and little.
deut. 2. 22. 9 Not that thou wast vnable to bring the vngodly under the
hand of the righteous in battell, or to destroy them at once
with cruel beastes, or with one rough word:
10 But executing thy iudgements vpon them by little and
little, thou gauest them place of repentance, not being
ignorant that they were a naughtie generation, and that their
malice, was bred in them, and that their cogitation would
neuer be changed.
* Gen. 9. 11 For it was a *cursed seed, from the beginning, neither
25. didst thou for feare of any man giue them pardon for those
things wherein they sinned.
* Rom. 9. 12 For who shall say, *What hast thou done? or who shall
20. withstand thy iudgement, or who shall accuse thee for the
nations that perish whom thou hast made? or who shall come
|| Or, in to ||stand against thee, to be ||reuenged for the vnrighteous men?
thy pre- 13 For neither is there any God but thou, that *careth for
sence.
|| Or, a re- all, to whom thou mightest shew that thy iudgement is not
uenger. vnright.
* 1. Pet. 5. 14 Neither shall king or tyrant bee able to set his face
7 against thee, for any whom thou hast punished.
15 For so much then as thou art righteous thy selfe, thou
* Iob 10. 2. orderest all things righteously: *thinking it not agreeable
with thy power to condemne him ỷ hath not deserued to be
punished.
16 For thy power is the beginning of righteousnesse, and
because thou art the Lord of all, it maketh thee to be gracious
vnto all.

17 For when men will not beleeue,

that thou art of a ||full power, thou shewest thy strength, || *Or, perfect.*
and among them that know it, thou makest their boldnesse
manifest.
18 But thou, mastering thy power, iudgest with equitie,
and orderest vs with great fauour: for thou mayest vse power
when thou wilt.
19 But by such workes hast thou taught thy people, that
the iust man should be mercifull, and hast made thy children
to be of a good hope, that thou giuest repentance for sinnes.
20 For if thou didst punish the enemies of thy children, and
the condemned to death with such deliberation, giuing them
time and place, wherby they might be deliuered from their
malice.
21 With how great circumspection diddest thou iudge thine
owne sonnes, vnto whose fathers thou hast sworne, and made
couenants of good promises?
23 Therefore whereas thou doest chasten vs, thou scourgest
our enemies a thousand times more, to the intent that when
wee iudge, wee should carefully thinke of thy goodnesse, and
when we our selues are iudged, wee should looke for mercy.
23 Wherefore, whereas men haue liued dissolutely and
vnrighteously, thou hast tormented them with their owne
||abominations. || *Or, abominable idoles.*
24 *For they went astray very farre in the wayes of errour,
& held them for gods (which euen amongst the beasts of *Chap. 11. 13. rom. 1. 23.
their enemies were despised) being deceiued as children of no
vnderstanding.
25 Therefore vnto them, as to children without the vse of
reason, thou didst send a iudgement to mocke them.
26 But they that would not bee refourmed by that correction wherein he dallied with them, shall feele a iudgement
worthy of God.
27 For looke, for what things they grudged when they were
punished, (that is) for them whom they thought to be gods,
[now] being punished in them; when they saw it, they
acknowledged him to be the true God, whome before they
denyed to know: and therefore came extreme damnation
vpon them.

CHAP. XIII.

1 They were not excused that worshipped any of Gods workes: 10 But most wretched are they that worship the works of mens hands.

SVrely vaine are all men by nature, who are ignorant of God, and could not out of the good things that are seene, know him that is: neither by considering the workes, did they acknowledge the worke-master;

*Rom. 1. 9. deut. 4. 19. and 17. 3.

2 *But deemed either fire, or wind, or the swift aire, or the circle of the stars, or the violent water, or the lights of heauen to be the gods which gouerne the world:

3 With whose beautie, if they being delighted, tooke them to be gods: let them know how much better the Lord of them is; for the first Author of beautie hath created them.

4 But if they were astonished at their power and vertue, let them vnderstand by them, how much mightier he is that made them.

5 For by the greatnesse and beautie of the creatures, proportionably the Maker of them is seene.

6 But yet for this they are the lesse to bee blamed: for they peraduenture erre seeking God, and desirous to finde him.

*Rom. 1. 21 || *Or, seeke.*

7 For being *conuersant in his workes, they ||search *him* diligently, and beleeue their sight: because the things are beautifull that are seene.

8 Howbeit, neither are they to bee pardoned.

9 For if they were able to know so much, that they could aime at the world; how did they not sooner finde out the Lord thereof?

10 But miserable are they, and in dead things is their hope, who called them gods which are the workes of mens hands, golde and siluer, to shewe arte in, and resemblances of beasts, or a stone good for nothing, the worke of an ancient hand.

*Isai 44. 13. || *Or, timber-wright.*

11 *Now a ||carpenter that felleth timber, after hee hath sawen downe a tree meet for the purpose, and taken off all the barke skilfully round about, and hath wrought it handsomely, & made a vessell thereof fit for the seruice of mans life:

|| *Or, chips.*

12 And after spending the ||refuse of his worke to dresse his meat, hath filled himselfe:

13 And taking the very refuse among those which serued to no vse (being a crooked piece of wood, and ful of knots)

hath carued it diligently when hee had nothing else to doe,
and formed it by the skill of his vnderstanding, and fashioned
it to the image of a man:
14 Or made it like some vile beast, laying it ouer with
vermilion, and with paint, colouring it red, and couering
euery spot therein:
15 And when he had made a conuenient roume for it, set
it in a wall, and made it fast with yron:
16 For he prouided for it, that it might not fall: knowing
that it was vnable to helpe it selfe, (for it is an image and
hath neede of helpe:)
17 Then maketh hee prayer for his goods, for his wife and
children, and is not ashamed to speake to that which hath no
life.
18 For health, hee calleth vpon that which is weake: for
life, prayeth to that which is dead: for aide, humbly besee-
cheth †that which hath least meanes to helpe: and for a
good iourney, hee asketh of that which cannot set a foot
forward:
19 And for gaining and getting, and for good successe of his
hands, asketh abilitie to doe, of him that is most vnable to
doe any thing.

† *Gr. that hath no experience at all.*

CHAP. XIIII.

1 Though men doe not pray to their shippes, 5 Yet are they saued rather by them then by their Idoles. 8 Idoles are accursed, and so are the makers of them. 14 The beginning of Idolatrie, 23 And the effects thereof. 30 God wil punish them that sweare falsely by their Idoles.

AGaine, one preparing himselfe to saile, and about to passe
through the raging waues, calleth vpon a piece of wood
more rotten then the ||vessell that carieth him.
2 For verely desire of gaine deuised ||that, and the worke-
man built it by his skill:
3 But thy prouidence, O Father, gouerneth it: for thou
hast *made a way in the Sea, and a safe path in the waues:
4 Shewing that thou canst saue from all danger: yea though
a man went to Sea without arte.
5 Neuerthelesse thou wouldest not that the works of thy
wisedome should be idle, and therefore doe men commit
their

|| *Or, ship.*

|| *Or, vessell or ship.*

* Exod. 14. 22.

their liues to a small piece of wood, and passing the rough sea
in a weake vessell, are saued.
*Gen. 6. 4. and 7. 10.
6 *For in the old time also when the proud gyants perished,
the hope of the world gouerned by thy hand, escaped in a
weake vessell, and left to all ages a seed of generation.
7 For blessed is the wood, whereby righteousnesse commeth.
*Psal. 115. 8. baruc. 6. 3
8 But that which is made with hands, is cursed, aswell *it,
as hee that made it: he, because he made it, and it, because
being corruptible it was called God.
*Psal. 5. 5.
9 *For the vngodly and his vngodlines are both alike hatefull vnto God.
10 For that which is made, shall bee punished together with
him that made it.
|| *Or, to or by.*
11 Therfore euen vpon ||the idoles of the Gentiles shall
there be a visitation: because in the creature of God they
*Ier. 10. 8. abac. 2. 18. † *Gre. scandales.* || *Or, trap.*
are become an abomination and *†stumbling blocks to the
soules of men, and a ||snare to the feet of the vnwise.
12 For the deuising of idoles was the beginning of *spiritual*
fornication, and the inuention of them the corruption of life.
13 For neither were they from the beginning, neither shall
they be for euer.
14 For by the vaine glory of men they entred into the
world, and therefore shall they come shortly to an end.
15 For a father afflicted with vntimely mourning, when he
hath made an image of his childe soone taken away, now
honoured him as a god, which was then a dead man, and
deliuered to those that were vnder him, ceremonies and
sacrifices.
† *Gre. in time*
16 Thus †in processe of time an vngodly custome growen
strong, was kept as a law, and grauen images were worshipped
|| *Or, tyrants* || *Or, in sight*
by the commandements of ||kings,
17 Whom men could not honour ||in presence, because they
dwelt farre off, they tooke the counterfeit of his visage from
farre, and made an expresse image of a king whom they
honoured, to the end that by this their forwardnes, they
might flatter him that was absent, as if he were present.
18 Also the singular diligence of the artificer did helpe to
set forward the ignorant to more superstition.
19 For he peraduenture willing to please one in authoritie,
forced all his

skill to make the resemblance †of the best fashion. † *Gre. to the better.*
20 And so the multitude allured by the grace of the worke,
tooke him now for a god, which a litle before was but honoured as a man.
21 And this was an occasion to deceiue the world: for men
seruing either calamitie or tyrannie, did ascribe vnto stones,
and stockes, the incommunicable ||Name. || *Of God.*
22 Moreouer this was not enough for them, that they erred
in the knowledge of God, but whereas they liued in the great
warre of ignorance, those so great plagues called they peace.
23 For whilest they *slew their children in sacrifices, or *Deut. 18. 10. ier. 7. 9. and 19. 4.
vsed secret ceremonies, or made reuellings of strange rites
24 They kept neither liues nor mariages any longer vndefiled: but either one slew another traiterously, or grieued
him by adulterie:
25 So that there reigned in all men ||without exception, || *Or, confusedly.*
blood, manslaughter, theft, and dissimulation, corruption,
vnfaithfulnesse, tumults, periurie,
26 Disquieting of good men, forgetfulnesse of good turnes,
defiling of soules, changing of ||kinde, disorder in mariages, || *Or, sexe.*
adulterie, and shameles vncleannesse.
27 For the worshipping of idoles †not to be named, is the † *Gre. namelesse.*
beginning, the cause, and the end of all euill.
28 For either they are mad when they be merry, or prophesie lies, or liue vniustly, or else lightly forsweare themselues.
29 For insomuch as their trust is in idoles which haue no
life, though they sweare falsly, yet they looke not to bee
hurt.
30 Howbeit for both causes shal they be iustly puuished:
both because they thought not well of God, ||giuing heed || *Or, deuoted.*
vnto idols, and also vniustly swore in deceit, despising holinesse.
31 For it is not the power of them by whom they sweare:
but it is the iust vengeance of sinners, that punisheth alwayes
the offence of the vngodly.

CHAP. XV.

1 We doe acknowledge the true God. 7 The follie of Idole-makers, 14 and of the enemies of Gods people: 15 because besides the idoles of the Gentiles, 18 they worshipped vile beasts.

But

BVt thou O God, art gracious and true: long suffering, and in mercy ordering all things.

2 For if we sinne we are thine, knowing thy power: but we will not sinne, knowing that we are counted thine.

3 For to know thee is perfect righteousnesse: yea to know thy power is the roote of immortality.

4 For neither did the mischieuous inuention of men deceiue vs: nor an image spotted with diuers colours, the painters fruitlesse labour.

|| *Or, turneth a reproch to the foolish.* 5 The sight wherof ||entiseth fooles to lust after it, and so they desire the forme of a dead image that hath no breath.

6 Both they that make them, they that desire them, and they that worship them, are louers of euill things, and are worthy to haue such things to trust vpon.

*Rom. 9. 11 7 For the *potter tempering soft earth fashioneth, euery vessell with much labour for our seruice: yea of the same clay hee maketh both the vessels that serue for cleane vses: and likewise also all such as serue to the contrary: but what is the vse of either sort, the potter himselfe is the iudge.

8 And employing his labours lewdly, he maketh a vaine God of the same clay, euen he which a little before was made of earth himselfe, and within a little while after returneth to the same out of the which he was taken: when his
*Luke 12. 20. *life which was lent him shall be demanded.

|| *Or, be sicke or die.* 9 Notwithstanding his care is, not that hee shall haue much labour, nor that ||his life is short: but strieueth to excel goldsmiths, and siluersmiths, and endeuoureth to doe like the workers in brasse, and counteth it his glory to make counterfeit things.

10 His heart is ashes, his hope is more vile then earth, and his life of lesse value then clay:

11 Forasmuch as hee knew not his maker, and him that inspired into him an actiue soule, and breathed in a liuing spirit.

† *Gre. life.* 12 But they counted our life a pastime, & our †time here a market for gaine: for, say they, we must be getting euery way, though it be by euil meanes.

|| *Or, so.* 13 ||For this man that of earthly mat-

ter maketh brickle vessels, and grauen images, knoweth himselfe to offend aboue all others.

14 And all the enemies of thy people, that hold them in subiection are most foolish and are more miserable then very babes.

15 For they counted all the idoles of the heathen to be gods: which neither haue the vse of eyes to see, nor noses to draw ||breath, nor eares to heare, nor fingers of hands to handle, and as for their feete they are slow to goe. || *Or, ayre.*

16 For man made them, and he that borrowed his owne spirit fashioned them, but no man can make a god like vnto himselfe.

17 For being mortall he worketh a dead thing with wicked hands: for hee himselfe is better then the things which he worshippeth: whereas he liued *once*, but they neuer.

18 Yea they worshipped those beasts also that are most hatefull: for being compared together, some are worse then others.

19 Neither are they beautifull, so much, as to bee desired in respect of beasts, but they went without the praise of God and his blessing.

CHAP. XVI.

2 God gaue strange meate to his people, to stirre vp their appetite, and vile beasts to their enemies to take it from them. 5 Hee stung with his serpents, 12 but soone healed them by his word onely. 17 The creatures altred their nature to pleasure Gods people, and to offend their enemies.

THerefore by the like were they punished worthily, and by the multitude of beasts *tormented. *Num. 21. 6. chap. 11. 15, 16.

2 In stead of which punishment, dealing graciously with thine owne people thou preparedst for them meate of a strange taste: euen *quailes to stirre vp their appetite: *Num. 11. 31.

3 To the end that they desiring food might for the ougly sight of the beasts sent among them, loath euen that which they must needs desire: but these suffering penury for a short space, might be made partakers of a strange taste.

4 For it was requisite, that vpon them excercising tyranny should come penury which they could not auoyde: but to these it should onely be shewed how their enemies were tormented.

5 For

5 For when the horrible fiercenesse of beasts came vpon
|| *Or, thy people.* ||these, and they perished with the *stings of crooked serpents,
*Num. 21. 6. 1. cor. 10. 9. thy wrath endured not for euer.
6 But they were troubled for a smal season that they might
*Num. 21. 9. be admonished, hauing a *signe of saluation, to put them in
remembrance of the commandement of thy Law.
7 For hee that turned himselfe towards it, was not saued
by the thing that he saw: but by thee that art the sauiour
of all.
8 And in this thou madest thine enemies confesse, that it is
thou who deliuerest from all euill:
*Exod. 8. 24. and 10. 4. reuel. 9. 7. 9 For *them the bitings of grassehoppers and flies killed,
neither was there found any remedy for their life: for they
were worthy to bee punished by such.
10 But thy sonnes, not the very teeth of venemous dragons
ouercame: for thy mercy was *euer* by them, and healed them.
† *Hebr. stung.* 11 For they were †pricked, that they should remember thy
words, and were quickly saued, that not falling into deep
|| *Or, neuer drawen from.* forgetfulnesse, they might be ||continually mindefull of thy
goodnesse.
12 For it was neither herbe, nor mollifying plaister that
restored them to health: but thy word, O Lord, which
healeth all things.
*Psal. 105. deut. 32. 39. 1. sam. 2. 6. 13 For thou hast power of life and death: thou *leadest to
the gates of hell, and bringest vp againe.
14 A man indeed killeth through his malice: and the spirit
when it is gone foorth returneth not; neither the soule
receiued vp, commeth againe.
15 But it is not possible to escape thine hand.
*Exod. 9. 23. 16 *For the vngodly that denied to know thee, were
scourged by the strength of thine arme: with strange raines,
hailes, and showers were they persecuted, that they could
not auoyd, and through fire were they consumed.
17 For, which is most to be wondered at, the fire had more
*Iud. 5. 20. force in the water that quencheth all things: for the *world
fighteth for the righteous.
18 For sometimes the flame was mitigated, that it might
not burne vp the beasts that were sent against the vngodly:
but themselues might see and perceiue that they were persecuted with the iudgement of God.

19 And at another time it burneth euen in the midst of
water, aboue the power of fire, that it might destroy the
fruits of an vniust land.
20 *In stead whereof thou feddest thine owne people, with
Angels food, and didst send them from heauen bread prepared
without their labour, able to content euery mans delight, and
agreeing to euery taste.
21 *For thy ||sustenance declared thy sweetnesse vnto thy
children, and seruing to the appetite of the eater ||tempered
it selfe to euery mans liking.
22 *But snow and yce endured the fire and melted not,
that they might know that fire burning in the haile, and
sparkling in the raine, did destroy the fruits of the enemies.
23 But this againe did euen forget his owne strength, that
the righteous might be nourished.
24 For the creature that serueth thee who art the maker,
encreaseth his strength against the vnrighteous for their punishment, and abateth his strength for the benefit of such as put
their trust in thee.
25 Therefore euen then was it altered into all ||fashions,
and was obedient to thy grace that nourisheth all things,
according to the desire ||of them that had need:
26 That thy children, O Lord, whom thou louest, might
know that *it is not the growing of fruits that nourisheth
man: but that it is thy word which preserueth them that
put their trust in thee.
27 For that which was not destroied of the fire, being
warmed with a litle Sunne beame, soone melted away,
28 That it might bee knowen, that wee must preuent the
Sunne, to giue thee thanks, and at the day-spring pray vnto
thee.
29 For the hope of the vnfaithfull, shal melt away as the
Winters hoarefrost, and shall runne away as vnprofitable
water.

* Exod. 16. 14. num. 11. 7. psal. 78. 25. ioh. 6. 31.

* Iudg. 6. 4.

|| *Or, Manna.*

|| *Or, was tempered.*

* Chap. 19. 20.

|| *Or, things.*

|| *Or, of them that prayed.*

* Deut. 8. 3. matth. 4. 4.

CHAP. XVII.

1 Why the Egyptians were punished with darkenesse. 4 The terrours of that darknes. 12 The terrours of an ill conscience.

FOr great are thy Iudgements, and cannot be expressed:
therefore ||vnnourtured soules haue erred.

|| *Or, soules that will not be reformed.*

2 For

2 For when vnrighteous men thought to oppresse the holy
nation: they being shut vp ||in their houses, the prisoners of
darkenesse, and fettered with the bondes of a long night, lay
[there] ||exiled from the eternall prouidence.

|| Or, vnder their roofes.
|| Or, fugitiues.

3 For while they supposed to lie hid in their secret sinnes,
they were scattered ||vnder a darke vaile of forgetfulnesse,
being horribly astonished, and troubled with (strange) ||apparitions.

|| Or, in.
|| Or, sights.

4 For neither might the corner that helde them keepe them
from feare: but noises (as of waters) falling downe, sounded
about them, and sadde visions appeared vnto them with
heauie countenances.

5 No power of the fire might giue them light: neither
could the bright flames of the starres endure to lighten that
horrible night.

6 Onely there appeared vnto them a fire kindled of it selfe,
very dreadfull: for being much terrified, they thought the
things which they saw to be worse then the sight they saw
not.

*Exo. 7. 12. and 8. 7, 19.

7 *As for the illusions of arte Magicke, they were put
downe, and their vaunting in wisedome was reprooued with
disgrace.

8 For they that promised to driue away terrours, and
troubles from a sicke soule, were sicke themselues of feare
worthy to be laughed at.

9 For though no terrible thing did feare them: yet being
skared with beasts that passed by, and hissing of serpents,

|| Or, refusing to looke vpon.

10 They died for feare, ||denying that they saw the ayre,
which could of no side be auoided.

11 For wickednesse condemned by her owne witnesse, is
very timorous, and being pressed with conscience, alwayes
forecasteth grieuous things.

12 For feare is nothing else, but a betraying of the succours
which reason offereth.

13 And the expectation from within being lesse, counteth
the ignorance more then the cause which bringeth the torment.

|| Or, wherein they could doe nothing.

14 But they sleeping the same sleepe that night ||which was
indeed intolerable, and which came vpon them out of the
bottomes of ineuitable hell:

15 Were partly vexed with monstrous apparitions, and partly
fainted,

their heart failing them: for a suddaine feare and not looked
for, came vpon them.
16 So then, whosoeuer there fell downe, was straitly kept,
shut vp in a prison without yron barres.
17 For whether hee were husbandman, or shepheard, or a
labourer in the ||field, he was ouertaken, and endured that || *Or,*
necessitie, which could not be auoided: for they were all *desert.*
bound with one chaine of darkenesse.
18 Whether it were a whistling winde, or a melodious noise
of birdes among the spreading branches, or a pleasing fall of
water running violently:
19 Or a ||terrible sound of stones cast downe, or a running || *Or,*
that could not be seene of skipping beasts, or a roaring voice *hideous.*
of most sauage wilde beasts, or a rebounding Eccho from the
hollow mountaines: these things made them to swoone for
feare.
20 For the whole world shined with cleare light, and none
were hindered in their labour.
21 Ouer them onely was spread an heauie night, an image
of that darkenesse which should afterwards receiue them:
but yet were they vnto themselues more grieuous then the
darkenesse.

CHAP. XVIII.

4 Why Egypt was punished with darkenesse, 5 and with the death of their children, 18 They themselues saw the cause thereof. 20 God also plagued his owne people. 11 By what meanes that plague was stayed.

NEuerthelesse, thy Saints had a very great *light, whose *Exod. 10.
voice they hearing and not seeing their shape, because 23.
they also had not suffered the same things, they counted them
happy.
2 But for that they did not hurt them *now*, of whom they
had beene wronged before, they thanked them, and besought
them pardon, for that they had beene enemies.
3 *In stead whereof thou gauest them a burning pillar of *Exo. 13.
fire, both to be a guide of the vnknowen iourney, and an 21 and 14.
harmelesse Sunne to entertaine them honourably. 24. psal. 78.
4 For they were worthy to be depriued of light, and im- 14. & 105.
prisoned in darknesse, who had kept thy sonnes shut vp, 29.

|| Or, incorruptible. by whom the ||vncorrupt light of the law was to be giuen
vnto the world.
*Exod. 14. 24, 25. 5 *And when they had determined to slay the babes of the
Saints, one child being cast forth, and saued: to reproue
them, thou tookest away the multitude of their children, and
destroyedst them altogether in a mightie water.
*Exod. 11. 4. 6 *Of that night were our fathers certified afore, that
assuredly knowing vnto what oathes they had giuen credence,
they might afterwards bee of good cheere.
7 So of thy people was accepted both the saluation of the
righteous, and destruction of the enemies.
8 For wherewith thou didst punish our aduersaries, by the
same thou didst glorifie vs whom thou hadst called.
*Exod. 12. 9 *For the righteous children of good men did sacrifice
|| Or, a couenant of God, or league, see psal. 50. 5. secretly, and with one consent made a ||holy lawe, that the
Saints should bee alike partakers of the same good and euill,
the fathers now singing out the songs of praise.
10 But on the other side there sounded an ill-according crie
of the enemies, and a lamentable noise was caried abroad for
children that were bewailed.
*Exo. 11. 5 and 12. 29. 11 *The master and the seruaunt were punished after one
maner, and like as the king, so suffered the common per-
son.
12 So they altogether had innumerable dead with one kind
of death, neither were the liuing sufficient to burie them:
for in one moment the noblest ofspring of them was destroyed.
13 For whereas they would not beleeue any thing by reason
of the enchantments, vpon the destruction of the first borne,
they acknowledged this people to be the sonnes of God.
14 For while all things were in quiet silence, and that night
was in the midst of her swift course,
15 Thine almighty word leapt downe from heauen, out of
thy royall throne, as a fierce man of warre into the midst of
a land of destruction,
16 And brought thine vnfained commandement as a sharpe
sword, and standing vp filled all things with death, and it
touched the heauen, but it stood vpon the earth.
|| Or, imaginations. 17 Then suddenly ||visions of horrible dreames troubled
them sore, and terrours came vpon them vnlooked for.

18 And one throwen here, another there halfe dead, shewed
the cause of his death.
19 For the dreames that troubled them, did foreshew this,
lest they should perish, and not know why they were afflicted.
20 Yea, the tasting of death touched the righteous also, and
there was a destruction of the * multitude in the wildernes: * Num. 16. 46.
but the wrath endured not long.
21 For then the blamelesse man made haste, and stood
foorth to defend them, and bringing the shield of his proper
ministerie, euen prayer and the propitiation of incense, set
himselfe against the wrath, and so brought the calamity to an
end, declaring that hee was thy seruant.
22 So hee ouercame the destroyer, not with strength of
body, nor force of armes, but with a word subdued he him
that punished, alleaging the oathes and couenants made with
the fathers.
23 For when the dead were now fallen downe by heaps
one vpon another, standing betweene, he staied the wrath,
and ||parted the way to the liuing. || *Or, cut off.*
24 * For in the long garment was the whole world, & in * Exo. 28. 6. and 11. 10.
the foure rowes of the stones was the glory of the fathers
grauen, and thy maiestie vpon the diademe of his head.
25 Vnto these the destroyer gaue place, and was afraid of
them: for it was enough that they onely tasted of the wrath.

CHAP. XIX.

1 Why God shewed no mercie to the Egyptians. 5 And how wonderfully hee dealt with his people. 14 The Egyptians were worse then the Sodomites. 18 The wonderfull agreement of the creatures to serue Gods people.

AS for the vngodly, wrath came vpon them without mercie
vnto the end: for he knew before what they would doe;
2 Howe that hauing giuen them leaue to depart, and sent
them hastily away, they would repent and pursue them.
3 For whilest they were yet mourning, and making lamentation at the graues of the dead, they added another
foolish

foolish deuice, and pursued them as fugitiues, whom they
|| Or, cast out by entreaty.
had ||entreated to be gone.
4 For the destiny, whereof they were worthy, drew them
vnto this end, and made them forget the things that had
already happened, that they might fulfill the punishment
which was wanting to their torments,
5 And that thy people might passe a wonderfull way: but
they might find a strange death.
6 For the whole creature in his proper kind was fashioned
againe anew, seruing the peculiar commandements that were
giuen vnto them, that thy children might be kept without hurt.
7 *As namely*, a cloud shadowing the campe, and where
water stood before drie land appeared, and out of the red
Sea a way without impediment, and out of the violent
streame a greene field:
8 Where-thorough all the people went that were defended
with thy hand, seeing thy marueilous strange wonders.
9 For they went at large like horses, and leaped like lambes,
praising thee O Lord, who hadst deliuered them.
10 For they were yet mindefull of the things that were
done while they soiourned in the strange land, how the
|| Or, lice.
ground brought forth ||flies in stead of cattell, and how the
riuer cast vp a multitude of frogs in stead of fishes.
11 But afterwards they saw a new generation of foules, when
being led with their appetite they asked delicate meates.
12 For quailes came vp vnto them from the Sea, for their
|| Or, comfort.
||contentment.
13 And punishments came vpon the sinners not without
former signes by the force of thunders: for they suffered
iustly, according to their owne wickednesse, insomuch as
they vsed a more

hard and hatefull behauiour towards strangers:
14 For the *Sodomits* did not receiue those whom they knew
not when they came: but these brought friends into bondage,
that had well deserued of them.
15 And not onely so: but peraduenture some respect shall
be had of those, because they vsed strangers not friendly.
16 But these very grieuously afflicted them, whom they
had receiued with feastings, and were already made partakers
of the same lawes with them.
17 Therefore euen with blindnesse were these stricken, as
those were at the doores of the righteous man: when being
compassed about with horrible great darknesse, euery one
sought the passage of his owne doores.
18 For the elements were changed †in themselues by a kind
of harmonie, like as in a Psaltery notes change the name of
the tune, and yet are alwayes sounds, which may well be
perceiued by the sight of the things that haue beene done.
19 For earthly things were turned into watry, and the
things that before swamme in the water, now went vpon
the ground.
20 The fire had power in the water, forgetting his owne
vertue: and the water forgat his owne quenching nature.
21 On the other side, the flames wasted not the flesh of
the corruptible liuing things, though they walked therin,
neither melted they the ycie kind of heauenly meate, that
was of nature apt to melt.
22 For in all things, O Lord, thou didst magnifie thy
people, and glorifie them, neither didst thou lightly regard
them: but didst assist them in euery time and place.

† *Gre. by themselues.*

¶ THE WISDOME OF
Iesus the sonne of Sirach,
Or Ecclesiasticus.

A Prologue made by an vncertaine Authour.

Some referre this Prologue to Athanasius, because it is found in his Synopsis.

THis Iesus was the sonne of Sirach, and grand-childe to Iesus of the same name with him; This man therefore liued in the latter times, after the people had bene led away captiue, and called home againe, and almost after all the Prophets. Now his grandfather Iesus (as he himselfe witnesseth) was a man of great diligence and wisedome among the Hebrewes, who did not onely gather the graue and short Sentences of wise men, that had bene before him, but himselfe also vttered some of his owne, full of much vnderstanding and wisedome. When as therefore the first Iesus died, leauing this booke almost ||perfected, Sirach his sonne receiuing it after him, left it to his owne sonne Iesus, who hauing gotten it into his hands, compiled it all orderly into one Volume, and called it Wisdome, Intituling it, both by his owne name, his fathers name, and his grandfathers, alluring the hearer by the very name of Wisedome, to haue a greater loue to the studie of this Booke. It conteineth therefore wise Sayings, darke Sentences, and Parables, and certaine particular ancient godly stories of men that pleased God. Also his Prayer and Song. Moreouer, what benefits God had vouchsafed his people, and what plagues he had heaped vpon their enemies. This Iesus did imitate Solomon, and was no lesse famous for Wisedome, and learning, both being indeed a man of great learning, and so reputed also.

|| Or, collected.

¶ *The Prologue of the Wisdome of Jesus the sonne of Sirach.*

WHereas many and great things haue bene deliuered vnto vs by the Law and the Prophets, and by others that haue followed their steps, for the which things Israel ought to be commended for learning and Wisedome, and whereof not onely the Readers must needs become skilful themselues, but also they that desire to learne, be able to profit them which are ||without, both by speaking and writing: My grandfather Iesus, when he had much giuen himselfe to the reading of the Law, and the Prophets, and other Bookes of our fathers, and had gotten therein good iudgement, was drawen on also himselfe, to write something pertayning to learning and Wisedome, to the intent that those which are desirous to learne, and are addicted to these things, might profit much more in liuing according to the Law. Wherefore, let me intreat you to reade it with fauour and attention, and to pardon Vs, wherein wee may seeme to come short of some words which we haue laboured to interprete. For the same things vttered in Hebrew, and translated into an other tongue, haue not the same force in them: and not onely these things, but the Law it selfe, and the †Prophets, and the rest of the Bookes, haue no small ||difference, when they are spoken in their owne language. For in the eight and thirtieth yeere comming into Egypt, when Euergetes was King, and continuing there some time, I found a ||Booke of no small learning, therefore I thought it most necessary for mee, to bestow some diligence and trauaile to interprete it: Vsing great watchfulnesse, and skill in that space, to bring the Booke to an end, and set it foorth for them also, which in a strange countrey are willing to learne, being prepared before in maners to liue after the Law.

|| *Or, of an other nation.*

† *Greeke, prophecies.*

|| *Or, excellencie.*

|| *Or, helpe of learning.*

CHAP.

CHAP. I.

1 All wisedome is from God. 10 He giueth it to them that loue him. 12 The feare of God is full of many blessings. 28 To feare God without hypocrisie.

*1. Kings ALL *wisedome *commeth* from the Lord, and is with him
3. 9. for euer.
2 Who can number the sand of the sea, and the drops of
raine, and the dayes of eternity?
3 Who can finde out the height of heauen, and the breadth
of the earth, and the deepe, and wisedome?
4 Wisedome hath beene created before all things, and the
vnderstanding of prudence from euerlasting.
5 The word of God most high, is the fountaine of wisdome,
& her wayes are euerlasting commandements.
*Rom. 11. 6 *To whom hath the root of wisdome beene reuealed? or
34. who hath knowen her wise counsels?
7 [Vnto whom hath the knowledge of wisedome beene
made manifest? and who hath vnderstood her great experience?]
8 There is one wise and greatly to bee feared; the Lord
sitting vpon his Throne.
9 He created her, and saw her, and numbred her, and
powred her out vpon all his workes.
10 Shee [is] with all flesh according to his gift, and hee
hath giuen her to them that loue him.
11 The feare of the Lord is honour, and glory, and gladnesse, and a crowne of reioycing.
*Prou. 1. 12 *The feare of the Lord maketh a merrie heart, and
7. giueth ioy and gladnesse, and a long life.
psal. 110. 10 13 Who so feareth the Lord, it shall goe well with
||*Or, shalbe* him at the last, & he ||shall finde fauour in the day of his
blessed. death.
14 To feare the Lord, is the beginning of wisedome: and it
was created with the faithfull in the wombe.
15 Shee hath built an euerlasting foundation with men, and
*2. Chron. she shal continue *with their seede.
20. 21. 16 To feare the Lord, is fulnesse of wisedome, and filleth
men with her fruits.
17 Shee filleth all their house with

things desireable, and the garners with her increase.
18 The feare of the Lord is a crowne of wisedome, making
peace and perfect health to flourish, both which are the gifts
of God: and it enlargeth their reioycing that loue him.
19 Wisedome raineth downe skill and knowledge of vnderstanding, and exalteth them to honour that holde her fast.
20 The root of wisedome is to feare the Lord, and the
branches thereof are long life.
21 The feare of the Lord driueth away sinnes: and where
it is present, it turneth away wrath.
22 A furious man cannot ||be iustified, for the sway of his || *Or, escape punishment.*
fury shalbe his destruction.
23 A patient man will beare for a time, and afterward ioy
shall spring vp vnto him.
24 He wil hide his words for a time, and the lippes of many
shall declare his wisedome.
25 The parables of knowledge are in the treasures of wisedome: but godlines is an abomination to a sinner.
26 If thou desire wisedome, keepe the commaundements,
and the Lord shall giue her vnto thee.
27 For the feare of the Lord is wisdome, and instruction:
and faith and meekenesse are his delight.
28 ||Distrust not the feare of the Lord when thou art poore: || *Or, be not disobedient to.*
and come not vnto him with a double heart.
29 Be not an hypocrite in the sight of men, and take good
heede what thou speakest.
30 Exalt not thy selfe, lest thou fall, and bring dishonor
vpon thy soule, and so God discouer thy secrets, and cast
thee downe in the midst of the congregation, because thou
camest not in trueth, to the feare of the Lord: but thy heart
is full of deceit.

CHAP. II.

1 Gods seruants must looke for trouble, 7 and be patient, and trust in him. 12 For woe to them that doe not so. 15 But they that feare the Lord, will doe so.

MY sonne, if *thou come to serue the Lorde, prepare *Mat. 4. 11. 2. tim. 3. 12. 1. pet. 4. 12.
thy soule for temptation.
2 Set thy heart aright,
and

‖ *Or, haste* and constantly endure, and ‖ make not haste in time of trouble.
not. 3 Cleaue vnto him, and depart not away, that thou mayest
be increased at thy last end.
4 Whatsoeuer is brought vpon thee, take cheerefully, and
bee patient when thou art changed to a lowe estate.
* Wisd. 3. 5 * For gold is tried in the fire, and acceptable men in the
6 furnace of aduersitie.
pro. 17. 3. 6 Beleeue in him, and he will helpe thee, order thy way
aright, and trust in him.
7 Ye that feare the Lord, waite for his mercie, and goe not
aside, lest ye fall.
8 Yee that feare the Lord, beleeue him, and your reward
shall not faile.
9 Ye that feare the Lord, hope for good, and for euerlasting
ioy and mercy.
10 Looke at the generations of old, and see, did euer any
trust in the Lord, and was confounded? or did any abide in
his feare, & was forsaken? or whom did hee euer despise,
that called vpon him?
* Psal. 37. 11 For the * Lord is full of compassion, and mercie, long
25 suffering, and very pitifull, and forgiueth sinnes, and saueth
in time of affliction.
12 Woe be to fearefull hearts, and faint hands, and the
sinner that goeth two wayes.
13 Woe vnto him that is faint hearted, for he beleeueth
not, therefore shall he not be defended.
14 Woe vnto you that haue lost patience: and what will
ye doe when the Lord shall visite you?
* Ioh. 14. 15 They * that feare the Lord, will not disobey his word,
20 and they that loue him, will keepe his wayes.
16 They that feare the Lord, will seeke that which is well
pleasing vnto him, and they that loue him, shall bee filled
with the Law.
17 They that feare the Lord, will prepare their hearts, and
humble their soules in his sight:
18 *Saying*, We will fal into the hands of the Lord, and not
into the hands of men: for as his maiestie is, so is his mercie.

CHAP. III.

3 Children must honour, and helpe both their parents. 21 We may not desire to knowe all things 26 The incorrigible must needes perish. 30 Almes are rewarded.

HEare mee your father, O children, and doe thereafter,
that ye may be safe.
2 For the Lord hath giuen *the father honour ouer the *Exo. 20.
children, and hath confirmed the ||authoritie of the mother 6. deut. 5. 10.
ouer the sonnes. || *Or, iudge-*
3 Who so honoureth his father, maketh an atonement for *ment.*
his sinnes.
4 And he that honoureth his mother, is as one that layeth
vp treasure.
5 Who so honoureth his father, shal haue ioy of *his owne*
children, and when he maketh his prayer, hee shall bee heard.
6 He that honoureth his father, shal haue a long life, and
he that is obedient vnto the Lord, shall bee a comfort to his
mother.
7 He that feareth the Lord, will honour his father, and will
doe seruice vnto his parents, as to his masters.
8 *Honour thy father and mother, both in word and deed, *Exod. 20.
that a blessing may come vpon thee from them. 12. deut. 5. 10.
9 For the *blessing of the father establisheth the houses of *Gene. 27.
children, but the curse of the mother rooteth out foundations. 27. deu. 33.
10 Glory not in the dishonour of thy father, for thy fathers 1.
dishonour is no glory vnto thee.
11 For the glory of a man, is from the honour of his father,
and a mother in dishonour, is a reproch to the children.
12 My sonne, helpe thy father in his age, and grieue him
not as long as hee liueth.
13 And if his vnderstanding faile, haue patience with him,
and despise him not, when thou art ||in thy ful strength. || *Or, in all*
14 For the relieuing of thy father shall not be forgotten: *thine habi-*
and in stead of sinnes it shall be added to build thee vp. *litie.*
15 In the day of thine affliction it shall be remembred, thy
sinnes also shal melt away, as the yce in yͤ faire warme
weather.
16 He that forsaketh his father, is as a blasphemer, and he
that angreth his mother, is cursed of God.
17 My sonne, goe on with thy businesse in meekenesse, so
shalt thou be beloued of him that is approued.
18 *The greater thou art, the more humble thy selfe, and *Phil. 2. 3.
thou shalt find fauour before the Lord.
19 Many are in high place and of re-
nowne:

*Psal. 25. 9, 14. nowne: but *mysteries are reueiled vnto the meeke.

20 For the power of the Lord is great, and hee is honoured of the lowly.

*Prou. 25. 27. rom. 12. 3. 21 *Seeke not out the things that are too hard for thee, neither search the things that are aboue thy strength.

22 But what is commaunded thee, thinke thereupon with reuerence, for it is not needfull for thee, to see *with thine eyes*, the things that are in secret.

23 Be not curious in vnnecessarie matters: for moe things are shewed vnto thee, then men vnderstand.

24 For many are deceiued by their owne vaine opinion, and an euill suspition hath ouerthrowen their iudgement.

25 Without eyes thou shalt want light: professe not the knowledge therfore that thou hast not.

26 A stubborne heart shall fare euill at the last, and he that loueth danger shall perish therein.

27 An obstinate heart shall be laden with sorrowes, and the wicked man shall heape sinne vpon sinne.

|| *Or, the proud man is not healed by his punishment.* 28 ||In the punishment of the proud there is no remedie: for the plant of wickednesse hath taken roote in him.

29 The heart of the prudent will vnderstand a parable, and an attentiue eare is the desire of a wise man.

*Psal. 40. 2. dan. 4. 24. matth. 5. 7. 30 *Water will quench a flaming fire, and almes maketh an attonement for sinnes.

31 And hee that requiteth good turnes, is mindfull of that which may come heereafter: and when he falleth he shall find a stay.

CHAP. IIII.

1 We may not despise the poore or fatherlesse, 11 but seeke for Wisedome, 20 and not be ashamed of some things, nor gainsay the trueth, 30 nor be as lyons in our houses.

MY sonne, defraude not the poore of his liuing, and make not the needy eies to waite long.

2 Make not an hungry soule sorrowfull, neither prouoke a man in his distresse.

3 Adde not more trouble to an heart that is vexed, and deferre not to giue to him that is in neede.

4 Reiect not the supplication of the

afflicted, neither turne away thy face from a poore man.
5 Turne not away thine eye from ||the needy, and giue || *Or, him that asketh.*
him none occasion to curse thee:
6 For if he curse thee in the bitternesse of his soule, his
prayer shall be heard of him that made him.
7 Get thy selfe the loue of the congregation, and bow thy
head to a great man.
8 Let it not grieue thee to bowe downe thine eare to the
poore, and giue him a friendly answere with meekenesse.
9 Deliuer him that suffreth wrong, from the hand of the
oppressour, and be not faint hearted when thou sittest in
iudgement.
10 Be as a father vnto the fatherlesse, and in stead of a
husband vnto their mother, so shalt thou be as the sonne of
the most high, and he shall loue thee more then thy mother
doeth.
11 Wisedome exalteth her children, and layeth hold of
them that seeke her.
12 He that loueth her, loueth life, and they that seeke to
her earely, shall be filled with ioy.
13 He that holdeth her fast shall inherit glory, and wheresoeuer she entreth, the Lord will blesse.
14 They that serue her shall minister ||to the Holy one, || *Or, in the sanctuary.*
and them that loue her, the Lord doth loue.
15 Who so giueth eare vnto her, shall iudge the nations,
and he that attendeth vnto her, shall dwell securely.
16 If a man commit himselfe vnto her, he shall inherite
her, and his generation shall hold her in possession.
17 For at the first she will walke with him by crooked
wayes, and bring feare and dread vpon him, and torment
him with her discipline, vntill she may trust his soule, and
try him by her Lawes.
18 Then wil she returne the straight way vnto him, and
comfort him, and shew him her secrets.
19 But if he goe wrong, she will forsake him, and giue him
ouer to his owne ruine.
20 Obserue the opportunitie, and beware of euill, and be
not ashamed when it concerneth thy soule.
21 For *there* is a shame that bringeth sinne, and there is a
shame which is glorie and grace.

22 Accept

22 Accept no person against thy soule, and let not the
reuerence of any man cause thee to fall:

† *Greeke, in time of sauing.*

23 And refraine not to speake, † *when* there is *occasion to doe*
good, and hide not thy wisedome in her beautie.
24 For by speach wisedome shall be knowen, and learning
by the word of the tongue.
25 In no wise speake against the trueth, but be abashed of
the errour of thine ignorance.

‖ *Or, and striue not against the streame.*

26 Bee not ashamed to confesse thy sinnes, ‖and force not
the course of the riuer.
27 Make not thy selfe an vnderling to a foolish man, neither
accept the person of the mighty.
28 Striue for the trueth vnto death, and the Lord shall fight
for thee.
29 Be not hastie in thy tongue, and in thy deeds slacke and
remisse.
30 Bee not as a Lion in thy house, nor franticke among
thy seruants.
31 Let not thine hand bee stretched out to receiue, and
shut when thou shouldest ‖repay.

‖ *Or, giue.*

CHAP. V.

1 Wee must not presume of our wealth and strength, 6 Nor of the mercie of God to sinne. 9 We must not be double tongued, 12 Nor answere without knowledge.

* Luke 12. 15.

SEt not thy heart vpon thy goods, and say not, *I haue
ynough for my life.
2 Folow not thine owne minde, and thy strength, to walke
in the wayes of thy heart:
3 And say not, Who shall controll mee for my workes? for
the Lord will surely reuenge thy pride.
4 Say not, I haue sinned, and what harme hath happened
vnto mee? for the Lord is long-suffering, he wil in no wise
let thee goe.
5 Concerning propitiation, bee not without feare to adde
sinne vnto sinne.

* Ecclus. 21. 1.

6 And say not, His *mercy is great, hee will be pacified for
the multitude of my sinnes: for mercy and wrath come from
him, and his indignation resteth vpon sinners.

* Chap. 16. 13.

7 *Make no tarying to turne to the Lord, and put not off
from day to day: for suddenly shal the wrath of the Lord
come foorth, and in thy securitie thou shalt be destroyed,
and perish in the day of vengeance.

8 *Set not thy heart vpon goods vniustly gotten: for they *Pro. 10.
shall not profit thee in the day of calamitie. 2. and 11. 4.
9 Winnow not with euery winde, and goe not into euery ezek. 7. 19.
way: for so doth the sinner that hath a double tongue.
10 Be stedfast in thy vnderstanding, and let thy word be
the same.
11 *Be swift to heare, and let thy life be sincere, & with *Iam. 1.
patience giue answere. 19.
12 If thou hast vnderstanding, answer thy neighbour, if
not, lay thy hand vpon thy mouth.
13 Honour and shame is in talke; and the tongue of man
is his fall.
14 Be not called a whisperer, and lye not in wait with thy
tongue: for a foule shame is vpon the thiefe, and an euill
condemnation vpon the double tongue.
15 Be not ignorant of any thing, in a great matter or a
small.

CHAP. VI.

2 Doe not extoll thy owne conceit, 7 But make choise of a friend. 18 Seeke wisedome betimes: 20 It is grieuous to some, 28 yet the fruits thereof are pleasant. 35 Be ready to heare wise men.

IN stead of a friend, become not an enemie; for [thereby]
thou shalt inherite an ill name, shame, and reproch:
euen so shall a sinner that hath a double tongue.
2 Extoll not thy selfe in the counsell of thine owne heart,
that thy soule bee not torne in pieces as a bull [straying alone.]
3 Thou shalt eat vp thy leaues, and loose thy fruit, and
leaue thy selfe as a dry tree.
4 A wicked soule shall destroy him that hath it, and shall
make him to be laughed to scorne of his enemies.
5 †Sweet language will multiply friends: and a faire †*Greeke, a*
speaking tongue will increase kinde greetings. *sweet throat.*
6 Be in peace with many: neuerthelesse haue but one
counseller of a thousand.
7 If thou wouldst get a friend, ||proue him first, and be not ||*Or, get*
hasty to credit him. *him in the time of*
8 For some man is a friend for his owne occasion, and will *trouble.*
not abide in the day of thy trouble.
9 And there is a friend, who being turned to enmitie, and
strife, will discouer thy reproch.

10 Againe

*Cha. 37. 5. 10 *Againe some friend is a companion at the table, and
will not continue in the day of thy affliction.
11 But in thy prosperitie hee will be as thy selfe, and will
be bould ouer thy seruants.
12 If thou be brought low, he will be against thee, and
will hide himselfe from thy face.
13 Separate thy selfe from thine enemies, and take heed of
thy friends.
14 A faithfull friend is a strong defence: and hee that hath
found such an one, hath found a treasure.
15 Nothing doeth counteruaile a faithful friend, and his
excellencie is vnualuable.
16 A faithfull friend is the medicine of life, and they that
feare the Lord shal finde him.
17 Who so feareth the Lord shall direct his friendship
aright, for as he is, so shall his neighbour be also.
18 My sonne, gather instruction from thy youth vp: so
shalt thou finde wisedome till thine old age.
19 Come vnto her as one that ploweth, and soweth, and
wait for her good fruits, for thou shalt not toile much in
labouring about her, but thou shalt eat of her fruits right soone.
20 She is very vnpleasant to the vnlearned: he that is with-
‖Or, heart. out ‖vnderstanding, will not remaine with her.
*Zech. 12. 4. 21 She wil lye vpon him as a *mightie stone of triall, and
hee will cast her from him ere it be long.
22 For wisedome is according to her name, and she is not
manifest vnto many.
23 Giue eare, my sonne, receiue my aduice, and refuse not
my counsell,
24 And put thy feet into her fetters, and thy necke into
‖Or, coller. her ‖chaine.
*Mat. 11. 29. 25 Bow *downe thy shoulder, and beare her, and be not
grieued with her bonds.
26 Come vnto her with thy whole heart, and keepe her
wayes with all thy power.
27 Search and seeke, and shee shall bee made knowen vnto
thee, and when thou hast got hold of her, let her not goe.
28 For at the last thou shalt finde her rest, and that shalbe
turned to thy ioy.
29 Then shall her fetters be a strong defence for thee, and
her chaines a robe of glory.

30 For there is a golden ornament vpon her, and her bandes
are ||purple lace. || Or, a
31 Thou shalt put her on as a robe of honour: and shalt *ribband of blew silke,*
put her about thee as a crowne of ioy. *Numb.* 15.
32 My sonne, if thou wilt, thou shalt bee taught: and if 38.
thou wilt apply thy minde, thou shalt be prudent.
33 If thou loue to heare, thou shalt receiue vnderstanding:
and if thou bow thine eare, thou shalt be wise.
34 Stand in the multitude of the *elders, and cleaue vnto *Ecclus.
him that is wise. 8. 9
35 Be willing to heare euery godly discourse, and let not
the parables of vnderstanding escape thee.
36 And if thou seest a man of vnderstanding, get thee
betimes vnto him, and let thy foote weare the steps of his
doore.
37 Let thy minde be vpon the ordinances of the Lord, &
*meditate continually in his commandements: he shal estab- *Psal. 1. 2.
lish thine heart, and giue thee wisedome at thine owne desire.

CHAP. VII.

1 Wee are exhorted from sinne, 4 from ambition, 8 presumption, 10 and fainting in prayer: 12 from lying and backebiting, 18 and how to esteeme a friend: 19 A good wife: 20 a seruant: 22 our cattell: 23 our children and parents: 31 the Lord and his Priests: 32 the poore and those that mourne.

DOe no euill, so shall no harme come vnto thee.
2 Depart from the vniust, and iniquitie shall turne
away from thee.
3 My sonne, sow not vpon the furrowes of vnrighteousnesse,
and thou shalt not reape them seuen folde.
4 Seeke not of the Lord preheminence, neither of the King
the seate of honour.
5 *Iustifie not thy selfe before the Lord, and boast not of *Psal. 142.
thy wisedome before the king. 2. eccles. 7.
6 Seeke not to be iudge, being not able to take away 17. iob 9.
iniquitie, lest at any time thou feare the person of the 20. luke
mightie, and lay a stumbling blocke in the way of thy 18. 11.
vprightnesse.
7 Offend not against the multitude of a city, and then thou
shalt not cast thy selfe downe among the people.
8 Bind not one sinne vpon another,
for

for in one thou shalt not be vnpunished.

9 Say not, God wil looke vpon the multitude of my oblations, and when I offer to the most High God, he will accept it.

10 Be not faint hearted when thou makest thy prayer, and neglect not to giue almes.

11 Laugh no man to scorne in the bitternesse of his soule: for there is one which humbleth and exalteth.

† *Gre. plough not.* 12 †Deuise not a lie against thy brother: neither doe the like to thy friend.

13 Vse not to make any maner of lie: for the custome thereof is not good.

* Mat. 6. 5, 7 14 Vse not many words in a multitude of Elders, *and *make not* ||*much babbling* when thou prayest.

|| *Or, vaine repetition.* † *Gre. created.* 15 Hate not laborious worke, neither husbandrie, which the most High hath †ordeined.

16 Number not thy selfe among the multitude of sinners, but remember that wrath will not tary long.

17 Humble thy soule greatly: for the vengeance of the vngodly is fire and wormes.

18 Change not a friend for any good by no meanes: neither a faithfull brother for the gold of Ophir.

19 Forgoe not a wise and good woman: for her grace is aboue gold.

* Leuit. 19. 15. 20 *Whereas thy seruant worketh truely, entreate him not euill, nor the hireling that bestoweth himselfe wholly for thee.

21 Let thy soule loue a good seruant, and defraud him not of liberty.

* Deu. 25. 4 22 *Hast thou cattell? haue an eye to them, and if they be for thy profit, keepe them with thee.

23 Hast thou children? instruct them, and bow downe their necke from their youth.

24 Hast thou daughters? haue care of their body, and shewe not thy selfe cheerefull toward them.

25 Marrie thy daughter, and so shalt thou haue performed a weightie matter: but giue her to a man of vnderstanding.

26 Hast thou a wife after thy minde? forsake her not, but giue not thy selfe ouer to a ||light woman.

|| *Or, hateful*

27 Honour thy father with thy whole heart, and forget not the sorrowes of thy mother.

28 Remember that thou wast begot of them, and how canst thou recom-

pense them the things that they haue done for thee?
29 Feare the Lord with all thy soule, and reuerence his
priests.
30 Loue him that made thee with all thy strength, and
forsake not his ministers.
31 Feare the Lord, and honour the priest: and giue him
his portion, as it is commanded thee, the first fruits, and the
trespasse offering, & the gift of the shoulders, and the sacrifice
of sanctification, and the first fruits of the holy things.
32 *And stretch thine hand vnto the poore, that thy
||*blessing* may be perfected
33 A gift hath grace in the sight of euery man liuing, and
for the dead deteine it not.
34 Faile not to bee with them that weepe, and mourne
with them that mourne.
35 Be not slow to visit the sicke: for that shall make thee
to be beloued.
36 Whatsoeuer thou takest in hand, remember the end, and
thou shalt neuer doe amisse.

*Deut. 15. 10.
|| *Or, thy liberality.*

CHAP. VIII.

1 Whom we may not striue with, 8 nor despise, 10 nor prouoke, 15 nor haue to doe with.

STriue not with a mighty man, lest thou fall into his hands.
2 Bee not at variance with a rich man, lest he ouerweigh
thee: for gold *hath destroyed many, and peruerted the
hearts of kings.
3 Striue not with a man that is ||full of tongue, and heape
not wood vpon his fire.
4 Iest not with a rude man, lest thy ancestours be disgraced.
5 Reproch not a man that turneth from sinne, but remember
that we are all worthy *of punishment.
6 *Dishonour not a man in his old age: for euen some of
vs waxe old.
7 Reioice not ouer thy greatest enemie being dead, but
remember that we die all.
8 *Despise not the discourse* of the wise, but acquaint thy selfe
with their prouerbs; for of them thou shalt learne instruction,
& how to serue great men with ease.
9 Misse not the discourse of the Elders: for they also
learned of their fathers, and of them thou shalt learne vnderstanding, and to giue answere as need requireth.

*Mat. 5. 25. chap. 31. 6
|| *Or, of an euill tongue.*
*Gal. 6. 2. 1. cor. 2. 6.
*Leuit. 19. 32.

10 Kindle

10 Kindle not the coales of a sinner, lest thou be burnt
with the flame of his fire.
11 Rise not vp (in anger) at the presence of an iniurious
|| Or, for thy mouth. person, least he lie in waite to ||entrap thee in thy words.
12 Lend not vnto him that is mightier then thy selfe; for
if thou lendest him, count it but lost.
13 Be not surety aboue thy power: for if thou be surety,
take care to pay it.
14 Goe not to law with a iudge, for they will iudge for
|| Or, opinion. him according to his ||honour.
* Gene. 4. 8. 15 *Trauaile not by the way with a bold fellow, least he
become grieuous vnto thee: for he will doe according to his
owne will, and thou shalt perish with him through his folly.
* Prou. 22. 24. 16 *Striue not with an angry man, and goe not with him
into a solitary place: for blood is as nothing in his sight, and
where there is no helpe, he will ouerthrow thee.
17 Consult not with a foole; for he cannot keepe counsell.
18 Doe no secret thing before a stranger, for thou knowest
not what he will bring forth.
19 Open not thine heart to euery man, least he requite
thee with a shrewd turne.

CHAP. IX.

1 We are aduised how to vse our wiues. 3 What women to auoide. 10 And not to change an old friend. 13 Not to be familiar with men in authority, 14 But to knowe our neighbours, 15 And to conuerse with wise men.

BE not iealous ouer the wife of thy bosome, and teach
her not an euil lesson against thy selfe.
2 Giue not thy soule vnto a woman, to set her foot vpon
thy substance.
3 Meete not with an harlot, least thou fall into her
snares.
|| Or, playeth vpon instruments. 4 Vse not much the companie of a woman that ||is a singer,
least thou be taken with her attempts.
5 Gaze not on a maide, that thou fall not by those things,
that are pretious in her.
6 Giue not thy soule vnto harlots, that thou loose not thine
inheritance.
7 Looke not round about thee, in the streets of the citie,
neither wander

thou in the solitary places thereof.
8 *Turne away thine eye from a beautifull woman, and *Gen. 34. 22. 2. sam. 11. 2. iudg. 10. 17.
looke not vpon anothers beautie: for many haue beene
deceiued by the beautie of a woman, for heerewith loue is
kindled as a fire.
9 Sit not at all with another mans wife, nor sit downe with
her in thine armes, and spend not thy money with her at
the wine, least thine heart incline vnto her, and so thorough
thy desire thou fall into destruction.
10 Forsake not an old friend, for the new is not comparable
to him: a new friend is as new wine: when it is old, thou
shalt drinke it with pleasure.
11 Enuy not the glory of a sinner: for thou knowest not
what shall be his end.
12 Delight not in the thing that the vngodly haue pleasure
in, but remember they shall not goe vnpunished vnto their
graue.
13 Keepe thee farre from the man that hath power to kill,
so shalt thou not doubt the feare of death: and if thou come
vnto him, make no fault, least he take away thy life pre-
sently: remember that thou goest in the midst of snares, and
that thou walkest vpon the battlements of the citie.
14 As neere as thou canst, ghesse at thy neighbour, and
consult with the wise.
15 Let thy talke be with the wise, and all thy communica-
tion in the law of the most High.
16 And let iust men eate and drinke with thee, and let thy
glorying be in the feare of the Lord.
17 For the hand of the artificer, the worke shall be commended: and the wise ruler of the people, for his speech.
18 A man of an ill tongue is dangerous in his citie, and he
that is rash in his talke shall be hated.

CHAP. X.

1 The commodities of a wise ruler. 4 God setteth him vp. 7 The inconueniences of pride, iniustice, and couetousnesse. 14 What God hath done to the proud. 19 Who shall be honored, 29 And who not.

A Wise iudge will instruct his people, & the gouernement
of a prudent man is well ordered.
2 *As the iudge of the people is himselfe, so are his officers, *Prou. 29. 12.
and what maner of man the ruler of

the

the citie is, such are all they that dwell therein.
3 An vnwise king destroyeth his people, but through the prudence of them which are in authoritie, the citie shalbe inhabited.
4 The power of the earth is in the hand of the Lord, and in due time hee will set ouer it one that is profitable.
5 In the hand of God is the prosperitie of man: and vpon
‖ *Or, face.* the ‖person of the scribe shall he lay his honour.
* Leuit. 19. 17. 6 Beare not hatred to thy neighbour for * euery wrong, and
do nothing at all by iniurious practises.
7 Pride is hatefull before God, and man: and by both doeth one commit iniquitie.
8 Because of vnrighteous dealings, iniuries, and riches got by deceit, the kingdome is translated from one people to another.
9 Why is earth and ashes proude? There is not a more wicked thing, then a couetous man: for such an one setteth his owne soule to sale, because while he liueth, he casteth away his bowels.
10 The Phisition cutteth off a long disease, and he that is to day a King, to morrow shall die.
11 For when a man is dead, hee shall inherite creeping things, beastes and wormes.
12 The beginning of pride is, when one departeth from God, and his heart is turned away from his maker.
13 For pride is the beginning of sinne, and hee that hath it, shall powre out abomination: and therefore the Lord brought vpon them strange calamities, and ouerthrew them vtterly.
14 The Lord hath cast downe the thrones of proud Princes, and set vp the meeke in their stead.
15 The Lord hath plucked vp the rootes of the proud nations: and planted the lowly in their place.
16 The Lord ouerthrew countreys of the heathen: and destroyed them to the foundations of the earth.
17 He tooke some of them away, and destroyed them, and hath made their memoriall to cease from the earth.
18 Pride was not made for men, nor furious anger for them that are borne of a woman.
19 They that feare the Lord are a sure seed, and they that loue him, an honourable plant: they that regard not

the Law, are a dishonourable seed, they that transgresse the
commandements, are a ||deceiuable seed. || *Or, vnstable generation.*
20 Among brethren he that is chiefe is honourable, so are
they that feare the Lord in his eyes.
21 The feare of the Lord goeth before ||the obtayning of || *Or, principalitie.*
authoritie: but roughnesse and pride, is the loosing thereof.
22 Whether hee bee rich, noble, or poore, their glorie is
the feare of the Lord.
23 It is not meet to despise the poore man that hath vnderstanding, neither is it conuenient to magnifie a sinnefull man.
24 Great men, and Iudges, and Potentates shall bee
honoured, yet is there none of them greater then he that
feareth the Lord.
25 Vnto the seruant that is wise, shall they that are free
doe seruice: and hee that hath knowledge, *will not grudge *Pro. 17. 2.
when he is reformed. 2. Sam. 12. 13.
26 Be not ouerwise in doing thy busines, and boast not thy
selfe in the time of thy distresse.
27 Better is he that laboureth and aboundeth in all things,
then hee that boasteth himselfe, and wanteth *bread. *Pro. 12. 9.
28 My sonne, glorifie thy soule in meekenesse, and giue it
honour according to the dignitie thereof.
29 Who wil iustifie him that sinneth against his owne
soule? and who will honour him that dishonoureth his
owne life?
30 The poore man is honoured for his skill, and the rich
man is honoured for his riches.
31 Hee that is honoured in pouertie, how much more in
riches? And he that is dishonourable in riches, how much
more in pouertie?

CHAP. XI.

4 Wee may not vaunt or set foorth our selues, 8 Nor answere rashly, 10 Nor meddle with many matters. 14 Wealth and all things else, are from God. 14 Bragge not of thy wealth, 29 Nor bring euery man into thy house.

WIsedome lifteth vp the head ||of him that is of low || *Or, of the lowly.*
degree, and *maketh him to sit among great men. *Gen. 40. 40. dan. 6. 3.
2 Commend not a man
for

for his beautie, neither abhorre a man for his outward
appearance.
3 The Bee is little among such as flie, but her fruite is
the chiefe of sweete things.
*Act. 12. 4 *Boast not of thy cloathing and raiment, and exalt not
21 thy selfe in the day of honour: for the workes of the Lord
are wonderfull, and his workes among men are hidden.
†*Gr. ty-* 5 Many †kings haue sit downe vpon the ground, and one
rants. that was neuer thought of, hath worne the crowne.
*1. Kin. 6 *Many mightie men haue beene greatly disgraced: and
15. 28. the honourable deliuered into other mens hands.
hest. 6. 10. *Deut. 12. 7 *Blame not before thou hast examined the trueth: vnder-
24. stand first, and then rebuke.
*Pro. 8. 8 *Answere not, before thou hast heard the cause: neither
13. interrupt men in the midst of their talke.
9 Striue not in a matter that concerneth thee not: and sit
‖ *Or, in the* not ‖in iudgement with sinners.
iudgement of sinners. 10 My sonne, meddle not with many matters: for if thou
meddle much, thou shalt not be innocent: and if thou follow
‖ *Or, escape* after, thou shalt not obtaine, neither shalt thou ‖escape by
hurt. flying.
*Mat. 19. 11 *There is one that laboureth and taketh paines, and
12. 1. tim. maketh haste, and is so much the more behinde.
6. 9. prou. 10. 13. 12 Againe, there is another that is slow, and hath neede of
*Iob 1. 12. helpe, wanting abilitie, and full of pouertie, *yet the eye of
ezek. 28. 4. the Lord looked vpon him for good, and set him vp from his
low estate,
13 And lifted vp his head from miserie, so that many that
saw it, marueiled at him.
14 Prosperitie and aduersitie, life and death, pouerty and
riches, come of the Lord.
15 Wisedome, knowledge, and vnderstanding of the Lawe,
are of the Lord: loue, & the way of good workes, are from
him.
16 Errour and darkenesse had their beginning together with
sinners: and euill shall waxe old with them that glory therein.
17 The gift of the Lord remaineth with the godly, and
his fauour bringeth prosperitie for euer.
18 There is that waxeth rich by his warinesse, and pinching,
and this is the portion of his reward:
*Luke 12. 19. 19 Whereas he sayth, *I haue found

rest, and now will eate continually of my goods, and *yet* hee
knoweth not what time shall ||come vpon him, and that hee || *Or, passe.*
must leaue those things to others, and die.
20 Be *stedfast in thy couenant, and be conuersant therein, *Matt. 10. 22.
and waxe olde in thy worke.
21 Marueile not at the workes of sinners, but trust in the
Lord, and abide in thy labour: for it is an easie thing in the
sight of the Lord, on the sudden to make a poore man rich.
22 The blessing of the Lord is ||in the reward of the godly, || *Or, for a reward.*
and suddenly he maketh his blessing to flourish.
23 Say not, *What profit is there of my seruice? and what *Mal. 3. 14.
good things shal I haue hereafter?
24 Againe, say not, I haue enough, and possesse many
things; and what euill can come to me hereafter?
25 In the day of prosperitie, there is a forgetfulnesse of
affliction: and in the day of affliction, there is no remembrance of prosperitie.
26 For it is an easie thing vnto the Lord in the day of death,
to reward a man according to his wayes.
27 The affliction of an houre, maketh a man forget pleasure: and in his end, his deeds shalbe discouered.
28 Iudge none blessed before his death: for a man shall bee
knowen in his children.
29 Bring not euery man into thine house, for the deceitfull
man hath many traines.
30 Like as a Partrich taken [and kept] in a cage, so is the
heart of the proud; aud like as a spie, watcheth hee for thy
fall.
31 For hee lieth in wait, and turneth good into euill, and
in things worthy praise, will lay blame vpon thee.
32 Of a sparke of fire, a heape of coales is kindled: and a
sinnefull man layeth waite for blood.
33 Take heed of a mischieuous man, (for hee worketh wickednesse) lest hee bring vpon thee a perpetuall blot.
34 Receiue a stranger into thine house, and hee will disturbe
thee, and turne thee out of thine owne.

CHAP. XII.

2 Be not liberall to the vngodly. 10 Trust not thine enemie, nor the wicked.

WHen thou wilt doe good, know to whō thou
doest it, so shalt thou be thanked for thy bene-
fites.
2 Do good to the godly man, and thou shalt find a recompence, and if not from him, yet from the most High.
3 There can no good come to him that is alwayes occupied
in euill: nor to him that giueth no almes.
4 Giue to the godly man, and helpe not a sinner.
5 Doe well vnto him that is lowly, but giue not to the
vngodly: hold backe thy bread, and giue it not vnto him, lest
he ouermaster thee thereby. For [else] thou shalt receiue
twice as much euill, for all the good thou shalt haue done
vnto him.
6 For the most High hateth sinners, and will repay vengeance vnto the vngodly, and keepeth them against the mightie
day of their punishment.
7 Giue vnto the good, and helpe not the sinner.
8 A friend cannot be knowen in prosperitie, and an enemy
cannot be hidden in aduersitie.
9 In the prosperitie of a man, enemies will be grieued, but
in his aduersitie, euen a friend will depart.
|| *Or, brasse.* 10 Neuer trust thine enemie: for like as ||yron rusteth, so
is his wickednesse.
11 Though he humble himselfe, and goe crouching, yet
take good heed, and beware of him, and thou shalt bee
vnto him, as if thou hadst wiped a looking glasse, and thou
shalt knowe that his rust hath not beene altogether wiped
away.
12 Set him not by thee, lest when he hath ouerthrowen
thee, he stand vp in thy place, neither let him sit at thy
right hand, lest he seeke to take thy seat, and thou at the
last remember my wordes, and be pricked therewith.
13 Who will pitie a charmer that is bitten with a serpent,
or any such as come nigh wilde beasts?
|| *Or, mingled.* 14 So one that goeth to a sinner, and is ||defiled with him
in his sinnes, who will pitie?
15 For a while hee will abide with thee, but if thou begin
to fall, he wil not tarie.
* Ier. 41. 6. 16 An enemie speaketh sweetly with *his lippes, but in
his heart he imagineth how to throw thee into a pit: hee

will weepe with his eyes, but if he find opportunitie, hee
will not be satisfied with blood.
17 If aduersitie come vpon thee, thou shalt find him there
first, & though he pretend to helpe thee, yet shal he ||vnder- || *Or, sup-*
mine thee. *plant.*
18 He will shake his head and clap his handes, and whisper
much, and change his countenance.

CHAP. XIII.

1 Keepe not companie with the proude, or a mightier then thy selfe. 15 Like will to like. 21 The difference betweene the rich and the poore. 25 A mans heart will change his countenance.

HE that toucheth pitch, shal be defiled therewith, and
*hee that hath fellowship with a proude man, shall *Deu. 7.
be like vnto him. 2.
2 Burthen not thy selfe aboue thy power, while thou liuest,
and haue no fellowship with one that is mightier, and richer
then thy selfe. For how agree the kettle and the earthen
pot together? †for if the one be smitten against the other, †*Gre. this*
it shall be broken. *shal smite against it, and be broken.*
3 The rich man hath done wrong, and yet he threatneth
withall: the poore is wronged, and he must intreat also.
4 If thou be for his profit, he will vse thee: but if thou
haue nothing, he will forsake thee.
5 If thou haue any thing, he will liue with thee, yea he will
make thee bare, and will not be sorie for it.
6 If he haue need of thee, hee will deceiue thee, and smile
vpon thee, and put thee in hope, he will speake thee faire,
and say, What wantest thou?
7 And hee will shame thee by his meates, vntill he haue
drawen thee drie twice or thrice, and at the last hee will
laugh thee to scorne: afterward when he seeth thee, he will
forsake thee, and shake his head at thee.
8 Beware that thou bee not deceiued, and brought downe
||in thy iolitie. || *Or, by thy simplicitie.*
9 If thou be inuited of a mighty man, withdraw thy selfe,
and so much the more will he inuite thee.
10 Presse thou not vpon him, lest thou be put backe, stand
not farre off, lest thou be forgotten.
11 ||Affect not to be made equall vnto him in talke, ||and || *Or, forbeare not.*
beleeue not his many words: for with much communication || *Or, but.*
will

will he tempt thee, and smiling vpon thee will get out thy secrets.

12 But cruelly he will lay vp thy words, and will not spare to doe thee hurt, and to put thee in prison.

13 Obserue and take good heed, for thou walkest in peril of thy ouerthrowing: when thou hearest these things, awake in thy sleepe.

14 Loue the Lord all thy life, and call vpon him for thy saluation.

15 Euery beast loueth his like, and euery man loueth his neighbour.

16 All flesh consorteth according to kind, and a man will cleaue to his like:

17 What fellowship hath the wolfe with the lambe? so the sinner with the godly.

18 What agreement is there betweene the Hyena and a dogge? and what peace betweene the rich and the poore?

19 As the wilde asse is the lyons pray in the wildernesse: so the rich eate vp the poore.

20 As the proud hate humilitie: so doth the rich abhorre the poore.

21 A rich man beginning to fall, is held vp of his friends: but a poore man being downe, is thrust also away by his friends.

22 When a rich man is fallen, he hath many helpers: he speaketh things not to be spoken, and yet men iustifie him: the poore man slipt, and yet they rebuked him too: he spake wisely, and could haue no place.

23 When a rich man speaketh, euery man holdeth his tongue, and looke what hee sayeth, they extoll it to the clouds: but if the poore man speake, they say, What fellow is this? and if he stumble, they will helpe to ouerthrowe him.

24 Riches are good vnto him that hath no sinne, and pouerty is euill in the mouth of the vngodly.

25 The heart of a man changeth his countenance, whether it be for good or euill: and a merry heart maketh a cheerefull countenance.

26 A cheerefull countenance is a token of a heart that is in prosperity, and the finding out of parables, is a wearisome labour of the minde.

CHAP. XIIII.

1 A good conscience maketh men happie. 5 The niggard doth good to none. 13 But

doe thou good. 10 Men are happy that draw neere to wisedome.

B*Lessed is the man that hath not slipt with his *Chap. 19. 16. and 25. 8. iam. 3. 2.
mouth, and is not pricked with the ||multitude of
sinnes. || Or, sorrow.
2 Blessed is hee whose conscience hath not condemned him,
and who is not fallen from his hope in the Lord.
3 Riches are not comely for a niggard: and what should
an enuious man doe with money?
4 He that gathereth by defrauding his owne soule, gathereth
for others, that shall spend his goods riotously.
5 Hee that is euill to himselfe, to whom will he be good?
he shall not take pleasure in his goods.
6 There is none worse then he that enuieth himselfe; and
this is a recompence of his wickednesse.
7 And if he doth good, he doth it vnwillingly, and at the
last he will declare his wickednesse.
8 The enuious man hath a wicked eye, he turneth away
his face and despiseth men.
9 A *couetous mans eye is not satisfied with his portion, *Prou. 17. 20.
and the iniquity of the wicked dryeth vp his soule.
10 A wicked eye enuieth [his] bread, and he is a niggard
at his table.
11 My sonne, according to thy habilitie doe good to thy
selfe, and giue the Lord his due offering.
12 Remember that death will not be long in comming,
and that the couenant of the graue is not shewed vnto
thee.
13 *Doe good vnto thy friend before thou die, and ac- *Tobit. 4. 7. luc. 14. 13.
cording to thy abilitie, stretch out thy hand and giue to
him. || Or, the feast day.
14 Defraud not thy selfe of ||the good day, and let not the
part of a good desire ouerpasse thee.
15 Shalt thou not leaue thy trauailes vnto another? and
thy labours to be diuided by lot?
16 Giue, and take, and sanctifie thy soule, for there is no
seeking of dainties in the graue.
17 *All flesh waxeth old as a garment: for the couenant *Isai. 40. 5. iam. 1. 10. 1. pet. 1. 24.
from the beginning is; thou shalt die the death.
18 As of the greene leaues on a thicke tree, some fall, and
some grow; so is the generation of flesh and blood, one com-

Ssss 2 meth

meth to an end, and another is borne.
19 Euery worke rotteth and consumeth away, and the
worker therof shal goe withall.
*Psal. 1. 2. 20 *Blessed is the man that doeth meditate good things in
wisdome, and that reasoneth of holy things by his vnderstanding.
21 He that considereth her wayes in his heart, shall also
haue vnderstanding in her secrets.
22 Goe after her as one that traceth, and lie in wait in her
wayes.
23 Hee that prieth in at her windowes, shal also hearken
at her doores.
24 Hee that doeth lodge neere her house, shall also fasten
‖ *Or, stake.* a ‖pin in her walles.
25 He shall pitch his tent nigh vnto her, and shall lodge in
a lodging where good things are.
26 He shal set his children vnder her shelter, and shall
lodge vnder her branches.
27 By her he shall be couered from heat, and in her glory
shall he dwell.

CHAP. XV.

2 Wisedome embraceth those that feare God. 7 The wicked shall not get her. 11 We may not charge God with our faults: 14 For he made, and left vs to our selues.

HE that feareth the Lord will doe good, and he that
hath the knowledge of the Law shal obtaine her.
2 And as a mother shall she meet him, and receiue him as
a wife maried of a virgin.
3 With the bread of vnderstanding shall she feed him, and
giue him the water of wisedome to drinke.
4 Hee shall be stayed vpon her, and shall not be moued,
and shall rely vpon her, and shall not be confounded.
5 Shee shall exalt him aboue his neighbours, and in the
midst of the congregation shall she open his mouth.
6 He shall finde ioy, and a crowne of gladnesse, and she
shall cause him to inherit an euerlasting name.
7 But foolish men shall not attaine vnto her, and sinners
shall not see her.
‖ *Or, a parable.* 8 For she is farre from pride, and men that are liers cannot
remember her.
‖ *Or, he was not sent of, &c.* 9 ‖Praise is not seemly in the mouth of a sinner, for ‖it was
not sent him of the Lord:

10 For ||praise shalbe vttered in wisdome, and the Lord wil || *Or, rather a parable.*
prosper it.
11 Say not thou, It is through the Lord, that I fell away,
for thou oughtest not to doe the things that he hateth.
12 Say not thou, He hath caused mee to erre, for hee hath
no need of the sinfull man.
13 The Lord hateth all abomination, and they that feare
God loue it not.
14 Hee himselfe made man from the *beginning, and left *Gene. 1. 20.
him in the hand of his counsell,
15 If thou wilt, to keepe the Commandements, and to
performe acceptable faithfulnesse.
16 He hath set fire and water before thee: stretch forth
thy hand vnto whether thou wilt.
17 *Before man is life and death, and whether him liketh *Iere. 21. 8.
shalbe giuen him.
18 For the wisedome of the Lord is great, and he is mighty
in power, and beholdeth all things,
19 And *his eyes are vpon them that feare him, & hee *Psal. 33. 16.
knoweth euery worke of man.
20 Hee hath commanded no man to do wickedly, neither
hath he giuen any man license to sinne.

CHAP. XVI.

1 It is better to haue none then many lewd children. 6 The wicked are not spared for their number. 12 Both the wrath and the mercy of the Lord are great. 17 The wicked cannot be hid. 20 Gods workes are vnsearchable.

DEsire not a multitude of vnprofitable children, neither
delight in vngodly sonnes.
2 Though they multiply, reioyce not in them, except the
feare of the Lord be with them.
3 Trust not thou in their life, neither respect their multitude:
for one that is iust, is better then a thousand, and better it is
to die without children, then to haue them that are vngodly.
4 For by one that hath vnderstanding, shall the city be
replenished, but the ||kindred of the wicked, shall speedily || *Or, tribe.*
become desolate.
5 Many such things haue I seene with mine eyes, and mine
eare hath heard greater things then these.
6 *In the congregation of the vngodly, shall a fire be kindled, *Chap. 21. 10.
and in a rebellious nation, wrath ||is set on fire. || *Or, hath bene.*

7 He

* Gen. 6. 4. 7 * Hee was not pacified towards the olde giants, who fell
away in the strength of their foolishnesse.
* Gen. 19. 8 * Neither spared he the place where Lot soiourned, but
24. abhorred them for their pride.
9 Hee pitied not the people of perdition, who were taken
away in their sinnes.
* Num. 14. 10 * Nor the sixe hundreth thousand footmen, who were
15. and 16. gathered together in the hardnesse of their hearts.
20. and 20. 51. 11 And if there be one stiffe-necked among the people, it
* Chap. 5. is marueile, if he escape vnpunished; for * mercy and wrath
6. are with him, hee is mighty to forgiue, and to powre out
displeasure.
12 As his mercy is great, so is his correction also: he
iudgeth a man according to his workes.
13 The sinner shall not escape with his spoiles, and the
patience of the godly shall not be frustrate.
14 Make way for euery worke of mercy: for euery man
shall finde according to his workes.
15 The Lord hardened Pharaoh, that hee should not know
him, that his powerfull workes might be knowen to the
world.
16 His mercy is manifest to euery creature, and hee hath
|| *Or, strong* separated his light from the darkenesse with an || Adamant.
partition. 17 Say not thou, I will hide my selfe from the Lord: shall
any remember me from aboue? I shall not be remembred
among so many people: for what is my soule among such
an infinite number of creatures?
* 1. King. 18 * Behold, the heauen, and the heauen of heauens, the
8. 27. 2. chron. deepe and the earth, and all that therein is, shall be mooued
6. 18. when he shall visit.
2. pet. 3. 10. 19 The mountaines also, and foundations of the earth shall
bee shaken with trembling, when the Lord looketh vpon
them.
20 No heart can thinke vpon these things worthily: and
who is able to conceiue his wayes?
21 It is a tempest, which no man can see: for the most
part of his workes are hidde.
22 Who can declare the workes of his iustice? or who can
endure them? for his Couenant is afarre off, and the triall
of all things is in the ende.
23 He that wanteth vnderstanding,

will thinke vpon vaine things: and a foolish man erring,
imagineth follies.
24 My sonne, hearken vnto mee, and learne knowledge,
and marke my words with thy heart.
25 I will shewe foorth doctrine in weight, and declare his
knowledge exactly.
26 The works of the Lord are done in iudgement from the
beginning: and from the time he made them, hee disposed
the parts thereof.
27 Hee garnished his workes for euer, and in his hand are
the ||chiefe of them vnto all generations: they neither labour, || *Or, beginnings.*
nor are weary, nor cease from their workes.
28 None of them hindreth another, and they shall neuer
disobey his word.
29 After this, the Lord looked vpon the earth, and filled it
with his blessings.
30 With all maner of liuing things hath hee couered the
face thereof, and they shall returne into it againe.

CHAP. XVII.

1 How God created and furnished man. 14 Auoid all sinne: 19 For
God seeth all things. 25 Turne to him while thou liuest.

THe Lord *created man of the earth, and turned him *Gen. 1. 27 and 5. 2. wisd. 2. 23. and 7. 1, 6. 1. cor. 11. 7. col. 3. 10.
into it againe.
2 *He gaue them few dayes, and a short time, and power
also ouer the things therein.
3 He endued them with strength by themselues, and made
them according to his image, *Gen. 1. 26. 1. cor. 11. 7.
4 And put the feare ||of man vpon all flesh, and gaue him
dominion ouer beasts and foules.
5 [They receiued the vse of the fiue operations of the || *Or, of him.*
Lord, and in the sixt place he imparted them vnderstanding, and in the seuenth, speech, an interpreter of
the cogitations thereof.]
6 Counsell, and a tongue, and eyes, eares, and a heart, gaue
he them to vnderstand.
7 Withall, hee filled them with the knowledge of vnderstanding, & shewed them good and euill.
8 Hee set his eye vpon their hearts, that he might shew
them the greatnesse of his workes.
9 He gaue them to glory in his marueilous actes for euer,
that they might declare his works with vnderstanding.

10 And the elect shall praise his holy Name.
11 Beside this he gaue them knowledge, and the law of life
for an heritage.
12 He made an euerlasting couenant with them, and shewed
them his iudgements.
13 Their eyes saw the maiestie of his glory, and their eares
heard his glorious voyce.
14 And he said vnto them, Beware of all vnrighteousnes,
*Exod. 20. 16. &. 22. 23.
and he *gaue euery man commandement concerning his
neighbour,
15 Their wayes are euer before him, and shall not be hid
from his eyes.
16 Euery man from his youth is giuen to euill, neither could
they make to themselues fleshie hearts for stonie.
17 For in the diuision of the nations of the whole earth,
*Deu. 32. 8. rom. 13. 1.
he set a *ruler ouer euery people, but *Israel is the Lords
portion.
*Deu. 4. 20 and 10. 15.
18 Whom being his first borne, hee nourisheth with discipline, and giuing him the light of his loue, doth not forsake
him.
19 Therefore all their workes are as the Sunne before him,
and his eyes are continually vpon their wayes.
20 None of their vnrighteous deeds are hid from him, but
all their sinnes are before the Lord:
21 But the Lord being gracious, and knowing his workemanship, neither left nor forsooke them, but spared them.
*Cha. 29. 13
22 The *almes of a man is as a signet with him, and he
will keep the good deedes of man, as the apple of the eye,
and giue repentance to his sonnes and daughters.
*Mat. 25. 35.
23 *Afterward he will rise vp and reward them, and render
their recompense vpon their heads.
*Acts 3. 19
24 *But vnto them that repent, he granted them returne,
and comforted those that faile in patience.
*Iere. 3. 12
25 *Returne vnto the Lord, and forsake thy sinnes, make
thy prayer before his face, and ||offend lesse.
|| *Or, lessen thy offence.*
26 Turne againe to the most High, and turne away from
iniquitie: for he will leade thee out of darkenesse into the
|| *Or, illumination.*
||light of health, and hate thou abomination vehemently.
*Psal. 6. 6. isa. 38. 19.
27 *Who shall praise the most High in the graue, in stead
of them which liue and giue thanks?
28 Thankesgiuing perisheth from

the dead, as from one that is not: the liuing and sound in
heart, shall praise the Lord.
29 How great is the louing kindnes of the Lord our God,
and his compassion vnto such as turne vnto him in holinesse?
30 For all things cannot bee in men, because ẏͤ sonne of
man is not immortal.
31 *What is brighter then the Sun? yet the light thereof *Iob 25. 4, 5.
faileth: and flesh and blood will imagine euill.
32 Hee vieweth the power of the height of heauen, and all
men are but earth and ashes.

CHAP. XVIII.

4 Gods workes are to be wondred at. 9 Mans life is short. 11 God is mercifull. 15 Doe not blemish thy good deeds with ill wordes. 22 Deferre not to bee iustified. 30 Followe not thy lustes.

HEe that liueth for euer, *created all things in generall. *Gen. 1.1.
2 The Lord onely is righteous, and there is none
other but he.
3 Who gouerneth the world with the palme of his hand,
and all things obey his will, for he is the king of all, by his
power *diuiding holy things among them from prophane. *Leuit. 10. 6.
4 To whom hath he giuen power to declare his works?
*and who shall finde out his noble actes? *Psal. 105.
5 Who shall number the strength of his maiestie? and who
shall also tel out his mercies?
6 As for the wonderous workes of the Lord, there may
nothing bee taken from them, neither may any thing bee put
vnto them, neither can the ground of them be found out.
7 When a man hath done, then he beginneth, and when
hee leaueth off, then he shall be doubtfull.
8 What is man, and whereto serueth he? what is his good,
& what is his euil?
9 *The number of a mans dayes at the most are an hundred *Psal. 90. 10
yeeres.
10 As a drop of water vnto the Sea, and a grauell stone in
comparison of the sand, so are a *thousand yeeres to the *2. Pet. 3. 8.
dayes of eternitie.
11 Therfore is God patient with them, & powreth forth
his mercy vpon them.
12 He saw and perceiued their end to be euill, therefore he
multiplied his compassion.

13 The

13 The mercy of man is toward his neighbour, but the mercy of the Lord is vpon all flesh: he reprooueth and nurtureth, and teacheth, & bringeth againe as a shepheard his flocke.

14 He hath mercy on them that receiue discipline, and that diligently seeke after his iudgements.

*Chap. 41. 23. 15 *My sonne, blemish not thy good deeds, neither vse vncomfortable words when thou giuest any thing.

16 Shall not the deaw asswage the heate? so is a word better then a gift.

17 Loe is not a word better then a gift? but both are with a gracious man.

18 A foole will vpbraide churlishly, and a gift of the enuious consumeth the eyes.

19 Learne before thou speake, and vse phisicke, or euer thou be sicke.

*1. Cor. 11. 28. 31. 20 Before iudgement *examine thy selfe, and in the day of visitation thou shalt find mercy.

21 Humble thy selfe before thou be sicke, and in the time of sinnes shew repentance.

22 Let nothing hinder thee to pay thy vowe in due time, and deferre not vntill death to be iustified.

23 Before thou prayest, prepare thy selfe, and be not as one that tempteth the Lord.

*Chap. 7. 17, 36. 24 *Thinke vpon the wrath that shall be at the end; and the time of vengeance when he shall turne away his face.

25 When thou hast enough remember the time of hunger, and when thou art rich thinke vpon pouerty and need.

26 From the morning vntill the euening the time is changed, and all things are soone done before the Lord.

*Prou. 28. 14. 27 *A wise man will feare in euery thing, and in the day of sinning he will beware of offence: but a foole will not obserue time.

28 Euery man of vnderstanding knoweth wisedome, and wil giue praise vnto him that found her.

29 They that were of vnderstanding in sayings, became also wise themselues, and powred forth exquisite parables.

*Rom. 6. 6. and 13. 14. 30 *Goe not after thy lustes, but refraine thy selfe from thine appetites.

31 If thou giuest thy soule the desires that please her, she will make thee a laughingstocke to thine enemies, that maligne thee.

32 Take not pleasure in much good

cheere, neither be tyed to the expence thereof.
33 Be not made a begger by banquetting vpon borrowing,
when thou hast nothing in thy purse, for thou shalt lie in
waite for thy owne life: and be talked on.

CHAP. XIX.

2 Wine and women seduce wise men. 7 Say not all thou hearest. 17 Reproue thy friend without anger. 22 There is no wisedome in wickednesse.

A Labouring man that is giuen to drunkennesse shal not
be rich, and hee that contemneth small things shall fall
by little & little.
2 Wine and women will make men of vnderstanding to fall
away, and he that cleaueth to harlots will become impudent.
3 Mothes and wormes shall haue him to heritage, and a
bold man shall be taken away.
4 *He that is hasty to giue credit is light minded, and he *Iosh. 22. 11.
that sinneth shall offend against his owne soule.
5 Who so taketh pleasure in wickednesse shall be condemned, but he that resisteth pleasures, crowneth his life.
6 He that can rule his tongue shall liue without strife, and
he that hateth babbling, shall haue lesse euill.
7 Rehearse not vnto another that which is told vnto thee,
and thou shalt fare neuer the worse.
8 Whether it be ‖to friend or foe, talk not of other mens ‖ *Or, of friend or foe.*
liues, and if thou canst without offence reueale them not.
9 For he heard and obserued thee, and when time commeth
he will ‖hate thee. ‖ *Or, shewe his hatred.*
10 If thou hast heard a word, let it die with thee, and be
bold it will not burst thee.
11 A foole trauaileth with a word, as a woman in labour of
a child.
12 As an arrowe that sticketh in a mans thigh, so is a word
within a fooles ‖belly. ‖ *Or, heart.*
13 *Admonish a friend, it may be he hath not done it, and *Leuit. 19. 17. matth. 18. 15.
if he haue [done it] that he doe it no more.
14 ‖Admonish thy friend, it may be he hath not said it, ‖ *Or, reproue.*
and if he haue, that he speake it not againe.
15 Admonish a friend: for many times it is a slander, &
beleeue not euery tale.

16 There

|| Or, wil- 16 There is one that slippeth in his speach, but not ||from
lingly. his heart, and who is he that hath not offended with his
* Iam. 3. 2. *tongue?
|| Or, re- 17 ||Admonish thy neighbour before thou threaten him, and
proue. not being angry giue place to the Law of the most high.
|| Or, of re- 18 The feare of the Lord is the first step ||to be accepted
ceiuing [of him,] and wisedome obtaineth his loue.
him. 19 The knowledge of the Commandements of the Lord, is
the doctrine of life, and they that do things that please him,
shall receiue the fruit of the tree of immortalitie.
20 The feare of the Lord is all wisedome, and in all wisedome is the performance of the Law, and the knowledge of
his omnipotencie.
21 If a seruant say to his master, I will not doe as it pleaseth
thee, though afterward hee doe it, hee angereth him that
nourisheth him.
22 The knowledge of wickednes is not wisedome, neither
at any time the counsell of sinners, prudence.
23 There is a wickednesse, and the same an abomination,
and there is a foole wanting in wisedome.
24 He that hath smal vnderstanding and feareth God, is
better then one that hath much wisedome, and transgresseth
the Law of the most High.
25 There is an exquisite subtilty, and the same is vniust, and
there is one that turneth aside to make iudgement appeare:
|| Or, iudg- and there is a wise man that ||iustifieth in iudgement.
eth. 26 There is a wicked man that hangeth downe his head
|| Or, in ||sadly; but inwardly he is full of deceit,
blacke. 27 Casting downe his countenance, and making as if he
heard not: where he is not knowen, he will do thee a
mischiefe before thou be aware.
28 And if for want of power hee be hindered from sinning,
yet when he findeth opportunitie he wil doe euil.
29 A man may bee knowen by his looke, and one that hath
vnderstanding, by his countenance, when thou meetest him.
30 A mans attire, and excessiue laughter, and gate, shew
what he is.

CHAP. XX.

1 Of silence and speaking. 10 Of gifts, and gaine. 18 Of slipping by the tongue. 24 Of lying. 27 Of diuers aduertisements.

THere is a reproofe that is not ||comely: againe some || *Or, seaso-*
man holdeth his tongue, and he is wise. *nable.*
2 It is much better to reprooue, then to be angry secretly,
and he that confesseth his fault, shall be preserued from
hurt.
3 How good is it when thou art reproued, to shew repentance? for so shalt thou escape wilfull sinne.
4 As is the lust of an *Eunuch to defloure a virgine; so is *Chap. 30.
he that executeth iudgement with violence. 20.
5 There is one that keepeth silence and is found wise: and
another by much babling becommeth hatefull.
6 Some man holdeth his tongue, because hee hath not to
answere, and some keepeth silence, *knowing his time. *Eccle. 3.
7 A wise man wil hold his *tongue till he see opportunitie: 7.
but a babler and a foole will regard no time. *Cha. 32.
8 He that vseth many words shalbe abhorred; and hee that 4.
taketh to himselfe authoritie therein, shalbe hated.
9 There is a sinner that hath good successe in euill things;
and there is a gaine that turneth to losse.
10 There is a gift that shall not profit thee; and there is a
gift whose recompence is double.
11 There is an abasement because of glory; and there is
that lifteth vp his head from a low estate.
12 There is that buyeth much for a little, and repayeth it
seuen fold.
13 *A wise man by his words maketh himselfe beloued: *Chap. 6.
but the ||graces of fooles shalbe ||powred out. 5.
14 The gift of a foole shall doe thee no good when thou || *Or, plea-sant con-*
hast it; neither yet of the enuious for his necessitie: for hee *ceits.*
†looketh to receiue many things for one. || *Lost, or spilt.*
15 Hee giueth little and vpbraideth much; hee openeth his † *Gr. for,*
mouth like a crier; to day he lendeth, and to morrow will *his eyes are*
he aske it againe: such an one is to be hated of God and *many for one to re-*
man. *ceiue.*
16 The foole saith, I haue no friends, I haue no thanke for
all my good deeds: and they that eate my bread speake euill
of me.
17 How oft, and of how many shall he be laughed to scorne?
for hee knoweth not aright what it is to haue; and it is all
one vnto him, as if he had it not.

18 To

18 To slip vpon a pauement, is better then to slip with the
tongue: so, the fall of the wicked shall come speedily.
|| *Or, an vnpleasant fellow.*
19 ||An vnseasonable tale will alwayes be in the mouth of
the vnwise.
20 A wise sentence shall be reiected when it commeth out
of a fools mouth: for he will not speake it in due season.
21 There is that is hindred from sinning through want: and
† *Gr. shall not be pricked.*
when hee taketh rest, he †shall not be troubled.
22 There is that destroyeth his owne soule through bashful-
nesse, and by accepting of persons ouerthroweth himselfe.
23 There is that for bashfulnes promiseth to his friend, and
maketh him his enemy for nothing.
*Cha. 25. 2.
24 *A lie is a foule blot in a man, yet it is continually in
the mouth of the vntaught.
25 A thiefe is better then a man that is accustomed to lie:
but they both shall haue destruction to heritage.
|| *Or, ignominie.*
26 The disposition of a liar is ||dishonourable, and his shame
is euer with him.
27 A wise man shall promote himselfe *to honour* with his
words: and hee that hath vnderstanding, will please great
men.
*Prou. 12. 11. and 28. 19.
28 *He that tilleth his land, shall increase his heape: and
he that pleaseth great men, shal get pardon for iniquity.
*Exo. 23. 8. deu. 16. 19.
|| *Or, as a muzzle in the mouth.*
29 *Presents and gifts blind the eyes of the wise, and
||stoppe vp his mouth that he cannot reprooue.
30 Wisedome that is hidde, and treasure that is hoarded vp,
what profit is in them both?
31 Better is he that hideth his folly, then a man that hideth
his wisedome.
32 Necessary patience in seeking the Lord, is better then he
that leadeth his life without a guide.

CHAP. XXI.

2 Flee from sinne as from a serpent. 4 His oppression will vndoe the rich. 9 The ende of the vniust shall be naught. 12 The differences betweene the foole and the wise.

*Psal. 41. 4. luk. 15. 21.
MY sonne, hast thou sinned? doe so no more, but *aske
pardon for thy former sinnes.
2 Flee from sinne as from the face of a Serpent: for if thou
commest too neere it, it will bite thee: the teeth thereof, are
as the teeth of a

lyon, slaying the soules of men.
3 All iniquitie is as a two edged sword, the wounds whereof
cannot be healed.
4 To terrifie and doe wrong, will waste riches: thus the
house of proude men shalbe made desolate.
5 A *prayer out of a poore mans mouth reacheth to the *Exod. 3. 9. and 22. 23.
eares of God, and his iudgement commeth speedily.
6 He that hateth to be reprooued, is in the way of sinners:
but hee that feareth the Lord, will †repent from his heart. † *Gr. be conuerted.*
7 An eloquent man is knowen farre and neere, but a man
of vnderstanding knoweth when he slippeth.
8 He that buildeth his house with other mens money, is like
one that gathereth himselfe stones for the tombe of his buriall.
9 *The congregation of the wicked is like tow wrapped *Chap. 16. 16.
together: and the end of them is a flame of fire to destroy
them.
10 The way of sinners is made plaine with stones, but at
the ende thereof is the pit of hell.
11 Hee that keepeth the Law of the Lord, getteth the
vnderstanding thereof: and the perfection of the feare of the
Lord, is wisedome.
12 *He that is not ||wise, will not be taught: but there is *Eccles. 1. 18.
a ||wisedome which multiplieth bitternesse. || *Or, wittie.* || *Or, subtiltie.*
13 The knowledge of a wise man shall abound like a flood:
and his counsell is like a pure fountaine of life.
14 *The inner parts of a foole, are like a broken vessell, and *Cha. 33. 5.
he will holde no knowledge as long as he liueth.
15 If a skilfull man heare a wise word, hee will commend
it, and *adde vnto it: but assoone as one of no vnderstanding *Pro. 9. 9.
heareth it, it displeaseth him, and he casteth it behinde his
backe.
16 The talking of a foole is like a burden in the way: but
grace shall be found in the lips of the wise.
17 They inquire at the mouth of the wise man in the congregation, and they shall ponder his words in their heart.
18 As is a house that is destroyed, so is wisedome to a foole:
and the knowledge of the vnwise, is as talke ||without sense. || *Or, not to be enquired after.*
19 Doctrine vnto fooles, is as fetters on the feete, and like
manacles on the right hand.

20 *A

*Chap. 19. 27, 28. 20 *A foole lifteth vp his voyce with laughter, but a wise man doeth scarce smile a litle.

21 Learning is vnto a wise man, as an ornament of gold, and like a bracelet vpon his right arme.

22 A foolish mans foote is soone in his [neighbours] house: but a man of experience is ashamed of him.

23 A foole will peepe in at the doore into the house, but he that is well nurtured, will stand without.

24 It is the rudenesse of a man to hearken at the doore: but a wise man will be grieued with the disgrace.

25 The lips of talkers will bee telling such things as pertaine not vnto them: but the words of such as haue vnderstanding, are weighed in the ballance.

26 The heart of fooles is in their mouth, but the mouth of the wise is in their heart.

27 When the vngodly curseth Satan, he curseth his owne soule.

*Chap. 28. 13. 28 *A whisperer defileth his owne soule, and is hated wheresoeuer hee dwelleth.

CHAP. XXII.

1 Of the slouthfull man, 3 and a foolish daughter. 11 Weepe rather for fooles, then for the dead. 13 Meddle not with them. 16 The wise mans heart will not shrinke. 20 What will lose a friend.

A Slouthful man is compared to a filthy stone, and euery one will hisse him out to his disgrace.

2 A slouthfull man is compared to the filth of a dunghill: euery man that takes it vp, will shake his hand.

3 An euill nurtured sonne is the dishonour of his father that begate him: and a [foolish] daughter is borne to his losse.

*Prou. 13. 22. 4 *A wise daughter shall bring an ||inheritance to her husband: but shee that liueth dishonestly, is her fathers heauinesse.

|| *Or, shalbe the heire of her husband*

5 Shee that is bold, dishonoureth both her father and her husband, but they both shall despise her.

6 A tale out of season [is as] musick in mourning: but stripes and correction of wisedome are neuer out of time.

7 Who so teacheth a foole, is as one that gleweth a potsheard together, and

as hee that waketh one from a sound sleepe.
8 Hee that telleth a tale to a foole, speaketh to one in
a slumber: when hee hath told his tale, he will say, What
is the matter?
9 If children liue honestly, and haue ||wherwithall, they || *Or, an*
shall couer the basenesse of their parents. *art.*
10 But children being haughtie through disdaine, and want
of nurture, doe staine the nobilitie of their kinred.
11 *Weepe for the dead, for hee hath lost the light: and *Chap. 38.
weepe for the foole, for he wanteth vnderstanding: make 16.
litle weeping for the dead, for hee is at rest: but the life of
the foole is worse then death.
12 Seuen dayes doe men mourne for him that is dead; but
for a foole, and an vngodly man, all the dayes of his life.
13 Talke not much with a foole, and goe not to him that
hath no vnderstanding, *beware of him lest thou haue *Cha. 12.
trouble, and thou shalt neuer be defiled ||with his fooleries: 12 || *Or, when*
depart from him, and thou shalt find rest, and neuer bee *he shakes*
||disquieted with madnesse. *off his*
14 What is heauier then lead? and what is the name thereof, *filth.* || *Or,*
but a foole? *wearied*
15 *Sand, and salt, and a masse of yron is easier to beare *Pro. 27.
then a man without vnderstanding. 3.
16 As timber girt and bound together in a building, cannot
be loosed with shaking: so the heart that is stablished by
aduised counsel, shal feare at no time.
17 A heart setled vpon a thonght of vnderstanding, is as
a faire plaistering ||on the wall of a gallerie. || *Or, of a*
18 Pales set on an high place will neuer stand against the *polished*
wind: so a feareful heart in the imagination of a foole, can *wall*
not stand against any feare.
19 He that pricketh the eye, wil make teares to fall: and he
that pricketh the heart, maketh it to shewe her knowledge.
20 Who so casteth a stone at the birds, frayeth them away,
and he that vpbraideth his friend, breaketh friendship.
21 Though thou drewest a sword at thy friend, yet despaire
not, for there way be a returning (to fauour.)
22 If thou hast opened thy mouth against thy friend, feare
not, for there may be a reconciliation: except for vpbraiding,
or pride, or disclosing of secrets,
or

or a treacherous wound, for, for these things euery friend will
depart.
23 Be faithfull to thy neighbour in his pouertie, that thou
mayest reioyce in his prosperitie: abide stedfast vnto him in
the time of his trouble, that thou mayest bee heire with him
in his heritage: for a meane estate is not alwayes to be con-
temned, nor the rich that is foolish, to be had in admiration.
24 As the vapour and smoke of a furnace goeth before the
fire: so reuiling before blood.
25 I will not be ashamed to defend a friend: neither will
I hide my selfe from him.
26 And if any euill happen vnto me by him, euery one that
heareth it will beware of him.
*Psal. 141. 27 *Who shall set a watch before my mouth, and a seale
3. of wisedome vpon my lippes, that I fall not suddenly by
them, & that my tongue destroy me not?

CHAP. XXIII.

1 A prayer for grace to flee sinne. 9 We may not vse swearing: 14 But remember our parents. 16 Of three sorts of sinne. 23 The adultresse wife sinneth many waies.

O Lord, father and gouernour of all my whole life, leaue
me not to their counsels, and let me not fall by them.
2 Who will set scourges ouer my thoughts, and the discipline of wisedome ouer mine heart? that they spare me not
for mine ignorances and it passe not by my sinnes:
3 Least mine ignorances increase, and my sinnes abound to
my destruction, and I fall before mine aduersaries, and mine
enemie reioyce ouer mee, whose hope is farre from thy mercy.
4 O Lord, father and God of my life, giue me not a proud
|| *Or, a* looke, but turne away from thy seruants alwaies a ||haughty
giant like. minde:
5 Turne away from mee vaine hopes, and concupiscence,
and thou shalt hold him vp that is desirous alwaies to serue
thee.
6 Let not the greedinesse of the belly, nor lust of the flesh
take hold of me, and giue not ouer me thy seruant into an
impudent minde.
7 Heare, O yee children, the discipline of the mouth: He
that keepeth it,

shall neuer be taken in his lippes.
8 The sinner shall be left in his foolishnesse: both the
euill speaker and the proud shall fall thereby.
9 *Accustome not thy mouth to swearing: neither vse thy *Exod. 20.
selfe to the naming of the holy one. 7. chap. 27.
10 For as a seruant that is continually beaten, shall not be 15. math.
without a blew marke: so hee that sweareth and nameth 5. 33.
God continually, shal not be faultlesse.
11 A man that vseth much swearing shall be filled with
iniquity, and the plague shall neuer depart from his house:
If he shall offend, his sinne shall be vpon him: and if he
acknowledge not his sinne, hee maketh a double offence, and
if he sweare in vaine, he shall not be †innocent, but his †*Gre. ius-*
house shall be full of calamities. *tified.*
12 There is a word that is clothed about with death: God
graunt that it be not found in the heritage of Iacob, for all
such things shall be farre from the godly, and they shall not
wallow in their sinnes.
13 Vse not thy mouth to vntemperate swearing, for therein
is the word of sinne.
14 Remember thy father and thy mother, when thou sittest
among great men. Be not forgetfull before them, and so
thou by thy custome become a foole, and wish that thou
hadst not beene borne, and curse the day of thy natiuitie.
15 *The man that is accustomed to opprobrious words, will *2. Sam.
neuer be reformed all the daies of his life. 16. 17.
16 Two sorts of men multiply sinne, and the third will
bring wrath: a hot minde is as a burning fire, it will neuer
be quenched till it be consumed: a fornicatour in the body
of his flesh, will neuer cease till he hath kindled a fire.
17 *All bread is sweete to a whoremonger, he will not *Prou. 9.
leaue off till he die. 17.
18 A man that breaketh wedlocke, saying thus in his heart,
*Who seeth me? I am compassed about with darknesse: *Isai. 29.
the walles couer me; & no body seeth me, what neede I to 15. iob. 24.
feare? The most high wil not remember my sinnes: 15.
19 Such a man only feareth the eies of men, and knoweth
not that the eies of the Lord are tenne thousand times brighter
then the Sunne, beholding all the waies of men, and considering the most secret parts.

20 He

20 He knew all things ere euer they were created, so also
after they were perfited, he looked vpon them all:
21 *This man shall bee punished in the streets of the citie, *Leuit. 20. 10. deut. 22. 22.
and where he suspecteth not, he shall be taken.
22 Thus shall it goe also with the wife, that leaueth her
husband, and bringeth in an heire by ||another: || Or, a stranger.
23 For *first she hath disobeyed the Law of the most High: *Exod. 20. 14.
and secondly, she hath trespassed against her owne husband,
and thirdly, she hath played the whore in adultery, and
brought children by another man.
24 Shee shall be brought out into the congregation, and
||inquisition shalbe made of her children. || Or, visitation.
25 Her *children shall not take root, and her branches shall *Wisd. 4. 3.
bring foorth no fruit.
26 She shall leaue her memorie to be cursed, and her reproch
shall not be blotted out.
27 And they that remaine, shall know that there is nothing
better then the feare of the Lord, and that there is nothing
sweeter then to take heed vnto the Commandement of the
Lord.
28 It is great glory to follow the Lord, & to be receiued of
him is long life.

CHAP. XXIIII.

2 Wisdome doeth praise herselfe, shew her beginning, 4 Her dwelling, 13 Her glory, 17 Her fruit, 26 Her increase, and perfection.

The praise of wisedome.

WIsedome shall praise her selfe, and shall glory in the
midst of her people.
2 In the Congregation of the most high, shall she open her
mouth, and triumph before his power.
3 I came out of the mouth of the most High, and couered
the earth as a ||cloud. || Or, a miste.
4 *I dwelt in high places, and my throne is in a cloudy pillar. *Iob. 22. 14.
5 I alone compassed the circuit of heauen, and walked in the
bottome of the deepe.
6 In the waues of the sea, and in all the earth, and in euery
people, and nation, I got a possession.
7 With all these I sought rest: and in whose inheritance
shall I abide?
8 So the creatour of all things gaue mee a commandement,
and hee that made me, caused my tabernacle to rest:

and said, Let thy dwelling be in Iacob, and thine inheritance
in Israel.
9 Hee *created mee from the beginning before the world, * Pro. 8.
and I shall neuer faile. 23.
10 In the *holy Tabernacle I serued before him: and so * Exod. 31.
was I established in Sion. 3.
11 *Likewise in the ||beloued citie he gaue mee rest, and in * Psal. 132.
Ierusalem was my power. 8. || *Or, holy.*
12 And I tooke roote in an honourable people, euen in the
portion of the Lords inheritance.
13 I was exalted like a Cedar in Libanus, and as a Cypresse
tree vpon the mountaines of Hermon.
14 I was exalted like a palme tree in ||Engaddi, and as a || *Or,*
rose-plant in Iericho, as a faire oliue tree in a pleasant fielde, *Cades.*
and grew vp as a planetree ||by the water. || *Or, in the*
15 I gaue a sweete smell like cinamon, and aspalathus, and *water.*
I yeelded a pleasant odour like the best mirrhe, as Galbanum
and Onix, and sweet Storax, and as the fume of franckincense
in the *Tabernacle. * Exod. 30
16 As the Turpentine tree, I stretched out my branches, 34.
and my branches are the branches of honour and grace.
17 As the Vine brought I foorth pleasant sauour, and my * Ioh. 15.
flowers are the fruit of honour and riches. 1.
18 I am the mother of faire loue, and feare, and knowledge,
and holy hope, I therefore being eternall, am giuen to all my
children which are ||named of him. || *Or,*
19 Come vnto me all ye that be desirous of mee, and fill *chosen.*
your selues with my fruits.
20 For my memorial is sweeter then hony, and mine in- * Psal. 19.
heritance then the hony combe. 10, 11.
21 They that eate mee shall yet be hungry, and they that
drinke me shall yet be thirstie.
22 He that obeyeth me, shall neuer be confounded, and
they that worke by me, shall not doe amisse.
23 All these things are the booke of the Couenant of the
most high God, *euen* the *Law which Moses commanded for * Exod. 20.
an heritage vnto the Congregations of Iacob. 1. and 24.
24 Faint not to bee strong in the Lord; that he may con- 1. deut. 4. 1. and 29.
firme you, cleaue vnto him: for the Lord Almightie is 2.
God

God alone, and besides him there is no other Sauiour.

*Gen. 2. 11.

25 He filleth all things with his wisdome, as *Physon, and as Tigris in the time of the new fruits.

*Iosh. 3. 15.

26 He maketh the vnderstanding to abound like Euphrates, and as *Iorden in the time of the haruest.

27 He maketh the doctrine of knowledge appeare as the light, and as Geon in the time of vintage.

28 The first man knew her not perfectly: no more shall the last finde her out.

29 For her thoughts are more then the Sea, and her counsels profounder then the great deepe.

‖ *Or, draine or ditch.*

30 I also came out as a ‖brooke from a riuer, and as a conduit into a garden.

31 I said, I will water my best garden, and will water abundantly my garden bedde: and loe, my brooke became a riuer, and my riuer became a sea.

32 I will yet make doctrine to shine as the morning, and will send forth her light afarre off.

33 I will yet powre out doctrine as prophecie, and leaue it to all ages for euer.

*Chap. 33. 16.

34 *Behold that I haue not laboured for my selfe onely, but for all them that seeke wisedome.

CHAP. XXV.

1 What things are beautifull, and what hatefull. 6 What is the crowne of age. 7 What things make men happy. 13 Nothing worse then a wicked woman.

‖ *Or, gloried.*
*Gen. 13. 2, 5. rom. 12. 10.

IN three things I ‖was beautified, and stoode vp beautiful, both before God and men: the *vnitie of brethren, the loue of neighbours, a man and a wife that agree together.

2 Three sorts of men my soule hateth, and I am greatly offended at their life: a poore man that is proud, a rich man that is a lyar, and an olde adulterer that doteth.

3 If thou hast gathered nothing in thy youth, how canst thou finde any thing in thine age?

4 Oh how comely a thing is iudgement for gray haires, and for ancient men to know counsell?

5 Oh how comely is the wisedome of olde men, and vnderstanding and counsell to men of honour?

6 Much experience is the crowne of olde men, and the feare
of God is their glory.
7 There be nine things which I haue iudged in mine heart
to be happy, and the tenth I will vtter with my tongue:
a man that hath ioy of his children, and he that liueth to see
the fall of his enemie.
8 Well is him that dwelleth with a wife of vnderstanding,
and that hath not *slipped with his tongue, and that hath *Cha. 14.
not serued a man more vnworthy then himselfe. 1. and 19.
16.
9 Well is him that hath found ||prudence, and he that iam. 3. 2.
speaketh in the eares of him that will heare. || *Or, a*
10 Oh how great is he that findeth wisedome! yet is there *friend*
none aboue him that feareth the Lord.
11 But the loue of the Lord passeth all things for illumina-
tion: he that holdeth it, ||whereto shall he be likened? || *Or, to*
12 The feare of the Lord is the beginning of his loue: and *whom.*
faith is the beginning of cleauing vnto him.
13 [Giue mee] any plague, but the plague of the heart:
and any wickednesse, but the wickednesse of a woman.
14 And any affliction, but the affliction from them that
hate me: and any reuenge, but the reuenge of enemies.
15 There is no head aboue the head of a serpent, and there
is no wrath aboue the wrath of an enemie.
16 *I had rather dwell with a lyon and a dragon, then to *Pro. 21.
keepe house with a wicked woman. 19
17 The wickednesse of a woman changeth her face, and
darkeneth her countenance like ||sackecloth. || *Or, like a*
18 Her husband shall sit among his neighbours: and when *Beare.*
hee heareth it, shall sigh bitterly.
19 All wickednesse is but little to the wickednesse of a
woman: let the portion of a sinner fall vpon her.
20 As the climbing vp a sandie way is to the feete of the
aged, so is a wife ||full of words to a quiet man. || *Or, scol-*
ding.
21 *Stumble not at the beautie of a woman, and desire her *2. Sam.
not for pleasure. 11. 2. chap.
22 A woman, if shee maintaine her husband, is full of 42. 2.
anger, impudencie, and much reproch.
23 A wicked woman abateth the courage, maketh a heauie
countenance, and a wounded heart: a woman that will not
comfort her husband in di-

Tttt stresse,

stresse maketh weake hands, and feeble knees.
*Gen. 3.6. 1. tim. 2. 14 24 Of *the woman came the beginning of sinne, & through
her wee all die.
25 Giue the water no passage: neither a wicked woman
libertie to gad abroad.
26 If she goe not as thou wouldest haue her, cut her off
from thy flesh, and giue her a bill of diuorce, and let her goe.

CHAP. XXVI.

1 A good wife, 4 and a good conscience doe glad men. 6 A wicked wife is a feareful thing. 13 Of good and bad wiues. 28 Of three things that are grieuous. 29 Merchants and hucksters are not without sinne.

BLessed is the man that hath a vertuous wife, for the
number of his dayes shall be double.
2 A vertuous woman reioyceth her husband, and he shall
fulfill the yeeres of his life in peace.
3 A good wife is a good portion, which shall be giuen in
the portion of them that feare the Lord.
4 Whether a man be rich or poore, if he haue a good heart
towards the Lord, he shall at all times reioyce with a cheerefull countenance.
5 There bee three things that mine heart feareth: and for
the fourth I was sore afraid: †the slander of a citie, the
gathering together of an vnruly multitude, and a false accusation: all these are worse then death.

† *Gr. an euill report.*

6 But a griefe of heart and sorrow, is a woman that is
ielous ouer another woman, and a scourge of the tongue
which communicateth withall.
7 An euil wife is a ||yoke shaken to and fro: he that hath
hold of her, is as though he held a scorpion.

|| *Or, a yoke of oxen.*

8 A drunken woman and a gadder abroad, causeth great
anger, and shee will not couer her owne shame.
9 The whordome of a woman may be knowen in her
haughtie lookes, and eye lids.
*Chap. 44. 11. 10 *If thy daughter be shamelesse, keepe her in straitly:
lest she abuse her selfe through ouermuch libertie.
11 Watch ouer an impudent eye: and marueile not, if shee
trespasse against thee.
12 Shee will open her mouth as a thirstie traueiler, when
he hath found a fountaine: and drinke of euery water

neere her: by euery ||hedge will she sit downe, and open her || Or, stake.
quiuer against euery arrow.
13 The grace of a wife delighteth her husband, and her
discretion will fat his bones.
14 A silent and louing woman is a gift of the Lord, and
there is nothing so much worth, as a mind well instructed.
15 A shamefast and faithfull woman is a double grace, and
her continent mind cannot be valued.
16 As the Sunne when it ariseth in the †high heauen: so
is the beautie of a good wife in the ||ordering of her house.
17 As the cleare light is vpon the holy candlesticke: so is
the beautie of the face ||in ripe age.
18 As the golden pillars are vpon the sockets of siluer: so
are the ||faire feete with a constant ||heart.
19 My sonne, keepe the flowre of thine age sound: and
giue not thy strength to strangers.
20 When thou hast gotten a fruitfull possession through all
the field: sowe it with thine owne seede, trusting in the
goodnesse of thy stocke.
21 So thy race which thou leauest shalbe magnified, hauing
the confidence of their good descent.
22 An harlot shall bee accounted as ||spittle: but a maried
woman is a towre against death to her husband.
23 A wicked woman is giuen as a portion to a wicked man:
but a godly woman is giuen to him that feareth the Lord.
24 A dishonest woman contemneth shame, but an honest
woman will reuerence her husband.
25 A shamelesse woman shalbe counted as a dog: but she
that is shamefast will feare the Lord.
26 A woman that honoureth her husband, shall bee iudged
wise of all: but she that dishonoureth him in her pride, shall
be counted vngodly of all.
27 A loude crying woman, and a scolde, shall be sought out
to driue away the enemies.
28 There be two things that grieue my heart: and the
third maketh me angry: a man of warre that suffereth
pouerty, and men of vnderstanding that are not set by: and
one that returneth from righteousnesse to sinne: the Lord
prepareth such a one for the sword.
29 A merchant shall hardly keepe
him-

† Gre. in the highest places of the Lord.
|| Or, ornament.
|| Or, in constant age.
|| Or, comely.
|| Or, brest.
|| Or, a swine.

himselfe from doing wrong: and an huckster shall not be freed from sinne.

CHAP. XXVII.

1 Of sinnes in selling and buying. 7 Our speach will tell what is in vs. 16 A friend is lost by discouering his secrets. 25 Hee that diggeth a pit shall fall into it.

* Prou. 28. 21. || Or, a thing indifferent.

*MAny haue sinned for ||a smal matter: & he that seeketh for abundance will turne his eies away.

* Prou. 23. 4. 1. tim. 6. 9.

2 *As a naile sticketh fast betweene the ioynings of the stones: so doth sinne sticke close betweene buying and selling.

3 Vnlesse a man hold himselfe diligently in the feare of the Lord, his house shall soone be ouerthrowen.

|| Or, thought

4 As when one sifteth with a sieue, the refuse remaineth, so the filth of man in his ||talke.

* Prou. 27. 21.

5 The furnace prooueth the potters vessell: so the *triall of man is in his reasoning.

* Matth. 7. 17.

6 *The fruite declareth if the tree haue beene dressed: so is the vtterance of a conceit in the heart of man.

7 Praise no man before thou hearest him speake, for this is the triall of men.

8 If thou followest righteousnesse, thou shalt obtaine her, and put her on, as a glorious long robe.

9 The birds will resort vnto their like, so will truth returne vnto them that practise in her.

10 As the Lyon lieth in waite for the pray: so sinne for them that worke iniquity.

11 The discourse of a godly man is alwaies with wisedome: but a foole changeth as the Moone.

12 If thou be among the vndiscreet, obserue the time: but be continually among men of vnderstanding.

13 The discourse of fooles is irksome, and their sport is in the wantonnesse of sinne.

14 The talke of him that sweareth much, maketh the haire stand vpright: and their braules make one stop his eares.

15 The strife of the proud is bloodshedding, and their reuilings are grieuous to the eare.

16 Who so discouereth secrets, looseth his credit: and shall neuer find friend to his minde.

17 Loue thy friend, and be faithfull vnto him: but if thou
bewrayest his secrets, follow no more after him.
18 For as a man hath destroyed his enemie: so hast thou
lost the loue of thy neighbour.
19 As one that letteth a bird goe out of his hand, so hast
thou let thy neighbour goe, and shalt not get him againe.
20 Follow after him no more, for he is too far off, he is as
a roe escaped out of the snare.
21 As for a wound it may be bound vp, and after reuiling
there may be reconcilement: but he that bewrayeth secrets
is without hope.
22 He *that winketh with the eies worketh euil, and he *Prou. 10.
that knoweth him will depart from him. 10.
23 When thou art present he will speake sweetly, and will
admire thy words: but at the last he will ||writhe his mouth, || *Or, alter*
and slander thy sayings. *his speach.*
24 I haue hated many things, but nothing like him, for the
Lord will hate him.
25 Who so casteth a stone on high, casteth it on his owne
head, and a deceitfull stroke shall make wounds.
26 Who so diggeth a *pit shall fall therein: and he that *Psal. 7.
setteth a trap shall be taken therein. 15.
27 He that worketh mischiefe, it shall fall vpon him, and prou. 26. 27. ecclesi.
he shall not know whence it commeth. 8. 10.
28 Mockery and reproach are from the proud: but *ven- *Deut. 32.
geance as a Lyon shall lie in waite for them. 35. rom.
29 They that reioyce at the fall of the righteous shalbe 12. 19.
taken in the snare, and anguish shall consume them before
they die.
30 Malice and wrath, euen these are abhominations, and
the sinfull man shall haue them both.

CHAP. XXVIII.

1 Against reuenge. 8 Quarrelling, 10 Anger, 15 And backbiting.

HE that reuengeth shall find vengeance from the Lord,
and he will surely keepe his sinnes (in remembrance.)
2 Forgiue thy neighbour the hurt that he hath done vnto
thee, so shall thy sinnes also be forgiuen when thou prayest.
3 One man beareth hatred against

another, and doeth he seeke pardon from the Lord?

4 Hee sheweth no mercy to a man, which is like himselfe: and doeth hee aske forgiuenesse of his owne sinnes?

5 If he that is but flesh nourish hatred, who will intreat for pardon of his sinnes?

6 Remember thy end, and let enimitie cease, [remember] corruption and death, and abide in the Commandements.

7 Remember the Commaundements, & beare no malice to thy neighbour: [remember] the Couenant of the highest, and winke at ignorance.

*Chap. 8. 1. 8 * Abstaine from strife, and thou shalt diminish thy sinnes: for a furious man will kindle strife.

9 A sinfull man disquieteth friends, and maketh debate among them that be at peace.

*Prou. 26. 21. 10 *As the matter of the fire is, so it burneth: and as a mans strength is, so is his wrath, and according to his riches his anger riseth, and the stronger they are which contend, the more they will be inflamed.

11 An hastie contention kindleth a fire, and an hasty fighting sheddeth blood.

12 If thou blow the sparke, it shall burne: if thou spit vpon it, it shall bee quenched, and both these come out of thy mouth.

*Chap. 21. 28. 13 *Curse the whisperer, and double tongued: for such haue destroyed many that were at peace.

14 A backbiting tongue hath disquieted many, and driuen them from nation to nation, strong cities hath it pulled down, and ouerthrowen the houses of great men.

|| *Or, third.* 15 A ||backbiting tongue hath cast out vertuous women, and depriued them of their labours.

16 Who so hearkeneth vnto it, shall neuer finde rest, and neuer dwel quietly.

17 The stroke of the whip maketh markes in the flesh, but the stroke of the tongue breaketh the bones.

18 Many haue fallen by the edge of the sword: but not so many as haue fallen by the tongue.

19 Well is hee that is defended from it, and hath not passed through the venime thereof: who hath not drawen the yoke thereof, nor hath bene bound in her bands.

20 For the yoke thereof is a yoke of yron, and the bands
thereof are bandes of brasse.
21 The death therof is an euil death, the graue were better
then it.
22 It shall not haue rule ouer them that feare God, neither
shall they be burnt with the flame thereof.
23 Such as forsake the Lord shall fall into it, and it shall
burne in them, and not be quenched, it shalbe sent vpon
them as a Lion, and deuoure them as a Leopard.
24 Looke that thou hedge thy possession about with thornes,
and binde vp thy siluer and gold:
25 And weigh thy words in a ballance, and make a doore
and barre for thy mouth.
26 Beware thou slide not by it, lest thou fall before him
that lieth in wait.

CHAP. XXIX.

2 Wee must shew mercy and lend: 4 but the borower must not defraud the lender. 9 Giue almes. 14 A good man will not vndoe his suretie. 18 To be suretie and vndertake for others is dangerous. 22 It is better to liue at home, then to soiourne.

HEe that is mercifull, will lende vnto his neighbour, and hee that strengthneth his hande, keepeth the Commandements.
2 Lend to thy neighbour in time of his *need, and pay *Deut. 15.
thou thy neighbour againe in due season. 8. matth.
3 Keepe thy word & deale faithfully with him, and thou 5. 42. luke 6. 35.
shalt alwaies finde the thing that is necessary for thee.
4 Many when a thing was lent them, reckoned it to be
found, and put them to trouble that helped them.
5 Till he hath receiued, he will kisse a mans hand: and for
his neighbours money he will speake submissely: but when
he should repay, he will prolong the time, and returne words
of griefe, and complaine of the time.
6 If he preuaile, he shall hardly receiue the halfe, and he ‖ *Or, if he*
will count as if he had found it: if not; he hath depriued *be able.*
him of his money, and he hath gotten him an enemy without cause: he payeth him with cursings, and raylings: and
for honour he will pay him disgrace.

7 Many

7 Many therefore haue refused to lend for other mens ill
dealing, fearing to be defrauded.
8 Yet haue thou patience with a man in poore estate, and
delay not to shew him mercy.
9 Helpe the poore for the commandements sake, and turne
him not away because of his pouertie.
10 Lose thy money for thy brother and thy friend, and let
it not rust vnder a stone to be lost.

*Dan. 4. 24 matt. 6. 20. luke 11. 41. and 12. 33. acts 10. 4. 1. tim. 6. 18, 19. *Iob 4 8, 9, 10.

11 *Lay vp thy treasure according to the commandements
of the most high, and it shall bring thee more profite then
golde.
12 *Shut vp almes in thy storehouses: and it shall deliuer
thee from all affliction.
13 It shal fight for thee against thine enemies, better then
a mightie shield and strong speare.
14 An honest man is suretie for his neighbour: but hee
that is impudent, will ||forsake him. ||*Or, faile.*
15 Forget not the friendship of thy suretie: for hee hath
giuen his life for thee.
16 A sinner will ouerthrow the good estate of his suretie:
17 And he that is of an vnthankfull minde, will leaue him
in [danger] that deliuered him.
18 Suretiship hath vndone many of good estate, and shaked
them as a waue of the Sea: mightie men hath it driuen from
their houses, so that they wandred among strange nations.
19 A wicked man transgressing the commandements of
the Lord, shall fall into suretiship: and hee that vndertaketh
and followeth other mens businesse for gaine, shall fall into
suits.
20 Helpe thy neighbour according to thy power, and beware
that thou thy selfe fall not into the same.

*Chap. 39. 26.

21 The *chiefe thing for life is water and bread, and
clothing, and an house to couer shame.
22 Better is the life of a poore man in a meane cottage, then
delicate fare in another mans house.
23 Be it little or much, holde thee contented, that thou
heare not the reproch of thy house.
24 For it is a miserable life to goe from house to house: for
where thou art a stranger, thou darest not open thy mouth.

25 Thou shalt entertaine and feast, and haue no thankes:
moreouer, thou shalt heare bitter words.
26 Come thou stranger, and furnish a table, and feede me
of that thou hast ready.
27 Giue place thou stranger to an honourable man, my
brother commeth to be lodged, and I haue neede of mine
house.
28 These things are grieuous to a man of vnderstanding:
the vpbraiding of house-roome, and reproching of the lender.

CHAP. XXX.

1 It is good to correct our children, 7 and not to cocker them. 14 Health is better then wealth. 22 Health and life are shortened by griefe.

HEe *that loueth his sonne, causeth him oft to feele *Of children.*
the rodde, that hee may haue ioy of him in the end. * Prou. 13.
2 He that chastiseth his sonne, shall haue ||ioy in him, and 24. and 23.
shall reioyce of him among his ||acquaintance. 13.
3 *He that teacheth his sonne, grieueth the enemie: and || *Or, good by him.*
before his friends he shall reioyce of him. || *Or, kinsefolke.*
4 Though his father die, yet he is as though hee were not
dead: for hee hath left one behinde him that is like himselfe. * Deut. 6.
5 While he liued, he *saw and reioyced in him: and when 7. * Psal. 128.
he died hee was not sorrowfull.
6 He left behinde him an auenger against his enemies, and
one that shall requite kindnesse to his friends.
7 He that maketh too much of his sonne, shall binde vp his
wounds, and his bowels wil be troubled at euery cry.
8 An horse not broken becommeth headstrong: and a childe
left to himselfe will be wilfull.
9 Cocker thy childe, and hee shall make thee ||afraid: play || *Or, astonished.*
with him, and he will bring thee to heauinesse.
10 Laugh not with him, lest thou haue sorrow with him,
and lest thou gnash thy teeth in the end.
11 *Giue him no liberty in his youth, and winke not at *Cha. 7.
his follies. 23.
12 Bow downe his necke while hee is young, and beate
him on the sides while he is a childe, lest hee waxe stubborne, and be disobedient vnto thee, and so bring sorrow to
thine heart.

13 Chastise thy sonne, and hold him to labour, lest his lewd
behauiour be an offence vnto thee.

Of health. 14 Better is the poore being sound and strong of constitu-
tion, then a rich man that is afflicted in his body.
15 Health and good state of body are aboue all gold, and a
strong body aboue infinite wealth.
16 There is no riches aboue a sound body, and no ioy
aboue the ioy of the heart.
17 Death is better then a bitter life, or continuall sickenesse.
18 Delicates powred vpon a mouth shut vp, are as messes
of meat set vpon a graue.
19 What good doth the offering vnto an idole? for neither
can it eat nor smell: so is he that is ||persecuted of the Lord.
20 Hee seeth with his eyes and groneth, as an Eunuch that
embraceth a virgine, and sigheth.
21 *Giue not ouer thy mind to heauinesse, and afflict not
thy selfe in thine owne counsell.
22 The gladnesse of the heart is the life of man, and the
||ioyfulnes of a man prolongeth his dayes.
23 Loue thine owne soule, and comfort thy heart, remoue
sorrow far from thee: for sorrow hath killed many, and
there is no profit therein.
24 Enuie and wrath shorten the life, and carefulnesse
bringeth age before the time.
25 ||A cherefull and good heart will haue a care of his meat
and diet.

|| *Or, afflicted.*
*Pro. 12. 25. & 15. 13. and 17. 22.
|| *Or, exultation.*
|| *Or, a noble.*

CHAP. XXXI.

1 Of the desire of riches. 12 Of moderation and excesse in eating, or drinking wine.

WAtching for *riches, consumeth the flesh, and the
care therof driueth away sleepe.
2 Watching care will not let a man slumber, as a sore
disease breaketh sleepe.
3 The rich hath great labour in gathering riches together,
and when he resteth, he is filled with his delicates.
4 The poore laboureth in his poore estate, and when he
leaueth off, hee is still needie.
5 He that loueth gold shall not bee iustified, and he that
followeth corruption, shall haue enough thereof.
6 *Gold hath bin the ruine of many, and their destruction
was present.

*1. Tim. 6. 9, 10.
*Chap. 8. 2

7 It is a stumbling block vnto them that sacrifice vnto it,
and euery foole shall be taken therewith.
8 *Blessed is the rich that is found without blemish, and *Luke 6.
hath not gone after gold: 24.
9 Who is he? and we will call him blessed: for wonderfull
things hath hee done among his people.
10 Who hath bene tried thereby, and found perfit? then
let him glory. Who might offend and hath not offended,
or done euill, and hath not done it?
11 His goods shall be established, and the congregatiō shall
declare his almes.
12 If thou sit at a bountifull table, *bee not greedy vpon *Psa. 111.
it, and †say not, There is much meate on it. 9 pro. 23. 1.
13 Remember that a wicked eye is an euill thing: and †*Gr. open not thy throat vpon it.*
what is created more wicked then an eye? therefore it
weepeth ||vpon euery occasion.
14 Stretch not thine hand whithersoeuer it looketh, and ||*Or, before euery thing that is presented.*
thrust it not with him into the dish.
15 Iudge of thy neighbour by thy selfe: and be discreet in
euery point.
16 Eate as it becommeth a man those things which are set
before thee: and deuoure not, lest thou be hated.
17 Leaue off first for maners sake, and be not vnsatiable,
lest thou offend.
18 *When thou sittest among many, reach not thine hand *Chap. 37.
out first of all. 29.
19 A very litle is sufficient for a man well nurtured, ||and ||*Or, & lieth not puffing and blowing.*
he fetcheth not his wind short vpon his bed.
20 Sound sleepe commeth of moderate eating: he riseth
early, and his wits are with him, but the paine of watching
and choller, and pangs of the bellie are with an vnsatiable man.
21 And if thou hast bin forced to eate, arise, goe forth,
vomit, and thou shalt haue rest.
22 My sonne, heare me, and despise me not, and at the
last thou shalt finde as I told thee: in all thy workes bee
quicke, so shall there no sickenesse come vnto thee.
23 *Who so is liberall of his meat, men shall speake well of *Prou. 22.
him, and the report of his good housekeeping will be beleeued. 9.
24 But against him that is a niggard of his meate, the
whole citie shall murmure; and the testimonies of his
niggardnesse shall not be doubted of.
25 Shew not thy *valiantnesse in *Isai. 5.
wine, 22. iudet. 13. 8

wine, for wine hath destroyed many.
26 The furnace prooueth the edge by dipping: so doth
wine the hearts of the proud by drunkennesse.
27 Wine is as good as life to a man if it be drunke
moderatly: what life is then to a man that is without wine?
for it was made to make men glad.
28 Wine measurably drunke, and in season, bringeth gladnesse of the heart and cheerefulnesse of the minde.
29 But wine drunken with excesse, maketh bitternesse of
the minde, with brawling and quarreling.
30 Drunkennesse increaseth the rage of a foole till he
offend, it diminisheth strength, and maketh wounds.
31 Rebuke not thy neighbour at the wine, and despise him
not in his mirth: giue him no despitefull words, and presse
not vpon him with vrging him (to drinke.)

CHAP. XXXII.

1 Of his duty that is cheefe or master in a feast. 14 Of the feare of God. 18 Of counsell. 20 Of a ragged and a smooth way. 23 Trust not to any but to thy selfe and to God.

IF thou be made the master (of the feast) lift not thy selfe
vp, but bee among them as one of the rest, take diligent
care for them, and so sit downe.
2 And when thou hast done all thy office, take thy place
that thou mayest be merry with them, and receiue a crowne
for thy well ordering of the feast.
3 Speake thou that art the elder, for it becometh thee, but
with sound iudgement, and hinder not musicke.
*Eccle. 3. 7. chap. 20. 7. 4 Powre not out words where *there is a musitian, and
shew not forth wisedome out of time.
5 A consort of musicke in a banket of wine, is as a signet
of Carbuncle set in gold.
6 As a signet of an Emeraud set in a worke of gold, so is
the melodie of musicke with pleasant wine.
7 Speake yong man, if there be need of thee: and yet
scarsely when thou art twise asked:
8 Let thy speach be short, comprehending much in few
words, be as one that knoweth, and yet holdeth his tongue.
*Iob. 33. 6. 9 *If thou be among great men,

make not thy selfe equall with them, and when ancient men
are in place, vse not many words.
10 Before the thunder goeth lightening: and before a
shamefast man shall goe fauour.
11 Rise vp betimes, and be not the last: but get thee home
without delay.
12 There take thy pastime, & do what thou wilt: but
sinne not by proud speach
13 And for these things blesse him that made thee, and
hath replenished thee with his good things.
14 Who so feareth the Lord, will receiue his discipline,
and they that seeke him early, shall find fauour.
15 He that seeketh the law, shall be filled therewith: but
the hypocrite will be offended thereat.
16 They that feare the Lord shall find iudgement, and
shall kindle iustice as a light.
17 A sinfull man will not be reproued, but findeth an
excuse according to his will.
18 A man of counsell will be considerate, but a strange
and proud man is not daunted with feare, euen when of
himselfe he hath done without counsell.
19 Doe nothing without aduice, and when thou hast once
done, repent not.
20 Goe not in a way wherein thou maiest fall, and stumble
not among the stones.
21 Be not confident in a plaine way.
22 And beware of thine owne children.
23 *In euery good worke trust thy owne soule: for this is *Rom. 14.
the keeping of the commandements. 5.
24 He that beleeueth in the Lord, taketh heed to the
commandement, and he that trusted in him, ||shall fare neuer ||*Or, shall*
the worse. *not be hurt.*

CHAP. XXXIII.

1 The safety of him that feareth the Lord. 2 The wise and the foolish. 7 Times and seasons are of God. 10 Men are in his hands, as clay in the hands of the potter. 18 Cheefely regard thy selfe. 24 Of seruants.

THere shall no euill happen vnto him that feareth the
Lord, but in temptation euen againe he wil deliuer him.
2 A wise man hateth not the Law, but he that is an
hypocrite therein, is as a ship in a storme.

3 A

3 A man of vnderstanding trusteth in the Law, and the
||Or, *as the asking of Vrim.*
Law is faithfull vnto him, ||as an oracle.
4 Prepare what to say, and so thou shalt be heard, and
binde vp instruction, and then make answere.
† Greeke, *bowels.*
*Chap. 21. 16.
5 The †heart of the *foolish is like a cartwheele: and his
thoughts are like a rolling axeltree.
6 A stallion horse is as a mocking friend, hee neigheth
vnder euery one that sitteth vpon him.
7 Why doth one day excell another? when as all the light
of euery day in the yeere is of the Sunne.
8 By the knowledge of the Lord they were distinguished:
and he altered seasons and feasts.
9 Some of them hath hee made high dayes, and hallowed
||Or, *ordained for the number of dayes.*
them, and some of them hath hee ||made ordinary dayes.
*Gen. 1. 27. and 2. 7.
10 And all men are from the ground, and *Adam was
created of earth.
11 In much knowledge the Lord hath diuided them, and
made their wayes diuers.
12 Some of them hath hee blessed, and exalted, and some
of them hath hee sanctified, and set neere himselfe: but
some of them hath hee cursed, and brought low, and turned
||Or, *standings.*
out of their ||places.
*Esay 45. 9. rom. 9. 20, 21.
13 *As the clay is in the potters hand to fashion it at his
pleasure: so man is in the hand of him that made him, to
render to them as liketh him best.
14 Good is set against euill, and life against death: so is
the godly against the sinner, and the sinner against the
godly.
15 So looke vpon all the workes of the most High, and
there are two and two, one against another.
||Or, *gleaneth.*
16 I awaked vp last of all, as one that ||gathereth after the
grape-gatherers: by the blessing of the Lord I profited, and
filled my wine-presse, like a gatherer of grapes.
*Chap. 24. 39.
17 *Consider that I laboured not for my selfe onely, but
for all them that seeke learning;
18 Heare me, O ye great men of the people, and hearken
with your eares ye rulers of the Congregation:
19 Giue not thy sonne, and wife, thy brother and friend
power ouer thee while thou liuest, and giue not thy goods to
another, lest it repent thee:

and thou intreat for the same againe.
20 As long as thou liuest and hast breath in thee, ||giue not ||Or, sell not.
thy selfe ouer to any.
21 For better it is that thy children should seeke to thee,
then that thou shouldst ||stand to their courtesie. ||Or, looke to their hands.
22 In all thy workes keepe to thy selfe the preheminence,
leaue not a staine in thine honour.
23 At the time when thou shalt end thy dayes, and finish
thy life, distribute thine inheritance.
24 Fodder, a wand, and burdens, *are* for the asse: and *Of seruants.*
bread, correction, and worke for a seruant.
25 If thou set thy seruant to labour, thou shalt finde rest:
but if thou let him goe idle, he shall seeke libertie.
26 A yoke and a collar doe bow the necke: so are tortures
and torments for an euill seruant.
27 Sende him to labour that hee be not idle: for idlenesse
teacheth much euill.
28 Set him to worke, as is fit for him; if he be not
obedient, put on more heauy fetters.
29 But be not excessiue toward any, and without discretion
doe nothing.
30 *If thou haue a seruant, let him bee vnto thee as thy *Chap. 7. 20.
selfe, because thou hast bought him †with a price.
31 If thou haue a seruant, intreate him as a brother: for †Greeke, in blood.
thou hast neede of him, as of thine owne soule: if thou
intreate him euill, and he runne from thee, which way wilt
thou goe to seeke him?

CHAP. XXXIIII.

1 Of dreames. 13 The praise and blessing of them that feare the Lord. 18 The offering of the ancient, and praier of the poore innocent.

THE hopes of a man voyd of vnderstanding are vaine, *Of dreames.*
and false: and dreames lift vp fooles.
2 Who so ||regardeth dreames, is like him that catcheth at ||Or, hath his minde vpon.
a shadow, and followeth after the winde.
3 The vision of dreames is the resemblance of one thing to
another, euen as the *likenesse of a face to a face. *Prou. 27. 19.
4 *Of an vncleane thing, what can be cleansed? and from *Iob 14. 4.
that thing which is false, what trueth can come?

5 Diui-

5 Diuinations, and soothsayings, and dreames are vaine:
and the heart fancieth as a womans heart in trauell.
6 If they be not sent from the most high in thy visitation,
||set not thy heart vpon them.
7 For dreames haue deceiued many, and they haue failed
that put their trust in them.
8 The Law shall be found perfect without lies: and wisedome is perfection to a faithfull mouth.
9 A man that hath trauailed knoweth many things: and
hee that hath much experience, wil declare wisedome.
10 He that hath no experience, knoweth little: but he that
hath trauailed, is full of prudence.
11 When I trauailed, I saw many things: and I vnderstand
more, then I can expresse.
12 I was oft times in danger of death, yet I was deliuered
because of these things.
13 The spirit of those that feare the Lord shall liue, for
their hope is in him that saueth them.
14 Who so feareth the Lord, shall not feare nor be afraid,
for hee is his hope.
15 Blessed is the soule of him that feareth the Lord: to
whom doeth hee looke? and who is his strength?
16 For *the eyes of the Lord are vpon them that loue him,
he is their mightie protection, and strong stay, a defence
from heat, and a couer from the Sunne at noone, a preserua-
tion from stumbling, and a helpe from falling.
17 He raiseth vp the soule, and lighteneth the eyes: hee
giueth health, life, and blessing.
18 *Hee that sacrificeth of a thing wrongfully gotten, his
offering is ridiculous, and the ||giftes of vniust men are not
accepted.
19 *The most high is not pleased with the offerings of the
wicked, neither is he pacified for sinne by the multitude of
sacrifices.
20 Who so bringeth an offering of the goods of the poore,
doeth as one that killeth the sonne before his fathers eyes.
21 The bread of the needie, is their life: he that defraudeth
him thereof, is a man of blood.
22 Hee that taketh away his neighbours liuing, slayeth
him: and hee that

|| *Or, regard them not.*

* Psal. 33. 18. and 61. 1, 2.

* Prou. 21. 27.

|| *Or, the mockeries.*

* Pro. 15. 8.

*defraudeth the labourer of his hire, is a bloodshedder. *Deut. 24.
23 When one buildeth, and another pulleth downe, what 14, 15. cha. 7. 20.
profite haue they then but labour?
24 When one prayeth, and another curseth, whose voice
will the Lorde heare?
25 *He that washeth himselfe after the touching of a dead *Num. 19.
body, if he touch it againe, what auaileth his washing? 11, 12.
26 So is it with a man that fasteth for his sinnes, and goeth
againe and doeth the same: who will heare his prayer, or
what doeth his humbling profit him?

CHAP. XXXV.

1 Sacrifices pleasing God. 14 The prayer of the fatherlesse, of the widow, and of the humble in spirit. 20 Acceptable mercy.

HEe *that keepeth the law, bringeth offerings enow: *1. Sam.
he that taketh heed to the commandement, offereth 15. 22. iere. 7. 3,
a peace offering. 5, 6, 7.
2 He that requiteth a good turne, offereth fine floure: and
he that giueth almes, sacrificeth praise.
3 To depart from wickednesse is a thing pleasing to the
Lord: and to forsake vnrighteousnesse, is a propitiation.
4 *Thou shalt not appeare emptie before the Lord: *Exod. 23.
5 For all these things [are to bee done] because of the 15. deut. 16. 16.
commandement.
6 The offering of the righteous maketh the Altar fat, and
the sweete sauour thereof *is* before the most high.
7 The sacrifice of a iust man is acceptable, and the
memoriall thereof shall neuer be forgotten.
8 Giue the Lord his honour with a good eye, and diminish
not the first fruits of thine hands. *2. Cor. 9.
9 *In all thy gifts shew a cheerefull countenance, and 7.
||dedicate thy tithes with gladnesse. ||*Or, set apart.*
10 *Giue vnto the most high, according as hee hath *Tob. 4.
enriched thee, and as thou hast gotten, giue with a cheere- 8.
full eye. ||*Or, diminish nothing of thy offerings.*
11 For the Lord recompenseth, and will giue thee seuen
times as much.
12 ||Doe not thinke to corrupt with gifts, *for such he will *Leuit. 22.
not receiue: and trust not to vnrighteous sacrifices, for 21, 22.
the deu. 15.21.

*Deut. 10. 17. 2. chr. 19 7. iob 34. 19 wisd. 6. 7. acts 10. 34. rom. 2. 11. gal. 2. 6. eph. 6. 9. colos. 3. 25. 1. pet. 1. 17.

the Lord is iudge, and with him is *no respect of persons.
13 Hee will not accept any person against a poore man:
but will heare the prayer of the oppressed.
14 He will not despise the supplication of the fatherlesse:
nor the widowe when she powreth out her complaint.
15 Doeth not the teares run downe the widowes cheeks?
and is not her crie against him that causeth them to fall?
16 He that serueth the Lord, shall be accepted with fauour,
and his prayer shall reach vnto the cloudes.
17 The prayer of the humble pierceth the clouds: and till
it come nigh he will not be comforted: and will not depart
till the most High shall beholde to iudge righteously, and
execute iudgement.
18 For the Lord will not be slacke, neither will the mightie
be patient towards them, till he hath smitten in sunder the
loines of the vnmercifull, and repaid vengeance to the heathen:
till he haue taken away the multitude of the ||proud, and
broken the scepter of the vnrighteous:
19 Till he haue rendred to euery man according to his
deeds, and to the works of men according to their deuises,
till he haue iudged the cause of his people: and made them
to reioyce in his mercie,
20 Mercie is †seasonable in the time of affliction, as cloudes
of raine in the time of drought.

||Or, cruell oppressours.

†Gre. faire.

CHAP. XXXVI.

1 A prayer for the Church against the enemies thereof. 18 A good heart and a froward. 21 Of a good wife.

HAue mercie vpon vs, O Lord God of all, and behold vs:
2 And send thy feare vpon all the nations that seeke
not after thee.
3 *Lift vp thy hand ||against the strange nations, and let
them see thy power.
4 As thou wast sanctified in vs before them: so be thou
magnified among them before vs.
5 And let them know thee, as we haue knowen thee, that
there is no God, but onely thou, O God.
6 Shew new signes, and make other strange wonders:
glorifie thy hand and thy right arme, that they may set

*Ier. 10. 25

||Or, vpon.

forth thy wonderous workes.
7 Raise vp indignation, and powre out wrath: take away
the aduersarie and destroy the enemie.
8 Make the time short, remember the †couenant, and let †*Gre. othe.*
them declare thy wonderfull works.
9 Let him that escapeth, be consumed by the rage of the
fire, and let them perish that oppresse the people.
10 Smite in sunder the heads of the rulers of the heathen,
that say, There is none other but we.
11 Gather all the tribes of Iacob together, and inherit thou
them, as from the beginning.
12 O Lord haue mercie vpon the people, that is called by thy
name, and vpon Israel, *whom thou hast named thy first borne. *Exo. 4.
13 O bee mercifull vnto Ierusalem thy holy citie, the place 22
of thy rest.
14 Fill Sion with ||thine vnspeakable oracles, and thy people ||*Or, that*
with thy glory. *it may*
15 Giue testimonie vnto those that thou hast possessed from the *magnifie thine*
beginning, and raise vp ||prophets that haue bin in thy name. *oracles.*
16 Reward them that wait for thee, and let thy prophets ||*Or, pro-*
be found faithfull. *phecies.*
17 O Lord heare the prayer of thy ||seruants, according to ||*Or, sup-*
the *blessing of Aaron ouer thy people, that all they which *pliants.*
dwel vpon the earth, may know that thou art the Lord, the *Num. 6. 25.
eternall God.
18 The belly deuoureth all meates, yet is one meat better
then another.
19 *As the palate tasteth diuers kinds of venison: so doth *Iob 34.
an heart of vnderstanding false speeches. 3.
20 A froward heart causeth heauinesse: but a man of
experience will recompense him.
21 A woman will receiue euery man, yet is one daughter
better then another
22 The beautie of a woman cheareth the countenance, and
a man loueth nothing better.
23 If there be kindnesse, meekenes, and comfort in her
tongue, then is not her husband like ||other men. ||*Or, com-*
24 He that getteth a wife, beginneth ||a *possession*, a helpe *mon.*
like vnto himselfe, and a pillar of rest. ||*Or, to thriue.*
25 Where no hedge is, there the possession is spoiled: and
he that hath no wife will wander vp and downe mourning.
26 Who

26 Who will trust a thiefe well appointed, that skippeth
from citie to citie? so [who will beleeue] a man that hath
no house? and lodgeth wheresoeuer the night taketh him?

CHAP. XXXVII.

1 How to know friends and counsellers. 12 The discretion and
wisedome of a godly man blesseth him. 27 Learne to refraine thine
appetite.

EVery friend saieth, I am his friend also: but there is a
friend which is onely a friend in name.
2 Is it not a griefe vnto death, when a companion and
friend is turned to an enemie?
3 O wicked imagination, whence camest thou in to couer
the earth with deceit?
4 There is a companion, which reioyceth in the prosperity
of a friend: but in the time of trouble will be against him.
5 There is a companion which helpeth his friend for the
belly, and taketh vp the buckler ||against the enemie.
|| Or, in presence of the enemie.
6 Forget not thy friend in thy minde, and be not vnmind-
full of him in thy riches.
7 Euery counseller extolleth counsell; but there is some
that counselleth for himselfe.
8 Beware of a counseller, and know before ||what neede he
|| Or, what vse there is of him.
hath (for he will counsell for himselfe) lest hee cast the lot
vpon thee:
9 And say vnto thee, Thy way is good: and afterward he
stand on the other side, to see what shall befall thee.
10 Consult not with one that suspecteth thee: and hide
thy counsell from such as enuie thee.
11 Neither consult with a woman touching her of whom
she is iealous; neither with a coward in matters of warre,
nor with a merchant concerning exchange; nor with a
buyer of selling; nor with an enuious man of thankfulnesse;
nor with an vnmercifull man touching kindnesse; nor with
the slouthfull for any worke; nor with an hireling for a
yeere, of finishing worke; nor with an idle seruant of much
businesse: Hearken not vnto these in any matter of counsell.
12 But be continually with a godly man, whom thou
knowest to keepe the

commandements of the Lord, whose minde is according to
thy minde, and will sorrow with thee, if thou shalt miscarry.
13 And let the counsell of thine owne heart stand: for
there is no man more faithfull vnto thee then it.
14 For a mans minde is sometime wont to tell him more
then seuen watchmen, that sit aboue in an high towre.
15 And aboue all this pray to the most high, that he will
direct thy way in trueth.
16 Let reason goe before euery enterprise, & counsell before
euery action.
17 The countenance is a signe of changing of the heart.
18 Foure maner of things appeare: good and euill, life and
death: but the tongue ruleth ouer them continually.
19 There is one that is wise and teacheth many, and yet is
vnprofitable to himselfe.
20 There is one that sheweth wisedome in words, and is
hated: he shall be destitute of all ||foode. || *Or, wisedome.*
21 For grace is not giuen him from the Lord: because he
is depriued of all wisedome.
22 Another is wise to himselfe: and the fruits of vnderstanding are commendable in his mouth.
23 A wise man instructeth his people, and the fruits of his
vnderstanding faile not.
24 A wise man shall be filled with blessing, and all they
that see him, shall count him happy.
25 The daies of the life of man may be numbred: but the
daies of Israel are innumerable.
26 A wise man shall inherite ||glory among his people, and || *Or, credit.*
his name shalbe perpetuall.
27 My sonne prooue thy soule in thy life, and see what is
euill for it, and giue not that vnto it.
28 For all things are not profitable for all men, neither hath
euery soule pleasure in euery thing.
29 Be not vnsatiable in any dainty thing: nor too greedy
vpon meates.
30 For ||excesse of meates, bringeth sicknesse, and surfetting || *Or, varietie of meates.*
will turne into choler.
31 By surfetting haue many perished, but hee that taketh
heed, prolongeth his life.

CHAP.

CHAP. XXXVIII.

1 Honour due to the Phisitian, and why. 16 How to weepe and mourne for the dead. 24 The wisedome of the learned man, and of the Labourer and Artificer: with the vse of them both.

HOnour a Phisitian with the honour due vnto him, for the vses which you may haue of him: for the Lord hath created him.

2 For of the most High commeth healing, and he shall
||Or, a gift. receiue ||honour of the King.
3 The skill of the Phisitian shall lift vp his head: and in
the sight of great men he shalbe in admiration.
4 The Lord hath created medicines out of the earth; and
he that is wise will not abhorre them.
5 Was not the water made sweet with wood, that the
*Exod. 15. 25. *vertue thereof might be knowen?
6 And he hath giuen men skill, that hee might be honoured
in his marueilous workes.
7 With such doeth he heale [men,] and taketh away their
paines.
8 Of such doeth the Apothecarie make a confection; and
of his workes there is no end, and from him is peace ouer all
the earth.
9 My sonne, in thy sickenesse be not negligent: but
*Esay. 38. 2. *pray vnto the Lord, and he will make thee whole.
10 Leaue off from sinne, and order thy hands aright, and
cleanse thy heart from all wickednesse.
11 Giue a sweet sauour, and a memoriall of fine flowre:
||Or, as a dead man. and make a fat offering, as ||not being.
12 Then giue place to the phisitian, for the Lord hath created
him: let him not go from thee, for thou hast need of him.
13 There is a time when in their hands there is good successe.
14 For they shall also pray vnto the Lord, that hee would
||Or, curing. prosper that, which they giue, for ease and ||remedy to prolong life.
15 He that sinneth before his maker, let him fal into the
hand of the Phisitian.
16 My sonne, let teares fall downe ouer the dead, and begin
to lament, as if thou hadst suffered great harme thy selfe:
and then couer his body according to the custome, & neglect
not his buriall.
17 Weepe bitterly, and make great

moane, and vse lamentation, as hee is worthy, and that a day
or two, lest thou be euill spoken of: and then comfort thy
selfe for thy heauinesse.
18 For of heauinesse commeth death, and the heauinesseof
the *heart, breaketh strength. *Prou. 15.
19 In affliction also sorrow remaineth: and the life of the 13. and 17. 22.
poore, is the curse of the heart.
20 Take no heauines to heart: driue it away, and remember
the last end.
21 Forget it not, for there is no turning againe: thou shalt
not doe him good, but hurt thy selfe.
22 Remember ||my iudgement: for thine also shall be so; ||*Or, the sentence vpon him.*
yesterday for me, and to day for thee.
23 When the dead is at *rest, let his remembrance rest, & *2. Sam.
be comforted for him, when his spirit is departed from him. 12. 20.
24 The wisedome of a learned man cōmeth by opportunitie
of leasure: & he that hath litle busines shal become wise.
25 How can he get wisdome that holdeth the plough, and
that glorieth in the goad; that driueth oxen, and is occupied
in their labours, and whose talke is †of bullocks? †*Greeke, of the breed of bullocks.*
26 He giueth his minde to make furrowes: and is diligent
to giue the kine fodder.
27 So euery carpenter, and workemaster, that laboureth
night and day: and they that cut and graue seales, and are
diligent to make great variety, and giue themselues to
counterfait imagerie, and watch to finish a worke.
28 The smith also sitting by the anuill, & considering the
iron worke; the vapour of the fire wasteth his flesh, and he
fighteth with the heat of the furnace: the noise of the
hammer & the anuill is euer in his eares, and his eies looke
still vpon the patterne of the thing that he maketh, he setteth
his mind to finish his worke, & watcheth to polish it perfitly.
29 So doeth the potter sitting at his worke, and turning the
wheele about with his feet, who is alway carefully set at his
worke: and maketh all his worke by number.
30 He fashioneth the clay with his arme, and ||boweth ||*Or, tempereth it with his feet.*
downe his strength before his feet: he applieth himselfe to
lead it ouer; and he is diligent to make cleane the furnace.
31 All these trust to their hands: and euery one is wise in
his worke.

32 With-

32 Without these cannot a citie be inhabited: and they shall not dwell where they will, nor goe vp and downe.

33 They shall not be sought for in publike counsaile, nor sit high in the congregation: they shal not sit on the Iudges seate, nor vnderstand the sentence of iudgement: they cannot declare iustice, and iudgement, and they shall not be found where parables are spoken.

34 But they will maintaine the state of the world, and [all] their desire is in the worke of their craft.

CHAP. XXXIX.

1 A description of him that is truely wise. 12 An exhortation to praise God for his workes, which are good to the good, and euill to them that are euill.

BVT hee that giueth his minde to the Law of the most high, and is occupied in the meditation thereof, wil seeke out the wisdome of all the ancient, and be occupied in prophecies.

2 Hee will keepe the sayings of the renowmed men: and where subtile parables are, he will be there also.

3 Hee will seeke out the secrets of graue sentences, and be conuersant in darke parables.

4 He shall serue among great men, and appeare before princes: he will trauaile through strange countreys, for hee hath tried the good, and the euill among men.

5 Hee will giue his heart to resort early to the Lord that made him, and will pray before the most high, and will open his mouth in prayer, and make supplication for his sinnes.

6 When the great Lord will, he shall bee filled with the spirit of vnderstanding: he shal powre out wise sentences, and giue thankes vnto the Lord in his prayer.

7 Hee shall direct his counsell and knowledge, and in his secrets shall hee meditate.

8 Hee shall shew foorth that which he hath learned, and shall glory in the Law of the couenant of the Lord.

9 Many shall commend his vnderstanding, and so long as the world endureth, it shall not be blotted out, his memoriall shall not depart away, and his name shall liue from generation to generation.

10 *Nations shall shewe foorth his wisedome, and the con- *Chap. 44. 15.
gregation shall declare his praise.
11 If hee die, he shall leaue a greater name then a thou-
sand: and if he liue, he shall ||increase it. || *Or, gaine vnto it.*
12 Yet I haue more to say which I haue thought vpon,
for I am filled as the Moone at the full.
13 Hearken vnto me, ye holy children, and budde foorth
as a rose growing by the ||brooke of the field: || *Or, riuers of water.*
14 And giue yee a sweete sauour as frankincense, and
flourish as a lilly, send foorth a smell, and sing a song of
praise, blesse the Lord in all his workes.
15 Magnifie his Name, and shewe foorth his praise with
the songs of your lips, and with harpes, and in praising him
you shall say after this maner:
16 *Al the works of the Lord are exceeding good, & what- *Gen. 1. 31. mark. 7. 37.
soeuer hee commandeth, shalbe *accomplished* in due season.
17 And none may say, What is this? wherefore is that?
for at time conuenient they shall all be sought out: at his
commaundement the waters stood as an heape, & at the
wordes of his mouth the receptacles of waters.
18 At his commandement is done whatsoeuer pleaseth him,
and none can hinder when he will saue.
19 The workes of all flesh are before him, & nothing can
be hid from his eyes.
20 He seeth from euerlasting to euerlasting, and there is
nothing wonderfull before him.
21 A man neede not to say, What is this? wherefore is
that? for hee hath made all things for their vses.
22 His blessing couered the dry land as a riuer, and watered
it as a flood.
23 As hee hath turned the waters into saltnesse: so shall
the heathen inherite his wrath.
24 *As his wayes are plaine vnto the holy, so are they *Ose 14. 10.
stumbling blockes vnto the wicked.
25 For the good, are good things created from the beginning: so euill things for sinners.
26 The principall things for the whole vse of mans life, are
water, fire, yron, and salt, floure of wheatc, honie, milke, and
the blood of the grape, and oyle, and clothing.
27 All these things are for good to the godly: so to the
sinners they are turned into euill.

28 There be spirits that are created for vengeance, which
in their furie lay on sore strokes, in the time of destruction
they powre out their force, and appease the wrath of him
that made them.
29 Fire, and haile, and famine, and death: all these were
created for vengeance:
‖Or, vipers. 30 Teeth of wild beasts, and scorpions, ‖serpents, & the
sword, punishing the wicked to destruction.
31 They shall reioice in his commandement, and they shall
bee ready vpon earth when neede is, and when their time is
come, they shall not transgresse his word.
32 Therefore from the beginning I was resolued, and thought
vpon these things, and haue left them in writing.
33 All the workes of the Lord are good: and he will giue
euery needefull thing in due season.
34 So that a man cannot say, This is worse then that: for
in time they shall all be well approued.
35 And therefore praise ye the Lord with the whole heart
and mouth, and blesse the Name of the Lord.

CHAP. XL.

1 Many miseries in a mans life. 12 The reward of vnrighteousnesse, and the fruit of true dealing. 17 A vertuous wife, & an honest friend reioyce the heart, but the feare of the Lord is aboue all. 28 A beggers life is hatefull.

*Eccles. 1. 3 GReat *trauaile is created for euery man, and an heauy
yoke is vpon the sons of Adam, from the day that
they goe out of their mothers wombe, till the day that they
returne to the mother of all things.
2 Their imagination of things to come, & the day of death
[trouble] their thoughts, and [cause] feare of heart:
3 From him that sitteth on a throne of glory, vnto him
that is humbled in earth and ashes.
‖*Or, to the porter.* 4 From him that weareth purple, and a crown, ‖vnto *him
that is clothed with a linnen* frocke.
5 Wrath, and enuie, trouble and vnquietnesse, feare of death,
and anger, and strife, and in the time of rest vpon his bed, his
night sleepe doe change his knowledge.
6 A litle or nothing is his rest, and afterward he is in his
sleepe, as in a day

of keeping watch, troubled in the vision of his heart, as if he
were escaped out of a battell:
7 When all is safe, he awaketh, and marueileth that the
feare was nothing.
8 [Such things happen] vnto all flesh, both man and beast,
and that is seuen fold more vpon sinners.
9 *Death and bloodshed, strife and sword, calamities, famine, *Chap. 39.
tribulation, and the scourge: 29, 30.
10 These things are created for the wicked, and for their
sakes came the *flood. *Gen. 7.
11 *All things that are of the earth shal turne to the earth 11 *Gen. 3.
againe: and that which is of the *waters doeth returne into 19 chap.
the Sea. 41. 10
12 All †briberie and iniustice shall be blotted out: but true *Eccles. 1. 7
dealing shall endure for euer. † *Gre. bribes*
13 The goods of the vniust shall bee dried vp like a riuer,
and shall vanish with noise, like a great thunder in raine.
14 While he openeth his hand he shal reioyce: so shall
transgressours come to nought.
15 The children of the vngodly shall not bring forth many
branches: but are as vncleane roots vpon a hard rocke.
16 *The weed growing vpon euery water, and banke of a *Iob. 8.
riuer, shall bee pulled vp before all grasse. 11. and 16.
17 Bountifulnes is as a most ||fruitfull garden, and merciful- 12. gen. 41. 2.
nesse endureth for euer. || *Or, a garden that*
18 To *labour & to be content with that a man hath, is a *is blessed.*
sweet life: but hee that findeth a treasure, is aboue them both. *Phil. 4.
19 Children and the building of a citie continue a mans 12. 1. tim.
name: but a blamelesse wife is counted aboue them both. 6. 6.
20 Wine & musicke reioyce the heart: but the loue of
wisedome is aboue them both.
21 The pipe and the psalterie make sweet melodie: but a
pleasant tongue is aboue them both.
22 Thine eye desireth fauour and beautie: but more then
both, corne while it is greene.
23 A friend and companion neuer meet amisse: but aboue
both is a wife with her husband.
24 Brethren and helpe are against time of trouble: but
almes shall deliuer more then them both.
25 Golde and siluer make the foote
stand

stand sure: but counsell is esteemed aboue them both.
26 Riches and strength lift vp the heart: but the feare of
the Lord is aboue them both: there is no want in the feare
of the Lord, and it needeth not to seeke helpe.
*Isai. 4. 15. 27 *The feare of the Lord is a ||fruitfull garden, and couereth
him aboue all glory.
||Or, a garden that is blessed. 28 My sonne, lead not a beggers life: for better it is to die
then to beg.
29 The life of him that dependeth on another mans table,
is not to be counted for a life: for he polluteth himselfe with
other mens meate, but a wise man well nurtured will beware
thereof.
30 Begging is sweet in the mouth of the shamelesse: but
in his belly there shall burne a fire.

CHAP. XLI.

1 The remembrance of Death. 3 Death is not to be feared. 5 The vngodly shall be accursed. 11 Of an euill and a good name. 14 Wisedome is to be vttered. 16 Of what things we should be ashamed.

O Death, how bitter is the remembrance of thee to a man
that liueth at rest in his possessions, vnto the man that
hath nothing to vexe him, and that hath prosperity in all
things: yea vnto him that is yet able to receiue meate?
2 O death, acceptable is thy sentence vnto the needy, and
vnto him whose strength faileth, that is now in the last age,
||Or, to whom euery thing is trouble-some. and is ||vexed with all things, and to him that despaireth and
hath lost patience.
3 Feare not the sentence of death, remember them that
haue beene before thee, and that come after, for this is the
sentence of the Lord ouer all flesh.
4 And why art thou against the pleasure of the most High?
there is no inquisition in the graue, whether thou haue liued
ten, or a hundred, or a thousand yeeres.
5 The children of sinners, are abhominable children: and
they that are conuersant in the dwelling of the vngodly.
6 The inheritance of sinners children shal perish, and their
posterity shal haue a perpetuall reproch.

7 The children will complaine of an vngodly father, because
they shall be reproched for his sake.
8 Woe be vnto you vngodly men which haue forsaken the
law of the most high God: for if you encrease, it shall be to
your destruction.
9 And if you be borne, you shall be borne to a curse: and
if you die, a curse shall be your portion.
10 *All that are of the earth shall turne to earth againe: *Chap. 40. 11.
so the vngodly shall goe from a curse to destruction.
11 The mourning of men is about their bodies: but an ill
name of sinners shall be blotted out.
12 Haue regard to thy name: for that shall continue with
thee aboue a thousand great treasures of gold.
13 A good life hath but few daies: but a good name endureth
for euer.
14 My children, keepe discipline in peace: for wisedome
that is hid, and a treasure that is not seene, what profit is in
them both?
15 A man that hideth his foolishnesse is better then a man
that hideth his wisedome.
16 Therefore be shamefast according to my word: for it is
not good to retaine all shamefastnesse, neither is it altogether
approoued in euery thing.
17 Be ashamed of whoredome before father and mother,
and of a lie before a prince and a mighty man:
18 Of an offence before a iudge and ruler, of iniquitie
before a congregation and people, of vniust dealing before
thy partner and friend:
19 And of theft in regard of the place where thou soiournest,
and in regard of the trueth of God and his couenant, and to
leane with thine elbow vpon the meate, and of scorning to
giue and take:
20 And of silence before them that salute thee, and to look
vpon an harlot:
21 And to turne away thy face from thy kinsman, or to take
away a portion or a gift, or to gaze vpon another mans wife,
22 Or to bee ouerbusie with his maide, and come not neere
her bed, or of vpbraiding speaches before friends; and after
thou hast giuen, vpbraide not:
23 Or of iterating and speaking againe that which thou
hast heard, and of reuealing of secrets.

24 So shalt thou be truely shamefast, and finde fauour before all men.

CHAP. XLII.

1 Whereof we should not be ashamed. 9 Be carefull of thy daughter. 12 Beware of a woman. 15 The workes and greatnes of God.

OF these things be not thou ashamed, and accept no person to sinne thereby.

2 Of the Law of the most High, and his Couenant, and of iudgement to iustifie the vngodly:

|| Or, of thy partners speech. *|| Or, companions.* *|| Or, of the giuing.* *|| Or, without profit.*

3 Of ||reckoning with thy partners, and ||traueilers: or of the ||gift of the heritage of friends:

4 Of exactnesse of ballance, and waights: or of getting much or little:

5 And of merchants ||indifferent selling, of much correction of children, and to make the side of an euill seruant to bleed.

6 Sure keeping is good where an euill wife is, and shut vp where many hands are.

7 Deliuer all things in number and waight, and put al in writing that thou ||giuest out, or receiuest in.

|| Or, dealest for. *|| Or, rebuke.* *|| Or, that is accused of fornication.*

8 Be not ashamed to ||informe the vnwise and foolish, and the extreeme aged ||that contendeth with those that are yong, thus shalt thou bee truely learned and approued of all men liuing.

9 The father waketh for the daughter when no man knoweth, and the care for her taketh away sleepe; when shee is yong lest shee passe away the flowre of her age, and being married, lest she should be hated:

10 In her virginitie lest she should be defiled, and gotten with childe in her fathers house; and hauing an husband, lest she should misbehaue herselfe: and when shee is married, lest shee should be barren.

11 Keepe a sure watch ouer a shamelesse daughter, lest shee make thee a laughing stocke to thine enemies, and a by-word in the citie, and a reproch among the people, and make thee ashamed before the multitude.

**Chap. 25. 23.*

12 Behold not euery bodies *beauty, and sit not in the midst of women.

**Gene. 3. 6.*

13 For from garments commeth a moth, and *from women wickednesse.

|| Or, wickednesse.

14 Better is the ||churlishnesse of a man, then a courteous woman, a wo-

man *I say*, which bringeth shame and reproch.
15 I will now remember the works of the Lord, and declare
the things that I haue seene: in the words of the Lord are
his workes.
16 The Sunne that giueth light, looketh vpon all things:
and the worke thereof is full of the glory of the Lord.
17 The Lord hath not giuen power to the Saints to
declare all his marueilous workes, which the Almightie
Lord firmely setled, that whatsoeuer is, might be established
for his glory.
18 He seeketh out the deepe and the heart, and considereth
their crafty deuices: for ||the Lord knoweth all that may be
knowen, and he beholdeth the signes of the world.
19 Hee declareth the things that are past, and for to come,
and reueileth the steps of hidden things.
20 No *thought escapeth him, neither any word is hidden
from him.
21 Hee hath garnished the excellent workes of his wisedome, and hee is from euerlasting to euerlasting, vnto him
may nothing be added, neither can he be diminished, and he
hath no need of any counseller.
22 O how desireable are all his workes: and that a man
may see euen to a sparke.
23 All these things liue and remaine for euer, for all vses,
and they are all obedient.
24 All things are double one against another: and hee hath
made nothing vnperfit.
25 One thing establisheth the good of another: and who
shalbe filled with beholding his glory?

|| *Or, the highest.*

* Iob 41. 4. esay 21. 15.

CHAP. XLIII.

1 The workes of God in heauen, and in earth, and in the sea, are exceeding glorious and wonderfull. 29 Yet God himselfe in his power and wisedome is aboue all.

THe pride of the height, the cleare firmament, the
beautie of heauen, with his glorious shew;
2 The Sunne when it appeareth, declaring at his rising, a
marueilous ||instrument, the worke of the most High.
3 At noone it parcheth the country, and who can abide the
burning heate thereof?

|| *Or, vessell.*

4 A

4 A man blowing a furnace is in works of heat, but the
Sunne burneth the mountaines three times more; breathing
out fiery vapours, and sending foorth bright beames, it
dimmeth the eyes.
5 Great is the Lord that made it, and at his commandement †it runneth hastily.
6 *He made the Moone also to serue in her season, for a
declaration of times, and a signe of the world.
7 *From the Moone is the signe of Feasts, a light that
decreaseth in her perfection.
8 The moneth is called after her name, encreasing wonderfully in her changing, being an instrument of the armies
aboue, shining in the firmament of heauen,
9 The beautie of heauen, the glory of the starres, an ornament giuing light in the highest places of the Lord.
10 At the commandement of the holy One, they will stand
in their order, and neuer faint in their watches.
11 *Looke vpon the rainebow, and praise him that made it,
very beautifull it is in the brightnesse thereof.
12 *It compasseth the heauen about with a glorious circle,
and the hands of the most high haue bended it.
13 By his commandement hee maketh the snow to fall apace,
and sendeth swiftly the lightnings of his iudgment.
14 Through this the treasures are opened, and clouds flie
forth as foules.
15 By his great power hee maketh the cloudes firme, and
the hailestones are broken small.
16 At his sight the mountaines are shaken, and at his will
the South wind bloweth.
17 The noise of the thunder maketh the earth to ||tremble:
so doth the Northren storme, and the whirlewinde: as birds
flying he scattereth the snow, and the falling downe thereof,
is as the lighting of grashoppers.
18 The eye marueileth at the beauty of the whitenesse
thereof, and the heart is astonished at the raining of it.
19 The hoare frost also as salt hee powreth on the earth,
and being congealed, ||it lieth on the toppe of sharpe stakes.
20 When the colde North-winde bloweth, and the water is
congealed into yce, it abideth vpon euery gathe-

† *Gr. hee stayed his course.*
*Gen. 1. 16.
*Exo. 12. 2.
*Gen. 9. 13.
*Esa. 40. 12.
|| *Or, to grone as a woman in her trauaile.*
|| *Or, it is as the point of sharp stakes.*

ring together of water, and clotheth the water as with a
brestplate.
21 It deuoureth the mountaines, and burneth the wildernesse, and consumeth the grasse as fire.
22 A present remedy of all is a miste *comming speedily:* a
dew comming ||after heate, refresheth. || *Or, vpon the heat.*
23 By his counsell he appeaseth the deepe, and planteth
Ilands therein.
24 They that saile on the Sea, tell of the danger thereof,
and when wee heare it with our eares, wee marueile thereat.
25 For therein be strange and wonderous workes, varietie * Psal. 107. 23.
of all kindes of beasts, and whales created.
26 By him the ende of them hath prosperous successe, and
by his word all things consist.
27 We may speake much, & yet come short: wherefore
in summe, he is all.
28 How shall wee be able to magnifie him? for hee is great
aboue all his workes.
29 *The Lord is terrible and very great, and marueilous is * Psal. 96. 42
his power.
30 When you glorifie the Lord exalt him as much as you
can: for euen yet wil he farre exceed, and when you exalt
him, put foorth all your strength, and be not weary: for you
can neuer goe farre enough.
31 *Who hath seene him, that hee might tell vs? and who * Psal. 106. 2 ioh. 1. 18.
can magnifie him as he is?
32 There are yet hid greater things then these be, for wee
haue seene but a few of his workes:
33 For the Lord hath made all things, and to the godly
hath hee giuen wisedome.

CHAP. XLIIII.

1 The praise of certaine holy men: 16 Of Enoch, 17 Noah, 19 Abraham, 22 Isaac, 23 and Iacob.

LEt vs now praise famous men, and our Fathers that *The praise of the fathers.*
begat vs.
2 The Lorde hath wrought great glory by them, through
his great power from the beginning.
3 Such as did beare rule in their kingdomes, men renowmed
for their power, giuing counsell by their vnderstanding, and
declaring prophecies:
4 Leaders of the people by their

Uuuu 3 coun-

counsels, and by their knowledge of learning meet for the
people, wise and eloquent in their instructions.
|| *Or, ditties.* 5 Such as found out musicall tunes, and reiected ||verses in
writing.
6 Rich men furnished with abilitie, liuing peaceably in
their habitations.
7 All these were honoured in their generations, and were
the glory of their times.
8 There be of them, that haue left a name behind them,
that their praises might be reported.
*Gen. 7. 22 9 And some there be, which haue no memorial, *who are
perished as though they had neuer bene, and are become as
though they had neuer bene borne, and their children after
them.
10 But these were mercifull men, whose righteousnesse hath
not beene forgotten.
11 With their seed shall continually remaine a good inheritance, and their children are within the couenant.
|| *Or, after them.* 12 Their seed stands fast, and their children ||for their sakes.
13 Their seed shall remaine for euer, and their glory shall
not be blotted out.
14 Their bodies are buried in peace, but their name liueth
for euermore.
*Chap. 39. 10. 15 *The people will tell of their wisdome, and the congre-
gation will shew forth their praise.
*Gen. 5. 24 heb. 11. 5. 16 *Enoch pleased the Lord, and was translated, being an
example of repentance, to all generations.
*Gen. 6. 9. and 7. 1. heb. 11. 7. 17 *Noah was found perfect and righteous, in the time of
wrath, he was taken in exchange (for the world) therefore was
he left as a remnant vnto the earth, when the flood came.
*Gen. 9. 11. 18 An *euerlasting Couenant was made with him, that all
flesh should perish no more by the flood.
*Gen. 12. 3 and 15. 5. and 17. 4. 19 Abraham was a *great father of many people: in glory
was there none like vnto him:
20 Who kept the Law of the most High, and was in coue-
*Gen. 21. 4. nant with him, hee established the Couenant in *his flesh,
and when he was proued, he was found faithfull.
*Gen. 22. 16, 17, 18. gal. 3. 8. 21 Therefore he assured him by an *othe, that he would
blesse the nations in his seed, and that he would multiply
him, as the dust of the earth, and exalt his seed as the starres,
and cause them to inherit from Sea to Sea, & from the riuer
vnto the vtmost part of the land.

22 With *Isaac did he establish likewise [for Abraham his *Gen. 27.
fathers sake] the blessing of all men and the couenant, 28. and 28. 14.
23 And made it rest vpon the head of Iacob. Hee acknowledged him in his blessing, and gaue him an heritage, and
diuided his portions, among the twelue tribes did he part
them.

CHAP. XLV.

1 The praise of Moses, 6 Of Aaron, 23 and of Phinees.

AND he brought out of him a mercifull man, which found
fauour in the sight of all flesh, euen *Moses beloued *Exo. 11.
of God and men, whose memoriall is blessed: 3
2 He made him like to the glorious Saints, and magnified
him, so that his enemies stood in feare of him.
3 By his words he caused the wonders to cease, and he
made him *glorious in the sight of kings, and gaue him a *Exod. 6.
commaundement for his people, and shewed him part of his 7, 8, 9. chap.
glory.
4 *He sanctified him *in* his faithfulnesse, and meekenesse, *Num. 12.
and chose him out of all men. 3
5 He made him to heare his voyce, and brought him into
the darke cloud, and *gaue him commandements before his *Exo. 17.
face, euen the law of life and knowledge, that hee might 4.
teach Iacob his Couenants, and Israel his iudgments.
6 He *exalted Aaron an holy man like vnto him, euen his *Exo. 4.
brother, of the tribe of Leui. 28.
7 An euerlasting couenant he made with him, and gaue him
the priesthood among the people, he †beautified him with †*Gr. he blessed.*
comely ornaments, and clothed him with a robe of glory.
8 Hee put vpon him perfect glory: and strengthened him
with †rich garments, with breeches, with a long robe, and †*Greeke, vessels or instruments.*
the Ephod:
9 And he compassed him with pomegranates, and with
many golden bels round about, that as he went, there might
be a *sound, and a noise made that might be heard in the *Exod. 28.
Temple, for a memoriall to the children of his people. 35.
10 With an holy garment, with gold and blew silke, and
purple the worke of the embroiderer; with a brestplate of
iudgement, and with Vrim & Thummim.
11 With twisted scarlet, the worke of
the

the cunning workeman, with precious stones grauen like seales, and set in gold, the worke of the Ieweller, with a writing engraued for a memoriall, after the number of the tribes of Israel.

12 He set a crowne of gold vpon the miter, wherein was engraued holinesse an ornament of honour, a costly worke, the desires of the eies goodly & beautiful.

13 Before him there were none such, neither did euer any stranger put them on, but onely his children, and his childrens children perpetually.

14 Their sacrifices shall be wholy consumed euery day twise continually.

15 Moises consecrated him, and annointed him with holy oile, this was appointed vnto him by an euerlasting couenant, and to his seed so long as the heauens should remaine, that they should minister vnto him, and execute the office of the priesthood, and blesse the people in his name.

16 He chose him out of all men liuing to offer sacrifices to the Lord, incense and a sweet sauour, for a memoriall, to make reconciliation for his people.

* Deut. 17. 10. and 21. 5.

17 * He gaue vnto him his commandements, and authority in the statutes of iudgements, that he should teach Iacob the testimonies, and informe Israel in his lawes.

* Num. 16. 12.

18 * Strangers conspired together against him, and maligned him in the wildernesse, euen the men that were of Dathans, and Abirons side, and the congregation of Core with fury and wrath.

19 This the Lord saw and it displeased him, and in his wrathfull indignation, were they consumed: he did wonders vpon them, to consume them with the fiery flame.

* Num. 17. 8.

20 * But he made Aaron more honourable, and gaue him an heritage, and diuided vnto him the first fruits of the encrease, especially he prepared bread in abundance:

21 For they eate of the sacrifices of the Lord, which he gaue vnto him and his seed:

* Deut. 12. 12. and 18. 10.

22 * Howbeit in the land of the people he had no inheritance, neither had he any portion among the people, for the Lord himselfe is his portion and inheritance.

* Num. 25. 12, 13. 1. mac. 2. 54.

23 * The third in glory is Phinees the sonne of Eleazar, because he had zeale in the feare of the Lord, and stood vp with

good courage of heart, when the people were turned backe,
and made reconciliation for Israel.
24 Therfore was there a couenant of peace made with him,
that he should be the cheefe of the sanctuary, and of his
people, and that he, and his posteritie should haue the
dignitie of the Priesthood for euer.
25 According to the couenant made with Dauid sonne of
Iesse, of the tribe of Iuda, that the inheritance of the king
should be to his posterity alone: so the inheritance of Aaron
should also be vnto his seed.
26 God giue you wisedome in your heart to iudge his people
in righteousnesse, that their good things be not abolished, and
that their glory may endure for euer.

CHAP. XLVI.

1 The praise of Ioshua, 9 Of Caleb, 13 Of Samuel.

I *Esus the sonne of Naue was valiant in the wars, and was *Num. 27.
the successor of Moses in prophesies, who according to 18. deut.
his name was made great for the sauing of the elect of God, 34 9. iosh.
and taking vengeance of the enemies that rose vp against 1. 2. and
them, that he might set Israel in their inheritance. 12. 7.
2 *How great glory gat he when he did lift vp his hands, *Iosh. 10.
and stretched out his sword against the cities? 12, 13, 14.
3 Who before him so stood to it? for the Lord himselfe
brought his enemies vnto him.
4 Did not the Sunne goe backe by his meanes? and was
not one day as long as two?
5 He called vpon the most high Lord, when the enemies
pressed vpon him on euery side, & the great Lord heard
him.
6 And with hailestones of mighty power he made the battell
to fall violently vpon the nations, and in the descent (of
Bethoron) hee destroyed them that resisted, that the nations
might know all their strength, because hee fought in the sight
of the Lord, and he followed the mightie one.
7 In the time of Moses also, he did a worke of mercie, hee
and Caleb the sonne of Iephunne, in that they withstood
the Congregation, and withheld the people from sinne, and
appeased the wicked murmuring.

8 And

*Num. 26. 8 *And of sixe hundred thousand people on foot, they two
65. deu. were preserued to bring them into the heritage, euen vnto
35. 36. the land that floweth with milk & hony.
9 The Lord gaue strength also vnto Caleb, which remained
with him vnto his old age, so that he entred vpon the high
places of the land, and his seed obtained it for an heritage.
10 That all the children of Israel might see that it is good
to follow the Lord.
11 And concerning the Iudges, euery one by name, whose
heart went not a whoring, nor departed from the Lord, let
their memory be blessed.
*Chap. 49. 12 Let their bones *flourish out of their place, and let the
12. name of them that were honoured, be continued vpon their
children.
*1. Sam. 13 *Samuel the Prophet of the Lord, beloued of his Lord,
1. 10. and established a kingdom, & anointed princes ouer his people.
16. 19. 14 By the Law of the Lord hee iudged the Congregation,
and the Lord had respect vnto Iacob.
15 By his faithfulnes he was found a true Prophet, and by
his word he was knowen to be faithfull in vision.
16 He called vpon the mighty Lord, when his enemies
pressed vpon him on euery side, when he offered the
*1. Sam. *sucking lambe.
7. 9. 17 And the Lord thundered from heauen, and with a great
noise made his voice to be heard.
18 And he destroyed the rulers of the Tyrians, and all the
princes of the Philistines.
*1. Sam. 19 And before his long sleepe hee made *protestations in
12. 3. the sight of the Lord, and his anoynted, I haue not taken
any mans goods, so much as a shoe, and no man did accuse
him.
*1. Sam. 20 And after his death he *prophesied, and shewed the King
28. 18, 19. his end, and lift vp his voyce from the earth in prophesie, to
blot out the wickednesse of the people.

CHAP. XLVII.

1 The praise of Nathan, 2 Of Dauid, 12 Of Solomon his glory, and infirmities. 23 Of his end and punishment.

*2. Sam. AND after him rose vp Nathan to *prophesie in the time
12. 1. of Dauid.
2 As is the fat taken away from the peace of-

fering, so was Dauid chosen out of the children of Israel.
3 Hee ||played with Lions as with kids, and with *beares || *Or, he smote Lions.*
as with lambs.
4 *Slew he not a gyant when hee was yet but yong? and *1. Sam.
did he not take away reproch from the people, when he lifted 17. 34.
vp his hand with the stone in the sling, and beat downe the *1. Sam.
boasting of Goliah? 17. 49, 50, 51.
5 For he called vpon the most high Lord, and he gaue him
strength in his right hand to slay that mighty warriour, and
set vp the horne of his people:
6 So the people honoured him with *ten thousands, and *1. Sam.
praised him in the blessings of the Lord, in that hee gaue 18. 7.
him a crowne of glory.
7 For hee destroyed the enemies on euery side, and *brought *2. Sam.
to nought the Philistines his ||aduersaries, and brake their horne 5. 7. || *Or, contemned.*
in sunder vnto this day.
8 In all his workes hee praised the holy one most High,
with words of glory, with his whole heart he sung songs,
and loued him that made him.
9 He set singers also before the *Altar, that by their voyces *1. Chr.
they might make sweet melody, and daily sing praises in their 16. 4.
songs.
10 He beautified their feasts, and set in order the solemne
times, ||vntill the ende, that they might praise his holy Name, || *Or, perfectly.*
and that the Temple might sound from morning.
11 The Lord tooke away his sinnes, and exalted his *horne *1. Sam.
for euer: he gaue him a couenant of kings, and a throne 12. 13.
||of glory in Israel. || *Or, of a kingdome.*
12 After him rose vp a wise sonne, and for his sake he
dwelt at large.
13 *Salomon reigned in a peaceable time, and was honoured; *1. King.
for God made all quiet round about him, that hee might build 4. 21, 24.
an house in his Name, and prepare his Sanctuary for euer.
14 *How wise wast thou in thy youth, & as a flood filled *1. King.
with vnderstanding. 4. 29, 30.
15 Thy soule couered the whole earth, and thou filledst it
with dark parables.
16 Thy name went farre vnto the Ilands, and for thy peace
thou wast beloued.
17 The countreys marueiled at thee for thy *Songs, and *1. King.
Prouerbs, and Parables, and interpretations. 4. 31, 32.
18 By the Name of the Lord God, which is called the
Lord God of Israel, thou didst *gather gold as tinne, *1. Kin.
and 10. 27.

and didst multiply siluer as lead.
*1. King. 11. 1. ‖Or, in. 19 *Thou didst bow thy loines vnto women, and ‖by thy
body thou wast brought into subiection.

20 Thou dist staine thy honour, and pollute thy seed, so
that thou broughtest wrath vpon thy children, and wast
grieued for thy folly.

*1. Kin. 12. 15, 16, 17. 21 *So the kingdome was diuided, and out of Ephraim
ruled a rebellious kingdome.

*2. Sam. 7. 15. 22 *But the Lord will neuer leaue off his mercy, neither
shall any of his workes perish, neither will hee abolish the
posterity of his elect, and the seed of him that loueth him he
will not take away: wherefore he gaue a remnant vnto
Iacob, and out of him a roote vnto Dauid.

23 Thus rested Solomon with his fathers, and of his seede
he left behinde him Roboam, euen the foolishnesse of the
*1. Kin. 12. 10, 11, 13, 14. people, and one that had no vnderstanding; who *turned
away the people through his counsell: there was also Ieroboam
*1. Kin. 12. 28, 30. the sonne of Nabat, who *caused Israel to sinne, and shewed
Ephraim the way of sinne:

24 And their sinnes were multiplied exceedingly, that they
were driuen out of the land.

25 For they sought out all wickednes, till the vengeance
came vpon them.

CHAP. XLVIII.

1 The praise of Elias, 12 of Elizeus, 17 and of Ezekias.

*1. King. 17. 1. THen stood vp *Elias the Prophet as fire, and his word
burnt like a lampe.

2 He brought a sore famine vpon them, and by his zeale he
‖Or, made heauen to holde vp. diminished their number.

3 By the word of the Lord he ‖shut vp the heauen, *and
*1. Kin. 18. 38. 2. king. 1. 10, 12. also three times brought downe fire.

4 O Elias, how wast thou honoured in thy wondrous
deedes! and who may glory like vnto thee!

*1. Kin. 17. 21, 22. 5 *Who didst raise vp a dead man from death, & his soule
‖Or, graue. from the ‖place of the dead by the word of the most Hie.

*2. Kings 1. 16. 6 *Who broughtest kings to destruction, and honourable
‖Or, seate. men from their ‖bedde.

*1. Kings 19. 15. 7 Who heardest the rebuke of the Lord in Sinai, *and in
Horeb the iudgment of vengeance.

*1. Kin. 19. 16. 8 *Who anointed kings to take re-

uenge, & Prophets to succeed after him:
9 *Who wast taken vp in a whirlewinde of fire, and in a *2. King.
charet of fierie horses: 2. 11.
10 Who wast ||ordained *for reproofes in their times, to ||*Or, writ-*
pacifie the wrath of the Lordes iudgement before it brake *ten of.* *Mal. 4. 3.
foorth into fury, and to turne the heart of the father vnto
the sonne, and to ||restore the tribes of Iacob. ||*Or, esta-*
11 Blessed are they that saw thee, and ||slept in loue, for we *blish.*
shal surely liue. ||*Or, were adorned*
12 *Elias it was, who was couered with a whirlewinde: *with loue.*
and Elizeus was filled with his spirit: whilest he liued he *2. King.
was not mooued [with the presence] of any prince, neither 2. 11, 15.
could any bring him into subiection.
13 ||No word could ouercome him, *& after his death his ||*Or, No-*
body prophecied. *thing.*
14 He did wonders in his life, and at his death were his *2. King. 13. 21.
works marueilous.
15 For all this the people repented not, neither departed
they from their sinnes, *till they were spoiled and caried out *2. Kin.
of their land, and were scattered through all the earth: yet 18. 11, 12.
there remained a small people, and a ruler in the house of
Dauid:
16 Of whom, some did that which was pleasing to God,
and some multiplied sinnes.
17 *Ezekias fortified his citie, and brought in water into *2. King.
the midst thereof: he digged the hard rocke with yron, and 18. 2.
made welles for waters.
18 In his time *Sennacherib came vp, and sent Rabsaces, *2. King.
and lift vp his hand against Sion, & boasted proudly. 18. 13.
19 Then trembled their hearts and handes, and they were
in paine as women in trauell.
20 But they called vpon the Lord which is mercifull, and
stretched out their hands towards him, and immediatly the
holy One heard them out of heauen, and deliuered them by
the ||ministery of Esay. ||*Or, hand.*
21 *He smote the hoste of the Assyrians, and his Angel *2. Kin.
destroyed them. 19. 35. isa. 37. 36.
22 For Ezekias had done the thing that pleased the Lord, tob. 1. 18.
and was strong in the wayes of Dauid his father, as Esay the 1. mac. 7.
Prophet, who was great and faithfull in his vision, had com- 41. 2. mac.
maunded him. 8. 19.
23 *In his time the Sunne went backeward, and hee *2. King.
lengthened the kings life. 20. 10. isa. 38. 8.

24 He

24 Hee sawe by an excellent spirit what should come to passe at the last, and hee comforted them that mourned in Sion.

25 He shewed what should come to passe for euer, and secret things or euer they came.

CHAP. XLIX.

1 The praise of Iosias, 4 Of Dauid and Ezekias, 6 Of Ieremie, 8 Of Ezechiel, 11 Zorobabel, 12 Iesus the sonne of Iosedec. 13 Of Nehemiah, Enoch, Seth, Sem, and Adam.

*2. King. 22 1. and 23. 2. 2. chr. 3. 34.

THe remembrance of *Iosias is like the composition of the perfume y^t is made by the arte of the Apothecarie: it is sweete as hony in all mouthes, and as musicke at a banquet of wine.

|| Or, prospered.

2 He ||behaued himselfe vprightly in the conuersion of the people, and tooke away the abominations of iniquitie.

*2. Kin. 23. 4.

3 *He directed his heart vnto the Lord, and in the time of the vngodly he established the worship of God.

4 All, except Dauid and Ezechias, and Iosias, were defectiue: for they forsooke the Law of the most High, (euen) the kings of Iudah failed:

|| Or, horne. *2. King. 25. 9.

5 Therefore he gaue their ||power vnto others, & their glory to a strange nation.

|| Or, by the hand of Ieremie.

6 *They burnt the chosen citie of the Sanctuarie, and made the streets desolate ||according to the prophecie of Ieremias:

*Ier. 38. 6. *Ier. 1. 5. *Eze. 1. 3, 15.

7 For they *entreated him euil, who neuerthelesse was a prophet *sanctified in his mothers wombe, that he might root out and afflict & destroy, and that he might build vp also and plant.

*Eze. 13. 11 and 38. 11, 16. & 46. 12 hag. 2. 24. ezr. 3. 2.

8 *It was Ezechiel who sawe the glorious vision, which was shewed him vpon the chariot of the Cherubims

|| Or, did good. * Ezek. 13. 13. & 38. 22

9 For he *made mention of the enemies vnder [the figure of] the raine, and ||directed them that went right.

10 *And of the twelue prophets let the memorial be blessed, and let their bones flourish againe out of their place: for they comforted Iacob, and deliuered them by assured hope.

*Zach. 3. 1. ezr. 3. 2. hag. 1. 12. and 2. 3.

11 *How shall we magnifie Zorobabel? euen he was as a signet on the right hand.

*Nehe. 7. 1.

12 *So was Iesus the sonne of Iosedec: who in their time builded the house, and set vp an holy Temple to the

Lord, which was prepared for euerlasting glory.
13 *And among the elect was Neemias whose renowme is *Gen. 5.
great, who raised vp for vs, the walles that were fallen, and 24 heb. 11.
set vp the gates & the barres, and raised vp our ruines againe. 5.
14 But vpon the earth was no man created like Enoch, for
he was taken from the earth.
15 Neither was there a man borne like vnto *Ioseph, a *Gen. 41.
gouernour of his brethren, a stay of the people, whose bones 44. and 42.
were regarded of the Lord. 6. & 45. 8.
16 *Sem and Seth were in great honour among men, and *Gen. 5. 3.
so was Adam aboue euery liuing thing in the creation. and 11. 10.

CHAP. L.

1 Of Simon the sonne of Onias. 22 How the people were taught to praise God, and pray. 27 The conclusion.

SImon *the high priest the sonne of Onias, who in his *2. Mac. 3,
life repaired the house againe, and in his dayes fortified 4
the Temple:
2 And by him was built from the foundation the double
height, the high fortresse of the wall about the Temple.
3 In his dayes the *cisterne to receiue water being in *1. King.
compasse as the sea, was couered with plates of brasse. 7. 23.
4 He tooke care of the Temple that it should not fall, and
fortified the citie against besieging.
5 How was he honoured in the midst of the people, in his
comming out of the †Sanctuarie? † *Gr. the house of the vaile.*
6 He was as the morning starre in the midst of a cloud:
and as the moone at the full.
7 As the Sunne shining vpon the Temple of the most High,
and as the rainebow giuing light in the bright cloudes.
8 And as the flowre of roses in the spring of the yeere, as
lillies by the riuers of waters, and as the branches of the
frankincense tree in the time of summer.
9 As fire and incense in the censer, and as a vessell of beaten
gold set with all maner of precious stones,
10 And as a faire oliue tree budding forth fruit, and as a
Cypresse tree which groweth vp to the cloudes.
11 When he put on the robe of honour, and was clothed
with the perfec-
tion

tion of glory, when he went vp to the holy altar, he made
the garment of holinesse honourable.
12 When he tooke the portions out of the priests hands, hee
himselfe stood by the hearth of the altar, compassed with his
brethren round about, as a yong cedar in Libanus, and as
palme trees compassed they him round about.
13 So were all the sonnes of Aaron in their glory, and the
oblations of the Lord in their hands, before all the congregation of Israel.
14 And finishing the seruice at the altar, that he might
adorne the offring of the most high Almighty,
15 He stretched out his hand to the cup, and powred of the
blood of the grape, he powred out at the foote of the altar, a
sweet smelling sauour vnto the most high King of all.
16 Then shouted the sonnes of Aaron, and sounded ‖the
siluer trumpets, and made a great noise to be heard, for a
remembrance before the most High.

‖ *Or, trumpets beaten forth with the hammer.*

17 Then all the people together hasted, and fell downe to
the earth vpon their faces to worship their Lord God almighty
the most High.
18 The singers also sang praises with their voices, with
great variety of sounds was there made sweete melodie.
19 And the people besought the Lord the most High by
prayer before him that is mercifull, till the solemnity of the
Lord was ended, and they had finished his seruice.
20 Then he went downe, and lifted vp his hands ouer the
whole congregation of the children of Israel, to giue the
blessing of the Lord with his lips, and to reioyce in his
name.
21 And they bowed themselues downe to worship the
second time, that they might receiue a blessing from the most
High.
22 Now therefore blesse yee the God of all, which onely
doth wonderous things euery where, which exalteth our daies
from the wombe, and dealeth with vs according to his mercy.
23 He grant vs ioyfulnesse of heart, and that peace may be
in our daies in Israel for euer.
24 That hee would confirme his mercy with vs, and deliuer
vs at his time.
25 There be two maner of nations

which my heart abhorreth, and the third is no nation.
26 They that sit vpon the mountaine of Samaria, and they
that dwell amongst the Philistines, and that foolish people
that dwell in Sichem.
27 Iesus the sonne of Sirach of Hierusalem hath written in
this booke, the instruction of vnderstanding and knowledge,
who out of his heart powred forth wisedome.
28 Blessed is he that shall be exercised in these things, and
hee that layeth them vp in his heart, shall become wise.
29 For if he doe them, hee shall be strong to all things, for
the light of the Lord leadeth him, who giueth wisedome to
the godly: blessed be the Lord for euer. Amen. Amen.

CHAP. LI.

¶ A Prayer of Iesus the sonne of Sirach.

I Will thanke thee, O Lord and king, and praise thee O
God my Sauiour, I doe giue praise vnto thy name:
2 For thou art my defeuder, and helper, and hast preserued
my body from destruction, and from the snare of the
slanderous tongue, and from the lippes that forge lies, and
hast beene my helper against mine aduersaries.
3 And hast deliuered me according to the multitude of thy
mercies, and greatnesse of thy name, from the †teeth of
them that were ready to deuoure me, and out of the hands of
such as sought after my life, and from the manifold afflictions
which I had:

† *Gre. the gnashing of the teeth.*

4 From the choking of fire on euery side, and from the mids
of the fire, which I kindled not:
5 From the depth of the belly of hel, from an vncleane
tongue, and from lying words.
6 By an accusation to the king from an vnrighteous tongue,
my soule drew neere euen vnto death, my life was neere to
the hell beneath:
7 They compassed me on euery side, and there was no man
to helpe me: I looked for the succour of men, but there was
none:
8 Then thought I vpon thy mercy, O Lord, and vpon thy
acts of old, how thou deliuerest such as waite for
thee,

thee, and sauest them out of the hands of the enemies:
9 Then lifted I vp my supplication from the earth, and
prayed for deliuerance from death.
10 I called vpon the Lord the father of my Lord, that he
would not leaue me in the dayes of my trouble, & in the
time of the proud when there was no helpe.
11 I will praise thy Name continually, and will sing praise
with thankesgiuing, and so my prayer was heard:
12 For thou sauedst me from destruction, and deliuerest
mee from the euill time: therefore will I giue thankes and
praise thee, and blesse thy Name, O Lord.
13 When I was yet yong, or euer I ||went abroad, I desired
wisedome openly in my prayer.
14 I prayed for her before the Temple, & will seeke her
out euen to the end:
15 Euen from the flowre till the grape was ripe, hath my
heart delighted in her, my foot went the right way, from my
youth vp sought I after her.
16 I bowed downe mine eare a litle and receiued her, &
gate much learning.
17 I profited therein, [therefore] will I ascribe the glory
vnto him that giueth me wisedome:
18 For I purposed to doe after her, and earnestly I followed
that which is good, so shall I not be confounded:

|| *Or, went astray.*

¶ BA

CHAP. I.

1 Baruch wrote a booke in Babylon. 5 The Iewes there wept at the reading of it. 7 They sende money and the booke, to the brethren at Hierusalem.

AND these are the wordes of the booke, which Baruch the sonne of Nerias, the sonne of Maasias, the sonne of Sedecias, the sonne of Asadias, the son of Chelcias, wrote in Babylon,

19 My soule hath wrestled with her, and in my doings I
was exact, I stretched foorth my hands to the heauen aboue,
& bewailed my ignorances of her.
20 ||I directed my soule vnto her, and I found her in pure- || *Or, I got*
nesse, I haue had my heart ioyned with her from the beginning, *vnderstan-*
therefore shall I not bee forsaken. *ding.*
21 My ||heart was troubled in seeking her: therefore haue || *Or,*
I gotten a good possession. *bowels.*
22 The Lord hath giuen mee a tongue for my reward, and
I wil praise him therewith.
23 Draw neere vnto me you vnlearned, and dwell in the
house of learning.
24 Wherefore are you slow, and what say you of these
things, seeing your soules are very thirstie?
25 *I opened my mouth, and said, buy her for your selues *Esay 55.
without money. 1.
26 Put your necke vnder the yoke, and let your soule receiue
instruction, she is hard at hand to finde.
27 *Behold with your eies, how that I haue had but little *Chap. 6.
labour, and haue gotten vnto me much rest. 18.
28 Get learning with a great summe of money, and get
much gold by her.
29 Let your soule reioyce in his mercy, and be not ashamed
of his praise.
30 Worke your worke betimes, & in his time he will giue
you your reward.

RVCH.

2 In the fift yere, and in the seuenth day of the moneth,
what time as the Caldeans tooke Ierusalem, and burnt it
with fire.
3 And Baruch did reade the words of this booke, in the
hearing of Iechonias, the sonne of ||Ioachim king of Iuda, and || *Or,*
in the eares of all the people, that came to [heare] the booke* *Ioacim.*
4 And in the hearing of the nobles, and of the kings sonnes,
and in the hearing of the Elders, and of all the people from
the lowest vnto the highest, euen of all them that dwelt at
Babylon, by the riuer Sud.
5 Whereupon they wept, fasted,
||and

|| *Or, and vowed vowes.* ||and prayed before the Lord.
6 They made also a collection of money, according to euery
mans power.
|| *Or, Ioacim.* 7 And they sent it to Ierusalem vnto ||Ioachim the hie
Priest the sonne of Chelcias, sonne of Salom, and to the
Priestes, and to all the people which were found with him at
Ierusalem,
8 At the same time, when he receiued the vessels of the
house of the Lord that were caried out of the Temple, to
returne them into the land of Iuda the tenth day of the
moneth Siuan, [namely] siluer vessels, which Sedecias the
sonne of Iosias king of Iuda had made,
9 After that Nabuchodonosor king of Babylon had caried
|| *Or, prisoners.* away Iechonias, and the Princes, and the ||captiues, and the
mightie men, and the people of the land from Ierusalem, and
brought them vnto Babylon:
10 And they said, Behold, we haue sent you money, to buy
you burnt offerings, and sinne offerings, and incense, and
† *Gr. corruptly for Mincha, a meat offering.* prepare yee †Manna, and offer vpon the Altar of the Lord
our God,
11 And pray for the life of Nabuchodonosor king of Babylon,
and for the life of Balthasar his sonne, that their dayes may
be vpon earth as the dayes of heauen.
12 And the Lord wil giue vs strength, and lighten our eyes,
and we shall liue vnder the shadow of Nabuchodonosor king
of Babylon, and vnder the shadow of Balthasar his sonne, and
wee shall serue them many dayes, and finde fauour in their
sight.
13 Pray for vs also vnto the Lord our God, (for wee haue
sinned against the Lord our God, and vnto this day the fury
of the Lord, and his wrath is not turned from vs)
14 And yee shall reade this booke, which we haue sent vnto
you, to make confession in the house of the Lord, vpon the
feasts and solemne dayes.
*Chap. 2. 6. 15 And yee shall say, *To the Lord our God belongeth
righteousnesse, but vnto vs the confusion of faces, as it is
come to passe this day vnto them of Iuda, & to the inhabitants
of Ierusalem,
16 And to our kings, and to our princes, and to our Priests,
and to our Prophets, and to our fathers.
*Dan. 9. 5. 17 For wee haue *sinned before the Lord,
18 And disobeyed him, aud haue not

hearkened vnto the voice of the Lord our God, to walke in
the commaundements that he gaue vs openly:
19 Since the day that the Lorde brought our forefathers out
of the land of Egypt, vnto this present day, wee haue beene
disobedient vnto the Lord our God, and we haue beene
negligent in not hearing his voice.
20 *Wherefore the euils cleaued vnto vs, and the curse *Deut. 28.
which the Lord appointed by Moses his seruant, at the time 15.
that he brought our fathers out of the land of Egypt, to giue
vs a land that floweth with milke and honie, like as it is to
see this day.
21 Neuerthelesse we haue not hearkened vnto the voice of
the Lord our God, according vnto all the wordes of the
Prophets, whom he sent vnto vs.
22 But euery man followed the imagination of his owne
wicked heart, to serue strange gods, and to doe euill in the
sight of the Lord our God.

CHAP. II.

The prayer and confession which the Iewes at Babylon made, and sent in that booke vnto the brethren in Ierusalem.

THerefore the Lord hath made good his worde, which
hee pronounced against vs, and against our Iudges that
iudged Israel, and against our kings, and against our princes,
and against the men of Israel and Iuda,
2 To bring vpon vs great plagues, such as neuer happened
vnder the whole heauen, as it came to passe in Ierusalem,
according to the things that were written in the Law of
Moses,
3 That a man should *eat the flesh of his owne sonne, and *Deut. 28.
the flesh of his owne daughter. 53.
4 Moreouer, he hath deliuered them to be in subiection to
all the kingdomes that are round about vs, to be as a reproch
and desolation among all the people round about, where the
Lord hath scattered them.
5 Thus wee †were cast downe and not exalted, because wee †*Gr. were*
haue sinned against the Lord our God, and haue not beene *beneath and not*
obedient vnto his voice. *aboue.*
6 *To the Lord our God appertaineth righteousnesse: but *Cha. 1.
vnto vs and to our fathers open shame, as appeareth this day. 15

7 For all these plagues are come vpon vs, which the Lord
hath pronounced against vs,
8 Yet haue we not prayed before the Lord, yͭ we might
turne euery one from the imaginations of his wicked heart.
9 Wherefore the Lord watched ouer vs for euill, and the
Lord hath brought it vpon vs: for the Lord is righteous in
all his works, which he hath commanded vs.
10 Yet we haue not hearkened vnto his voice, to walk in
the cōmandements of the Lord, that he hath set before vs.
*Dan. 9. 15 11 *And now O Lord God of Israel, that hast brought thy
people out of the land of Egypt with a mighty hand, and
high arme, and with signes & with wonders, & with great
power, and hast gotten thy selfe a name, as appeareth this day:
12 O Lord our God, we haue sinned, we haue done vngodly,
wee haue dealt vnrighteously in all thine ordinances.
13 Let thy wrath turne from vs: for we are but a few left
among the heathen, where thou hast scattered vs.
14 Heare our prayers, O Lord, and our petitions, and deliuer
vs for thine owne sake, and giue vs fauour in the sight of
them which haue led vs away:
15 That all the earth may know that thou art yͤ Lord our
†*Gr. thy name is called vpon Israel.* God, because Israel & his posterity is †called by thy name.
16 O Lord *looke downe from thy holy house, & consider
vs: bow downe thine eare, O Lord, to heare vs.
*Deut. 26. 15. esa. 63. 15. 17 *Open thine eyes and behold: for the dead that are in
the graues, whose †soules are taken from their bodies, wil
*Psal. 6. 5. and 115. 17 esa. 38. 18, 19. giue vnto the Lord neither praise nor righteousnesse.
18 But yͤ soule that is greatly vexed, which goeth stouping
& feeble, and the eyes that faile, and the hungry soule wil
giue thee praise & righteousnes O Lord.
†*Gr. spirit or life.* 19 *Therfore wee doe not make our humble supplication
*Dan. 9. 20 before thee, O Lord our God, for the righteousnes of our
fathers, and of our kings.
20 For thou hast sent out thy wrath & indignation vpon vs,
as thou hast spoken by thy seruants yͤ prophets, saying,
*Ier. 27. 7, 8 21 *Thus saith the Lord, bow down your shoulders to
serue the king of Babylon: so shall ye remaine in the lande
that I gaue vnto your fathers.
22 But if ye will not heare the voice of the Lord to serue
yͤ king of Babylon,

23 I will cause to cease out of the cities of Iuda, and from
without Ierusalem the voice of mirth, and the voice of ioy:
the voice of the bridegrome, and the voice of the bride, and
the whole land shall be desolate of inhabitants.
24 But we would not hearken vnto thy voyce, to serue the
king of Babylon: therefore hast thou made good the wordes
that thou spakest by thy seruants the prophets, namely that
the bones of our kings, and the bones of our fathers should
be taken out of their places.
25 And loe, they are cast out to the heat of the day, and to
the frost of the night, and they died in great miseries, by
famine, by sword, and by pestilence.
26 And the house which is called by thy name (hast thou
laid waste) as it is to be seene this day, for the wickednesse
of the house of Israel, and the house of Iuda.
27 O Lord our God, thou hast dealt with vs after all thy
goodnesse, and according to all that great mercie of thine.
28 As thou spakest by thy seruant Moses in the day when
thou didst command him to write thy Law, before the
children of Israel, saying,
29 *If ye will not heare my voyce, surely †this very great
multitude shalbe turned into a smal [number] among the
nations, where I will scatter them.
30 For I knew that they would not heare me: because it is
a stiffenecked people: but in the land of their captiuities,
they shall ‖remember themselues,
31 And shall know that I am the Lord their God: For I
giue them an heart, and eares to heare.
32 And they shal praise me in the land of their captiuitie,
and thinke vpon my name,
33 And returne from their stiffe †neck, and from their
wicked deeds: for they shal remember the way of their
fathers which sinned before the Lord.
34 And I will bring them againe into the land which I
promised with an oath vnto their fathers, Abraham, Isaac,
and Iacob, and they shall bee lords of it, and I will increase
them, and they shall not be diminished.
35 And I will make an euerlasting couenant with them, to
be their God, and they shall be my people: and I will no
more driue my people of Israel out of the land that I haue
giuen them.

* Leuit. 26. 14. deut. 28 15.
† *Gr. this great swarme.*
‖ *Or, come to themselues.*
† *Gr. backe.*

CHAP.

CHAP. III.

3 The rest of their prayer & confession contained in that book, which Baruch writ and sent to Hierusalem. 30 Wisdome was shewed first to Iacob, and was seene vpon the earth.

O Lord almighty, God of Israel, the soule in anguish, the troubled spirit crieth vnto thee.
2 Heare O Lord, and haue mercy: for thou art mercifull, and haue pitty vpon vs, because we haue sinned before thee.
3 For thou endurest for euer, and we perish vtterly.
4 O Lord almighty, thou God of Israel, heare now the prayers of the dead Israelites, and of their children, which haue sinned before thee, and not hearkened vnto the voice of thee their God: for the which cause these plagues cleaue vnto vs.
5 Remember not the iniquities of our forefathers: but thinke vpon thy power and thy name, now at this time.
6 For thou art the Lord our God, and thee, O Lord, will we praise.
7 And for this cause thou hast put thy feare in our hearts, to the intent that we should call vpon thy name, and praise thee in our captiuity: for *we haue called to minde all the iniquity of our forefathers that sinned before thee.

* Deut. 30. 1.

8 Behold, we are yet this day in our captiuity, where thou hast scattered vs, for a reproch and a curse, and to be subiect to payments, according to all the iniquities of our fathers which departed from the Lord our God.
9 Heare, Israel, the commandements of life, giue eare to vnderstand wisedome.
10 How happeneth it, Israel, that thou art in thine enemies land, that thou art waxen old in a strange countrey, that thou art defiled with the dead?
11 That thou art counted with them that goe downe into the graue?
12 Thou hast forsaken the fountaine of wisedome.
13 For if thou hadst walked in the way of God, thou shouldest haue dwelled in peace for euer.
14 Learne where is wisedome, where is strength, where is vnderstanding, that thou mayest know also where is length of daies, and life, where is the light of the eyes and peace.

15 Who hath found out her *place? or who hath come *Iob. 28. 12. 20.
into her treasures?
16 Where are the princes of the heathen become, and such
as ruled the beasts vpon the earth.
17 They that had their pastime with the foules of the aire,
and they that hoorded vp siluer and gold wherein men trust,
and made no end of their getting?
18 For they that wrought in siluer, and were so careful,
and whose workes are vnsearchable,
19 They are vanished, and gone downe to the graue, and
others are come vp in their steads.
20 Young men haue seene light, and dwelt vpon the earth:
but the way of knowledge haue they not knowen,
21 Nor vnderstood the pathes thereof, nor laid hold of it:
their children were farre off from that way.
22 It hath not beene heard of in Chanaan: neither hath it
beene seene in Theman.
23 The Agarenes that seek wisdome vpon earth, the
marchants of Merran, and of Theman, the ||authors of fables, ||*Or, expounders.*
and searchers out of vnderstanding: none of these haue
knowen the way of wisedome, or remember her pathes.
24 O Israel, how great is the house of God? and how large
is the place of his possession?
25 Great, and hath none end: high, and vnmeasurable.
26 There were the gyants, famous from the beginning, that
were of so great stature, and so expert in warre.
27 Those did not the Lord chuse, neither gaue he the way
of knowledge vnto them.
28 But they were destroyed, because they had no wisedome,
and perished through their owne foolishnesse.
29 Who hath gone vp into heauen and taken her, and
brought her downe from the clouds?
30 Who hath gone ouer the Sea, and found her, & wil
bring her for pure gold?
31 No man knoweth her way, nor thinketh of her path.
32 But he that knoweth all things, knoweth her, and hath
found her out with his vnderstanding: he that prepared the
earth for euermore, hath filled it with fourefooted beasts.
33 He that sendeth forth light, and it goeth: calleth it
againe, and it obeyeth him with feare.

34 The starres shined in their watches, and reioyced: when
he calleth them, they say, Here we be, and so with cheerefulnesse they shewed light vnto him that made them.
35 This is our God, and there shall none other be accounted
of in comparison of him.
36 He hath found out all the way of knowledge, and hath
giuen it vnto Iacob his seruant, & to Israel his beloued.
37 *Afterward did he shew himselfe vpon earth, and con-
uersed with men.

*Pro. 8. 31. iohn 1. 14.

CHAP. IIII.

1 The booke of Commandements, is that Wisdome which was commended in the former chapter. 25 The Iewes are mooued to patience, and to hope for the deliuerance.

THis is the Booke of the commandements of God: and
the Law that endureth for euer: all they that keepe
it shall come to life: but such as leaue it, shall die.
2 Turne thee, O Iacob, & take heed of it: walke †in the
presence of the light therof, that thou mayest be illuminated.
3 Giue not thine honour to another, nor the things that
are profitable vnto thee, to a strange nation.
4 O Israel, happie are wee: for things that are pleasing to
God, are made knowen vnto vs.
5 Be of good cheare, my people, the memoriall of Israel.
6 Ye were sold to the nations, not for [your] destruction:
but because you moued God to wrath, ye were deliuered vnto
the enemies.
7 For yee prouoked him that made you, by *sacrificing
vnto deuils, and not to God.
8 Ye haue forgotten the euerlasting God, that brought you
vp, and ye haue grieued Ierusalem that noursed you.
9 For when shee saw the wrath of God cōming vpon you,
she said; Hearken, O ye that dwell about Sion: God hath
brought vpō me great mourning.
10 For I saw the captiuitie of my sonnes and daughters,
which the euerlasting brought vpon them.
11 With ioy did I nourish them: but sent them away with
weeping and mourning.
12 Let no man reioyce ouer me a widow, and forsaken of
many, who for the sinnes of my children, am left desolate:

†*Greeke, to the shining, before the light thereof.*

*1. Cor. 10. 20.

because they departed from the Law of God.
13 They knew not his statutes, nor walked in the waies of
his Commandements, nor trode in the pathes ||of discipline in || *Or, of his discipline in righteousnes.*
his righteousnesse.
14 Let them that dwell about Sion come, and remember ye
the captiuity of my sonnes and daughters, which the euerlasting hath brought vpon them.
15 For he hath brought a nation vpon them from far: a
shamelesse nation, and of a strange language, who neither
reuerenced old man, nor pitied childe.
16 These haue caried away the deare beloued children of
the widow, and left her that was alone, desolate without
daughters.
17 But what can I helpe you?
18 For he that brought these plagues vpon you, will deliuer
you from the hands of your enemies.
19 Goe your way, O my children, goe your way: for I am
left desolate.
20 I haue put off the clothing of ||peace, and put vpon me || *Or, prosperitie.*
the sackcloth of my prayer. I will cry vnto the euerlasting
||* in my dayes. || *Or, in the time of mine affliction.*
21 Be of good cheare, O my children, cry vnto the Lord:
& he shal deliuer you from the power & hand of the enemies.
22 For my hope is in the Euerlasting that hee will saue * Psa. 116. 2. and 137. 7.
you, and ioy is come vnto me from the Holy one, because of
the mercy which shall soone come vnto you from the euerlasting our Sauiour.
23 For I sent you out with mourning and weeping: but
God will giue you to mee againe, with ioy and gladnesse for euer.
24 Like as now the neighbours of Sion haue seene your
captiuity: so shall they see shortly your saluation from our
God, which shall come vpon you with great glory, and
brightnesse of the euerlasting.
25 My children, suffer patiently the wrath that is come
vpon you from God: for thine enemy hath persecuted thee:
but shortly thou shalt see his destruction, & shalt tread vpon
his necke.
26 My ||delicate ones haue gone rough wayes, and were || *Or, my dearelings.*
taken away as a flocke caught of the enemies.
27 Be of good comfort, O my children, and cry vnto God:
for you shall be remembred of him that brought these things
vpon you.
28 For as it was your minde to goe
astray

astray from God: so being returned seeke him ten times more.
29 For he that hath brought these plagues vpon you, shall bring you euerlasting ioy againe with your saluation.
30 Take a good heart, O Ierusalem: for hee that gaue thee that name, will comfort thee.
31 Miserable are they that afflicted thee, and reioyced at thy fall.
32 Miserable are the cities which thy children serued: miserable is she that receiued thy sonnes.
33 For as shee reioyced at thy ruine, and was glad of thy fall: so shall she be grieued for her owne desolation.
34 For I will take away the reioycing of her great multitude, and her pride shalbe turned into mourning.
35 For fire shal come vpon her frō the euerlasting, long to endure: and she shal be inhabited of deuils for a great time.
36 O Ierusalem, looke about thee toward the East, and behold the ioy that commeth vnto thee from God.
37 Loe, thy sonnes come whom thou sentest away: they come gathered together from the East to the West, by the word of the holy One, reioycing in the glory of God.

CHAP. V.

1 Ierusalem is moued to reioyce, 5 and to behold their returne out of captiuity with glory.

PVt off, O Ierusalem, the garment of thy mourning and affliction, and put on the comelinesse of the glory that commeth from God for euer.
2 Cast about thee a double garment of the righteousnesse which commeth from God, and set a diademe on thine head of the glory of the euerlasting.
3 For God wil shew thy brightnesse vnto euery countrey vnder heauen.
4 For thy name shall bee called of God for euer, The peace of righteousnesse, and the glory of Gods worship.
5 Arise, O Ierusalem, and stand on high, and looke about toward the East, and behold thy children gathered from the West vnto the East by the word of the holy One, reioycing in the remembrance of God.
6 For they departed from thee on foote, and were ledde away of their enemies: but God bringeth them vnto thee exalted with glory, as children of the kingdome.

7 For God hath appointed that euery high hill, and banks
of long continuance should be cast downe, and valleys filled
vp, to make euen the ground, that Israel may goe safely in
the glory of God.
8 Moreouer, euen the woods, & euery sweet smelling tree,
shall ouershadow Israel by the commandement of God.
9 For God shall leade Israel with ioy, in the light of his
glory, with the mercy and righteousnes that commeth from
him.

¶ *The Epistle of Ieremie.*

CHAP. VI.

1 The cause of the captiuity is their sinne. 3 The place whereto they were caried, is Babylon: the vanitie of whose idols and idolatry are set foorth at large in this Chapter.

A Copy of an Epistle which Ieremie sent vnto them which
were to be led captiues into Babylon, by the king of
the Babylonians, to certifie them as it was commanded him
of God.
2 Because of ye sinnes which ye have committed before God,
ye shall be led away captiues vnto Babylon by Nabuchodonosor king of the Babylonians.
3 So when ye be come vnto Babylon, ye shal remaine there
many yeeres, and for a long season, namely seuen generations: and after that I will bring you away peaceably from
thence.
4 *Now shal ye see in Babylon gods of siluer, and of gold, *Esai. 44.
and of wood, borne vpon shoulders, which cause the nations 8, 9, 10.
to feare. and 46. 5, 7. psal. 115.
5 Beware therefore that yee in no wise be like to strangers, 4. wis. 13.
neither be yee afraid of them, when yee see the multitude 10.
before them, and behinde them, worshipping them.
6 But say yee in your hearts, O Lord, we must worship thee.
7 For mine Angel is with you, and I my selfe caring for
your soules.
8 As for their tongue, it is polished by the workeman, and
they themselues are guilded and laid ouer with siluer, yet are
they but false and cannot speake.
9 And taking golde, as it were for a virgine that loues to go
gay, they make crownes for the heads of their gods.
10 Sometimes also the Priests conuey from their gods golde
and siluer, and bestow it vpon themselues.

|| *Or, which prostitute themselues openly.*

11 Yea they will giue thereof to the ||common harlots, and
decke them as men with garments [being] gods of siluer, and
gods of gold, and wood.
12 Yet cannot these gods saue themselues from rust and
moths, though they be couered with purple raiment.
13 They wipe their faces because of the dust of the Temple,
when there is much vpon them.
14 And he that cannot put to death one that offendeth him,
holdeth a scepter as though hee were a iudge of the countrey.
15 Hee hath also in his right hand a dagger, and an axe:
but cannot deliuer himselfe from warre and theeues.
16 Whereby they are knowen not to bee gods, therefore
feare them not.
17 For like as a vessell that a man vseth, is nothing worth
when it is broken: euen so it is with their gods: when they
be set vp in the Temple, their eyes be full of dust, thorow
the feet of them that come in.

|| *Or, courts.*

18 And as the ||doores are made sure on euery side, vpon
him that offendeth the king, as being committed to suffer
death: euen so the priests make fast their temples, with
doores, with lockes and barres, lest their gods bee spoiled
with robbers.
19 They light them candles, yea, more then for themselues,
whereof they cannot see one.

† *Gr. licked.*

20 They are as one of the beames of the temple, yet they
say, their hearts are †gnawed vpon by things creeping out of
the earth, & when they eate them and their clothes, they
feele it not.
21 Their faces are blacked, thorow the smoke that comes
out of the temple.
22 Vpon their bodies and heads, sit battes, swallowes, and
birds, and the cats also.
23 By this you may know that they are no gods: therefore
feare them not.
24 Notwithstanding the gold that is about them, to make
them beautifull, except they wipe off the rust they will not
shine: for neither when they were molten did they feele it.
25 The things wherein there is no breath, are bought for
||a most hie price.

|| *Or, any price.*
* Esa. 46. 7.

26 * They are borne vpon shoulders, hauing no feete, whereby they declare vnto men that they be nothing worth.
27 They also that serue them, are ashamed: for if they fall
to the ground at

any time, they cannot rise vp againe of themselues: neither
if one set them vpright can they moue of themselues: neither
if they be bowed downe, can they make themselues streight:
but they set ||gifts before them as vnto dead men. || Or, of-
28 As for the things that are sacrificed vnto them, their frings
priests sell and ||abuse: in like maner their wiues lay vp part || Or,
thereof in salt: but vnto the poore and impotent, they giue spend.
nothing of it.
29 Menstruous women, and women in childbed *eate their * Leu. 12.
sacrifices: by these things ye may know that they are no 4.
gods: feare them not.
30 For how can they be called gods? because women set
meate before the gods of siluer, gold, and wood.
31 And the priests sit in their temples, hauing their clothes
rent, and their heads and beards shauen, and nothing vpon
their heads.
32 They roare and crie before their gods: as men doe at
the feast when one is dead.
33 The priestes also take off their garments, and clothe
their wiues and children.
34 Whether it be euill that one doth vnto them, or good:
they are not able to recompense it: they can neither set vp
a king, nor put him downe.
35 In like maner, they can neither giue riches nor money:
though a man make a vowe vnto them, and keepe it not, they
will not require it.
36 They can saue no man from death, neither deliuer the
weake from the mightie.
37 They cannot restore a blind man to his sight, nor helpe
any man in his distresse.
38 They can shew no mercie to the widow: nor doe good
to the fatherlesse.
39 Their gods of wood, and which are ouerlaid with gold,
and siluer, are like the stones that be hewen out of the
mountaine: they that worship them shall be confounded.
40 How should a man then thinke and say that they are
gods? when euen the Chaldeans thēselues dishonor them.
41 Who if they shall see one dumbe that cannot speake,
they ||bring him and intreate Bel that he may speake, as || Or, bid
though he were able to vnderstand. him call
42 Yet they cannot vnderstand this themselues, and leaue vpon Bel.
them: for they haue no ||knowledge. || Or, sence.

43 The

43 The women also with cordes about them, sitting in the
wayes, burne branne for perfume: but if any of them drawen
by some that passeth by, lie with him, she reproacheth her
fellow that she was not thought as worthy as her selfe, nor
her cord broken.
44 Whatsoeuer is done among them is false: how may it
then be thought or said that they are gods?
45 They are made of carpenters, and goldsmiths, they can
be nothing else, then the workman will haue them to be.
46 And they themselues that made them, can neuer continue long, how should then the things that are made of them,
be gods?
47 For they left lies and reproaches to them that come after.
48 For when there commeth any warre or plague vpon
them, the priests consult with themselues, where they may
be hidden with them.
49 How then cannot men perceiue, that they be no gods,
which can neither saue themselues from warre nor from
plague?
*Psal. 115. 50 *For seeing they be but of wood, and ouerlaide with
4. wisdom. siluer and gold: it shall be knowen heereafter that they are
13. 10. false.
51 And it shall manifestly appeare to all nations and kings,
that they are no gods: but the workes of mens hands, and
that there is no worke of God in them.
52 Who then may not know that they are no gods?
53 For neither can they set vp a king in the land, nor giue
raine vnto men.
54 Neither can they iudge their owne cause, nor redresse a
wrong being vnable: for they are as crowes between heauen
and earth.
55 Whereupon when fire falleth vpon the house of gods of
wood, or layd ouer with gold or siluer, their priests will fly
away, & escape: but they themselues shall be burnt asunder
like beames.
56 Moreouer they cannot withstand any king or enemies:
how can it then be thought or said that they be gods?
57 Neither are those gods of wood, and layd ouer with
siluer or gold able to escape either from theeues or robbers.
58 Whose gold, and siluer, and garments wherwith they
are clothed, they that are strong doe take, and goe away

withall: neither are they able to helpe themselues.
59 Therefore it is better to be a king that sheweth his
power, or else a profitable vessell in an house, which the
owner shall haue vse of, then such false gods: or to be a
doore in an house to keepe such things safe as be therein,
then such false gods: or a pillar of wood in a palace, then
such false gods.
60 For Sunne, Moone, and starres, being bright and sent to
doe their offices, are obedient.
61 In like maner the lightning when it breaketh forth is
easie to bee seene, and after the same maner ||the wind blow- || *Or, the same wind.*
eth in euery country.
62 And when God commandeth the clouds to goe ouer the
whole world: they doe as they are bidden:
63 And the fire sent from aboue to consume hilles and
woods, doth as it is commanded: but these are like vnto
them neither in shew, nor power.
64 Wherefore it is neither to be supposed nor said, that
they are gods, seeing they are able, neither to iudge causes,
nor to doe good vnto men.
65 Knowing therefore that they are no gods, feare them
not.
66 For they can neither curse nor blesse kings.
67 Neither can they shew signes in the heauens among the
heathen: nor shine as the Sunne, nor giue light as the Moone.
68 The beasts are better then they: for they can get vnder
a couert, and helpe themselues.
69 It is then by no meanes manifest vnto vs that they are
gods: therefore feare them not.
70 For as a scarcrow in a garden of Cucumbers keepeth
nothing: so are their gods of wood, and laid ouer with siluer
and gold.
71 And likewise their gods of wood, and laid ouer with
siluer and gold, are like to a white thorne in an orchard that
euery bird sitteth vpon: as also to a dead body, that is cast
into the darke.
72 And you shall know them to be no gods, by the ||bright || *Or purple and brightnesse.*
purple that rotteth vpon them: and they themselues after-
ward shall be eaten, and shall be a reproach in the country.
73 Better therefore is the iust man that hath none idoles:
for he shall be farre from reproach.

¶ The

¶ The Song of the

which followeth in the third

this place, [And they walked in the

and blessing the Lord.] That which followeth is
stood vp] vnto these wordes,

1 Azarias his praier and confession in the flame, 24 wherewith the Chaldeans about the ouen were consumed, but the three children within it were not hurt. 28 The Song of the three children in the ouen.

THEN Azarias stood vp & prayed on this manner, and
opening his mouth in the midst of the fire, said,
2 Blessed art thou, O Lord God of our fathers: thy Name
is worthy to be praised, and glorified for euermore.
3 For thou art righteous in all the things that thou hast
done to vs: yea, true are all thy workes: thy wayes are
right, and *all thy iudgements trueth.
4 In all the things that thou hast brought vpon vs, and
vpon the holy citie of our fathers, euen Ierusalem, thou hast
executed true iudgement: for according to trueth and iudgement, didst thou bring all these things vpon vs, because of
our sinnes.
5 For wee haue sinned and committed iniquitie, departing
from thee.
6 In all things haue we trespassed, and not obeyed thy
Commandements, nor kept them, neither done as thou hast
commanded vs, that it might goe well with vs.
7 Wherefore all that thou hast brought vpon vs, and euery
thing that thou hast done to vs, thou hast done in true
iudgement.
8 And thou didst deliuer vs into the hands of lawlesse
enemies, most hatefull forsakers [of God] and to an vniust
King, and the most wicked in all the world.
9 And now wee can not open our

*Psal. 25. 10,

three holy children,

Chapter of Daniel after

midst of the fire, praising God,

not in the Hebrew; to wit, [Then Azarias
[And Nabuchodonosor.]

mouthes, we are become a shame, and reproch to thy seruants, and to them that worship thee.
10 Yet deliuer vs not vp wholy for thy Names sake, neither
disanull thou thy Couenant:
11 And cause not thy mercy to depart from vs: for thy
beloued Abrahams sake: for thy seruant Isaacs sake, and for
thy holy Israels sake.
12 To whom thou hast spoken and promised, That thou
wouldest multiply their seed as the starres of heauen, and as
the sand that lyeth vpon the sea shore.
13 For we, O Lord, are become lesse then any nation, and
bee kept vnder this day in all the world, because of our
sinnes.
14 Neither is there at this time, Prince, or Prophet, or leader,
or burnt offering, or sacrifice, or oblation, or incense, or place
to sacrifice before thee, and to finde mercie.
15 Neuerthelesse in a contrite heart, and an humble spirit,
let vs be accepted.
16 Like as in the burnt offering of rammes and bullockes,
and like as in ten thousands of fat lambes: so let our sacrifice bee in thy sight this day, and [grant] that wee may
wholy goe after thee: for they shall not bee confounded that
put their trust in thee.
17 And now wee follow thee, with all our heart, wee feare
thee, and seeke thy face.
18 Put vs not to shame: but deale with vs after thy louing
kindenesse, and according to the multitude of thy mercies.
19 Deliuer vs also according to thy marueilous workes, and
giue glory to thy Name, O Lord, and let all them that doe
thy seruants hurt be ashamed.
20 And let them be ||confounded in all

|| *Or, by thy power and might.*

all their power and might, and let their strength be broken.
21 And let them know that thou art Lord, the onely God,
and glorious ouer the whole world.
22 And the kings seruants that put them in, ceased not to
make the ouen hote with ||rosin, pitch, towe, and small wood.

|| *Or, Naptha, which is a certaine kind of fat and chalkie clay, Plin. lib.* 2. *c.* 105.

23 So that the flame streamed forth aboue the fornace,
fourtie and nine cubites:
24 And it passed through, and burnt those Caldeans it
found about the fornace.
25 But the Angel of the Lord came downe into the ouen,
together with Azarias and his fellowes, and smote the flame
of the fire out of the ouen:
26 And made the mids of the fornace, as it had bene a
||moist whistling wind, so that the fire touched them not at
all, neither hurt nor troubled them.

|| *Or, coole.*

27 Then the three, as out of one mouth, praised, glorified,
and blessed God in the fornace, saying;
28 Blessed art thou, O Lord God of our fathers: and to be
praised and exalted aboue all for euer.
29 And blessed is thy glorious and holy Name: and to be
praised and exalted aboue all for euer.
30 Blessed art thou in the Temple of thine holy glory: and
to be praised and glorified aboue all for euer.
31 Blessed art thou that beholdest the depths, and sittest
vpon the Cherubims, and to be praised and exalted aboue all
for euer.
32 Blessed art thou on the glorious Throne of thy kingdome: and to bee praised and glorified aboue all for euer.
33 Blessed art thou in the firmament of heauen: and aboue
all to be praised and glorified for euer.
34 O all yee workes of the Lorde, blesse ye the Lord:
praise and exalt him ||aboue all for euer.

|| *Or, highly exalt: and so in the rest.*
* Psal. 148. 4

35 *O ye heauens, blesse ye the Lord: praise and exalt
him aboue all for euer.
36 O yee Angels of the Lord, blesse ye the Lord: praise
and exalt him aboue all for euer.
37 O all ye waters that be aboue the heauen, blesse yee the
Lord: praise and exalt him aboue all for euer.
38 O all yee powers of the Lord, blesse ye the Lord: praise
and exalt him aboue all for euer.

39 O yee Sunne and Moone, blesse ye the Lord: praise
and exalt him aboue all for euer.
40 O ye starres of heauen, blesse ye the Lord: praise and
exalt him aboue all for euer.
41 O euery showre and dew, blesse ye the Lord: praise
and exalt him aboue all for euer.
42 O all ye windes, blesse yee the Lord: praise and exalt
him aboue all for euer.
43 O yee fire and heate, blesse ye the Lord: praise and
exalt him aboue all for euer.
44 O yee Winter and Summer, blesse ye the Lord: praise
and exalt him aboue all for euer.
45 O ye dewes and stormes of snow, blesse ye the Lord:
praise and exalt him aboue all for euer.
46 O ye nights and dayes, blesse ye the Lord: praise and
exalt him aboue all for euer.
47 O ye light and darkenesse, blesse ye the Lord: praise
and exalt him aboue all for euer.
48 O yee yce and colde, blesse ye the Lord: praise and
exalt him aboue all for euer.
49 O ye frost and snow, blesse ye the Lord: praise and
exalt him aboue all for euer.
50 O ye lightnings and clouds, blesse ye the Lord: praise
and exalt him aboue all for euer.
51 O let the earth blesse the Lord: praise and exalt him
aboue all for euer.
52 O ye mountaines and little hils, blesse ye the Lord:
praise and exalt him aboue all for euer.
53 O all ye things that grow on the earth, blesse ye the
Lord: praise and exalt him aboue all for euer.
54 O yee fountaines, blesse yee the Lord: praise and exalt
him aboue all for euer.
55 O ye seas and riuers, blesse ye the Lord: praise and
exalt him aboue all for euer.
56 O ye whales and all that mooue in the waters, blesse ye
the Lord: praise and exalt him aboue all for euer.
57 O all ye foules of the †aire, blesse ye the Lord: praise † *Gr. heauen.*
and exalt him aboue all for euer.
58 O all ye beasts and cattell, blesse ye the Lord: praise
and exalt him aboue all for euer.

59 O ye

59 O ye children of men, blesse yee the Lord: praise and
exalt him aboue all for euer.
60 O Israel blesse ye the Lord: praise and exalt him aboue
all for euer.
61 O ye priests of the Lord, blesse ye the Lord: praise and
exalt him aboue all for euer.
62 O ye seruants of the Lord, blesse ye the Lord: praise
and exalt him aboue all for euer.
63 O ye spirits and soules of the righteous, blesse ye the
Lord, praise and exalt him aboue all for euer.
64 O ye ‖holy and humble men of heart, blesse ye the
Lord: praise and ex-

‖ *Or, Saints*

¶ The historie of Susanna,

the beginning of Daniel,

brew, as neither the narration of

16 Two Iudges hide themselues in the garden of Susanna to haue their pleasure of her: 28 which when they could not obteine, they accuse and cause her to be condemned for adulterie, 46 but Daniel examineth the matter againe, and findeth the two iudges false.

THere dwelt a man in Babylon, called Ioacim.
2 And hee tooke a wife, whose name was Susanna, the
daughter of Chelcias, a very faire woman, and one that feared
the Lord.
3 Her parents also were righteous, and taught their daughter according to the Law of Moses.
4 Now Ioacim was a great rich man, and had a faire garden
ioyning vnto his house, and to him resorted the Iewes: because he was more honourable then all others.
5 The same yeere were appointed two of the Ancients of
the people to be iudges, such as the Lord spake of, that
wickednesse came from Babylon from ancient iudges, who
seemed to gouerne the people.
6 These kept much at Ioacims house: and all that had any
suits in lawe, came vnto them.

alt him aboue all for euer.
65 O Ananias, Azarias, and Misael, blesse ye the Lord,
praise and exalt him aboue all for euer: for hee hath de-
liuered vs from ||hell, and saued vs from the hand of death, and || *Or, graue.*
deliuered vs out of the mids of the furnace, [and] burning
flame: euen out of the mids of the fire hath he deliuered vs.
66 O giue thanks vnto the Lord, because he is gracious:
for his mercie endureth for euer.
67 O all ye that worship the Lord, blesse the God of gods,
praise him, and giue him thankes: for his mercie endureth
for euer.

set apart from

because it is not in He-

†Bel and the Dragon.

† *Gr, Bels Dragon.*

7 Now when the people departed away at noone, Susanna
went into her husbands garden to walke.
8 And the two Elders saw her going in euery day and walking: so that their lust was inflamed toward her.
9 And they peruerted their owne mind, and turned away
their eyes, that they might not looke vnto heauen, nor remember iust iudgements.
10 And albeit they both were wounded with her loue: yet
durst not one shew another his griefe.
11 For they were ashamed to declare their lust, that they
desired to haue to doe with her.
12 Yet they watched diligently from day to day to see her.
13 And the one said to the other, Let vs now goe home:
for it is dinner time.
14 So when they were gone out, they parted the one from
the other, and turning backe againe they came to the same
place, and after that they had asked one another the cause,
they acknowledged their lust: then appointed they a time
both together, when they might find her alone.
15 And it fell out as they watched a fit time, she went in
†as before, with two maids onely, and she was desirous
to

† *Gr. as yesterday and the day before.*

to wash her selfe in the garden: for it was hot.
16 And there was no body there saue the two Elders, that
had hid themselues, and watched her.
17 Then she said to her maids, Bring me oile and washing
bals, and shut the garden doores, that I may wash me.
18 And they did as she bad them, and shut the garden
doores, and went out themselues at ‖priuie doores to fetch
the things that she had commaunded them: but they saw not
the Elders, because they were hid.

‖ *Or, side doores.*

19 Now when the maids were gone forth, the two Elders
rose vp, and ran vnto her, saying,
20 Behold, the garden doores are shut, that no man can see
vs, and we are in loue with thee: therefore consent vnto vs,
and lie with vs.
21 If thou wilt not, we will beare witnesse against thee,
that a young man was with thee: and therefore thou didst
send away thy maides from thee.
22 Then Susanna sighed and said, I am straited on euery
side: for if I doe this thing, it is death vnto me: and if I doe
it not, I cannot escape your hands.
23 It is better for me to fall into your hands, and not doe
it: then to sinne in the sight of the Lord.
24 With that Susanna cried with a loud voice: and the two
Elders cried out against her.
25 Then ranne the one, and opened the garden doore.
26 So when the seruants of the house heard the crie in the
garden, they rushed in at a priuie doore to see what was done
vnto her.
27 But when the Elders had declared their matter, the seruants were greatly ashamed: for there was neuer such a
report made of Susanna.
28 And it came to passe the next day, when the people
were assembled to her husband Ioacim, the two Elders came
also full of mischieuous imagination against Susanna to put
her to death,
29 And said before the people, Send for Susanna, the
daughter of Chelcias, Ioacims wife. And so they sent.
30 So she came with her father and mother, her children
and all her kinred.
31 Now Susanna was a very delicate woman, and beauteous
to behold.
32 And these wicked men commanded to vncouer her face
(for she was co-

uered) that they might be filled with her beautie.
33 Therefore her friends, and all that saw her, wept.
34 Then the two Elders stood vp in the mids of the people,
and laid their hands vpon her head.
35 And she weeping looked vp towards heauen: for her
heart trusted in the Lord.
36 And the Elders said, As we walked in the garden alone,
this woman came in, with two maides, and shut the garden
doores, & sent the maides away.
37 Then a young man who there was hid, came vnto her
& lay with her.
38 Then we that stood in a corner of the garden, seeing
this wickednesse, ran vnto them.
39 And when we saw them together, the man we could
not hold: for he was stronger then we, and opened the
doore, and leaped out.
40 But hauing taken this woman, we asked who the young
man was: but she would not tell vs: these things doe we
testifie.
41 Then the assembly beleeued them, as those that were
the Elders and Iudges of the people: so they condemned her
to death.
42 Then Susanna cried out with a loud voice and said: O
euerlasting God that knowest the secrets, and knowest all
things before they be:
43 Thou knowest that they haue borne false witnesse a-
gainst me, and behold I must die: whereas I neuer did such
things, as these men haue maliciously inuented against me.
44 And the Lord heard her voice.
45 Therefore when she was led to be put to death: the
Lord raised vp the holy spirit of a young youth, whose name
was Daniel,
46 Who cried with a loud voice: I am cleare frō the blood
of this woman.
47 Then all the people turned them towards him, & said:
what meane these words that thou hast spoken?
48 So he standing in the mids of them, said, Are ye such
fooles ye sonnes of Israel, that without examination or knowledge of the truth, ye haue condemned a daughter of Israel?
49 Returne againe to the place of iudgement: for they
haue borne false witnesse against her
50 Wherefore all the people turned
againe

againe in hast, and the Elders said vnto him, Come sit downe
among vs, and shew it vs, seeing God hath giuen thee the
honour of an Elder.
51 Then said Daniel vnto them, Put these two aside one
farre from another, and I will examine them.
52 So when they were put asunder one from another, hee
called one of them, and said vnto him, O thou that art waxen
old in wickednesse: now thy sinnes which thou hast committed aforetime, are come [to light.]
53 For thou hast pronounced false iudgement, and hast
condemned the innocent, and hast let the guiltie goe free,
*Exod. 23. 7. albeit the Lord saith, *The innocent and righteous shalt
thou not slay.
54 Now then if thou hast seene her: tell me, Vnder what
tree sawest thou them companying together? who answered,
†Gr. lentiske tree. Vnder a †masticke tree.
55 And Daniel said, Very wel; Thou hast lied against
thine owne head: for euen now the Angel of God hath
receiued the sentence of God, to cut thee in two.
56 So hee put him aside, and commanded to bring the
other, & said vnto him, O thou seed of Chanaan, and not of
Iuda, beauty hath deceiued thee, and lust hath peruerted
thine heart.
57 Thus haue yee dealt with the

¶ The history of the
and the Dragon, cut off

19 The fraud of Bels Priests, is discouered by Daniel, 27 and the Dragon slaine, which was worshipped. 33 Daniel is preserued in the Lions denne. 42 The King doeth acknowledge the God of Daniel, and casteth his enemies into the same denne.

AND King Astyages was gathered to his fathers, and Cyrus
of Persia receiued his kingdome.
‖Or, liued with the King. 2 And Daniel ‖conuersed with the king, and was honored
aboue all his friends.
3 Now the Babylonians had an Idol called Bel, and there
were spent

daughters of Israel, and they for feare companied with you:
but the daughter of Iuda would not abide your wickednesse.
58 Now therefore tell mee, Vnder what tree didst thou
take them companying together? who answered, Vnder a
||holme tree. || *Or, kinde of oake.*
59 Then said Daniel vnto him, Well: thou hast also lied
against thine owne head: for the Angel of God waiteth with
the sword to cut thee in two, that he may destroy you.
60 With that all the assembly cried out with a lowd voice,
and praised God who saueth them that trust in him.
61 And they arose against the two Elders, (for Daniel had
conuicted them of false witnesse by their owne mouth)
62 And according to the Law of Moses, they did vnto them
in such sort as they *malitiously intended to doe to their * Deut. 19. 19. prou. 19. 5.
neighbour: And they put them to death. Thus the inno-
cent blood was saued the same day.
63 Therefore Chelcias and his wife praised God for their
daughter Susanna, with Ioacim her husband, and all the
kinred: because there was no dishonestie found in her.
64 From that day foorth was Daniel had in great reputation
in the sight of the people.

destruction of †Bel

† *Gr. Bels Dragon.*

from the end of Daniel.

vpon him euery day twelue great measures of fine flowre, and
fourtie sheepe, and sixe vessels of wine.
4 And the king worshipped it, and went daily to adore it:
but Daniel worshipped his owne God. And the king said
vnto him, Why doest not thou worship Bel?
5 Who answered and said, Because I may not worship idols
made with hands, but the liuing God, who hath created the
heauen, and the earth, and hath soueraigntie ouer all flesh.
6 Then saide the King vnto him, Thinkest thou not that
Bel is a liuing god? seest thou not how much he
eateth

eateth and drinketh euery day ?
7 Then Daniel smiled, and said, O king, be not deceiued:
for this is but clay within, and brasse without, and did neuer
* Ecclus. *eate or drinke any thing.
30. 19. 8 So the king was wroth, and called for his Priests, and
said vnto them, If yee tell me not who this is that deuoureth
these expenses, ye shall die.
9 But if ye can certifie me that Bel deuoureth them, then
Daniel shall die: for hee hath spoken blasphemie against
Bel. And Daniel sayd vnto the king, Let it be according
to thy word.
10 (Now the Priests of Bel were threescore and tenne,
beside their wiues and children) and the king went with
Daniel into the temple of Bel.
11 So Bels Priests said, Loe, wee goe out: but thou, O
king, set on the meate, and make ready the wine, and shut
the doore fast, and seale it with thine owne signet:
12 And to morrow, when thou commest in, if thou findest
not that Bel hath eaten vp all, wee will suffer death; or
else Daniel, that speaketh falsely against vs.
13 And they little regarded it: for vnder the table they
had made a priuie entrance, whereby they entred in continually, and consumed those things.
14 So when they were gone forth, the king set meates
before Bel. Now Daniel had commanded his seruants to
bring ashes, and those they strewed throughout all the
temple, in the presence of the king alone: then went they
out and shut the doore, & sealed it with the kings signet,
and so departed.
15 Now in the night came the Priests with their wiues and
children (as they were woont to doe) and did eate and drinke
vp all.
16 In the morning betime the king arose, and Daniel with him.
17 And the king said, Daniel, are the seales whole? And
he said, Yea, O king, they be whole.
18 And assoone as he had opened the doore, the king looked
vpon the table, and cried with a loude voice, Great art thou,
O Bel, and with thee is no deceit at all.
19 Then laughed Daniel, and helde the king that he should
not goe in, and sayd, Behold now the pauement, and marke
well whose footsteps are these.
20 And the king said, I see the foot-

steps of men, women and children: and then the king was
angry,
21 And tooke the Priests, with their wiues and children,
who shewed him the priuy doores, where they came in, and
consumed such things as were vpon the table.
22 Therefore the king slewe them, and deliuered Bel into
Daniels power, who destroyed him and his temple.
23 ‖And in that same place there was a great Dragon,
which they of Babylon worshipped.
24 And the king said vnto Daniel, Wilt thou also say that
this is of brasse? loe, he liueth, he eateth and drinketh, thou
canst not say, that he is no liuing God: therefore worship
him.
25 Then said Daniel vnto the king, I will worship the
Lord my God: for he is the liuing God.
26 But giue me leaue, O king, and I shall slay this dragon
without sword or staffe. The king sayde, I giue thee leaue.
27 Then Daniel tooke pitch, fat, and haire, and did seethe
them together, and made lumpes thereof: this hee put in
the Dragons mouth, and so the Dragon burst in sunder:
and Daniel said, ‖Loe, these are the gods you worship.
28 When they of Babylon heard that, they tooke great
indignation, and conspired against the king, saying, The
king is become a Iew, and he hath destroyed Bel, he hath
slaine the Dragon, and put the Priests to death.
29 So they came to the king, and said, Deliuer vs Daniel,
or else we will destroy thee and thine house.
30 Now when the king sawe that they pressed him sore,
being constrained, he *deliuered Daniel vnto them:
31 Who cast him into the lions den, where he was sixe
dayes.
32 And in the den there were seuen lyons, and they had
giuen them euery day ‖two carkeises, and two sheepe:
which then were not giuen to them, to the intent they
might deuoure Daniel.
33 Now there was in Iury a Prophet called Habacuc, who
had ‖made pottage, & had broken bread in a boule, and was
going into the field, for to bring it to the reapers.
34 But the Angel of the Lord said vnto Habacuc, Goe
carrie the dinner

‖ *Some adde this title: Of the Dragon.*

‖ *Or, Behold what you worship.*

* Dan. 6. 16.

‖ *Or, two slaues.*

‖ *Or, sodde.*

that thou hast into Babylon vnto Daniel, who is in the lions
denne.
35 And Habacuc said, Lord, I neuer saw Babylon: neither
do I know where the denne is.
36 Then the Angel of the Lord tooke him by the crown,
*Ezek. 8. and *bare him by the haire of his head, and through the
3. vehemencie of his spirit, set him in Babylon ouer the den.
*1. King. 37 And Habacuc cryed, saying, O Daniel, Daniel, *take
17. 4. the dinner which God hath sent thee.
38 And Daniel saide, Thou hast remembred mee, O God:
neither hast thou forsaken them that seeke

¶ The prayer of Manasses
when he was holden

O Lord, Almightie God of our Fathers, Abraham, Isaac, and Iacob, and of their righteous seed: who hast made heauen and earth, with all the ornament thereof: who hast bound the Sea by the word of thy Commandement: who hast shut vp the deepe, and sealed it by thy terrible and glorious Name, whome all men feare, and tremble before thy power: for the Maiestie of thy glory cannot bee borne, and thine angry threatning towards sinners is importable: but thy mercifull promise is vnmeasurable and vnsearchable: for thou art the most High Lord, of great compassion, long suffering, very mercifull, and repentest of the euils of men. Thou, O Lord, according to thy great goodnesse hast promised repentance, and forgiuenesse to them that haue sinned against thee: and of thine infinite mercies hast appointed repentance vnto sinners that they may be saued. Thou therefore, O Lord, that art the God of the iust, hast not appointed repentance to the iust, as to Abraham, and Isaac, and Iacob, which haue not sinned against thee: but thou hast appointed repentance vnto me that am a sinner: for I haue sinned aboue the number of the sands of the Sea.

thee, and loue thee.
39 So Daniel arose and did eate: and the Angel of the
Lord set Habacuc in his owne place againe immediatly.
40 Vpon the seuenth day the king went to bewaile Daniel:
and when he came to the den, he looked in, and behold,
Daniel was sitting.
41 Then cried the king with a loud voyce, saying, Great
art thou, O Lord God of Daniel, and there is none other
besides thee.
42 *And he drew him out: and cast those that were the
cause of his destruction into the den: and they were deuoured in a moment before his face.

*Ier. 37. 17

King of Iuda,

captiue in Babylon.

My transgressions, O Lord, are multiplied: my transgressions are multiplied, and I am not worthy to behold and see the height of heauen, for the multitude of mine iniquitie. I am bowed downe with many yron bands, that I cannot lift vp mine head, ‖neither haue any release: For I haue prouoked thy wrath, and done euill before thee, I did not thy will, neither kept I thy Commandements: I haue set vp abominations, and haue multiplied offences. Now therefore I bow the knee of mine heart, beseeching thee of grace: I haue sinned, O Lord, I haue sinned, and I acknowledge mine iniquities: wherefore I humbly beseech thee, forgiue me, O Lord, forgiue me, and destroy me not with mine iniquities. Be not angry with me for euer, by reseruing euill for me, neither condemne mee into the lower parts of the earth. For thou art the God, euen the God of them that repent: and in me thou wilt shew all thy goodnesse: for thou wilt saue me that am vnworthy, according to thy great mercie. Therefore I will praise thee for euer all the dayes of my life: for all the powers of the heauens doe praise thee, and thine is the glory for euer and euer, Amen.

‖ *Or, neither take my breath.*

¶ The

¶ The first booke

CHAP. I.

14 Antiochus gaue leaue to set vp the fashions of the Gentiles in Hierusalem, 22 And spoiled it, & the temple in it, 57 And set vp therin the abomination of desolation, 63 And slew those that did circumcise their children.

‖Or, Chethiim.

ANd it happened, after that Alexander sonne of Philip, the
Macedonian, who came out of the land of ‖Chettiim,
had smitten Darius king of the Persians and Medes, that hee
reigned in his stead, the first ouer Greece,
2 And made many wars, and wan many strong holds, and
slew the kings of the earth,
3 And went through to the ends of the earth, and tooke
spoiles of many nations, insomuch, that the earth was quiet
before him, whereupon ‖he was exalted, and his heart was
lifted vp.
4 And he gathered a mighty strong hoste, and ruled ouer
countries, and nations and ‖kings, who became tributaries
vnto him.
5 And after these things he fell sicke, and perceiued †that
he should die.
6 Wherefore he called his seruants, such as were honourable,
and had bin brought vp with him from his youth, and parted
kis kingdome among them, while he was yet aliue:
7 So Alexander reigned twelue yeeres, and (then) died.
8 And his seruants bare rule euery one in his place.
9 And after his death they all put crownes [vpon them-
selues] so did their sonnes after them, many yeeres, and euils
were multiplied in the earth.
10 And there came out of them a wicked roote, Antiochus
[surnamed] Epiphanes, sonne of Antiochus the king, who
had beene an hostage at Rome, and he reigned in the
hundreth and thir-

‖Or, his heart was exalted and lifted vp.
‖Or, kingdomes which became &c.
†Gre. that he dieth.

of the Maccabees.

ty and seuenth yeere of the kingdome of the Greekes.
11 In those daies went there out of Israel wicked men, who
perswaded many, saying, Let vs goe, and make a couenant
with the heathen, that are round about vs: for since we
departed from them, †we haue had much sorrow.
12 So this deuise pleased them well.
13 Then certaine of the people were so forward heerein,
that they went to the king, who gaue them licence to doe
after the ordinances of the heathen.
14 Whereupon ||they built a place of exercise at Ierusalem,
according to the customes of the heathen,
15 And made themselues, vncircumcised, and forsooke the
holy couenant, and ioyned themselues to the heathen, and
were sold to doe mischiefe.
16 Now when the kingdome was established, before Antiochus, hee thought to reigne ouer Egypt, that he might
haue ye dominion of two realms:
17 Wherefore he entred into Egypt with a great multitude,
with chariots, and elephants, and horsemen, and a great
nauie,
18 And made warre against Ptolomee king of Egypt, but
Ptolomee was afraide of him, and fled: and many were
wounded to death.
19 Thus they got the strong cities in the land of Egypt,
and hee tooke the spoiles thereof.
20 And after that Antiochus had smitten Egypt, he returned
againe in the hundreth fortie and third yeere, and went vp
against Israel and Ierusalem with a great multitude,
21 And entred proudly into the sanctuarie, and tooke away
the golden altar, and the candlesticke of light, and all the
vessels thereof,
22 And the table of the shewbread, and the powring vessels,
and the vials, and the censers of gold, & the vaile, and the
crownes, & the golden ornaments that were before the temple,
||all which he pulled off.

† Gre. many euils haue found vs.

|| Or, set vp an open schoole at Ierusalem.

|| Or, he pilled all things.

† *Gr. desireable.* 23 Hee tooke also the siluer and the gold, and the †pretious
vessels: also he tooke the hidden treasures which hee found:
24 And when hee had taken all away, he went into his
owne land, hauing made a great massacre, and spoken very
proudly.
25 Therfore there was great mourning in Israel, in euery
place where they were;
26 So that the Princes and Elders mourned, the virgines
and yong men were made feeble, and the beautie of women
was changed.
27 Euery bridegrome tooke vp lamentation, and she that
sate in the marriage chamber, was in heauinesse.
28 The land also was moued for the inhabitants thereof,
and all the house of Iacob was couered with confusion.
29 And after two yeeres fully expired, the king sent his
chiefe collectour of tribute vnto the cities of Iuda, who came
vnto Ierusalem with a great multitude,
30 And spake peaceable wordes vnto them, but [all was]
deceit: for when they had giuen him credence, he fell suddenly vpon the citie, and smote it very sore, & destroyed
much people of Israel.
31 And when hee had taken the spoiles of the citie, hee set
it on fire, and pulled downe the houses, and walles thereof
on euery side.
32 But the women & children tooke they captiue, and
possessed the cattell.
33 Then builded they the citie of Dauid with a great and
strong wall, [and] with mightie towers, and made it a strong
hold for them,
34 And they put therein a sinfull nation, wicked men, and
fortified [themselues] therein.
35 They stored it also with armour and victuals, and when
they had gathered together the spoiles of Ierusalem, they
layd them vp there, and so they became a sore snare:
36 For it was a place to lie in wait against the Sanctuary,
and an euill aduersary to Israel.
37 Thus they shed innocent blood on euery side of the
Sanctuary, and defiled it.
38 In so much that the inhabitants of Ierusalem fledde because of them, whereupon [the citie] was made an habitation
of strangers, & became strange

to those that were borne in her, and her owne children
left her:
39 Her Sanctuary was laid waste like a wildernesse, her
feasts were turned into mourning, her Sabbaths into reproch,
her honour into contempt.
40 As had bene her glory, so was her dishonour encreased,
and her excellencie was turned into mourning.
41 Moreouer king Antiochus wrote to his whole kingdome,
that all should be one people,
42 And euery one should leaue his lawes: so all the heathen
agreed, according to the commandement of the king.
43 Yea many also of the Israelites consented to his religion,
and sacrificed vnto idols, and prophaned the Sabbath.
44 For the king had sent letters by messengers vnto Ieru-
salem, and the cities of Iuda, that they should follow ||the
strange lawes of the land,
45 And forbid burnt offerings, and sacrifice, and drinke
offerings in the temple; and that they should prophane the
Sabbaths, and festiuall dayes:
46 And pollute the Sanctuarie and holy people:
47 Set vp altars, and groues, and chappels of idols, and
sacrifice swines flesh, and vncleane beasts:
48 That they should also leaue their children vncircumcised,
and make their soules abominable with all maner of vncleannesse, and prophanation:
49 To the end they might forget the Law, and change all
the ordinances.
50 And whosoeuer would not doe according to the commandement of the king [he said] he should die.
51 In the selfe same maner wrote he to his whole kingdome,
and appointed ouerseers ouer all the people, commanding the
cities of Iuda to sacrifice, citie by citie.
52 Then many of the people were gathered vnto them, to
wit, euery one that forsooke the Lawe, and so they committed euils in the land:
53 ||And droue the Israelites into secret places, euen where-
soeuer they could flie for succour.
54 Now the fifteenth day of the moneth Casleu, in the
hundreth fourtie and fift yeere, they set vp the abomination
of desolation vpon the Altar, and builded idole altars throughout the cities of Iuda, on euery side:

|| *Or, the lawes and rites of the strangers of the land.*

|| *Or, and they made Israel hide themselues in holes, in euery place of succour.*

55 And

55 Aud burnt incense at the doores of their houses, and in the streetes.

56 And when they had rent in pieces the bookes of the Lawe which they found, they burnt them with fire.

57 And wheresoeuer was found with any, the booke of the Testament, or if any consented to the Lawe, †the kings commandement was, that they should put him to death.

† Gr. the kings commandement put him to death.

58 Thus did they by their authority, vnto the Israelites euery moneth, to as many as were found in the cities.

59 Now the fiue and twentieth day of the moneth, they did sacrifice vpon the idole altar, which was vpon the Altar of God.

60 At which time, according to the commandement, they put to death certaine women †that had caused their children to be circumcised.

† Gr. that had circumcised their children.

61 And they hanged the infants about their neckes, and rifled their houses, and slewe them that had circumcised them.

62 Howbeit, many in Israel were fully resolued and confirmed in themselues, not to eate any vncleane thing.

63 Wherfore they chose rather to die, that they might not be defiled with meats, and that they might not profane the holy Couenant: So then they died.

64 And there was very great wrath vpon Israel.

CHAP. II.

6 Mattathias lamenteth the case of Ierusalem. 24 He slayeth a Iewe that did sacrifice to Idoles in his presence, and the Kings messenger also. 34 He and his are assailed vpon the Sabbath, and make no resistance. 50 Hee dieth, and instructeth his sons: 66 and maketh their brother Iudas Maccabeus generall.

IN those daies ‖arose Mattathias the son of Iohn, the sonne of Simeon, a Priest of the sonnes of Ioarib, from Ierusalem, and dwelt in Modin.

2 And he had fiue sonnes, Ioannan ‖called ‖Caddis:

3 Simon, called Thassi:

4 Iudas, who was called Maccabeus:

5 Eleazar, called ‖Auaran, and Ionathan, whose surname was Apphus.

6 And when hee saw the blasphemies that were committed in Iuda and Ierusalem,

‖ Or, Mattathias the son of Iohn, &c. arose from Ierusalem, or out of Ierusalem.
‖ Or, who was called: and so afterward in the rest.
‖ Gaddis.
‖ Or, Auaron, or Abaron.

7 He said, Woe is me, wherfore was I borne to see this
misery of my people, and of the holy citie, and to dwell
there, when it was deliuered into the hand of the enemie,
and the Sanctuary into the hand of strangers?
8 Her Temple is become as a man without glory.
9 Her glorious vessels are caried away into captiuitie, her
infants are slaine in the streets, her yong men with the
sword of the enemie.
10 What nation hath not had a part in her kingdome, and
gotten of her spoiles?
11 All her ornaments are taken away, of a free-woman shee
is become a bondslaue.
12 And behold, our ||Sanctuarie, euen our beautie, aud our ||*Or, holy thing.*
glory is laid waste, & the Gentiles haue profaned it.
13 To what ende therefore shall we liue any longer?
14 Then Mattathias and his sons rent their clothes, and put
on sackcloth, and mourned very sore.
15 In the meane while the kings officers, such as compelled
the people to reuolt, came into the city Modin to make them
sacrifice.
16 And when many of Israel came vnto them, Mattathias
also and his sonnes came together.
17 Then answered the kings officers, and said to Mattathias
on this wise; Thou art a ruler, and an honourable and great
man in this citie, and strengthened with sons and brethren:
18 Now therefore come thou first and fulfill the kings commandement, like as all the heathen haue done; yea and the
men of Iuda also, and such as remaine at Ierusalem: so shalt
thou and thine house be in the number of the kings friends,
and thou and thy children shall be honoured with siluer, and
golde, and many rewards.
19 Then Mattathias answered, and spake with a loude voice,
Though all the nations that are vnder the kings dominion
obey him, and fall away euery one from the religion of their
fathers, and giue consent to his commandements:
20 Yet will I, and my sonnes, and my brethren walke in
the couenant of our fathers.
21 God forbid that we should forsake the Law, and the
ordinances:

22 We will not hearken to the kings words, to goe from
our religion, either on the right hand, or the left.
23 Now when he had left speaking these words, there came
one of the Iewes in the sight of all, to sacrifice on the altar,
which was at Modin, according to the kings commandement.
24 Which thing when Mattathias saw, he was inflamed
with zeale, and his reines trembled, neither could hee forbeare to shew his anger according to iudgement: wherefore
he ranne, and slew him vpon the altar.
25 Also the kings commissioner who compelled men to
sacrifice, he killed at that time, & the altar he pulled downe.
26 Thus dealt he zealously for the Law of God, like as
*Num. 25. 9. *Phineas did vnto Zambri the sonne of Salom.
27 And Mattathias cried throughout the citie with a loud
voyce, saying, Whosoeuer is zealous of the law, and main-
taineth the couenant, let him follow me.
28 So he and his sonnes fled into the mountaines, and left
all that euer they had in the citie.
29 Then many that sought after iustice and iudgement,
† Gr. sit, abide. went downe into the wildernesse to †dwell there.
30 Both they and their children, and their wiues, and their
† Gr. euils were multiplied vpon them. cattell, †because afflictions increased sore vpon them.
31 Now when it was told the kings seruants, and the hoste
that was at Ierusalem, in the citie of Dauid, that certaine
men, who had broken the kings commandement, were gone
downe into the secret places in the wildernesse.
32 They pursued after them, a great number, and hauing
ouertaken them, they camped against them, and made war
against them on the Sabbath day.
33 And they said vnto them, Let that which you haue
done hitherto, suffice: Come foorth, and doe according to
the commandement of the king, and you shall liue.
34 But they said, We will not come forth, neither will we
do the kings commandement to profane the Sabbath day.
† Gr. the Iewes. 35 So then †they gaue them the battell with all speed.
36 Howbeit, they answered them not, neither cast they a
stone at them, nor stopped the places where they lay hid,
† Gr. simplicitie. 37 But said, Let vs die all in our †in-

nocencie: heauen and earth shall testifie for vs, that you put
vs to death wrongfully.
38 So they rose vp against them in battell on the Sabbath,
and they slew them with their wiues & children, and their
cattell, to the number of a thousand †people. †*Gr. soules of men.*
39 Now when Mattathias and his friends vnderstood hereof,
they mourned for them right sore.
40 And one of them said to another: If we all do as our
brethren haue done, and fight not for our liues, and lawes
against the heathen, they wil now quickly root vs out of the
earth.
41 At that time therfore they decreed, saying, Whosoeuer
shall come to make battell with vs on the Sabbath day, we
will fight against him, neither will wee die all, as our brethren
that were murdered in the secret places.
42 Then came there vnto him a company of Assideans,
who were mightie men of Israel, euen all such as were
voluntarily deuoted vnto the Lawe.
43 Also all they that fled for persecution ioyned themselues
vnto them, and were a stay vnto them.
44 So they ioyned their forces, and smote sinfull men in
their anger, and wicked men in their wrath: but the rest
fled to the heathen for succour.
45 Then Mattathias & his friends went round about, and
pulled downe the altars.
46 And what children soeuer they found within the coast
of Israel vncircumcised, those they circumcised ||valiantly. ||*Or, by force*
47 They pursued also after ẏe proud men, & the work
prospered in their hand.
48 So they recouered the Law out of the hand of the
Gentiles, and out of the hande of Kings, neither †suffered †*Gr. gaue they the horne to the sinner.*
they the sinner to triumph.
49 Now when the time drew neere, that Mattathias should
die, he said vnto his sonnes, Now hath pride & rebuke gotten
strength, and the time of destruction, and the wrath of indignation:
50 Now therefore, my sonnes, be ye zealous for the Law,
& giue your liues for the couenant of your fathers.
51 Call to remembrance what actes our fathers did in their
†time, so shall ye receiue great honour, & an euerlasting †*Gr. generations.*
name.

52 *Was

*Gene. 22. 52 *Was not Abraham found faithfull intentation, and it
9, 10. rom. was imputed vnto him for righteousnesse?
4. 3. *Gene. 41. 53 *Ioseph in the time of his distresse kept the commaunde-
40. ment, and was made Lord of Egypt.
*Num. 25. 54 *Phineas our father in being zealous and feruent, ob-
13. ecclus. tained the couenant of an euerlasting priesthood.
45. 23, 24. *Iosh. 1. 2. 55 *Iesus for fulfilling the word, was made a iudge in Israel.
*Num. 14. 56 *Caleb for bearing witnesse, before the congregation,
6, 7. iosh. receiued the heritage of the land.
14. 13. *2. Sam. 57 *Dauid for being mercifull, possessed the throne of an
2. 4. euerlasting kingdome.
*2. Kin. 2. 58 *Elias for being zealous and feruent for the law, was
11. taken vp into heauen.
*Dan. 3. 59 *Ananias, Azarias, and Misael, by beleeuing were saued
16. 17. 18, out of the flame
and 26. *Dan. 6. 60 *Daniel for his innocencie was deliuered from the mouth
22. of Lyons.
61 And thus consider ye throughout all ages, that none that
put their trust in him shall be ouercome.
62 Feare not then the words of a sinfull man: for his glory
shall bee dung and wormes.
63 To day he shall be lifted vp, and to morrow hee shall
*Psal. 146. not be found, because he is *returned into his dust, and his
4. thought is come to nothing.
64 Wherefore you my sonnes be valiant, and shew your
selues men in the behalfe of the law, for by it shall you
obtaine glory.
65 And behold, I know that your brother Simon is a man
of counsell, giue eare vnto him alway: he shall be a father
vnto you.
66 As for Iudas Maccabeus hee hath bin mighty and strong,
||*Or fight* euen from his youth vp, let him be your captaine, and ||fight
yee the battaile of the battaile of the people.
the people. 67 Take also vnto you, all those that obserue the law, and
auenge ye the wrong of your people.
68 Recompence fully the heathen, and take heed to the
commandements of the law.
69 So he blessed them, and was gathered to his fathers.
70 And he died in the hundreth fortie, and sixth yeere,
and his sonnes buried him in the Sepulchre of his fathers, at
Modin, and all Israel made great lamentation for him.

CHAP. III.

1 The valour and fame of Iudas Maccabeus. 10 He ouerthroweth the forces of Samaria and Syria. 27 Antiochus sendeth a great power against him. 44 He and his fall to fasting and prayer, 58 and are encouraged.

THen his sonne Iudas, called Maccabeus, rose vp in his
stead.
2 And all his brethren helped him, and so did all they that
held with his father, and they fought with cheerefulnesse,
the battaile of Israel.
3 So he gate his people great honor, and put on a brestplate
as a giant, and girt his warlike harnesse about him, and he
made battels, protecting the host with his sword.
4 In his acts he was like a lyon, and like a lyons whelp
roaring for his pray.
5 For hee pursued the wicked, and sought them out, and
burnt vp those that vexed his people.
6 Wherefore the wicked shrunke for feare of him, and all
the workers of iniquity were troubled, because saluation prospered in his hand.
7 He grieued also many kings, and made Iacob glad with
his acts, and his memoriall is blessed for euer.
8 Moreouer he went through the citties of Iuda, destroying
the vngodly out of them, and turning away wrath from Israel.
9 So that he was renowned vnto the vtmost part of the
earth, & he †receiued vnto him such as were ready to perish. † *Gre. gathered together.*
10 Then Apollonius gathered the Gentiles together, and a
great host out of Samaria to fight against Israel.
11 Which thing when Iudas perceiued he went forth to
meete him, and so he smote him, and slew him, many also
fell downe slaine, but the rest fled.
12 Wherefore Iudas tooke their spoiles, and Apollonius
sword also, and therewith he fought, all his life long.
13 Now when Seron a prince of the armie of Syria, heard
say that Iudas had gathered vnto him a multitude and company of the faithfull, to goe out with him to warre.
14 He said, I will get me a name and honour in the kingdome, for I will goe fight with Iudas, and them that are with
him, who despise the kings commandement.

15 So

15 So he made him ready to goe vp, and there went with
him a mighty host of the vngodly to helpe him, and to be
auenged of the children of Israel.

16 And when hee came neere to the going vp of Bethoron,
Iudas went forth to meet him with a smal company.

17 Who when they saw the host comming to meet them,
said vnto Iudas; How shall wee be able, being so few to
fight against so great a multitude, and so strong, seeing wee
are ready to faint with fasting all this day?

*1. Sam. 14. 6. 2. chron. 14. 11.

18 Vnto whom Iudas answered: *It is no hard matter for
many to bee shut vp in the hands of a few; and with the
God of heauen it is all one, to deliuer with a great multitude,
or a small company:

19 For the victory of battell standeth not in the multitude
of an hoste, but strength commeth from heauen.

|| Or, vnto vs.
† Greek. in multitude of pride, or enuie, and iniquitie.

20 They come ||against vs †in much pride and iniquitie to
destroy vs, and our wiues & children, and to spoile vs:

21 But wee fight for our liues, and our Lawes.

22 Wherefore the Lord himselfe will ouerthrow them before our face: and as for you, be ye not afraid of them.

23 Now as soone as hee had left off speaking, he lept suddenly vpon them, and so Seron and his host was ouerthrowen
before him.

† Gr. in the going downe.

24 And they pursued them †from the going downe of
Bethoron, vnto the plaine, where were slaine about eight
hundred men of them; and the residue fledde into the land
of the Philistines.

25 Then began the feare of Iudas and his brethren, & an
exceeding great dread to fall vpon the nations round about
them:

26 In so much, as his fame came vnto the king, and all
nations talked of the battels of Iudas.

27 Now when King Antiochus heard these things, he was
full of indignation: wherefore hee sent and gathered together
all the forces of his realme [euen] a very strong armie.

† Gr. or at euery need.
† Gr. that the collectors of tribute in the countrey were few.

28 He opened also his treasure, and gaue his souldiers pay
for a yeere, commanding them to be ready, †whensoeuer he
should need them.

29 Neuerthelesse, when he saw that the money of his
treasures failed, and †that the tributes in the countrey were

small, because of the dissention, and plague which he had
brought vpon the land, ||in taking away the Lawes which
had bene of old time,
30 Hee feared †that he should not be able to beare the
charges any longer, nor to haue such gifts to giue so liberally,
as he did before: for hee had abounded aboue the Kings
that were before him.
31 Wherefore, being greatly perplexed in his minde, hee
determined to goe into Persia, there to take the tributes of
the countreys, and to gather much money.
32 So hee left Lysias a noble man, and one of the blood
royall, to ouersee the affaires of the King, from the riuer
Euphrates, vnto the borders of Egypt:
33 And to bring vp his sonne Antiochus, vntill he came
againe.
34 Moreouer he deliuered vnto him the halfe of his forces,
and the Elephants, and gaue him charge of all things that
he would haue done, as also concerning them that dwelt in
Iuda and Ierusalem.
35 To wit, that he should send an armie against them, to
destroy and root out the strength of Israel, and the remnant
of Ierusalem, and to take away their memoriall from that
place:
36 And that he should place strangers in all their quarters,
and diuide their land by lot.
37 So the king tooke the halfe of the forces that remained,
and departed from Antioch †his royall city, the hundreth
fourtie and seuenth yeere, and hauing passed the riuer Euphrates, hee went through the high countreys.
38 Then Lysias chose Ptoleme, the son of Dorymenes and
Nicanor, & Gorgias, mighty men of the kings friends:
39 And with them hee sent fourtie thousand footmen, and
seuen thousand horsemen to goe into the land of Iuda, and to
destroy it as the king cōmanded.
40 So they went forth with all their power, and came and
pitched by Emmaus in the plaine countrey.
41 And the merchants of the countrey, hearing the fame of
them, tooke siluer, & gold very much, with ||seruants, and
came into the campe to buy the children of Israel for slaues;
A power also of Syria, and of the land ||of the Philistines,
ioyned themselues vnto them.

|| *Or, for the taking away of the Lawes*

† *Gr. that he should not haue.*

† *Gr. a citie of his kingdome.*

|| *Or, fetters.*

|| *Or, of strangers.*

42 Now

42 Now when Iudas and his brethren saw that miseries were multiplied, & that the forces did encampe themselues in their borders, (for they knewe how the king had giuen commaundement to destroy the people, and vtterly abolish them.)

43 They said one to another, Let vs restore the decayed estate of our people, and let vs fight for our people and the Sanctuarie.

44 Then was the Congregation gathered together, that they might be ready for battell, and that they might pray, and aske mercy and compassion.

45 Now Ierusalem lay voide as a wildernesse, there was none of her children that went in or out: the Sanctuarie also was troden downe, and aliens kept the strong holde: the heathen had their habitation in that place, and ioy was taken from Iacob, and the pipe with the harpe ceased.

46 Wherefore the Israelites assembled themselues together, and came to ||Maspha ouer-against Ierusalem; for in Maspha was the place where they prayed aforetime in Israel.

|| *Or, Mitzpa.*

47 Then they fasted that day, and put on sackecloth, and cast ashes vpon their heads, and rent their clothes:

48 And laide open the booke of the Law, ||wherein yͤ heathen had sought to paint the likenesse of their images.

|| *Or, for the which the heathen had made diligent search that they might paint therein the likenesse of their idols.*

49 They brought also the Priestes garments, and the first fruits, and the tithes, and the *Nazarites they stirred vp, who had accomplished their dayes.

*Num. 6. 2.

50 Then cried they with a loud voice toward heauen, saying, What shall we doe with these, and whither shall wee cary them away?

51 For thy Sanctuarie is troden downe and profaned, and thy Priestes are in heauinesse, and brought low.

52 And loe, the heathen are assembled together against vs, to destroy vs: what things they imagine against vs, thou knowest.

53 How shall wee be able to stand against them, except thou (O God) be our helpe?

54 Then sounded they with trumpets, and cryed with a loude voice.

55 And after this, Iudas ordained captains ouer the people, euen captains ouer thousands, and ouer hundreds, and ouer fifties, and ouer tennes.

*Deu. 20. 5.

56 But as for such as *were building

houses, or had betrothed wiues, or were planting vineyards,
or *were fearefull, those hee commanded that they should *Iudg. 7.
returne, euery man to his owne house, according to the Law. 3.
57 So the campe remooued, and pitched vpon the South
side of Emmaus.
58 And Iudas sayde, Arme your selues, and be valiant men,
and see that ye be in readinesse against the morning, that yee
may fight with these nations, that are assembled together
against vs, to destroy vs and our Sanctuarie.
59 For it is better for vs to die in battell, then to behold the
calamities of our people, and our Sanctuarie.
60 Neuerthelesse, as the will [of God] is in heauen, so let
him doe.

CHAP. IIII.

6 Iudas defeateth the plot 14 and forces of Gorgias, 23 and spoileth their tents, 34 and ouerthroweth Lysias. 45 He pulleth downe the Altar which the heathen had prophaned, and setteth vp a newe, 60 and maketh a wall about Sion.

THen tooke Gorgias fiue thousand footmen, and a thousand of the best horsemen, and remooued out of the
campe by night:
2 To the end he might rush in vpon the camp of the Iewes,
and smite them suddenly. And the men of the fortresse
were his guides.
3 Now when Iudas heard thereof, hee himselfe remooued,
and the valiant men with him, that hee might smite the
Kings armie which was at Emmaus,
4 While as yet the forces were dispersed from the campe.
5 In the meane season came Gorgias by night into the
campe of Iudas: and when hee found no man there, hee
sought them in the mountaines: for said hee, these fellowes
flee from vs.
6 But assoone as it was day, Iudas shewed himselfe in the
plaine with three thousand men, who neuerthelesse had
neither ||armour, nor swordes to their mindes. || *Or,*
7 And they sawe the campe of the heathen, that it was *targets.*
strong, and well harnessed, and compassed round about with
horsemen; and these were expert of warre.
8 Then said Iudas to the men that
were

were with him: feare ye not their multitude, neither be ye
afraid of their assault
9 Remember how our fathers were deliuered in the red Sea,
when Pharao pursued them with an armie.
10 Now therfore let vs crie vnto heauen, if peraduenture
the Lord wil haue mercie vpon vs, and remember the
couenant of our fathers, and destroy this hoste before our face
this day.
11 That so all the heathen may know that there is one,
who deliuereth and saueth Israel.
12 Then the strangers lift vp their eyes, & saw them comming ouer against them.
13 Wherefore they went out of the campe to battell, but
they that were with Iudas sounded their trumpets.
14 So they ioyned battell, and the heathen being discomfited,
fled into the plaine.
15 Howbeit all the hindmost of them were slaine with the
sword: for they pursued them vnto Gazera, and vnto the
plaines of Idumea, and Azotus, and Iamnia, so that there
were slaine of them, vpon a three thousand men.
16 This done, Iudas returned againe with his hoste frō
pursuing them,
17 And said to the people, Bee not greedie of the spoiles, in
as much as there is a battell before vs,
18 And Gorgias and his hoste are here by vs in the mountaine, but stand ye now against your enemies, and ouercome
them, & after this you may boldly take the spoiles.
19 As Iudas was yet speaking these words, there appeared
a part of them looking out of the mountaine.
20 Who when they perceiued that the Iewes had put their
hoste to flight, and were burning the tents: (for the smoke
that was seene declared what was done)
21 When therefore they perceiued these things, they were
sore afraid, and seeing also the hoste of Iudas in the plaine
ready to fight:
22 They fled euery one into the land of strangers.
23 Then Iudas returned to spoile the tents, where they got
much golde, and siluer, and blew silke, and purple of the sea,
and great riches.
24 After this, they went home, and sung a song of thankesgiuing, & praised the Lord in heauen: because it is good,

because his mercie endureth for euer.
25 Thus Israel had a great deliuerance that day.
26 Now all the strangers that had escaped, came and told
Lysias what had happened.
27 Who when hee heard thereof, was confounded, and discouraged, because neither such things as he would, were
done vnto Israel, nor such things as the king commanded
him were come to passe.
28 The next yeere therefore following, Lysias gathered
together threescore thousand choice men of foote, and fiue
thousand horsemen, that he might subdue them.
29 So they came into Idumea, and pitched their tents at
Bethsura, and Iudas met with them ten thousand men.
30 And when he saw that mighty armie, he prayed, and
said, Blessed art thou, O sauiour of Israel, *who diddest
quaile the violence of the mighty man by the hand of thy
seruant Dauid, and gauest, the host of ||strangers into the
hands of *Ionathan the sonne of Saul, and his armour bearer.
31 Shut vp this armie in the hand of thy people Israel, and
let them be confounded in their power and horsemen.
32 Make them to be of no courage, and cause the boldnesse
of their strength to †fall away, & let them quake at their
destruction.
33 Cast them downe with the sword of them that loue
thee, and let all those that know thy name, praise thee with
thanksgiuing.
34 So they ioyned battaile, and there were slaine of the
host of Lysias about fiue thousand men, euen before them
were they slaine.
35 Now when Lysias saw his armie put to flight, and the
manlinesse of Iudas souldiers, and how they were ready,
either to liue or die valiantly, he went into Antiochia, and
gathered together a company of strangers, and hauing made
his armie greater then it was, he purposed to come againe
into Iudea.
36 Then saide Iudas and his brethren, behold our enemies
are discomfited: let vs goe vp to cleanse, and ||dedicate the
Sanctuarie.
37 Vpon this all the host assembled themselues together,
and went vp into mount Sion.

38 And

*1. Sam. 17 50, 51.
|| *Or, Philistines.*
*1. Sam. 14 13, 14.
† *Gr. melt.*
|| *Or, repaire*

38 And when they saw the sanctuarie desolate, and the
altar prophaned, and the gates burnt vp, and shrubs growing
in the courts, as in a forrest, or in one of the mountaines, yea
and the priests chambers pulled downe,
39 They rent their clothes, and made great lamentation,
and cast ashes vpon their heads,
40 And fell downe flat to the ground vpon their faces, and
blew an alarme with the trumpets, and cried towards heauen.
41 Then Iudas appointed certaine men to fight against
those that were in the fortresse, vntill he had clensed the
Sanctuarie.
42 So he chose priests of blamelesse conuersation, such as
had pleasure in the law.
43 Who cleansed the Sanctuarie, and bare out the defiled
stones into an vncleane place.
44 And when as they consulted what to doe with the altar
of burnt offrings which was prophaned,
45 They thought it best to pull it downe, lest it should be
a reproch to them, because the heathen had defiled it; wherefore they pulled it downe,
46 And laide vp the stones in the mountaine of the temple
in a conuenient place, vntill there should come a Prophet, to
shew what should be done with them.
47 Then they tooke whole stones *according to the law, and
built a new altar, according to the former:
48 And made vp the Sanctuarie, and the things that were
within the temple, and hallowed the courts.
49 They made also new holy vessels, and into the temple
they brought the candlesticke, and the altar of burnt offerings,
and of incense, and the table.
50 And vpon the altar they burnt incense, and the lamps
that were vpon the candlesticke they lighted, that they might
giue light in the temple.
51 Furthermore they set the loaues vpon the table, and
||spread out the veiles, and finished all the workes which they
had begunne to make.
52 Now on the fiue and twentieth day of the ninth moneth,
(which is called the moneth Casleu) in the hundreth fourty
and eight yeere they rose vp betimes in the morning,
53 And offered sacrifice according to

* Exod. 20. 25. deut. 27 5, & iosh. 8.

|| *Or, spread abroad the hangings, or hanged vp the vailes.*

the law vpon the new altar of burnt offerings, which they had made.

54 Looke at what time, and what day the heathen had prophaned it, euen in that was it dedicated with songs, and citherns, and harpes, & cimbals.

55 Then all the people fell vpon their faces, worshipping and praising the God of heauen, who had giuen them good successe.

56 And so they kept the dedication of the altar eight dayes, and offered burnt offerings with gladnesse, and sacrificed the sacrifice of ||deliuerance and praise.

|| Or, peace offerings.

57 They deckt also the forefront of the temple with crownes of gold; and with shields, and the gates, and the chambers they ||renewed and ||hanged doores vpon them.

|| Or, dedicated.
|| Or, made doores for them.

58 Thus was there very great gladnesse among the people, for that the reproch of the heathen was put away.

59 Moreouer Iudas and his brethren with the whole congregation of Israel ordained that the daies of the dedication of the altar, should be kept in their season from yeere to yeere by the space of eight dayes, from the fiue and twentieth day of the moneth Casleu, with mirth and gladnesse.

60 At that time also they builded vp the mount Sion with high walles, and strong towres round about, lest the Gentiles should come & tread it downe, as they had done before.

61 And they set there a garison to keepe it: and fortified Bethsura to preserue it, that the people might haue a defence against Idumea.

CHAP. V.

3 Iudas smiteth the children of Dan, Bean, and Ammon. 17 Simon is sent into Galile. 15 The exploits of Iudas in Galaad. 51 He destroyeth Ephron, for denying him to passe through it. 56 Diuerse, that in Iudas absence would fight with their enemies, are slaine.

NOw when the nations round about heard that the Altar was built, & the Sanctuarie renewed as before, it displeased them very much.

2 Wherfore they thought to destroy the generation of Iacob that was among them, and thereupon they began to slay and destroy the people.

3 Then

|| Or, *Arabathene, or Arabattan, or Arabettine.*
|| Or, *malice.*
|| Or, *Haran, Gene.* 36. 27. & *num.* 33. 3, 32.

3 Then Iudas fought against the children of Esau in Idumea
at ||Arabattine, because they besieged Israel: and hee gaue
them a great ouerthrow, and abated their courage, and tooke
their spoiles.
4 Also he remembred the ||iniurie of the children of ||Bean,
who had bene a snare and an offence vnto the people, in that
they lay in waite for them in the wayes.
5 Hee shut them vp therefore in the towres, and incamped
against them, and destroyed them vtterly, and burnt the
towers of that place with fire, and all that were therein.
6 Afterward he passed ouer to the children of Ammon,
where he found a mighty power, and much people, with
Timotheus their captaine.
7 So he fought many battels with them, till at length they
were discomfited before him; and he smote them.
8 And when hee had taken Iazar, with the townes belonging thereto, he returned into Iudea.
9 Then the heathen that were at Galead, assembled themselues together against the Israelites that were in their
quarters to destroy them: but they fled to the fortresse of
Dathema;
10 And sent letters vnto Iudas and his brethren: The
heathen that are round about vs, are assembled together
against vs to destroy vs;
11 And they are preparing to come and take the fortresse
whereunto wee are fled, Timotheus being captaine of their
host.
12 Come now therefore and deliuer vs from their handes,
for many of vs are slaine.
13 Yea all our brethren that were in the places of Tobie,
are put to death, their wiues and their children; Also they
haue caried away captiues, and borne away their stuffe, and
they haue destroied there about a thousand men.
14 While these letters were yet reading, behold there came
other messengers from Galilee with their clothes rent, who
reported on this wise,
15 And said: They of Ptolemais, and of Tyrus, and Sidon,
and all Galilee of the Gentiles are assembled together against
vs to consume vs.
16 Now when Iudas and the people heard these wordes,
there assembled a great congregation together, to con-

sult what they should doe for their brethren, that were in
trouble and assaulted of them.
17 Then said Iudas vnto Simon his brother, Choose thee
out men, and goe, and deliuer thy brethren that are in
Galilee, for I and Ionathan my brother, will goe into the
countrey of Galaad.
18 So hee left Ioseph the sonne of Zacharias, and Azarias
captaines of the people, with the remnant of the hoste in
Iudea to keepe it,
19 Vnto whom he gaue commandement, saying, Take yee
the charge of this people, and see that you make not warre
against the heathen, vntill the time that we come againe.
20 Now vnto Simon were giuen three thousand men to goe
into Galilee, and vnto Iudas eight thousand men for the
countrey of Galaad.
21 Then went Simon into Galilee, where hee fought many
battels with the heathen, so that the heathen were discomfited
by him.
22 And hee pursued them vnto the gate of Ptolemais; And
there were slaine of the heathen about three thousand men,
whose spoiles he tooke.
23 And ||those that were in Galilee and in Arbattis, with
their wiues and their children, and all that they had, tooke
he away [with him] and brought them into Iudea, with great ioy.
24 Iudas Maccabeus also and his brother Ionathan, went
ouer Iordan, and trauailed three dayes iourney in the wildernesse,
25 Where they met with the Nabathites, who came vnto
them in peaceable maner, and told them euery thing that
had happened to their brethren in the land of Galaad,
26 And how that many of them were shut vp in ||Bosora,
and Bosor, in Alema, ||Casphor, Maked & Carnaim (all these
cities are strong and great.)
27 And that they were shut vp in the rest of the cities of
the countrey of Galaad, and that against to morrow ||they
had appointed to bring their host against the forts, and to
take them, and to destroy them all in one day.
28 Hereupon Iudas and his host turned suddenly by the
way of the wildernesse vnto ||Bosorra, and when he had
wonne the citie, hee slew all the males with the edge of the
sword, and
tooke

|| *Or, captiue Iewes.*

|| *Or, Bosorra.*

|| *Or, Chascor.*

|| *Or, the heathen.*

|| *Or, Bosor.*

tooke all their spoiles, and burnt the citie with fire.

29 From whence hee remooued by night, and went till he came to the fortresse.

† *Gr. lift vp their eyes.*
|| *The heathen assaulted the Iewes.*

30 And betimes in the morning they †looked vp, & behold, there was an innumerable people bearing ladders, and other engines of warre, to take the fortresse: for ||they assaulted them.

31 When Iudas therefore saw that the battaile was begun, and that the cry of the citie went vp to heauen, with trumpets, and a great sound,

32 He said vnto his hoste, Fight this day for your brethren.

33 So he went foorth behinde them in three companies, who sounded their trumpets, and cryed with prayer.

34 Then the hoste of Timotheus knowing that it was Maccabeus, fled from him: wherefore hee smote them with a great slaughter: so that there were killed of them that day about eight thousand men.

35 This done, Iudas turned aside to Maspha, and after he had assaulted it, hee tooke it, and slewe all the males therein, and receiued the spoiles therof, and burnt it with fire.

36 From thence went he, and tooke Casphon, Maged, Bosor, and the other cities of the countrey of Galaad.

37 After these things, gathered Timotheus another hoste, and encamped against Raphon beyond the brooke.

38 So Iudas sent [men] to espie the hoste, who brought him word, saying; All the heathen that be round about vs, are assembled vnto them, euen a very great hoste.

39 Hee hath also hired the Arabians to helpe them, and they haue pitched their tents beyond the brooke, readie to come and fight against thee: vpon this Iudas went to meet them.

40 Then Timotheus said vnto the captaines of his hoste, When Iudas and his hoste come neere the brooke, if he passe ouer first vnto vs, we shall not be able to withstand him, for hee will mightily preuaile against vs.

41 But if he be afraid, and campe beyond the riuer, we shall goe ouer vnto him, and preuaile against him.

42 Now when Iudas came neere the brooke, he caused the Scribes of the people to remaine by the brooke: vnto whom hee gaue commandement, say-

ing, Suffer no man to remaine in the campe, but let all come to the battell.

43 So he went first ouer vnto them, and all the people after him: then all the heathen being discomfited before him, cast away their weapons, and fled vnto the Temple that was at Carnaim.

44 But ||they tooke the citie, and burnt the Temple, with all that were therein. Thus was Carnaim subdued, neither could they stand any longer before Iudas.

|| *Iudas and his company.*

45 Then Iudas gathered together all the Israelites that were in the countrey of Galaad from the least vnto the greatest, euen their wiues and their children, and their stuffe, a very great hoste, to the ende they might come into the land of Iudea.

46 Now when they came vnto Ephron (this was a great city in the way as they should goe, very well fortified) they could not turne from it, either on the right hand or the left, but must needs passe through the midst of it.

47 Then they of the city shut them out, and stopped vp the gates with stones.

48 Whereupon Iudas sent vnto them in peaceable maner, saying; Let vs passe through your land to goe into our owne countrey, and none shall doe you any hurt, we will onely passe thorow on foote: howbeit they would not open vnto him.

49 Wherefore Iudas commaunded a proclamation to be made throughout the hoste, that euery man should pitch his tent in the place where he was.

50 So the souldiers pitched, and assaulted the city all that day, and all that night, till at the length the city was deliuered into his hands:

51 Who then slew all the males with the edge of the sword, and rased the city, and tooke the spoiles therof, and passed through the city ouer them that were slaine.

52 After this went they ouer Iordan, into the great plaine before Bethsan.

53 And Iudas gathered together those that ||came behind, and ||exhorted the people all the way through, till they came into the land of Iudea.

|| *Or, went hindmost,* *Num.* 10. 25

|| *Or, comforted, or encouraged.*

54 So they went vp to mount Sion with ioy and gladnesse, where they offered ||burnt offerings, because not one of them were slaine, vntill they had returned in peace.

|| *Peace offerings, Ioseph. Antiq.* 12. 12.

55 Now what time as Iudas and Ionathan were in the land
of Galaad, and Simon his brother in Galilee before Ptolemais,
56 Ioseph the sonne of Zacharias, and Azarias, captaines of
the garisons, heard of the valiant actes and warlike deeds
which they had done.
57 Wherefore they said, Let vs also get vs a name, and goe
fight against the heathen that are round about vs.
58 So when they had giuen charge vnto the garison that
was with them, they went towards Iamnia.
59 Then came Gorgias and his men out of the citie †to
fight against them.
60 And so it was, that Ioseph and Azarias were put to
flight, and pursued vnto the borders of Iudea, and there were
slaine that day of the people of Israel about two thousand
men.
61 Thus was there a great ouerthrow among the children
of Israel, because they were not obedient vnto Iudas, and his
brethren, but thought to doe some valiant act.
62 Moreouer these men came not of the seed of those, by
whose hand deliuerance was giuen vnto Israel.
63 Howbeit the man Iudas and his brethren were greatly
renowned in the sight of all Israel, and of all the heathen
wheresoeuer their name was heard of,
64 Insomuch as the people assembled vnto them with ioyfull
acclamations.
65 Afterward went Iudas foorth with his brethren, and
fought against the children of Esau in the land toward the
South, where he smote Hebron, and the †*townes* thereof, and
pulled downe the fortresse of it, and burnt the townes thereof
round about.
66 From thence he remoued to goe into the land of the
†Philistines, and passed through Samaria.
67 At that time certaine priests desirous to shew their
valour, were slaine in battell, for that they went out to fight
vnaduisedly.
68 So Iudas turned to Azotus in the land of the Philistines,
and when he had pulled downe their altars, and burnt their
carued images with fire, and spoiled their cities, he returned
into the land of Iudea.

† Gr. to meet them in battell.

† Gr. daughters.

† Gr. strangers.

CHAP. VI.

8 Antiochus dieth, 12 and confesseth that he is plagued for the wrong done to Ierusalem. 20 Iudas besiegeth those in the towre at Hierusalem. 28 They procure Antiochus the yonger to come into Iudea. 51 He besiegeth Sion, 60 and maketh peace with Israel: 62 yet ouerthroweth the wall of Sion.

ABout that time king Antiochus trauailing through the high countreys, heard say that Elimais in the countrey of Persia, was a citie greatly renowned for riches, siluer, and gold,

2 And that there was in it a very rich temple, wherein were ||couerings of gold, and brestplates, and ||shields which Alex- || *Or, shields.*
ander sonne of Philippe the Macedonian King, who reigned || *Or, armour*
first among the Grecians, had left there.

3 Wherefore he came and sought to take the citie, and to spoile it, but he was not able, because they of the citie hauing had warning thereof,

4 Rose vp against him in battell: So he fled and departed thence with great heauinesse, and returned to Babylon.

5 Moreouer there came one, who brought in tidings into Persia, that the armies which went against the land of Iudea, were put to flight:

6 And that Lysias who went forth first with a great power, was driuen away of the Iewes, and that they were made strong by the armour, and power, and store of spoiles, which they had gotten of the armies, whom they had destroyed.

7 Also that they had pulled downe the abomination which hee had set vp vpon the altar in Ierusalem, and that they had compassed about the Sanctuarie with high wals as before, and his citie Bethsura.

8 Now when the king heard these words, he was astonished, and sore moued, whereupon hee laide him downe vpon his bedde, and fell sicke for griefe, because it had not befallen him, as hee looked for.

9 And there hee continued many dayes: for his griefe was euer more and more, and he made account that he should die.

10 Where-

10 Wherefore he called for all his friends, and said vnto them, The sleepe is gone from mine eyes, and my heart faileth for very care.

11 And I thought with my selfe: Into what tribulation am I come, and how great a flood [of miserie] is it wherein now I am? for I was bountifull, and beloued in my power.

12 But now I remember the euils that I did at Ierusalem, and that I tooke all the vessels of gold and siluer that were therein, and sent to destroy the inhabitants of Iudea without a cause.

13 I perceiue therefore that for this cause these troubles are come vpon me, and behold I perish through great griefe in a strange land.

14 Then called he for Philip one of his friends whom he made ruler ouer all his realme:

15 And gaue him the crowne and his robe, and his signet, to the end ‖hee should bring vp his sonne Antiochus, and nourish him vp for the kingdome.

‖ *Or, hee should take his sonne Antiochus to him.*

16 So king Antiochus died there in the hundreth forty and ninth yeere.

17 Now when Lysias knew that the king was dead, he set vp Antiochus his sonne (whom he had brought vp being yong) to reigne in his stead, and his name he called Eupator.

18 About this time they that were in the towre shut vp the Israelites round about the Sanctuarie, and sought alwayes their hurt, and the strengthening of the heathen.

19 Wherefore Iudas purposing to destroy them, called all the people together to besiege them.

20 So they came together, and besieged them in the hundred and fiftith yeere, and he made mounts for shot against them, and [other] engines:

21 Howbeit certaine of them that were besieged got forth, vnto whom some vngodly men of Israel ioyned themselues.

22 And they went vnto the king and said, How long will it be ere thou execute iudgement, and auenge our brethren?

23 We haue beene willing to serue thy father, and to doe as he would haue vs, and to obey his commandements.

24 For which cause they of our nation besiege the towre, and are alienated from vs: Moreouer as many of vs as

they could light on, they slew, and spoiled our inheritance.
25 Neither haue they stretched out their hand against vs
only, but also against all their borders.
26 And behold this day are they besieging the towre at
Ierusalem to take it: the Sanctuary also, and Bethsura haue
they fortified.
27 Wherefore if thou doest not preuent them quickly, they
wil doe greater things then these, neither shalt thou be able
to rule them.
28 Now when the king heard this, he was angry, and
gathered together all his friends, and the captaines of his
armie, and those that had charge of the horse.
29 There came also vnto him from other kingdomes, and
from Isles of the Sea bands of hired souldiers.
30 So that the number of his armie was an hundred thousand foote men, and twentie thousand horsemen, and two
and thirty Elephants exercised in battell.
31 These went through Idumea, and pitched against Bethsura which they assaulted many daies, making engines of
warre: but they [of Bethsura] came out, and burnt them
with fire, and fought valiantly.
32 Vpon this Iudas remoued from the towre, and pitched in
Bathzacharias, ouer against the kings campe.
33 Then the king rising very earely marched fiercely with
his host toward Bathzacharias, where his armies made them
ready to battell, and sounded the trumpets.
34 And to the end they might prouoke the elephants to
fight, they shewed them the blood of grapes & mulberies.
35 Moreouer, they diuided the beasts among the armies, and
for euery elephant they appointed a thousand men, armed
with coats of male, and with helmets of brasse on their heads,
and besides this, for euery beast were ordained fiue hundred
horsemen of the best.
36 These were ready at euery occasion: wheresoeuer the
beast was, and whithersoeuer ẏͤ beast went, they went also,
neither departed they from him.
37 And vpon the beastes were there strong towres of wood,
which couered euery one of them, and were girt fast vnto
them with deuices: there were also vpon euery one

two and thirtie strong men that fought vpon them, besides
the Indian that ruled him.
38 As for the remnant of the horsemen they set them
on this side, and that side, at the two parts of the host ||giuing
them signes what to do, and being harnessed all ouer amidst
the rankes.

|| *Or, stirring them vp, and being compassed with the ranckes, or defended with the valleys.*

39 Now when the Sunne shone vpon the shields of golde,
and brasse, the mountaines glistered therewith, and shined
like lampes of fire.
40 So part of the kings armie being spred vpon the high
mountaines, and part on the valleyes below, they marched on
safely, and in order.
41 Wherefore all that heard the noise of their multitude,
and the marching of the company, and the ratling of the
harnesse, were moued: for the army was very great and mighty.
42 Then Iudas and his host drew neere, and entred into
battell, and there were slaine of the kings army, sixe hundred
men.
43 ¶ Eleazar also (syrnamed) Sauaran, perceiuing that one
of the beasts, armed with royall harnesse, was higher then all
the rest, and supposing that the king was vpon him,
44 Put himselfe in ieopardie, to the end hee might deliuer
his people, and get him a perpetuall name:
45 Wherefore hee ranne vpon him courageously through
the midst of the battell, slaying on the right hand, and on
the left, ||so that they were diuided from him on both sides.

|| *Or, so that he cut them in pieces.*

46 Which done, he crept vnder the Elephant, and thrust
him vnder and slew him: whereupon the Elephant fell
downe vpon him, and there he died.
47 How be it [the rest of the Iewes] seeing the strength of
the king, and the violence of his forces, turned away from
them.
48 ¶ Then the kings armie went vp to Ierusalem to meet
them, and the king pitched his tents ||against Iudea, and
against mount Sion.

|| *Or, in Iudea.*

49 But with them that were in Bethsura hee made ||peace:
for they came out of the citie, because they had no victuals
there, to endure the siege, it being a yeere of rest to the land.

|| *Adde out of Iosephus,* and yeelded themselues.

50 So the King tooke Bethsura, and set a garison there to
keepe it.
51 As for the Sanctuarie hee besieged it many dayes: ||and
set there ar-

|| *Or, made there mounts for shot.*

tillerie with engins, and instruments to cast fire and stones,
and pieces to cast darts, and slings.
52 Whereupon ‖they also made engins, against their engins, ‖ *Or, the Iewes.*
and helde them battell a long season.
53 Yet at the last their vessels being without victuals, (for
that it was the seuenth yeere, and they in Iudea that were
deliuered from the Gentiles, had eaten vp the residue of the
store)
54 There were but a few left in the Sanctuary, because the
famine did so preuaile against them, that they were faine to
disperse themselues, euery man to his owne place.
55 At that time Lysias heard say, that Philip (whom
Antiochus the King whiles hee liued had appointed to bring
vp his sonne Antiochus, that he might be king)
56 Was returned out of Persia, and Media, and the Kings
host also that went with him, and that hee sought to take
vnto him the ruling of the affaires.
57 Wherefore hee went in all haste, and said to the King,
and the captaines of the host, and the company, Wee decay
dayly, and our victuals are but small, and the place wee lay
siege vnto is strong: and the affaires of the kingdome lie
vpon vs.
58 Now therefore let vs †be friends with these men, and † *Gr. giue hands.*
make peace with them, and with all their nation.
59 And couenant with them, that they shall liue after their
Lawes, as they did before: for they are therefore displeased,
& haue done all these things because wee abolished their
Lawes.
60 So the King and the Princes were content: wherefore
hee sent vnto them to make peace, and they accepted thereof.
61 Also the King and the Princes made an oath vnto them:
whereupon they went out of the strong hold.
62 Then the King entred into mount Sion, but when hee
saw the strength of the place, hee brake his oath that hee
had made, and gaue commandement to pull downe the wall
round about.
63 Afterward departed hee in all haste, and returned vnto
Antiochia, where hee found Philip to bee master of the citie;
So he fought against him, and tooke the citie by force.

CHAP.

CHAP. VII.

1 Antiochus is slaine, and Demetrius reigneth in his stead. 5 Alcimus
would be hie Priest, and complaineth of Iudas to the king. 16 He
slayeth threescore Asideans. 43 Nicanor is slaine, and the kings
forces are defeated by Iudas. 49 The day of this victorie is kept
holy euery yeere.

IN the hundreth and one and fiftieth yeere, Demetrius the
sonne of Seleucus departed from Rome, and came vp
with a fewe men vnto a ||citie of the Sea coast, and reigned
there.
2 And as he entred into the †palace of his ancestors, so it
was, that his forces had taken Antiochus and Lysias to bring
them vnto him.
3 Wherefore when he knew it, hee said; Let me not see
their faces.
4 So his hoste slewe them. Now when Demetrius was set
vpon the throne of his kingdome,
5 There came vnto him all the wicked and vngodly men of
Israel, hauing Alcimus (who was desirous to be high Priest)
for their captaine.
6 And they accused the people to the king, saying; Iudas
and his brethren haue slaine all thy friends, and driuen vs out
of our owne land.
7 Now therefore send some man whom thou trustest, and
let him goe and see what hauocke he hath made amongst vs,
and in the kings land, and let him punish them with all them
that aide them.
8 Then the king chose Bacchides a friend of the king, who
ruled beyond the flood, and was a great man in the kingdome,
and faithfull to the king.
9 And him hee sent with that wicked Alcimus, whom hee
made high Priest, and commanded that he should take vengeance of the children of Israel.
10 So they departed, and came with a great power into the
land of Iudea, where they sent messengers to Iudas and his
brethren with peaceable words deceitfully.
11 But they gaue no heede to their words, for they sawe
that they were come with a great power.
12 Then did there assemble vnto Alcimus and Bacchides,
a company of ||Scribes, to require iustice.

|| *Tripolis: Ioseph. Ant. lib. 10, 12. cap. 16.*

† *Gr. house of the kingdome of his father.*

|| *Or, officers, gouernours, chiefe men, or men in authoritie.*

13 Now the Assideans were the first among the children of
Israel, that sought peace of them:
14 For, said they, one that is a Priest of the seede of Aaron,
is come with this armie, and he will doe vs no wrong.
15 So he spake vnto them peaceably, and sware vnto them,
saying; We will procure the harme neither of you nor your
friends.
16 Whereupon they beleeued him: howbeit hee tooke of
them threescore men, and slewe them in one day, according
to the words which he wrote:
17 *The flesh of thy Saints [haue they cast out] and their *Psal. 79.
blood haue they shed round about Ierusalem, and there was 2, 3.
none to bury them.
18 Wherefore the feare and dread of them fell vpon all the
people, who said, There is neither trueth, nor †righteous- †*Gr. iudge-*
nesse in them; for they haue broken the couenant and othe *ment.*
that they made.
19 After this remooued Bacchides from Ierusalem, and
pitched his tents in Bezeth, where he sent and tooke many
of the men that had forsaken him, and certaine of the people
also, and when he had slaine them, [he cast them] into the
great pit.
20 Then committed he the countrey to Alcimus, and left
with him a power to aide him: so Bacchides went vnto the king.
21 But Alcimus ‖contended for the high Priesthood. ‖*Or,*
22 And vnto him resorted all such as troubled the people, *laboured to defend*
who after they had gotten the land of Iuda into their power, *his high*
did much hurt in Israel. *Priesthood.*
23 Now when Iudas saw all the mischiefe that Alcimus and
his company had done among the Israelites, euen aboue the
heathen,
24 He went out into all the coast of Iudea round about, and
tooke vengeance of them that had ‖reuolted from him, so that ‖*Or, fledde from him*
they durst no more ‖goe foorth into the countrey. *to the*
25 On the other side, when Alcimus saw that Iudas and his *enemie.*
company ‖had gotten the vpper hand, and knew that he was ‖*Or, inuade the*
not able to †abide their force, he went againe to the king, *countrey.*
and said all the worst of them that he could. ‖*Or, were*
26 Then the king sent Nicanor one of his honourable *growen very*
princes, a man that bare deadly hate vnto Israel, with com- *strong.*
mandement to destroy the people. †*Gr. to*

 abide them.

27 So Nicanor came to Ierusalem with a great force: and
† *Gr. peaceable.* sent vnto Iudas and his brethren deceitfully with †friendly
words, saying,
28 Let there be no battell betweene me and you, I will
† *Gr. see your faces.* come with a fewe men, that I may †see you in peace.
29 He came therefore to Iudas, and they saluted one another
peaceably. Howbeit the enemies were prepared to take away
Iudas by violence.
30 Which thing after it was knowen to Iudas (to wit) that
he came vnto him with deceit, he was sore afraid of him, and
would see his face no more.
31 Nicanor also when he saw that his counsell was dis-
† *Gr. meet Iudas in battell.* couered, went out to †fight against Iudas besides ||Caphar-
salama.
|| *Or, Carphasalama.*
32 Where there were slaine of Nicanors side, about fiue
thousand men, and [the rest] fled into the citie of Dauid.
33 After this went Nicanor vp to mount Sion, and there
came out of the Sanctuarie certaine of the priestes, and
certaine of the elders of the people to salute him peaceably,
and to shewe him the burnt sacrifice that was offred for
the king.
† *Gr. defiled them.* 34 But he mocked them, and laughed at them, and †abused
them shamefully, and spake proudly,
35 And swore in his wrath, saying, vnlesse Iudas and his
hoste be now deliuered into my hands, if euer I come againe
† *Gr. in peace* †in safetie, I will burne vp this house: and with that he went
out in a great rage.
36 Then the priests entred in, and stood before the altar,
and the Temple, weeping, and saying,
37 Thou O Lord didst choose this house, to be called by
thy Name, and to be a house of prayer and petition for thy
people.
38 Be auenged of this man and his hoste, and let them fall
by the sword: Remember their blasphemies, and suffer them
not to continue any longer.
39 So Nicanor went out of Ierusalem, & pitched his tents in
* 2. Kings 19. 35. esai. 37. 36. ecclus. 48. 22. 2. mac. 8. 19 Bethoron, where an hoste out of Syria met him.
40 But Iudas pitched in Adasa with three thousand men,
and there he prayed, saying,
41 *O Lord, when they that were sent from the king of
the Assyrians blasphemed, thine Angel went out, and smote
a hundred, fourescore, and fiue

thousand of them.
42 Euen so destroy thou this host before vs this day, that
the rest may know that he hath spoken blasphemously against
thy Sanctuary, and iudge thou him according to his wickednesse.
43 So the thirteenth day of the moneth Adar, the hostes
ioyned battell, but Nicanors host was discomfited, & he himselfe was first slaine in the battell.
44 Now when Nicanors host saw that he was slaine, they
cast away their weapons, and fled.
45 Then ||they pursued after them a dayes iourney from
Adasa, vnto Gasera, sounding an alarme after them with their
trumpets.
46 Whereupon they came forth out of all the townes of
Iudea round about, and closed them in, so that they turning
backe vpon them that pursued them, were all slaine with the
sword, and not one of them was left.
47 Afterwards they tooke ẏ spoiles, and the pray, and smote
off Nicanors head, & his right hand, which he stretched out
so proudly, and brought them away, and hanged them vp,
towards Ierusalem.
48 For this cause the people reioyced greatly, and they kept
that day, a day of great gladnesse.
49 Moreouer they ordeined to keepe yeerely this day, being
the thirteenth of Adar.
50 Thus the land of Iuda was in rest a litle while.

|| *Or, the Iewes.*

CHAP. VIII.

1 Iudas is informed of the power and policie of the Romanes, 20 and maketh a league with them. 24 The articles of that league.

NOw Iudas had heard of the fame of the Romanes, that
they were mighty and valiant men, and such as
would louingly accept all that ioyned themselues vnto them,
and make a league of amitie with all that came vnto them,
2 And that they were men of great valour: It was told him
also of their warres and noble acts which they had done
amongst the ||Galatians, and how they had conquered them,
and brought them vnder tribute.
3 And what they had done in ẏ countrey of Spaine, for the
winning of the mines of the siluer & gold which is there

|| *Or, French men.*

4 And

4 And that by their policie and patience, they had conquered
|| Or, euery place. ||all that place (though it were very farre from them) and the
kings also that came against them from the vttermost part
of the earth, till they had discomfited them, & giuen them a
great ouerthrow, so that the rest did giue them tribute euery
yere.
5 Besides this, how they had discomfited in battell Philip,
|| Or, Macedonians. and Perseus king of the ||Citims, with others that lift vp them-
selues against them, and had ouercome them.
6 How also Antiochus the great king of Asia that came
against them in battaile, hauing an hundred and twentie
Elephants with horsemen and chariots, and a very great armie,
was discomfited by them.
7 And how they tooke him aliue, and couenanted that hee
and such as reigned after him, should pay a great tribute, and
giue hostages, and that which was agreed vpon,
8 And the country of India, and Media, and Lidia, and of
the goodliest countries: which they tooke of him, and gaue
to king Eumenes.
9 Moreouer how the Grecians had determined to come and
destroy them.
10 And that they hauing knowledge thereof sent against
them a certaine captaine, and fighting with them slew many
of them, and caried away captiues, their wiues, and their
children, and spoiled them, and tooke possession of their lands,
and pulled downe their strong holds, and brought them to be
their seruants vnto this day.
11 [It was told him besides] how they destroyed and brought
vnder their dominion, all other kingdomes and isles that at
any time resisted them.
12 But with their friends, and such as relied vpon them
they kept amitie: and that they had conquered kingdomes
both farre and nigh, insomuch as all that heard of their name
were afraid of them.
13 Also that whom they would helpe to a kingdome, those
raigne, and whom againe they would, they displace: finally
that they were greatly exalted.
14 Yet for all this, none of them wore a crowne, or was
clothed in purple to be magnified thereby.
15 Moreouer how they had made for themselues a senate
house, wherin three hundred and twentie men sate in coun-

sell daily, consulting alway for the people, to the end they
might be wel ordered
16 And that they committed their gouernment to one man
euery yeere, who ruled ouer all their countrie, and that all
were obedient to that one, and that there was neither enuy,
nor emulation amongst them.
17 In consideration of these things Iudas chose Eupolemus
the sonne of Iohn, the sonne of Accas, and Iason the sonne
of Eleazar, and sent them to Rome to make a league of amitie
and confederacie with them,
18 [And to intreate them] that they would take the yoke
from them, for they saw that the kingdome of the Grecians
did oppresse Israel with seruitude
19 They went therefore to Rome (which was a very great
iourney) and came into the Senate, where they spake and said,
20 Iudas Maccabeus with his brethren, and the people of
the Iewes, haue sent vs vnto you, to make a confederacie,
and peace with you, and that we might be registred, your
confederats and friends.
21 So that matter pleased the Romanes well.
22 And this is the copie of the Epistle which (the Senate)
wrote backe againe, in tables of brasse: and sent to Ierusalem,
that there they might haue by them a memorial of peace &
confederacy.
23 Good successe be to the Romans and to the people of the
Iewes, by Sea, and by land for euer: the sword also and
enemie, be farre from them.
24 If there come first any warre vpon the Romans or any
of their confederats throughout all their dominion,
25 The people of the Iewes shall helpe them, as the time
shall be appointed, with all their heart.
26 Neither shal they giue any thing, vnto them that make
war vpon them, or aide them with victuals, weapons, money,
or ships, as it hath seemed good vnto the Romans, but they
shall keepe their couenant without taking any thing therefore.
27 In the same maner also, if warre come first vpon the
nation of the Iewes, the Romans shall helpe them with all
their heart, according as the time shall be appointed them.
28 Neither shal victuals be giuen to thē that take part
against thē, or weapons,
or

or money, or ships, as it hath seemed good to the Romanes; but they shall keepe their couenants, and that without deceit.
29 According to these articles did the Romanes make a couenant with the people of the Iewes.
30 Howbeit, if hereafter the one partie or the other, shall thinke meete to adde or diminish any thing, they may doe it at their pleasures, and whatsoeuer they shall adde or take away, shalbe ratified.
31 And as touching the euils that Demetrius doeth to the Iewes, wee haue written vnto him, saying, Wherefore hast thou made thy yoke heauie vpon our friends, and confederats the Iewes?
32 If therefore they complaine any more against thee: wee will doe them iustice, and fight with thee by sea and by land.

CHAP. IX.

1 Alcimus and Bacchides come againe with new forces into Iudea. 7 The armie of Iudas flee from him, 17 and he is slaine. 30 Ionathan is in his place, 40 and reuengeth his brother Iohns quarrell. 55 Alcimus is plagued, and dieth. 70 Bacchides maketh peace with Ionathan.

FVrthermore, when Demetrius heard that Nicanor and his hoste were slaine in battell, †hee sent Bacchides and Alcimus into the land of Iudea the second time, and with them the ||chiefe strength of his hoste.
2 Who went forth by the way that leadeth to ||Galgala, and pitched their tents before Masaloth, which is in Arbela, and after they had wonne it, they slew much people.
3 Also the first moneth of the hundred fiftie and second yeere, they encamped before Ierusalem.
4 From whence they remoued and went to ||Berea, with twentie thousand footmen, and two thousand horsemen.
5 Now Iudas had pitched his tents at Eleasa, and three thousand chosen men with him.
6 Who seeing the multitude of the other army to be so great, were sore afraide, whereupon many conueyed themselues out of the hoste, insomuch

† Gr. he added or proceeded to send.
|| Or, the right wing.
|| Or, Galilea.
|| Or, Beretho. Ios.

as there abode of them no moe but eight hundred men.
7 When Iudas therefore saw that his hoste slipt away, and
that the battell pressed vpon him, he was sore troubled in
mind, and much distressed, for that he had no time to gather
them together.
8 Neuerthelesse vnto them that remained, he said; Let vs
arise and goe vp against our enemies, if peraduenture we may
be able to fight with them.
9 But they dehorted him, saying, Wee shall neuer be able:
||Let vs now rather saue onr liues, and hereafter we will
returne with our brethren, and fight against them: for we
are but few.
10 Then Iudas said, God forbid that I should doe this
thing, and flee away from them: If our time be come, let vs
die manfully for our brethren, and †let vs not staine our
honour.
11 With that the hoste [of Bacchides] remoued out of their
tents, and stood ouer against ||them, their horsemen being
diuided into two troupes, and their slingers and archers going
before the hoste, and they that marched in the foreward were
all mighty men.
12 As for Bacchides, hee was in the right wing, so the
hoste drew neere on the two parts, and sounded their trumpets.
13 They also of Iudas side, euen they sounded their trumpets
also, so that the earth shooke at the noise of the armies, and
the battell continued from morning till night.
14 Now when Iudas perceiued that Bacchides and the
strength of his armie were on the right side, he tooke with
him all the hardy men,
15 Who discomfited the right wing, and pursued them vnto
the mount Azotus.
16 But when they of the left wing, saw that they of the
right wing were discomfited, they followed vpon Iudas and
those that were with him hard at the heeles from behinde:
17 Whereupon there was a sore battell, insomuch as many
were slaine on both parts.
18 Iudas also was killed, and the remnant fled.
19 Then Ionathan and Simon tooke Iudas their brother,
and buried him in the sepulchre of his fathers in Modin.
20 Moreouer they bewailed him,
and

|| We follow here the Romane copie.

† Gr. let vs not leaue any iust cause behinde vs, why our glory should be spoken against.

|| Or the Iewes.

and all Israel made great lamentation for him, and mourned
many dayes, saying;
21 How is the valiant man fallen, that deliuered Israel?
22 As for the other things concerning Iudas and his warres,
and the noble actes which he did, and his greatnesse, they
are not written: for they were very many.
23 ¶ Now after the death of Iudas, the wicked began to put
foorth their heads in all the coasts of Israel, and there rose vp
all such as wrought iniquitie.
24 In those dayes also was there a very great famine, by
reason whereof the countrey reuolted, and went with ||them.
25 Then Bacchides chose the wicked men, and made them
lordes of the countrey.

|| *Bacchides and his company.*

26 And they made enquirie & search for Iudas friends,
and brought them vnto Bacchides, who tooke vengeance of
them, and †vsed them despitefully.

† *Gr. mocked them.*

27 So was there a great affliction in Israel, the like whereof
was not since the time that a Prophet was not seene amongst
them.
28 For this cause all Iudas friends came together, & said
vnto Ionathan,
29 Since thy brother Iudas died, we haue no man like him
to goe foorth against our enemies, and Bacchides, and against
them of our nation that are aduersaries to vs.
30 Now therefore wee haue chosen thee this day to be our
prince, and captaine in his stead, that thou mayest fight our
battels.
31 Vpon this, Ionathan tooke the gouernance vpon him at
that time, and rose vp in stead of his brother Iudas.
32 But when Bacchides gat knowledge thereof, he sought
for to slay him.
33 Then Ionathan and Simon his brother, and all that were
with him, perceiuing that, fled into the wildernes of Thecoe,
and pitched their tents by the water of the poole Asphar.
34 ||Which when Bacchides vnderstood, he came neere to
Iordan with all his hoste vpon the Sabbath day.

|| *Or, Which when Bacchides vnderstood, on the Sabbath day he came neere.*

35 Now Ionathan had sent his brother [||Iohn] a captaine of
the people, to pray his friendes the Nabbathites †that they
might leaue with them their cariage, which was much.

|| *Ios. Antiq. lib.* 13. *c.* 1.

† *Gr. that he might leaue with them their cariage or stuffe.*

36 But the children of Iambri came out of Medaba, and
tooke Iohn and all that hee had, and went their way with it.
37 After this came word to Ionathan and Simon his brother,
that the children of Iambri made a great mariage, and were
bringing the bride from ||Nadabatha with a great traine, as
being the daughter of one of the great princes of Canaan.
38 Therfore they remembred Iohn their brother, and went
vp and hidde themselues vnder the couert of the mountaine.
39 Where they lift vp their eyes, and looked, & behold,
there was much adoe and great cariage: and the bridegrome
came foorth, and his friends & brethren to meet them with
||drums and ||instruments of musicke, and many weapons.
40 Then Ionathan and they that were with him, rose vp
against them from the place where they lay in ambush, and
made a slaughter of them in such sort, as many fell downe
dead, and the remnant fledde into the mountaine, and they
tooke all their spoiles.
41 Thus was the mariage turned into mourning, and the
noise of their melody into lamentation.
42 So when they had auenged fully the blood of their
brother, they turned againe to the marish of Iordan.
43 Now when Bacchides heard hereof, hee came on the
Sabbath day vnto the banks of Iordan with a great power.
44 Then Ionathan sayde to his company, Let vs goe vp
now and fight for our liues, for it standeth not with vs to day,
as in time past:
45 For behold, the battell is before vs and behinde vs, and
the water of Iordan on this side and that side, the marish
likewise and wood, neither is there place for vs to turne aside.
46 Wherefore cry ye now vnto heauen, that ye may be
deliuered from the hand of your enemies.
47 With that they ioyned battel, and Ionathan stretched
foorth his hand to smite Bacchides, but hee turned backe
from him.
48 Then Ionathan and they that were with him, leapt into
Iordan, and swamme ouer vnto the farther banke: howbeit
the other passed not ouer Iordan vnto them.

|| *Or, Medaba.*

|| *Or, timbrels*

|| *Or, musicians.*

49 So

49 So there were slaine of Bacchides side that day about a
†thousand men
50 Afterward returned [Bacchides] to Ierusalem, and
||repaired the strong cities in Iudea: the fort in Iericho, and
Emmaus, and Bethoron, and Bethel, and Thamnatha, Phara-
thoni, and ||Taphon (these did he strengthen with high wals,
with gates, & with barres.)
51 And in them he set a garison, that they might worke
malice vpon Israel.
52 He fortified also †the citie Bethsura, and Gazara, and
the towre, and put forces in them, and prouision of victuals.
53 Besides, he tooke the chiefe mens sonnes in the country
for hostages, and put them into the towre at Ierusalem to
be kept.
54 Moreouer, in the hundred, fiftie and third yere, in the
second moneth, Alcimus commanded that the wall of the
inner court of the Sanctuarie should be pulled downe, he
pulled downe also the works of the prophets.
55 And as he began to pull downe, euen at that time was
Alcimus plagued, and his enterprises hindered: for his mouth
was stopped, and he was taken with a palsie, so that hee
could no more speake any thing, nor giue order concerning
his house.
56 So Alcimus died at that time with great torment.
57 Now when Bacchides saw that Alcimus was dead, he
returned to the king, wherupon the land of Iudea was in
rest two yeere.
58 Then all the vngodly men held a counsell, saying,
Behold, Ionathan and his companie are at ease, and dwell
without care: now therefore wee will bring Bacchides hither,
who shall take them all in one night.
59 So they went, and consulted with him.
60 Then remoued he, and came with a great hoste, and
sent letters priuily to his adherents in Iudea, that they should
take Ionathan, and those that were with him: Howbeit they
could not, because their counsell was knowen vnto them.
61 Wherefore they tooke of the men of the countrey that
were authours of that mischiefe, about fiftie persons, and
slew them.
62 Afterward Ionathan and Simon, and they that were with
him, got them away to Bethbasi, which is in the

† Two thousand men. Ioseph. ant. lib. 13. cap. 1
|| Or, built.
|| Ioseph. Techoa.
† Gr. the citie in Bethsura.

wildernesse, and they repaired the decayes thereof, and made it strong.

63 Which thing when Bacchides knew, he gathered together all his host, and sent word ||to them that were of Iudea.

64 Then went he and laid siege against Bethbasi, & they fought against it a long season, and made engines of warre.

65 But Ionathan left his brother Simon in the citie, and went forth himselfe into the countrey, and with a certaine number went he forth.

|| Or, to such of the countrey as were his friends to take his part.

66 And he smote ||Odonarkes and his brethren, and the children of Phasiron in their tent.

|| Or, Odomarra.

67 And when he began to smite them, and came vp with his forces, Simon and his company went out of the citie, and burnt vp the engines of warre,

68 And fought against Bacchides, who was discomfited by them, and they afflicted him sore. For his counsell and trauaile was in vaine.

69 Wherefore he was very wroth at the wicked men that gaue him counsell to come into the countrey, insomuch as he slew many of them, and purposed to returne into his owne countrey.

70 Whereof when Ionathan had knowledge, he sent ambassadours vnto him, to the end he should make peace with him, & deliuer them the prisoners.

71 Which thing hee accepted, and did according to his demaunds, and sware vnto him that hee would neuer doe him harme all the dayes of his life.

72 When therefore hee had restored vnto him the prisoners that he had taken aforetime out of the land of Iudea, he returned and went his way into his owne land, neither †came he any more into their borders.

† Gr. added he to come any more.

73 Thus the sword ceased from Israel: but Ionathan dwelt at Machmas, and began to †gouerne the people, and he destroyed the vngodly men out of Israel.

† Gr. iudge.

CHAP. X.

1 Demetrius maketh large offers to haue peace with Ionathan. 25 His letters to the Iewes. 47 Ionathan maketh peace with Alexander, 50 Who killeth Demetrius, 58 and marieth the daughter of Ptolomeus. 62 Ionathan is sent for by him, and much honoured, 75 and preuaileth against the forces of Demetrius the yonger, 84 & burneth the temple of Dagon.

In

|| Ios. the sonne of Antiochus Epiphanes.

IN the hundreth & sixtieth yere, Alexander the ||sonne of Antiochus surnamed Epiphanes, went vp and tooke Ptolemais: for the people had receiued him, by meanes whereof he reigned there.

2 Now when king Demetrius heard thereof, he gathered together an exceeding great host, and went foorth against him to fight.

3 Moreouer Demetrius sent letters vnto Ionathan with louing wordes, so as he magnified him.

4 For, said hee, Let vs first make peace with him before he ioyne with Alexander against vs.

5 Else he wil remember allthe euils that we haue done against him, and against his brethren and his people.

6 Wherefore he gaue him authority to gather together an host, and to prouide weapons that hee might aide him in battell: he commaunded also that the hostages that were in the towre, should be deliuered him.

7 Then came Ionathan to Ierusalem, and read the letters in the audience of all the people, and of them that were in the towre.

8 Who were sore afraid when they heard that the king had giuen him authoritie to gather together an host.

9 Whereupon they of the towre deliuered their hostages vnto Ionathan, & he deliuered them vnto their parents.

10 This done, Ionathan setled himselfe in Ierusalem, and began to build and repaire the citie.

11 And he commaunded the workemen to build the wals, and the mount Sion round about with square stones, for fortification, and they did so.

12 Then the strangers that were in the fortresses which Bacchides had built, fled away:

13 Insomuch as euery man left his place, and went into his owne country.

14 Onely at Bethsura certaine of those that had forsaken the law, and the commaundements remained still: for it was their place of refuge.

15 Now when king Alexander had heard what promises Demetrius had sent vnto Ionathan: when also it was told him of the battels and noble acts which he & his brethren had done, and of the paines that they had indured,

16 He said, Shal we find such another

man? Now thereforee we will make him our friend, and
confederate.
17 Vpon this he wrote a letter and sent it vnto him according to these words, saying:
18 King Alexander to his brother Ionathan, sendeth greeting:
19 We haue heard of thee, that thou art a man of great
power, and meete to be our friend.
20 Wherefore now this day we ordaine thee to bee the high
priest of thy nation, and to be called the kings friend, (and
therewithall he sent him a purple robe and a crowne of gold)
[and require thee] to take our part, and keepe friendship
with vs.
21 So in the seuenth moneth of the hundreth and sixtieth
yere, at the feast of the Tabernacles, Ionathan put on the
holy robe, and gathered together forces, and prouided much
armour.
22 Wherof when Demetrius heard, he was very sory,
and said,
23 What haue we done that Alexander hath preuented vs,
in making amity with the Iewes to strengthen himself?
24 I also will write vnto them words of encouragement [and
promise them] dignities and gifts, that I may haue their ayde.
25 He sent vnto him therefore, to this effect: King Demetrius vnto the people of the Iewes, sendeth greeting:
26 Whereas you haue kept couenants with vs, & continued
in our friendship, not ioyning your selues with our enemies,
we haue heard hereof, & are glad:
27 Wherefore now continue yee still to be faithful vnto vs,
and we will well recompence you for the things you doe in
our behalfe,
28 And will grant you many immunities, and giue you
rewards.
29 And now I doe free you, and for your sake I release all
the Iewes from tributes, and from the customes of salt, and
from crowne taxes,
30 And frō that which appertaineth vnto me to receiue for
the third part of the seed, and the halfe of the fruit of
the trees, I release it from this day forth, so that they shall
not be taken of the land of Iudea, nor of the three gouernments which are added thereunto out of the country of
Samaria and Galile, from this day forth for euermore.
31 Let Ierusalem also bee holy and free, with the borders
thereof,

both

both from tenths and tributes.
32 And as for the towre which is at Ierusalem, I yeeld vp
my authoritie ouer it, and giue it to the high Priest, that he
may set in it such men as he shall choose to keepe it.
33 Moreouer I freely set at libertie euery one of the Iewes
that were carried captiues out of the land of Iudea, into any
part of my kingdome, and I will that all my officers remit the
tributes, euen of their cattell.
34 Furthermore, I will that all the Feasts and Sabbaths, &
New moones and solemne dayes, and the three dayes before
the Feast, and the three dayes after the Feast, shall be all
dayes of immunitie and freedom for all the Iewes in my
realme.
35 Also no man shall haue authoritie to meddle with them,
or to molest any of them in any matter.
36 [I will further] that there be enrolled amongst the kings
forces about thirtie thousand men of the Iewes, vnto whom
pay shall be giuen as belongeth to all the kings forces.
37 And of them some shalbe placed in the kings strong
holds, of whom also some shall be set ouer the affaires of the
kingdome, which are of trust: and I will that their ouerseers
and gouernours be of themselues, and that they †liue after
their owne lawes, euen as the King hath commanded in the
land of Iudea.

† *Gr. walke.*

38 And concerning the three gouernments that are added
to Iudea from the countrey of Samaria, let them be ioyned
with Iudea, that they may be reckoned to be vnder one, nor
bound to obey other authoritie then ỹ high priests
39 As for Ptolemais and the land pertaining thereto, I giue
it as a free gift to the Sanctuary at Ierusalem, for the neces-
sary expences ||of the Sanctuary.

|| *Or, of the holy things.*

40 Moreouer, I giue euery yeere fifteene thousand shekels
of siluer, out of the Kings accompts from the places appertaining.
41 And all the ouerplus which the officers payed not in as
in former time, from henceforth shalbe giuen towards the
workes of the Temple.
42 And besides this, the fiue thousand shekels of siluer,
which they tooke from the vses of the Temple out of the
accompts yeere by yeere, euen those

things shall be released, because they appertaine to the Priests
that minister.
43 And whosoeuer they be that flee vnto the Temple at
Ierusalem, or be within the liberties thereof, being indebted
vnto the King, or for any other matter, let them be at libertie,
and all that they haue in my realme.
44 For the building also and repairing of the workes of the
Sanctuary, expences shalbe giuen of the Kings accompts.
45 Yea, and for the building of the walles of Ierusalem, and
the fortifying thereof round about, expences shall bee giuen
out of the Kings accompts, as also for building of the walles
in Iudea.
46 Now when Ionathan and the people heard these words,
they gaue no credite vnto them, nor receiued them, because
they remembred the great euill that he had done in Israel;
for hee had afflicted them very sore.
47 But with Alexander they were well pleased, because hee
was the first that entreated of ‖peace with them, and they ‖ *True.*
were confederate with him alwayes.
48 Then gathered king Alexander great forces, and camped
ouer against Demetrius.
49 And after the two Kings had ioyned battell, Demetrius
hoste fled: but Alexander followed after him, and preuailed
against them.
50 And he continued the battell very sore vntill the Sunne
went downe, and that day was Demetrius slaine.
51 Afterward Alexander sent Embassadors to Ptoleme king
of Egypt, with a message to this effect;
52 Forsomuch as I am come againe to my realme, and am
set in the throne of my progenitors, and haue gotten the
dominion, and ouerthrowen Demetrius, and recouered our
countrey,
53 (For after I had ioyned battell with him, both he, and
his hoste was discomfited by vs, so that we sit in the throne
of his kingdome)
54 Now therefore let vs make a league of amitie together,
and giue me now thy daughter to wife: & I will be thy son
in law, and will giue both thee and her, gifts according to
thy dignity.
55 Then Ptoleme the king gaue answere, saying, Happy be
the day wherein thou diddest returne into the land of
thy

thy fathers, and satest in the throne of their kingdome.
56 And now will I doe to thee, as thou hast written: meet
me therefore at Ptolemais, that wee may see one another, for
I will marry my daughter to thee according to thy desire.
57 So Ptolome went out of Egypt with his daughter
Cleopatra, and they came vnto Ptolemais in the hundred
threescore and second yeere.
58 Where king Alexander meeting him, gaue vnto him his
daughter Cleopatra, and celebrated her marriage at Ptolemais
with great glory, as the maner of kings is.
59 Now king Alexander had written vnto Ionathan, that
hee should come and meete him.
60 Who thereupon went honourably to Ptolemais, where
he met the two kings, and gaue them and their friends siluer
and golde, and many presents, and found fauour in their
sight.
61 At that time certaine pestilent fellowes of Israel, men
of a wicked life, assembled themselues against him, to accuse
him: but the king would not heare them.
62 Yea more then that, the king commanded to take off his
garments, and clothe him in purple: and they did so.
63 Also he made him sit by himselfe, and said vnto his
princes, Goe with him into the midst of the city, and make
proclamation, that no man complaine against him of any
matter, and that no man troble him for any maner of cause.
64 Now when his accusers sawe that he was honoured
according to the proclamation, and clothed in purple, they
fled all away.
65 So the king honoured him, and wrote him amongst his
chiefe friends, and made him a duke, and ||partaker of his
dominion.

|| *Or, gouernour of a prouince.*

66 Afterward Ionathan returned to Ierusalem with peace
and gladnes.
67 Furthermore, in the hundreth threescore and fifth yeere,
came Demetrius sonne of Demetrius, out of Crete into the
land of his fathers.
68 Whereof when king Alexander heard tell, he was right
sory, and returned into Antioch.
69 Then Demetrius made Apollonius the gouernour of
Coelosyria his general, who gathered together a great hoste,
and camped in Iamnia, and sent

vnto Ionathan the high Priest, saying,
70 Thou alone liftest vp thy selfe against vs, and I am
laughed to scorne for thy sake, and reproched, and why doest
thou vaunt thy power against vs in the mountaines?
71 Now therefore if thou trustest in thine owne strength,
come downe to vs into the plaine field, and there let vs trie
the matter together, for with me is the power of the cities.
72 Aske and learne who I am, and the rest that take our
part, and they shal tel thee that thy foot is not able to stand
before our face; for thy fathers haue bene twice put to flight
in their owne land.
73 Wherefore now thou shalt not be able to abide the
horsemen and so great a power in the plaine, where is
neither stone nor flint, nor place to flee vnto.
74 So when Ionathan heard these words of Apollonius, he
was moued in his mind, & choosing ten thousand men, he
went out of Ierusalē, where Simon his brother met him for
to helpe him.
75 And hee pitched his tents against Ioppe: but they of
Ioppe shut him out of the citie, because Apollonius had a
garison there.
76 Then Ionathan laid siege vnto it: whereupon they of
the city let him in for feare: & so Ionathan wan Ioppe.
77 Wherof when Apollonius heard, he tooke three thousand
horsemen with a great hoste of footmen, and went to Azotus
||as one that iourneyed, & therewithal ||drew him forth into
the plaine, because he had a great number of horsemen, in
whom he put his trust.
78 Then Ionathan followed after him to Azotus, where the
armies ioyned battell.
79 Now Apollonius had left a thousand horsemen in ambush.
80 And Ionathan knew that there was an ambushment behinde him; for they had compassed in his host, and cast darts
at the people, from morning till euening.
81 But the people stood still, as Ionathan had commanded
them: and so the ||enemies horses were tired.
82 Then brought Simon forth his hoste, and set them
against the footmen, (for the horsmen were spent) who
were discomfited by him, and fled.
83 The horsemen also being scattered in the field, fled to
Azotus, and went into Bethdagō their idols temple for safety.

|| *Or, as thogh he wouldpasse thorow it.*

|| *Or, led his company.*

|| *Ios. Antiq. lib.* 13. *c.* 8.

84 But Ionathan set fire on Azotus, and the cities round
about it, and tooke their spoiles, and the temple of Dagon,
with them that were fled into it, he burnt with fire.
85 Thus there were burnt and slaine with the sword, well
nigh eight thousand men.
86 And from thence Ionathan remoued his hoste, and
camped against Ascalon, where the men of the city came
forth, and met him with great pompe.
87 After this, returned Ionathan and his hoste vnto Ierusalem, hauing many spoiles.
88 Now when king Alexander heard these things, he
honoured Ionathan yet more,
89 And sent him a buckle of golde, as the vse is to be giuen
to such as are of the kings blood: he gaue him also Accaron
with the borders thereof in possession.

CHAP. XI.

12 Ptolomeus taketh away his daughter from Alexander, and entreth vpon his kingdome. 17 Alexander is slaine, and Ptolemeus dieth within three dayes. 20 Ionathan besiegeth the towre at Ierusalem. 26 The Iewes and he are much honoured by Demetrius, 48 Who is rescued by the Iewes from his owne subiects in Antioch. 57 Antiochus the yonger honoureth Ionathan. 61 His exploits in diuers places

AND the king of Egypt gathered together a great host like
the sand that lieth vpon the Sea shore, and many ships,
and went about through deceit to get Alexanders kingdome,
and ioyne it to his owne.
2 Whereupon he tooke his iourney into Syria in peaceable
maner, so as they of the cities opened vnto him, and met
him: for king Alexander had commanded them so to doe,
because he was his father in law.
3 Now as Ptolomee entred into the cities, he set in euery
one of them a garison of souldiers to keepe it.
4 And when he came neere to Azotus, they shewed him
the temple of Dagon that was burnt, and Azotus, and the
suburbs thereof that were destroyed, and the bodies that
were cast abroad, and them that he had burnt in the battell,
for they had made heapes of them by the way where he
should passe.

5 Also they told the king whatsoe-

uer Ionathan had done, to the intent he might blame him:
but the king helde his peace.
6 Then Ionathan met the king with great pompe at Ioppa,
where they saluted one another, and †lodged. †Gr. slept.
7 Afterward Ionathan when he had gone with the king to
the riuer called Eleutherus, returned againe to Ierusalem.
8 King Ptolomee therefore hauing gotten the dominion of
the cities by the sea, vnto Seleucia vpon the sea coast, imagined
wicked counsels against Alexander.
9 Whereupon he sent embassadours vnto king Demetrius,
saying, Come, let vs make a league betwixt vs, and I will
giue thee my daughter whome Alexander hath, and thou
shalt reigne in thy fathers kingdome:
10 For I repent ỳ I gaue my daughter vnto him, for he
sought to slay me.
11 Thus did he slander him, because he was desirous of his
kingdome.
12 Wherefore he tooke his daughter from him, and gaue
her to Demetrius, and forsooke Alexander, so that their
hatred was openly knowen.
13 Then Ptolomee entred into Antioch, where he set two
crownes vpō his head, the crowne of Asia, and of Egypt.
14 In the meane season was king Alexander in Cilicia, because those ỳ dwelt in those parts, had reuolted from him.
15 But when Alexander heard of this, hee came to warre
against him, whereupon king Ptolomee brought forth his
hoste, and met him with a mightie power, and put him to
flight.
16 So Alexander fled into Arabia, there to be defended,
but king Ptolomee was exalted.
17 For Zabdiel the Arabian tooke off Alexanders head, and
sent it vnto Ptolomee.
18 King Ptolemee also died the third day after, †& they
that were in the strong holds, were slaine one of another.
19 By this meanes Demetrius reigned in the hundreth,
threescore and seuenth yeere.
20 At the same time Ionathan gathered together them that
were in Iudea, to take the towre that was in Ierusalem, and
he made many engines of warre against it.
21 Then certaine vngodly persons who hated their owne
people, went vn-
to

†Gr. and those that were in the holds were slaine of those that were in the holds.

to the king, and told him that Ionathan besieged the towre.
22 Whereof when he heard, he was angry, and immediately
remouing, he can to Ptolemais, and wrote vnto Ionathan,
that he should not lay siege to the towre, but come and
speake with him at Ptolemais in great haste.
23 Neuerthelesse Ionathan when he heard this, commanded
to besiege it [still] and he chose certaine of the Elders of
Israel, and the priests, and put himselfe in perill,
24 And tooke siluer and gold, and rayment, and diuers
presents besides, and went to Ptolemais, vnto the king,
where he found fauour in his sight.
25 And though certaine vngodly men of the people, had
made complaints against him,
26 Yet the king entreated him as his predecessors had done
before, & promoted him in the sight of all his friends,
27 And confirmed him in the high priesthood, and in all
the honours that hee had before, and gaue him preeminence
among his chiefe friends.
28 Then Ionathan desired the king, that hee would make
Iudea free from tribute, as also the three gouernments with
the countrey of Samaria, & he promised him three hundred
talents
29 So the king consented and wrote letters vnto Ionathan,
of all these things after this maner.
30 King Demetrius vnto his brother Ionathan, and vnto
the nation of the Iewes, sendeth greeting.
31 We send you heere a copie of the letter, which we did
write vnto our cousin Lasthenes, concerning you, that you
might see it.
32 King Demetrius vnto his father Lasthenes, sendeth
greeting:
33 We are determined to doe good to the people of the
Iewes, who are our friends, and keepe couenants with vs,
because of their good will towards vs.
34 ||Wherefore we haue ratified vnto them the borders of
Iudea, with the three gouernments of Apherema, and Lidda,
and Ramathem, that are added vnto Iudea, from the countrie
of Samaria, and all things appertaining vnto them, for all
such, as doe sacrifice in Ierusalem, in stead of the paiments,
which the king receiued of them yeerely aforetime out of
the fruits of the earth, and of trees.

|| *Josep. antiq. lib.* 13. *cap.* 8.

35 And as for other things that belong vnto vs of the tithes
and customes pertaining vnto vs, as also the salt pits, and the
crowne taxes, which are due vnto vs, we discharge them of
them all for their reliefe.
36 And nothing heereof shall be reuoked from this time
foorth for euer.
37 Now therefore see that thou make a copie of these
things, and let it be deliuered vnto Ionathan, and set vpon
the holy mount in a conspicuous place.
38 After this, when king Demetrius saw that the land was
quiet before him, and that no resistance was made against
him, he sent away all his forces euery one to his owne place,
except certaine bands of strangers, whom he had gathered
from the iles of the heathen, wherefore all the forces of his
fathers hated him.
39 Moreouer there was one Tryphon, that had beene of
Alexanders part afore, who seeing that all the hoste murmured against Demetrius, went to Simalcue the Arabian,
that brought vp Antiochus ye yong sonne of Alexander,
40 And lay sore vpon him, to deliuer him [this young
Antiochus] that he might raigne in his fathers stead: he
told him therefore all that Demetrius had done, and how
his men of warre were at enmitie with him, and there he
remained a long season.
41 In the meane time Ionathan sent vnto king Demetrius,
that hee would cast those of the towre out of Ierusalem, and
those also in the fortresses. For they fought against Israel.
42 So Demetrius sent vnto Ionathan, saying, I will not
onely doe this for thee, and thy people, but I will greatly
honour thee and thy nation, if opportunitie serue.
43 Now therefore thou shalt do wel if thou send me men
to helpe me; for all my forces are gone from me.
44 Vpon this Ionathan sent him three thousand strong men
vnto Antioch, and when they came to ye king, the king was
very glad of their comming.
45 Howbeit, they that were of the citie, gathered themselues together into the midst of the citie, to the number of
an hundreth and twentie thousand men, and would haue
slaine the king.
46 Wherefore the king fled into the court, but they of the
citie kept the passages of the citie, and began to fight.

47 Then the king called to the Iewes for helpe, who came
vnto him all at once, and dispersing themselues through the
city, slew that day in the citie to the number of an hundred
thousand.
48 Also they set fire on the citie, and gat many spoiles that
day, and deliuered the king.
49 So when they of the city saw, that the Iewes had got
the city as they would, their courage was abated, wherefore
they made supplication to the king, and cried, saying:

|| *Or, bee friends with vs.*

50 ||Graunt vs peace, and let the Iewes cease from assaulting
vs and the citie.
51 With that they cast away their weapons, and made
peace, and the Iewes were honoured in the sight of the
king, and in the sight of all that were in his realme, and
they returned to Ierusalem hauing great spoiles.
52 So king Demetrius sate on the throne of his kingdome,
and the land was quiet before him.
53 Neuerthelesse hee dissembled in all that euer hee spake,
and estranged himselfe from Ionathan, neither rewarded he
him, according to the benefits which hee had receiued of him,
but troubled him very sore.
54 After this returned Tryphon, and with him the yong
childe Antiochus, who reigned and was crowned.
55 Then there gathered vnto him all the men of warre
whom Demetrius had put away, and they fought against
Demetrius, who turned his backe and fled.

† *Gr. beasts.*

56 Moreouer Triphon tooke the †Elephants, and wonne
Antioch.
57 At that time yong Antiochus wrote vnto Ionathan,
saying; I confirme thee in the high Priesthood, and appoint
thee ruler ouer the foure gouernments, and to be one of the
kings friends.
58 Vpon this he sent him golden vessels †to be serued in,
and gaue him leaue to drinke in gold, and to bee clothed in
purple, and to weare a golden buckle.
59 His brother Simon also he made captaine from the place
called the ladder of Tyrus, vnto the borders of Egypt.
60 Then Ionathan ||went foorth and passed through the
cities beyond the water, and all the forces of Syria,

† *Gr. and seruice.*
|| *Or, went beyond the riuer,* and passed through the cities: *Or, went and passed beyond the riuer, and through the cities, Gr.*

gathered themselues vnto him for to helpe him: and when
he came to Ascalon, they of the city met him honorably.
61 From whence he went to Gaza, but they of Gaza shut
him out; wherefore hee layd siege vnto it, and burned ||the
suburbs thereof with fire, and spoiled them.
62 Afterward when they of Gaza made supplication vnto
Ionathan, †he made peace with them, and tooke the sonnes
of the chiefe men for hostages, and sent them to Ierusalem,
and passed through the countrey vnto Damascus.
63 Now when Ionathan heard that Demetrius Princes
were come to Cades which is in Galilee, with a great
power, purposing to ||remoue him out of the countrey,
64 Hee went to meet them, and left Simon his brother in
the countrey.
65 Then Simon encamped against Bethsura, and fought
against it a long season, and shut it vp:
66 But they desired to haue peace with him, which he
granted them, and then put them out from thence, and
tooke the city, and set a garrison in it.
67 As for Ionathan and his hoste, they pitched at the
water of Gennesar, from whence betimes in the morning
they gate them to the plaine of Nasor.
68 And behold, the hoste of strangers met them in the
plaine, who hauing layed men in ambush for him in the
mountaines, came themselues ouer against him.
69 So when they that lay in ambush rose out of their places,
and ioyned battel, al that were of Ionathans side fled.
70 In so much as there was not one of them left, except
Mattathias the sonne of Absolon, and Iudas the sonne of
Calphi the captaines of the hoste.
71 Then Ionathan rent his clothes, and cast earth vpon his
head, and prayed.
72 Afterwards turning againe to battell, he put them to
flight, and so they ranne away.
73 Now when his owne men that were fled saw this, they
turned againe vnto him, and with him pursued them to Cades,
euen vnto their owne tents, and there they camped.
74 So there were slaine of the heathen that day, about three
thousand men, but Ionathan returned to Ierusalem.

CHAP.

|| *Or, the places thereabout.*

† *Gr. he gaue them the right hand.*

|| *Or, to remooue him from the affaires of the kingdome.*

CHAP. XII.

1 Ionathan reneweth his league with the Romanes and Lacedemonians.
28 The forces of Demetrius thinking to surprise Ionathan, flee away
for feare. 35 Ionathan fortifieth the castles in Iudea, 48 and is shut
vp by the fraud of Tryphon in Ptolemais.

NOwe when Ionathan saw that the time serued him, he
chose certaine men and sent them to Rome, for to
confirme and renew the friendship that they had with them.
2 He sent letters also to the Lacedemonians, and to other
places, for the same purpose.
3 So they went vnto Rome, and entred into the Senate,
and said, Ionathan the high Priest, and the people of the
Iewes sent vs vnto you, to the end you should renew the
friendship which you had with them, and league, as in
former time.
4 Vpon this the Romanes gaue them letters vnto the
gouernours of euery place, that they should bring them
into the land of Iudea peaceably.
5 And this is the copy of the letters which Ionathan wrote
to the Lacedemonians:
6 Ionathan the hie Priest, and the Elders of the nation, and
the Priestes and the other people of the Iewes, vnto the
Lacedemonians their brethren, send greeting.
7 There were letters sent in times past vnto Onias the
high Priest from ||Darius, who reigned then among you,
to signifie that you are our brethren, as the copy here
vnder-written doeth specifie.
8 At which time Onias intreated the Embassador that was
sent, honourably, and receiued the letters, wherein declara-
tion was made of the ||league and friendship.
9 Therefore we also, albeit we need none of these things,
for that wee haue the holy bookes of Scripture in our hands
to comfort vs,
10 Haue neuerthelesse attempted to send vnto you, for
the renewing of brotherhood and friendship, lest we should
become strangers vnto you altogether: for there is a long
time passed since you sent vnto vs.
11 We therefore at all times without ceasing, both in our
Feasts, and other

|| *Areus: looke Ioseph. Ant. lib.* 13. *cap.* 8.

|| *Or, kinred, Ios. Ant.*

conuenient dayes, doe remember you in the sacrifices which
we offer, and in our prayers, as reason is, and as it becommeth
vs to thinke vpon our brethren:
12 And wee are right glad of your honour.
13 As for our selues, wee haue had great troubles and warres
on euery side, forsomuch as the kings that are round about
vs haue fought against vs.
14 Howbeit wee would not be troublesome vnto you, nor
to others of our confederates & friends in these warres:
15 For wee haue helpe from heauen that succoureth vs, so
as we are deliuered from our enemies, and our enemies are
brought vnder foote.
16 For this cause we chose Numenius the son of Antiochus,
and Antipater the sonne of Iason, and sent them vnto the
Romanes, to renew the amitie that we had with them, and
the former league.
17 We commanded them also to goe vnto you, and to salute
you, and to deliuer you our letters, concerning the renewing
of our brotherhood.
18 Wherefore now ye shall doe well to giue vs an answere
thereto.
19 And this is the copy of the letters which ||Omiares sent: || *Read out of Ios.*
20 Areus king of the Lacedemonians, to Onias the hie
Priest, greeting.
21 It is found in writing, that the Lacedemonians and Iewes
are brethren, and that they are of the stocke of Abraham:
22 Now therefore, since this is come to our knowledge, you
shall doe well to write vnto vs of your †prosperitie. † *Gr. peace.*
23 We doe write backe againe to you, that your cattell and
goods are ours, and ours are yours. We doe command therefore [our Embassadours] to make report vnto you on this wise.
24 Now when Ionathan heard that Demetrius princes were
come to fight against him with a greater hoste then afore,
25 Hee remooued from Ierusalem, and met them in the
land of Amathis: for he gaue them no respite ||to enter || *Or, to set foote in his countrey: or, to inuade his countrey.*
his countrey.
26 He sent spies also vnto their tents, who came againe,
and tolde him, that they were appointed to come vpon them
in the night season.
27 Wherefore so soone as the Sunne was downe, Ionathan
commaunded his men to watch, and to be in armes,

which Areus sent to Onias.

that all the night long they might bee ready to fight: Also
he sent foorth sentinels round about the hoste.
28 But when the aduersaries heard that Ionathan and his
men were ready for battell, they feared, and trembled in
their hearts, and ||they kindled fires in their campe.
29 Howbeit Ionathan and his company knew it not till the
morning: for they saw the lights burning.
30 Then Ionathan pursued after them, but ouertooke them
not: for they were gone ouer the riuer Eleutherus.
31 Wherefore Ionathan turned to the Arabians, who were
called †Zabadeans, and smote them, and tooke their spoiles.
32 And remouing thence, he came to Damascus, and so
passed through all the countrey.
33 Simon also went foorth, and passed through the countrey
vnto Ascalon, and the holds there adioyning, from whence
he turned aside to Ioppe, and wanne it.
34 For he had heard that they would deliuer the hold vnto
them that tooke Demetrius part, wherefore he set a garison
there to keepe it.
35 After this came Ionathan home againe, and calling the
Elders of the people together, hee consulted with them about
building steong holdes in Iudea,
36 And making the walles of Ierusalem higher, and raising
a great mount betweene the towre and the city, for to separate it from the city, that so it might be alone, that men
might neither sell nor buy in it.
37 Vpon this they came together, to build vp the citie
||forasmuch as [part of] the wall toward the brooke on the
East side was fallen down, & they repaired that which was
called Caphenatha
38 Simon also set vp Adida, in Sephela, and made it strong
with gates and barres.
39 Now Tryphon went about to get the kingdome of Asia,
and to kill Antiochus the king, that hee might set the crowne
vpon his owne head.
40 Howbeit, he was afraid that Ionathan would not suffer
him, and that he would fight against him, wherefore he
sought a way, howe to take Ionathan, that he might kill
him. So he remoued, and came to Bethsan.

|| *Joseph. lib. ant. 13. 9. they went away.*

† *Ios. gr. Nabatheans, or Zabatheans.*

|| *Or, according to the Romane reading, and he came neere to the wall of the brooke toward the East.*

41 Then Ionathan went out to meet him with fourtie thousand men, chosen for the battell, and came to Bethsan.
42 Now when Tryphon saw that Ionathan came with so great a force, hee durst not stretch his hande against him,
43 But receiued him honourably, and cōmended him vnto all his friends, and gaue him gifts, and commaunded his men of warre to be as obedient vnto him, as to himselfe.
44 Vnto Ionathan also hee said, Why hast thou put all this people to so great trouble, seeing there is no warre betwixt vs?
45 Therefore send them now home againe, and chuse a few men to waite on thee, and come thou with me to Ptolemais, for I will giue it thee and the rest of the strong holds and forces, and all that haue any charge: as for me, I will returne and depart: for this is the cause of my comming.
46 So Ionathan beleeuing him, did as he bade him, and sent away his host, who went into the land of Iudea.
47 And with himselfe hee retained but three thousand men, of whome he †sent two thousand into Galile, and one thousand went with him.
48 Now assoone as Ionathan entred into Ptolemais, they of Ptolemais shut the gates, and tooke him, and all them that came with him, they slewe with the sword.
49 Then sent Tryphon an hoste of footmen, and horsemen into Galile, and into the great plaine, to destroy all Ionathans company.
50 But when they knew that Ionathan and they that were with him were taken and slaine, they encouraged one another, and went close together, prepared to fight.
51 They therfore that followed vpon them, perceiuing ỷ they were ready to fight for their liues, turned back againe.
52 Whereupon they all came into the land of Iudea peaceably, and there they bewailed Ionathan & them that were with him, & they were sore afraid, wherfore all Israel made great lamentation.
53 Then all the heathen that were round about them, sought to destroy them. For, said they, they haue no captaine, nor any to helpe them. Now therfore let vs make war vpon them, & take away their memorial frō amongst men.

† *Gr. left two thousand in Galile.*

CHAP.

CHAP. XIII.

8 Simon is made captaine in his brother Ionathans roume. 19 Tryphon getteth two of Ionathans sonnes into his hands, and slayeth their father. 27 The tombe of Ionathan. 36 Simon is fauoured by Demetrius, 46 and winneth Gaza, and the towre at Hierusalem.

NOw when Simon heard that Tryphon had gathered
together a great hoste to inuade the land of Iudea,
and destroy it,
2 And saw that the people was in great trembling and
feare, he went vp to Ierusalem, and gathered the people
together,
3 And gaue them exhortation, saying: Yee your selues
know, what great things I and my brethren, and my
fathers house haue done for the lawes, and the Sanctuarie,
the battels also, and troubles which we haue seene,
4 By reason whereof all my brethren are slaine for Israels
sake, and I am left alone.
5 Now therefore be it farre from me, that I should spare
mine owne life in any time of trouble: for I am no better
then my brethren.
6 Doubtlesse I will auenge my nation and the Sanctuarie,
& our wiues, and our children: for all the heathen are
gathered to destroy vs, of very malice.
7 Now as soone as the people heard these words, their
spirit reuiued.
8 And they answered with a loud voice, saying, Thou shalt
bee our leader in stead of Iudas and Ionathan thy brother.
9 Fight thou our battels, & what soeuer thou commandest
vs, that will we doe.
10 So then he gathered together all the men of warre, and
made hast to finish the walles of Ierusalem, and he fortified
it round about.
11 Also he sent Ionathan, the sonne of Absolom, & with
him a great power to Ioppe, who casting out them that were
therein, remained there in it.
12 So Tryphon remoued from Ptolemais, with a great
power to inuade the land of Iudea, and Ionathan was with
him in warde.
13 But Simon pitched his tents at Adida, ouer against the
plaine.
14 Now when Tryphon knew that Simon, was risen vp in
stead of his bro-

ther Ionathan, and meant to ioyne battell with him, he sent
messengers vnto him, saying,
15 Whereas we haue Ionathan thy brother in hold, it is for
money that he is owing vnto the kings treasure, ||concerning
the businesse that was committed vnto him.
16 Wherefore, now send an hundred talents of siluer, and
two of his sonnes for hostages, that when he is at liberty he
may not reuolt from vs, and we will let him goe.
17 Heereupon Simon, albeit he perceiued that they spake
deceiptfully vnto him, yet sent he the money, and the
children, lest peraduenture he should procure to himselfe
great hatred of the people:
18 Who might haue said, Because I sent him not the money,
and the children, therefore is [Ionathan] dead.
19 So he sent them the children, and the hundred talents:
Howbeit [Tryphon] dissembled, neither would he let Ionathan goe.
20 And after this came Tryphon to inuade the land, and
destroy it, going round about by the way that leadeth vnto
Adora, but Simon and his host marched against him in euery
place wheresoeuer he went.
21 Now they that were in the towre, sent messengers vnto
Tryphon, to the end that he should hasten his comming vnto
them by the wildernesse, and send them victuals.
22 Wherefore Tryphon made readie all his horsemen to
come that night, but there fell a very great snow, by reason
whereof he came not: So he departed & came into the
countrey of Galaad.
23 And when he came neere to Bascama, he slew Ionathan,
who was buried there.
24 Afterward Tryphon returned, and went into his owne
land.
25 Then sent Simon and tooke the bones of Ionathan his
brother, and buried them in Modin the citie of his fathers.
26 And all Israel made great lamentation for him, and
bewailed him many daies.
27 Simon also built a monument vpon the Sepulchre of his
father and his brethren, and raised it aloft to the sight, with
hewen stone behind and before.

28 Moreouer

|| *Or, for the affaires, or officers that he had, for the necessary vses which he had.*

28 Moreouer hee set vp seuen pyramides one against another, for his father and his mother, and his foure brethren.

29 And in these he made cunning deuices, about the which he set great pillars, and vpon the pillars he made all their armour for a perpetuall memory, and by the armour, ships carued, that they might be seene of all that saile on the sea.

30 This is the Sepulchre which he made at Modin, and it standeth yet vnto this day.

31 Now Tryphon dealt deceitfully with the yong king Antiochus, and slew him,

32 And he raigned in his stead, and crowned himselfe king of Asia, and brought a great calamitie vpō the land.

33 Then Simon built vp the strong holds in Iudea, and fensed them about with high towres, and great walles and gates and barres, and layd vp victuals †therein.

† Gr. in the strong holds.

34 Moreouer Simon chose men, and sent to king Demetrius, to the end he should giue the land an immunitie, because †all that Tryphon did, was to spoyle.

† Gr. All Tryphons doings were robberies.

35 Vnto whom king Demetrius answered and wrote after this maner.

36 King Demetrius vnto Simon the high Priest, and friend of kings, as also vnto the Elders and nation of the Iewes, sendeth greeting.

37 The golden crowne, and the scarlet robe which ye sent vnto vs, we haue receiued, and wee are ready to make a stedfast peace with you, yea and to write vnto our officers to confirme the immunities which we haue granted.

38 And whatsoeuer couenants we haue made with you, shall stand, and the strong holdes which yee haue builded shalbe your owne.

39 As for any ouersight or fault committed vnto this day, we forgiue it, and the crowne taxe also which yee owe vs, if there were any other tribute paide in Ierusalem, it shall no more be paide.

40 And looke who are meet among you to be in our court, let them be inrolled, and let there be peace betwixt vs.

41 Thus the yoke of the heathen was taken away from Israel, in the hundred and seuentieth yeere.

42 Then the people of Israel be-

gan to write in their instruments, and contracts, in the first
yeere of Simon the high Priest, the gouernour, and leader of
the Iewes.
43 In those dayes Simon camped against Gaza, and besieged
it round about; he made also an engine of warre, and set it
by the city, and battered a certaine towre, and tooke it.
44 And they that were in the Engine leapt into the citie,
whereupon there was a great vproare in the citie:
45 Insomuch as the people of the citie rent their clothes,
and climed vpon the walles, with their wiues and children,
and cried with a lowd voice, beseeching Simon †to grant
them peace.
46 And they said, Deale not with vs according to our
wickednesse, but according to thy mercy.
47 So Simon was appeased towards them, and fought no
more against them, but put them out of the citie, and
cleansed the houses wherein the idols were: and so entred
into it, with songs, and thankesgiuing.
48 Yea, he put all vncleannesse out of it, and placed such
men there, as would keepe the Law, and made it stronger
then it was before, and built therein a dwelling place for
himselfe.
49 They also of the towre in Ierusalem were kept so strait,
that they could neither come foorth, nor goe into the countrey,
nor buy, nor sell, wherefore they were in great distresse for
want of victuals, and a great number of them perished through
famine.
50 Then cried they to Simon, beseeching him ‖to bee at
one with them, which thing hee graunted them, and when
he had put them out from thence, he cleansed the towre
from pollutions:
51 And entred into it the three and twentieth day of the
second moneth, in the hundred seuentie and one yere, with
thankesgiuing, and branches of palme trees, and with harpes,
and cymbals, and with viols and hymnes, and songs: because
there was destroyed a great enemy out of Israel.
52 Hee ordained also that that day should be kept euery
yeere with gladnes. Moreouer, the hill of the Temple that
was by the towre he made stronger then it was, and there
hee dwelt himselfe with his company.
53 And when Simon sawe that Iohn his sonne was a valiant
man, he
made

† *Gr. to giue them his right hand.*

‖ *Or, to make peace with them.*

made him captaine of all the hostes and dwelt in Gazara.

CHAP. XIIII.

3 Demetrius is taken by the King of Persia. 4 The good deedes of Simon to his countrey. 18 The Lacedemonians and Romans renew their league with him. 26 A memoriall of his actes is set vp in Sion.

NOw in the hundred threescore and twelfth yeere, king
Demetrius gathered his forces together, and went into
Media, to get him helpe to fight against Tryphon.
2 But when Arsaces the king of Persia & Media, heard
that Demetrius was entred within his borders, he sent one of
his princes to take him aliue.
3 Who went and smote the hoste of Demetrius, and tooke
him and brought him to Arsaces, by whom hee was put in
warde.
4 As for the land of Iudea, that was quiet all the dayes of
Simon: for he sought the good of his nation, in such wise,
as that euermore his authoritie and honour pleased them well.
5 And as he was honourable (in all his acts) so in this, that
he tooke Ioppe for an hauen, and made an entrance to the
yles of the Sea,
6 And enlarged the boundes of his nation, and recouered
the countrey,
7 And gathered together a great number of captiues, and
had the dominion of Gazara and Bethsura, and the towre,
out of the which he tooke all vncleannesse, neither was there
any that resisted him.
8 Then did they till their ground in peace, and the earth
gaue her increase, and the trees of the field their fruit.
9 The ancient men sate all in the streetes, communing
together of ||good things, and the young men put on glorious
and warrelike apparell.

|| *Or, the wealth of the land.*

10 He prouided victuals for the cities, and set in them all
maner of munition, so that his honourable name was renowmed vnto the end of the world.
11 He made peace in the land, and Israel reioyced with
great ioy:
12 For *euery man sate vnder his vine, and his figgetree,
and there was none to fray them:

*1. Kings 4. 25.

13 Neither was there any left in the lande to fight against
them: yea, the Kings themselues were ouer-

throwen in those dayes.
14 Moreouer hee strengthened all those of his people that
were brought low: the Law he searched out, and euery
contemner of the Law, and wicked person, he tooke away.
15 He beautified the Sanctuary, and multiplied the vessels
of the Temple.
16 Now when it was heard at Rome, & as far as Sparta,
that Ionathan was dead, they were very sorie.
17 But assoone as they heard that his brother Simon was
made high Priest in his stead, and ruled the countrey, and
the cities therein,
18 They wrote vnto him in tables of brasse, to renew the
friendship & league which they had made with Iudas and
Ionathan his brethren:
19 Which writings were read before the Congregation at
Ierusalem.
20 And this is the copy of the letters that the Lacedemonians sent: The rulers of the Lacedemonians, with the
city, vnto Simon the high Priest, and the Elders and Priestes,
and residue of the people of the Iewes, our brethren, send
greeting.
21 The Embassadors that were sent vnto our people, certified vs of your glory and honour, wherefore we were glad
of their comming,
22 And did register the things that they spake, in the
counsell of the people, in this maner: Numenius sonne of
Antiochus, and Antipater sonne of Iason, the Iewes Embassadours, came vnto vs, to renew the friendship they had
with vs.
23 And it pleased the people to entertaine the men honourably, and to put the copy of their embassage in publike
records, to the end the people of the Lacedemonians might
haue a memoriall therof: furthermore we haue written a
copy thereof vnto Simon the hie Priest.
24 After this, Simon sent Numenius to Rome, with a great
shield of golde of a thousand pound weight, to confirme the
league with them.
25 Whereof when the people heard, they said, What
thankes shall wee giue to Simon and his sonnes?
26 For hee and his brethren, and the house of his father,
haue established Israel, and chased away in fight their
enemies from them, and confirmed their libertie.
27 So then they wrote [it] in tables
of

of brasse, which they set vpon pillars in mount Sion, and
this is the copie of the writing. The eighteenth day of the
moneth Elul, in the hundred threescore and twelft yeere,
being the third yeere of Simon the hie priest,

|| Or, Ierusalem, peraduenture by corruption and transposition of letters, or as some thinke, the common hall where they met to consult of matters of estate.

28 At ||Saramel in the great congregation of the priests and
people, and rulers of the nation, & elders of the country,
were these things notified vnto vs.
29 Forsomuch as often times there haue bin warres in the
countrey, wherin for the maintenance of their Sanctuarie,
and the law, Simon the sonne of Mattathias of the posteritie
of Iarib, together with his brethren, put themselues in
ieopardie, and resisting the enemies of their nation, did
their nation great honour.
30 (For after that Ionathan hauing gathered his nation
together, and bene their hie priest, was added to his people,
31 Their enemies purposed to inuade their countrey that
they might destroy it, and lay hands on the Sanctuary.

|| Or, the men of warre.

32 At which time Simon rose vp, and fought for his nation,
and spent much of his own substance, & armed ||the valiant
men of his nation, & gaue them wages,

|| Or, weapons.

33 And fortified the cities of Iudea, together with Bethsura
that lieth vpon the borders of Iudea, where the ||armour of
the enemies had bin before, but he set a garison of Iewes
there.

|| Or, Gaza.

34 Moreouer, hee fortified Ioppe which lieth vpon the Sea,
and ||Gazara that bordereth vpon Azotus, where the enemies
had dwelt before: but hee placed Iewes there, and furnished
them with all things conuenient for the reparation thereof.)
35 The people therefore seeing the acts of Simon, and vnto
what glory he thought to bring his nation, made him their
gouernor and chiefe priest, because he had done all these
things, and for the iustice and faith which hee kept to his
nation, and for that hee sought by all meanes to exalt his
people.
36 For in his time things prospered in his hands, so that
the heathen were taken out of their countrey, and they also
that were in the citie of Dauid in Ierusalem, who had made
themselues a towre, out of which they issued, and polluted

|| Or, vnto religion.

all about the Sanctuarie, and did much hurt ||in the holy
place.
37 But he placed Iewes therein, and fortified it for the
safetie of the coun-

trey, and the city, and raised vp the wals of Ierusalem.
38 King Demetrius also confirmed him in the high priesthood, according to those things,
39 And made him one of his friends, and honoured him
with great honour.
40 For he had heard say, that the Romanes had called the
Iewes their friends, and confederates, and brethren, and that
they had entertained the Embassadours of Simon honourably.
41 Also that the Iewes & priests were wel pleased that
Simon should be their gouernour, and high priest for euer
vntil there should arise a faithfull prophet.
42 Moreouer, that he should be their captaine, and should
take charge of the Sanctuarie, to set them ouer their workes,
and ouer the countrey, and ouer the armour, and ouer the
fortresses, that (I say) he should take charge of the Sanctuarie.
43 Besides this, that he should be obeyed of euery man,
and that all the writings in the countrey should be made
in his name, and that he should be clothed in purple, and
weare gold.
44 Also that it should be lawfull for none of the people
or priests, to breake any of these things, or to gainesay his
words, or to gather an assembly in the countrey without him,
or to bee clothed in purple, or weare a buckle of gold.
45 And whosoeuer should do otherwise, or breake any of
these things, he should be punished.
46 Thus it liked all ẏͤ people to deale with Simon, & to do
as hath bene said.
47 Then Simon accepted hereof, and was well pleased to
be high Priest, and captaine, and gouernour of the Iewes, &
priests, & to defend them all.
48 So they commanded that this writing should be put in
tables of brasse, and that they should be set vp within the
compasse of the Sanctuary in a conspicuous place.
49 Also ẏͭ the copies therof should be laid vp in the treasurie,
to the ende that Simon & his sonnes might haue them.

CHAP. XV.

4 Antiochus desireth leaue to passe through Iudea, & granteth great honours to Simon and the Iewes. 16 The Romanes write to diuerse kings & nations to fauour the Iewes. 27 Antiochus quarrelleth with Simon, 38 and sendeth some to annoy Iudea.

More-

MOreouer Antiochus sonne of Demetrius the king, sent
letters from the isles of the Sea, vnto Simon the
priest, and prince of the Iewes, and to all the people.
2 The contents whereof were these: King Antiochus, to
Simon the high Priest, and prince of his nation, and to the
people of the Iewes, greeting,
3 For as much as certaine pestilent men, haue vsurped the
kingdome of our fathers, and my purpose is to chalenge it
againe, that I may restore it to the old estate, and to that
end haue gathered a multitude of forraine souldiers together,
and prepared shippes of warre,
4 My meaning also being to goe through the countrey, that
I may be auenged of them that haue destroyed it, and made
many cities in the kingdome desolate:
5 Now therefore I confirme vnto thee, all the oblations
which the kings before me granted thee, and whatsoeuer
gifts besides they granted.
6 I giue thee leaue also to coine money for thy countrey
with thine owne stampe.
7 And as concerning Ierusalem, and the Sanctuarie, let
them be free, and al the armour that thou hast made, and
fortresses that thou hast built, and keepest in thy hands, let
them remaine vnto thee.
8 And if any thing bee, or shall be owing to the king, let
it be forgiuen thee, from this time forth for euermore.
9 Furthermore, when we haue obtained our kingdome, we
will honour thee, and thy nation, and thy temple with great
honour, so that your honour shall bee knowen throughout
the world.
10 In the hundred threescore and fourteenth yeere, went
Antiochus into the land of his fathers, at which time all the
forces came together vnto him, so that few were left with
Tryphon.
11 Wherefore being pursued by king Antiochus, he fled
vnto Dora, which lieth by the Sea side.
12 For he saw, that troubles came vpon him all at once,
and that his forces had forsaken him.
13 Then camped Antiochus against Dora, hauing with him,
an hundred and twentie thousand men of warre,

and eight thousand horsemen.
14 And when he had compassed the citie round about, and
ioyned ships close to the towne on the Sea side, hee vexed
the citie by land, and by Sea, neither suffered he any to goe
out or in.
15 In the meane season came Numenius, & his company
from Rome hauing letters to the kings and countries, wherein
were written these things.
16 Lucius, Consul of the Romanes, vnto king Ptolomee
greeting.
17 The Iewes Embassadors our friends and confederates,
came vnto vs to renew the old friendship and league, being
sent from Simon the high Priest, and from the people of the
Iewes.
18 And they brought a shield of gold, of a thousand pound:
19 We thought it good therefore, to write vnto the kings
and countries, that they should doe them no harme, nor fight
against them, their cities, or countries, nor yet aide their
enemies against them.
20 It seemed also good to vs, to receiue the shield of them.
21 If therefore there be any pestilent fellowes, that haue
fled from their countrie vnto you, deliuer them vnto Simon
the high priest, that hee may punish them according to their
owne lawe.
22 The same thing wrote hee likewise vnto Demetrius the
king, and Attalus, to ||Ariarathes, and Arsaces, *|| Or, Arathes.*
23 And to all the countries, and to ||Sampsames, & the *|| Or, Sampsaces.*
Lacedemonians, and to Delus, and Myndus, and Sycion, and
Caria, and Samos, and Pamphylia, and Lycia, and Halicar-
nassus, and Rhodus, and ||Phaseilis, and Cos, and Sidee, and *|| Or, Basilis.*
Aradus, and Gortina, and Cnidus, and Cyprus, and Cyrene.
24 And the copy heereof they wrote, to Simon the high Priest.
25 So Antiochus the king camped against Dora, the second
day, †assaulting it continually, and making engins, by which *† Gre. bringing his forces to it.*
meanes he shut vp Tryphon, that he could neither goe out
nor in.
26 At that time Simon sent him two thousand chosen men
to aide him: siluer also, and gold, and much armour.
27 Neuerthelesse, he would not receiue them, but brake
all the couenants which he had made with him afore, and
became strange vnto him.

28 Further-

28 Furthermore hee sent vnto him Athenobius, one of his
friends to commune with him and say: you withhold Ioppe
and Gazara with the towre that is in Ierusalem, which are
cities of my realme.
29 The borders thereof yee haue wasted and done great
hurt in the land, and got the dominion of many places within
my kingdome.
30 Now therefore deliuer the cities which ye haue taken,
and the tributes of the places whereof yee haue gotten
dominion ||without the borders of Iudea.
31 Or else giue me for them fiue hundred talents of siluer,
and for the harme that you haue done, and the tributes of
the cities other fiue hundred talents: if not, we wil come
and ||fight against you.
32 So Athenobius the kings friend came to Ierusalem, and
when hee saw the glory of Simon, and the cupboard of gold,
and siluer plate, and his great attendance, he was astonished
and told him the kings message.
33 Then answered Simon, and said vnto him, We haue
neither taken other mens land, nor holden that which ap-
perteineth to others, but the inheritance of our fathers, which
our enemies had wrongfully in possession a certaine time.
34 Wherefore we hauing opportunitie, hold the inheritance
of our fathers.
35 And whereas thou demaundest Ioppe and Gazara; albeit
they did great harme vnto the people in our countrey, yet
will we giue an hundred talents for them. Hereunto Athenobius answered him not a word,
36 But returned in a rage to the king, and made report
vnto him of these speaches, and of the glory of Simon, and
of all that hee had seene: whereupon the king was exceeding
wroth.
37 In the meane time fled Tryphon by ship vnto Orthosias.
38 Then the king made Cendebeus captaine of the sea
coast, and gaue him an hoste of footmen and horsemen,
39 And commanded him to remoue his hoste toward Iudea:
also hee commanded him to build vp Cedron, and to fortifie
the gates, & to warre against the people, but as for the king
[himselfe] he pursued Tryphon.
40 So Cendebeus came to Iamnia, and began to prouoke
the people,

|| *Or, except the borders, &c.*

|| *Or, subdue you in fight.*

and to inuade Iudea, and to take the people prisoners, and slay them.

41 And when hee had built vp Cedron, he set horsemen there, and an host [of footmen] to the end that issuing out, they might make outroades vpon the wayes of Iudea, as the king had commanded him.

CHAP. XVI.

3 Iudas and Iohn preuaile against the forces sent by Antiochus. 11 The captaine of Hierico inuiteth Simon and two of his sonnes into his castle, and there treacherously murdereth them. 19 Iohn is sought for, 22 and escapeth, and killeth those that sought for him.

THen came vp Iohn from Gazara, and told Simon his father, what Cendebeus had done.

2 Wherefore Simon called his two eldest sonnes, Iudas and Iohn, and said vnto them, I and my brethren, and my fathers house haue euer from our youth vnto this day fought against the enemies of Israel, and things haue prospered so well in our hands, that wee haue deliuered Israel oftentimes.

3 But now I am old, and yee [by Gods mercy] are of a sufficient age: Be ye in stead of mee, and my brother, and goe and fight for our nation, and the helpe from heauen be with you.

4 So hee chose out of the countrey twentie thousand men of warre with horsemen, who went out against Cendebeus, and rested that night at Modin.

5 And when as they rose in the morning, and went into the plaine, behold, a mighty great hoste both of footmen, and horsmen, came against them: Howbeit there was a water brooke betwixt them.

6 So hee and his people pitched ouer against them, and when hee saw that the people were afraid to goe ouer the water brooke, hee went first ouer himselfe, and then the men seeing him, passed through after him.

7 [That done] he diuided his men, and set the horsemen in the midst of the footemen: for the enemies horsemen were very many.

8 Then sounded they with the holy Trumpets: whereupon Cendebeus and his hoste were put to flight, so that many of them were slaine, and the remnant gat them to the strong hold.

9 At

9 At that time was Iudas Iohns brother wounded: But Iohn still followed after them, vntill he came to Cedron which [Cendebeus] had built.

10 ‖So they fled euen vnto the towres in the fields of Azotus, wherefore hee burnt it with fire: So that there were slaine of them about two thousand men. Afterward hee returned into the land of Iudea in peace.

‖Or, which when he had set fire, they fled vnto the towres in the fields of Azotus, and there were slaine, &c.

11 Moreouer, in the plaine of Iericho was Ptolomeus the sonne of Abubus made captaine, and hee had abundance of siluer and golde.

12 For he was the hie Priests sonne in lawe.

13 Wherefore his heart being lifted vp, hee thought to get the countrey to himselfe, and thereupon consulted deceitfully against Simon and his sons, to destroy them.

14 Now Simon was visiting the cities that were in the countrey, and taking care for the good ordering of them, at which time hee came downe himselfe to Iericho with his sons, Mattathias and Iudas, in the hundreth threescore and seuenth yeere, in the eleuenth moneth called Sabat.

15 Where the sonne of Abubus receiuing them deceitfully into a little holde called Docus, which he had built, made them a great banquet: howbeit he had hidde men there.

16 So when Simon and his sonnes

¶ The second booke

CHAP. I.

1 A letter of the Iewes from Ierusalem to them of Egypt, to thanke God for the death of Antiochus. 19 Of the fire that was hidde in the pit. 24 The prayer of Nehemias.

THe brethren the Iewes that bee at Ierusalem, and in the lande of Iudea, wish vnto the brethren the Iewes that are throughout Egypt, health and peace.

2 God be gracious vnto you, and remember his Couenant that hee made with Abraham, Isaac, and Iacob, his faithfull seruants:

3 And giue you all an heart to serue him, and to doe his will, with a good courage, and a willing minde:

had drunke largely, Ptolome and his men rose vp, and tooke
their weapons, and came vpon Simon into the banketting
place, and slewe him and his two sonnes, and certaine of his
seruants.
17 In which doing, he committed a great treachery, and
recompensed euill for good.
18 Then Ptolome wrote these things, and sent to the king,
that he should send him an hoste to aide him, and he would
deliuer him the countrey and cities.
19 He sent others also to Gazara to kill Iohn, & vnto the
†tribunes he sent letters to come vnto him, that he might
giue them siluer, and golde, & rewards.
20 And others he sent to take Ierusalem, and the mountaine
of the temple.
21 Now one had runne afore to Gazara, and tolde Iohn
that his father and brethren were slaine, and [quoth he]
Ptolome hath sent to slay thee also.
22 Hereof when he heard, hee was sore astonished: So he
laide hands on them that were come to destroy him, and
slew them, for hee knew that they sought to make him away.
23 As concerning the rest of the actes of Iohn, and his
wars & worthy deeds which hee did, and the building of the
walles which he made, and his doings,
24 Behold, these are written in the Chronicles of his Priesthood, from the time he was made high Priest after his father.

† *Gr. captaines of thousands.*

of the Maccabees.

4 And open your hearts in his law and commandements, &
send you peace:
5 And heare your prayers, and be at one with you, and
neuer forsake you in time of trouble.
6 And now wee be here praying for you.
7 What time as Demetrius reigned, in the hundred threescore and ninth yeere, wee the Iewes wrote vnto you, in the
extremitie of trouble, that came vpon vs in those yeeres,
from the time that Iason and his company reuolted from the
holy land, and kingdome,
8 And burnt the porch, and shed innocent blood. Then
we prayed vnto the Lord, and were heard: we offered also
sacrifices, and fine flowre, and lighted the lampes, and set
forth the loaues.
9 And now see that ye keepe the feast

* Leuit. 23. 34. of * Tabernacles in the moneth Casleu.
10 In the hundreth, fourescore, and eight yeere, the people
that were at Ierusalem, and in Iudea, and the counsel, and
Iudas, sent greeting and health vnto Aristobulus, king Ptolomeus master, who was of the stock of the anointed priests,
and to the Iewes that were in Egypt.
11 Insomuch as God hath deliuered vs from great perils,
wee thanke him highly, as hauing bin in battell against a
king.
12 For he cast them out that fought within the holy citie.
13 For when the leader was come into Persia, and the
armie with him that seemed inuincible, they were slaine in
the temple of Nanea, by the deceit of Naneas priests.
14 For Antiochus, as though hee would marrie her, came
into the place, and his friends that were with him, to receiue
money in name of a dowrie.
15 Which when the priests of Nanea had set forth, and
he was entred with a small company into the compasse of
the temple, they shut the temple assoone as Antiochus was
come in.
16 And opening a priuie doore of the roofe, they threw
stones like thunderbolts, and stroke downe the captaine,
hewed them in pieces, smote off their heads, and cast them
to those that were without.
17 Blessed be our God in all things, who hath deliuered vp
the vngodly.
18 Therefore whereas we are nowe purposed to keep the
purification of the Temple vpon the fiue & twentieth day of
* Leuit. 23. the moneth * Casleu, we thought it necessary to certifie you
numb. 29. thereof, that ye also might keepe it, as the [feast] of the
tabernacles, and of the fire [which was giuen vs] when
Neemias offered sacrifice, after that he had builded the
Temple, and the Altar.
19 For when our fathers were led into Persia, the Priests
that were then deuout, took the fire of the Altar priuily, &
hid it in a hollow place of a pit without water, where they
kept it sure, so that the place was vnknowen to all men.
20 Now after many yeeres, when it pleased God, Neemias
being sent from the king of Persia, did send of the posteritie
of those Priests that had hid it, to the fire: but when they
tolde vs they found no fire, but thicke water,

21 Then cōmanded he them to draw it vp, and to bring it:
and when the sacrifices were laid on, Neemias cōmanded the
Priests to sprinkle ẏ wood, and the things laid therupon with
ẏ water.
22 When this was done, and the time came that the Sun
shone which afore was hid in the cloude, there was a great
fire kindled, so that euery man marueiled.
23 And the Priests made a prayer whilest the sacrifice was
consuming, [I say] both the Priests, and all the rest, Ionathan
beginning, and the rest answering thereunto, as Neemias did.
24 And the prayer was after this maner, O Lord, Lord
God, Creatour of all things, who art fearefull, and strong,
and righteous, and mercifull, and the onely, and gracious king,
25 The onely giuer of all things, the onely iust, almightie
& euerlasting, thou that deliuerest Israel from al trouble, &
didst choose the fathers, & sanctifie them:
26 Receiue the sacrifice for thy whole people Israel, and
preserue thine owne portion, and sanctifie it.
27 Gather those together that are scattered frō vs, deliuer
them that serue among the heathen, looke vpon them that
are despised & abhorred, and let the heathen know that thou
art our God.
28 Punish them that oppresse vs, and with pride doe vs wrong.
29 Plant thy people againe in thy holy place, as Moises
hath spoken.
30 And the Priests sung psalmes of thankesgiuing.
31 Now when the sacrifice was consumed, Neemias commanded the water that was left, to bee powred on the great
stones.
32 When this was done, there was kindled a flame: but it
was consumed by the light that shined from the Altar.
33 So when this matter was knowen, it was told the king
of Persia, that in the place, where the Priests that were led
away, had hid the fire, there appeared water, and that
||Neemias had purified the sacrifices therewith. || *Or, Neemias his company.*
34 Then the king inclosing the place, made it holy after he
had tried ẏ matter.
35 And the king tooke many gifts, and bestowed thereof,
on those whom he would gratifie.
36 And Neemias called this thing Naphthar, which is as
much to say as a cleansing: but many men call it Nephi.

CHAP.

CHAP. II.

1 What Ieremie the Prophet did. 5 How he hid the Tabernacle, the Arke, and the Altar. 13 What Neemias, and Iudas wrote. 20 What Iason wrote in fiue bookes, 25 And how those were abridged by the author of this booke.

IT is also found in the records, that Ieremie the Prophet, commaunded them that were caried away, to take of the fire as it hath beene signified,
2 And how that the Prophet hauing giuen them the law, charged them not to forget the commaundements of the Lord, and that they should not erre in their minds, when they see images of siluer, and gold, with their ornaments.
3 And with other such speeches exhorted he them, that the law should not depart from their hearts.
4 It was also contained in the same writing, that the Prophet being warned of God, commanded the Tabernacle, and the Arke to goe with him, as he went forth into the mountaine, where Moises climed vp, and sawe the heritage of God.
5 And when Ieremie came thither, he found an hollow caue wherin he laid the Tabernacle, and the Arke, and the altar of incense, & so stopped the doore.
6 And some of those that followed him, came to marke the way, but they could not find it.
7 Which when Ieremie perceiued, hee blamed them, saying, As for that place, it shall be vnknowen vntill the time that God gather his people againe together, and receiue them vnto mercy.
8 Then shall the Lord shew them these things, and the glory of the Lord shall appeare, and the cloud also as it was shewed vnder Moises, and as when Solomon desired that the place might be honourably sanctified.
9 It was also declared that he being wise, offered the sacrifice of dedication, and of the finishing of the Temple.
10 And as when Moises prayed vnto the Lord, the fire came down from heauen, and consumed the sacrifices: euen so prayed Solomon also, and the fire came downe from heauen, and consumed the burnt offerings.
11 And Moises said, because the sinne

offering was not to be eaten, it was consumed.
12 So Solomon kept those eight dayes.
13 The same things also were reported in the writings, and
commentaries of Neemias, and how he founding a librarie,
gathered together the acts of the Kings, and the Prophets,
and of Dauid, and the Epistles of the Kings concerning the
holy gifts.
14 In like maner also, Iudas gathered together all those
things that were lost, by reason of the warre we had, and
they remaine with vs.
15 Wherefore if yee haue neede thereof, send some to fetch
them vnto you.
16 Whereas we then are about to celebrate the purification,
we haue written vnto you, and yee shall doe well if yee
keepe the same dayes.
17 †We hope also that the God, that deliuered all his
people, and gaue them all an heritage, and the kingdome,
and the priesthood, and the Sanctuarie,
18 As he promised in the lawe, will shortly haue mercy
vpon vs, and gather vs together out of euery land vnder
heauen into the holy place: for he hath deliuered vs out of
great troubles, and hath purified the place.
19 Now as concerning Iudas Maccabeus, and his brethren,
and the purification of the great Temple, and the dedication
of the altar,
20 And the warres against Antiochus Epiphanes, & Eupator
his sonne,
21 And the manifest signes that came from heauen, vnto
those that behaued themselues manfully to their honour for
Iudaisme: so that being but a few, they ouercame the whole
country, and chased barbarous multitudes,

† Gre. now God it is that saued all his people, and rendred the heritage, and the kingdome, and the priesthood, and the Sanctuarie, as he promised in the lawe. For we hope in God that he will shortly, &c.

22 And recouered againe the Temple renowned all the
world ouer, and freed the citie, and vpheld the lawes, which
were going downe, the Lord being gracious vnto them with
al fauour:
23 All these things (I say) being declared by Iason of Cyrene
in fiue books, we will assay to abridge in one volume.
24 For considering the infinite number, and the difficulty,
which they find that desire to looke into the narrations of
the story, for the variety of ẏͤ matter,
25 We haue beene carefull, that they that will read might
haue delight, and that they that are desirous to commit to
memorie, might haue ease, and that

all, into whose hands it comes might haue profit.
26 Therefore to vs that haue taken vpon vs this paineful
labour of abridging, it was not easie, but a matter of sweat,
and watching.
|| *Or, to deserue well of many.*
27 Euen as it is no ease vnto him, that prepareth a banquet,
and seeketh the benefit of others: yet ||for the pleasuring of
many we will vndertake gladly this great paines:
28 Leauing to the authour the exact handling of euery particular, and labouring to follow the rules of an abridgement.
29 For as the master builder of a new house, must care for
the whole building: but hee that vndertaketh to set it out,
and paint it, must seeke out fit things for the adorning
thereof: euen so I thinke it is with vs.
30 To stand vpon euery point, and goe ouer things at large,
and to be curious in particulars, belongeth to the first authour
of the storie.
31 But to vse breuitie, and auoyde much labouring of the
worke, is to bee granted to him that will make an abridgement.
32 Here then will we begin the story: onely adding thus
much to that which hath bene said, That it is a foolish
thing to make a long prologue, and to be short in the story
it selfe.

CHAP. III.

1 Of the honour done to the Temple by the Kings of the Gentiles. 4 Simon vttereth what treasures are in the Temple. 7 Heliodorus is sent to take them away. 24 He is stricken of God, and healed at the praier of Onias.

NOw when the holy Citie was inhabited with all peace,
and the Lawes were kept very well, because of the godlinesse of Onias the high Priest, and his hatred of wickednesse,
2 It came to passe that euen the Kings themselues did
honour the place, and magnifie the Temple with their best
gifts;
3 Insomuch that Seleucus king of Asia, of his owne reuenues,
bare all the costes belonging to the seruice of the sacrifices.
4 But one Simon of the tribe of Beniamin, who was made
gouernour of the Temple, fell out with the high

Priest about disorder in the citie.
5 And when he could not ouercome Onias, he gate him to
Apollonius the sonne of Thraseas, who then was gouernour
of Coelosyria, and Phenice,
6 And told him that the treasurie in Ierusalem was full of
infinite summes of money, so that the multitude of their
riches which did not pertaine to the account of the sacrifices,
was innumerable, and that it was possible to bring all into
the kings hand.
7 Now when Apollonius came to the king, and had shewed
him of the money, whereof he was told, the king chose out
Heliodorus his treasurer, and sent him with a commaundement, to bring him the foresaid money.
8 So foorthwith Heliodorus tooke his iourney vnder a colour
of visiting the cities of Coelosyria, and Phenice, but indeed
to fulfill the kings purpose.
9 And when he was come to Ierusalem, & had bene cour-
teously receiued of the high Priest of the citie, hee told him
what intelligence was giuen of the money, & declared wherefore hee came, and and asked if these things were so in deed.
10 Then the high Priest tolde him that there was such
money layde vp for the reliefe of widowes, and fatherlesse
children,
11 And that some of it belonged to Hircanus, sonne of
Tobias, a man of great dignitie, and not as that wicked
Simon had misinformed: the summe whereof in all was
foure hundred talents of siluer, and two hundred of gold,
12 And that it was altogether impossible that such wrong
should be done vnto them, that had committed it to the
holinesse of the place, and to the maiestie and inuiolable
sanctitie of the Temple, honoured ouer all the world.
13 But Heliodorus because of the kings commandement
giuen him, said, That in any wise it must be brought into
the kings treasury.
14 So at the day which hee appointed, hee entred in to
order this matter, wherefore, there was no small agonie
throughout the whole citie.
15 But the Priests prostrating themselues before the Altar
in their Priests Vestments, called vnto heauen vpon him
that made a Lawe concerning things giuen to bee kept, that
they should safely bee preserued for such as had committed
them to be kept.

16 Then

16 Then whoso had looked the hie Priest in the face, it
would haue wounded his heart: for his countenance, and
the changing of his colour, declared the inward agonie of his
minde:
17 For the man was so compassed with feare, and horror of
the body, that it was manifest to them that looked vpon him,
what sorrow hee had now in his heart.
18 Others ran flocking out of their houses ‖to the generall
Supplication, because the place was like to come into contempt.
19 And the women girt with sackecloth vnder their breasts,
abounded in the streetes; and the virgins that were kept
in, ran some to the gates, and some to the walles, and others
looked out of the windowes:
20 And all holding their handes towards heauen, made
supplication.
21 Then it would haue pitied a man to see the falling
downe of the multitude of all sorts, and the †feare of the
hie Priest, being in such an agony.
22 They then called vpon the Almightie Lord, to keepe
the things committed of trust, safe and sure, for those that
had committed them.
23 Neuerthelesse Heliodorus executed that which was
decreed.
24 Now as hee was there present himselfe with his guard
about the treasurie, the ‖Lord of spirits, & the Prince of all
power caused a great apparition, so that all that presumed to
come in with him, were astonished at the power of God, and
fainted, and were sore afraid.
25 For there appeared vnto them a horse, with a terrible
rider vpon him, and adorned with a very faire couering, and
he ranne fiercely, and smote at Heliodorus with his forefeet,
and it seemed that hee that sate vpon the horse, had complete
harnesse of golde.
26 Moreouer two other yong men appeared before him,
notable in strength, excellent in beautie, and comely in
apparell, who stood by him on either side, and scourged him
continually, and gaue him many sore stripes.
27 And Heliodorus fell suddenly vnto the ground, and was
compassed with great darkenesse: but they that were with
him, tooke him vp, and put him into a litter.
28 Thus him that lately came with

‖ Or, to make generall supplication.

† Gr. expectation.

‖ Or, Lord of our fathers.

a great traine, and with all his guard into the said treasury,
they caried out, being vnable to helpe himselfe with his
weapons: and manifestly they acknowledged the power of
God.
29 For hee by the hand of God was cast downe, and lay
speechlesse without all hope of life.
30 But they praised the Lord that had miraculously honoured
his owne place: for the Temple which a little afore was full
of feare and trouble, when the Almightie Lord appeared, was
filled with ioy and gladnesse.
31 Then straightwayes certaine of Heliodorus friends,
prayed Onias that hee would call vpon the most High to
graunt him his life, who lay ready to giue vp the ghost.
32 So the high Priest suspecting lest the king should mis-
conceiue that some treachery had beene done to Heliodorus
by the Iewes, offered a sacrifice for the health of the man.
33 Now as the high Priest was making an atonement, the
same yong men, in the same clothing, appeared and stood
beside Heliodorus, saying, Giue Onias the high Priest great
thankes, insomuch as for his sake the Lord hath granted thee
life.
34 And seeing that thou hast beene scourged from heauen,
declare vnto all men the mightie power of God: and when
they had spoken these wordes, they appeared no more.
35 So Heliodorus after he had offered sacrifice vnto the
Lord, and made great vowes vnto him that had saued his
life, and saluted Onias, returned with his hoste to the king.
36 Then testified hee to all men, the workes of the great
God, which he had seene with his eyes.
37 And when the king asked Heliodorus, who might be a
fit man to be sent yet once againe to Ierusalem, he said,
38 If thou hast any enemy or traitor, send him thither, and
thou shalt receiue him well scourged, if he escape with his
life: for in that place, no doubt, there is an especiall power
of God.
39 For hee that dwelleth in heauen hath his eye on that
place, and defendeth it, and hee beateth and destroyeth them
that come to hurt it.
40 And the things concerning Heliodorus, and the keeping
of the treasurie, fell out on this sort.

CHAP. IIII.

1 Simon slandereth Onias. 7 Iason by corrupting the king, obteineth the office of the hie Priest. 24 Menelaus getteth the same from Iason by the like corruption. 34 Andronicus traiterously murdereth Onias. 36 The King being informed thereof, causeth Andronicus to be put to death. 39 The wickednes of Lysimachus, by the instigation of Menelaus.

THis Simon now (of whō wee spake afore) hauing bin a
bewrayer of the money, and of his countrey, slandered
Onias, as if he had terrified Heliodorus, and bene the worker
of these euils.
2 Thus was hee bold to call him a traitour, that had
deserued well of the citie, and tendred his owne nation, and
was so zealous of the lawes.
3 But when their hatred went so farre, that by one of
Simons faction murthers were committed,
4 Onias seeing the danger of this contention, and that
Appollonius, as being the gouernour of Coelosyria and
Phenice, did rage, and increase Simons malice,
5 He went to the king, not to be an accuser of his countrey
men, but seeking the good of all, both publike, & priuate.
6 For he saw that it was impossible, that the state should
continue quiet, and Simon leaue his folly, vnlesse the king
did looke thereunto.
7 But after the death of Seleucus, when Antiochus called
Epiphanes, tooke the kingdom, Iason the brother of Onias,
laboured vnder hand to bee hie Priest,
8 Promising vnto the king by intercession, three hundred
and threescore talents of siluer, and of another reuenew,
eightie talents:
9 Besides this, he promised to assigne an hundred and fiftie
more, if he might haue licence to set him vp a place for
exercise, and for the training vp of youth in the fashions of
the heathen, and to write them of Ierusalem [by the name
of] Antiochians.
10 Which when the king had granted, and hee had gotten
into his hand the rule, he foorthwith brought his owne nation
to the Greekish fashion.
11 And the royal priuiledges granted of speciall fauour to
the Iewes, by the meanes of Iohn the father of Eupole-

mus, who went Embassador to Rome, for amitie and aid, he
tooke away, and putting down the gouernments which were
according to the law, he brought vp new customes against
the law.
12 For he built gladly a place of exercise vnder the towre
it selfe, and brought the chiefe yong men vnder his subiection,
and made them weare a hat.
13 Now such was the height of Greek fashions, and increase
of heathenish maners, through the exceeding profanenes of
Iason that vngodly wretch, and no high priest:
14 That the priests had no courage to serue any more at
the altar, but despising the Temple, and neglecting the
sacrifices, hastened to be partakers of the vnlawfull allowance
in the place of exercise, after the game of ||Discus called
them forth.
15 Not setting by the honours of their fathers, but liking
the glory of the Grecians best of all.
16 By reason whereof sore calamity came vpon them: for
they had them to be their enemies and auengers, whose
custome they followed so earnestly, and vnto whom they
desired to be like in all things.
17 For it is not a light thing to doe wickedly against the
lawes of God, but the time following shall declare these
things.
18 Now when the game that was vsed euery fift yere was
kept at Tyrus, the king being present,
19 This vngracious Iason sent †speciall messengers from
Ierusalem, who were Antiochians, to carie three hundred
drachmes of siluer to the sacrifice of Hercules, which euen
the bearers therof thought fit not to bestow vpon the
sacrifice, because it was not conuenient, but to be reserued
for other charges.
20 This money then in regard of the sender, was appointed
to Hercules sacrifice, but because of the bearers thereof, it
was imployed to the making of gallies.
21 Now when Apollonius the sonne of Manastheus was
sent vnto Egypt, for the ||*coronation* of king Ptolomeus
Philometor, Antiochus vnderstanding him not to bee well
affected to his affaires, prouided for his owne safetie: whereupon he came to Ioppe, & from thence to Ierusalem.
22 Where he was honourably recei-
ued

|| *Or, the Discus which was a stone with an hole in the midst.*

† *Gr. who were religious embassadours.*

|| *Or, inthronizing.*

ued of Iason, and of the citie, and was brought in with torch-
light, and with great shoutings: and so afterward went with
his hoste vnto Phenice.
23 Three yeere afterward, Iason sent Menelaus the foresaid
Simons brother, to beare the money vnto the king, and to
put him in minde of certaine necessary matters.
24 But he being brought to the presence of the king, when
he had magnified him, for the glorious appearance of his
power, got the priesthood to himselfe, offering more then
Iason by three hundred talents of siluer.
25 So he came with the kings Mandate, bringing nothing
worthy the high priesthood, but hauing the fury of a cruell
Tyrant, and the rage of a sauage beast.
26 Then Iason, who had vndermined his owne brother,
being vndermined by another, was cōpelled to flee into the
countrey of the Ammonites.
27 So Menelaus got the principalitie: but as for the money
that he had promised vnto the king, hee tooke no good order
for it, albeit Sostratus the ruler of the castle required it.
28 For vnto him appertained the gathering of the customes.
Wherefore they were both called before the king.
29 Now Menelaus left his brother Lysimachus in his stead
in the priesthood, and Sostratus left Crates, who was gouernour
of the Cyprians.
30 While those things were in doing, they of Tharsus and
Mallos made insurrection, because they were giuen to the
kings concubine called Antiochis.
31 Then came the king in all haste to appease matters,
leauing Andronicus a man in authority, for his deputy.
32 Now Menelaus supposing that he had gotten a conuenient time, stole certaine vessels of gold, out of the temple,
and gaue some of them to Andronicus, and some he sold into
Tyrus, and the cities round about.
33 Which when Onias knew of a surety, he reprooued him,
and withdrew himselfe into a Sanctuarie at Daphne, that lieth
by Antiochia.
34 Wherefore Menelaus, taking Andronicus apart, prayed
him to get Onias into his hands, who being perswaded thereunto, and comming to Onias in deceit, gaue him his right
hand with othes, and though hee were sus-

pected (by him) yet perswaded he him to come forth of the
Sanctuarie: whom forthwith he shut vp without regard of
Iustice.
35 For the which cause not onely the Iewes, but many also
of other nations tooke great indignation, and were much
grieued for the vniust murder of the man.
36 And when the king was come againe from the places
about Cilicia, the Iewes that were in the citie, and certaine
of the Greekes, that abhorred the fact also, complained because Onias was slaine without cause.
37 Therefore Antiochus was heartily sorry, and mooued to
pity, and wept, because of the sober and modest behauiour
of him that was dead.
38 And being kindled with anger, forthwith he tooke away
Andronicus his purple, and rent off his clothes, and leading
him through the whole city vnto that very place, where he
had committed impietie against Onias, there slew he the
cursed murtherer. Thus the Lord rewarded him his punishment, as he had deserued.
39 Now when many sacriledges had beene committed in
the citie by Lysimachus, with the consent of Menelaus, and
the bruit therof was spread abroad, the multitude gathered
themselues together against Lysimachus, many vessels of gold
being already caried away.
40 Whereupon the common people rising, and being filled
with rage, Lysimachus armed about three thousand men, and
beganne first to offer violence on ||Auranus, being the leader, || *Or, Tyrannus.*
a man farre gone in yeeres, & no lesse in folly.
41 They then seeing the attempt of Lysimachus, some of
them caught stones, some clubs, others taking handfuls of
dust, that was next at hand, cast them all together vpon
Lysimachus, and those that set vpon them.
42 Thus many of them they wounded, & some they stroke
to the ground, and all [of them] they forced to flee: but as
for the Churchrobber himselfe, him they killed besides the
treasury.
43 Of these matters therefore there was an accusation laide
against Menelaus.
44 Now when the king came to Tyrus, three men that
were sent from the Senate, pleaded the cause before him:

45 But

45 But Menelaus being now conuicted, promised Ptolomee the sonne of Dorymenes, to giue him much money, if hee would pacifie the King towards him.

46 Whereupon Ptolomee taking the king aside into a certaine gallerie, as it were to take the aire, brought him to be of another minde;

47 Insomuch that hee discharged Menelaus from the accusations, who notwithstanding was cause of all the mischiefe: and those poore men, who if they had told their cause, yea, before the Scythians, should haue bene iudged innocent, them he condemned to death.

48 Thus they that followed the matter for the citie, and for the people, and for the holy vessels, did soone suffer vniust punishment.

49 Wherefore euen they of Tyrus mooued with hatred of that wicked deed, caused them to bee honourably buried.

50 And so through the couetousnesse of them that were in power, Menelaus remained still in authority, increasing in malice, and being a great traitour to the citizens.

CHAP. V.

2 Of the signes and tokens seene in Ierusalem. 6 Of the end and wickednesse of Iason. 11 The pursuit of Antiochus against the Iewes. 15 The spoiling of the Temple. 27 Maccabeus fleeth into the wildernes.

ABout the same time Antiochus prepared his second voyage into Egypt:

2 And then it happened, that through all the citie, for the space almost of fourtie dayes, there were seene horsemen running in the aire, in cloth of golde, and armed with lances, like a band of souldiers,

3 And troupes of horsemen in aray, incountring, and running one against another with shaking of shieldes, and multitude of ||pikes, and drawing of swords, and casting of darts, and glittering of golden ornaments, and harnesse of all sorts.

|| *Or, staues.*

4 Wherefore euery man praied that that apparition might turne to good.

5 Now when there was gone forth a false rumour, as though Antiochus had bene dead, Iason tooke at the least a thousand men, and suddenly made an assault vpon the citie, and they that

were vpon the walles, being put backe, and the citie at length
taken, Menelaus fled into the castle:
6 But Iason slew his owne citizens without mercy, (not
considering that to get the day of them of his owne nation,
would be a most vnhappy day for him: but thinking *they
had bene his enemies*, and not his countrey men whom he
conquered.)
7 Howbeit, for all this hee obtained not the principalitie,
but at the last receiued shame for the reward of his treason,
and fled againe into the countrey of the Ammonites.
8 In the end therefore hee had an vnhappy returne, being
accused before Aretas the king of the Arabians, fleeing from
city to city, pursued of all men, hated as a forsaker of the
Lawes, and being had in abomination, as an open ||enemie of
his countrey, and countreymen, he was cast out into Egypt.
9 Thus hee that had driuen many out of their countrey,
perished in a strange land, retiring to the Lacedemonians,
and thinking there to finde succour by reason of his kindred.
10 And hee that had cast out many vnburied, had none to
mourne for him, nor any solemne funerals at all, nor sepulchre
with his fathers.
11 Now when this that was done came to the kings eare,
he thought that Iudea had reuolted, whereupon remouing
out of Egypt in a furious minde, he tooke the citie by force
of armes,
12 And commaunded his men of warre not to spare such as
they met, and to slay such as went vp vpon the houses.
13 Thus there was killing of yong and old, making away
of men, women and children, slaying of virgins and infants.
14 And there were destroyed within the space of three
whole daies, fourescore thousand, whereof fourty thousand
were slaine in the conflict; and no fewer sold, then slaine.
15 Yet was he not content with this, but presumed to goe
into the most holy Temple of all the world: Menelaus that
traitour to the Lawes, and to his owne countrey, being his
guide.
16 And taking the holy vessels with polluted handes, and
with prophane handes, pulling downe the things that were
dedicated by other kings, to the
augmen-

|| *Or, executioner.*

augmentation and glory and honour of the place, he gaue them away.

17 And so haughtie was Antiochus in minde, that hee considered not that the Lord was angry for a while for the sinnes of them that dwelt in the citie, and therefore his eye was not vpon the place.

18 For had they not beene formerly wrapped in many sinnes, this man as soone as hee had come, had foorthwith beene scourged, and put backe from his presumption, as Heliodorus was, whom Seleucus the king sent to view the treasurie.

19 Neuerthelesse God did not choose the people for the places sake, but the place for the peoples sake.

20 And therefore the place it selfe that was partaker with them of the aduersities that happened to the nation, did afterward communicate in the benefits sent from the Lord: and as it was forsaken in the wrath of the Almighty, so againe the great Lord being reconciled, it was set vp with all glory.

21 So when Antiochus had caried out of the Temple, a thousand and eight hundred talents, hee departed in all haste into Antiochia, weening in his pride to make the land nauigable, and the Sea passable by foot: such was the haughtinesse of his minde.

22 And he left gouernours to vexe the nation: at Ierusalem Philip, for his countrey a Phrygian, and for manners more barbarous then hee that set him there:

23 And at Garizim, Andronicus; and besides, Menelaus, who worse then all the rest, bare an heauie hand ouer the citizens, hauing a malicious minde against his countreymen the Iewes.

24 He sent also that detestable ringleader Apollonius, with an armie of two and twentie thousand, commaunding him to slay all those that were in their best age, and to sell the women and the yonger sort:

25 Who comming to Ierusalem, and pretending peace, did forbeare till the holy day of the Sabbath, when taking the Iewes keeping holy day, hee commanded his men to arme themselues.

26 And so hee slewe all them that were gone to the celebrating of the Sabbath, and running through the city with weapons, slewe great multitudes.

27 But Iudas Maccabeus, †with nine others, or thereabout, †Gr. *who*
withdrew himselfe into the wildernesse, and liued in the *was the*
mountaines after the maner of beasts, with his company, *tenth.*
who fed on herbes continually, lest they should be partakers
of the pollution.

CHAP. VI.

1 The Iewes are compelled to leaue the Law of God. 4 The Temple is defiled. 8 Crueltie vpon the people and the women. 12 An exhortation to beare affliction, by the example of the valiant courage of Eleazarus, cruelly tortured.

NOT long after this, the king sent an olde man of
||Athens, to compell the Iewes to depart from the ||*Antioch:*
lawes of their fathers, and not to liue after the Lawes of *the Latine*
God: *interpreters.*
2 And to pollute also the Temple in Ierusalem, and to call
it the Temple of Iupiter Olympius: and that in Garizim,
of Iupiter the defender of strangers, as they ||did desire that || *Out of*
dwelt in the place. *Ios. lib.* 12.
3 The comming in of this mischiefe was sore and grieuous *c.* 7. *or, as they were.*
to the people:
4 For the Temple was filled with riot and reuelling, by the
Gentiles, who dallied with harlots, and had to doe with
women within the circuit of the holy places, and besides
that, brought in things that were not lawfull.
5 The Altar also was filled with profane things, which the
Law forbiddeth.
6 Neither was it lawfull for a man to keepe Sabbath dayes,
or ancient Feasts, or to professe himselfe at all to be a Iewe.
7 And in the day of the kings birth, euery moneth they
were brought by bitter constraint to eate of the sacrifices;
and when the Feast of Bacchus was kept, the Iewes were
compelled to goe in procession to Bacchus, carying Iuie.
8 Moreouer there went out a decree to the neighbour
cities of the †heathen, by the suggestion of Ptolomee, against †Gr. *Gre-*
the Iewes, that they should obserue the same fashions, and be *cians.*
partakers of their sacrifices.
9 And whoso would not conforme themselues to the maners
of the Gentiles, should be put to death: then might a man
hane seene the present misery.
10 For there were two women
brought

brought, who had circumcised their children, whom when
they had openly led round about the citie, the babes hanging
at their breasts, they cast them downe headlong from the wall.
11 And others that had run together into caues neere by,
to keepe the Sabbath day secretly, being discouered to Philip,
were all burnt together, because they made a conscience to
helpe themselues, for the honour of the most sacred day.
12 Now I beseech those that reade this booke, that they be
not discouraged for these calamities, but that they iudge those
punishments not to be for destruction, but for a chastening
of our nation.
13 For it is a token of his great goodnesse, when wicked
doers are not suffered any long time, but forthwith punished.
14 For not as with other nations whom the Lord patiently
forbeareth to punish, till they be come to the fulnesse of their
sinnes, so dealeth he with vs,
15 Lest that being come to the height of sinne, afterwards
hee should take vengeance of vs.
16 And therfore he neuer withdraweth his mercie from vs:
and though he punish with aduersitie, yet doeth he neuer
forsake his people.
17 But let this that we haue spoken be for a warning vnto
vs: And nowe will wee come to the declaring of the matter
in few words.
18 Eleazar one of the principall Scribes, an aged man, and
of a well fauoured countenance, was constrained to open his
mouth, and to eate swines flesh.
19 But he chusing rather to die gloriously, then to liue
stained with such an abomination, spit it forth, and came of
his owne accord to the torment,
20 As it behoued them to come, that are resolute to stand
out against such things, as are not lawfull for loue of life to
be tasted.
21 But they that had the charge of that wicked feast, for
the olde acquaintance they had with the man, taking him
aside, besought him to bring flesh of his owne prouision, such
as was lawfull for him to vse, and make as if he did eate of
the flesh, taken from the sacrifice commanded by the king,
22 That in so doing hee might bee deliuered from death,
and for the olde

friendship with them, find fauour.
23 But he began to consider discreetly, and as became his
age, and the excellencie of his ancient yeeres, and the honour
of his gray head, whereunto hee was come, and his most
honest education from a child, or rather the holy lawe made,
and giuen by God: therefore hee answered accordingly, and
willed them straightwaies to send him to the graue.
24 For it becommeth not our age, said he, in any wise to
dissemble, whereby many yong persons might thinke, that
Eleazar being fourescore yeres old and ten, were now gone
to a strange religion,
25 And so they through mine hypocrisie, and desire to liue
a litle time, and a moment longer, should bee deceiued by
me, and I get a staine to mine olde age, and make it
abominable.
26 For though for the present time I should be deliuered
from the punishment of men: yet should I not escape the
hand of the Almightie, neither aliue nor dead.
27 Wherefore now manfully changing this life, I will shew
my selfe such an one, as mine age requireth,
28 And leaue a notable example to such as bee yong, to die
willingly, and couragiously, for the honourable and holy
lawes: and when he had said these words, immediatly he
went to the torment,
29 They that led him, changing the good will they bare
him a litle before, into hatred, because the foresaid speaches
proceeded as they thought, from a ||desperate minde.
30 But when hee was readie to die with stripes, he groned,
and said, It is manifest vnto the Lord, that hath the holy
knowledge, that wheras I might haue bin deliuered from
death, I [now] endure sore paines in body, by being beaten:
but in soule am well content to suffer these things, because
I feare him.
31 And thus this man died, leauing his death for an example
of a noble courage, and a memoriall of vertue not only vnto
yong men, but vnto all his nation.

|| *Or, madnes or pride.*

CHAP. VII.

The constancie and cruell death of seuen brethren and their mother in one day, because they would not eate swines flesh at the kings commandement.

It

IT came to passe also that seuen brethren with their mother were taken, and compelled by the king against the lawe to taste swines flesh, and were tormented with scourges, and whips:

2 But one of them that spake first said thus: What wouldest thou aske, or learne of vs? we are ready to die, rather then to transgresse the lawes of our fathers.

3 Then the king being in a rage, commanded pannes, and caldrons to be made whot.

4 Which forthwith being heated, he commanded to cut out the tongue of him that spake first, and to cut off the vtmost parts of his body, the rest of his brethren, and his mother looking on.

5 Now when he was thus maimed in all his members, he commanded him being yet aliue, to be brought to the fire, and to be fried in the panne: and as the vapour of the panne was for a good space dispersed, they exhorted one another, with the mother, to die manfully, saying thus:

6 The Lord God looketh vpon vs, and in trueth hath comfort in vs, as *Moises in his song, which witnessed to their faces declared, saying, And he shall be comforted in his seruants.

*Deut. 32. 36.

7 So when the first was dead, after this maner, they brought the second to make him a mocking stocke: and when they had pulled off the skin of his head with the haire, they asked him, Wilt thou eate before thou bee punished throughout euery member of thy body?

8 But hee answered in his owne language, and said, No. Wherefore hee also receiued the next torment in order, as the former did.

9 And when hee was at the last gaspe, hee said, Thou like a fury takest vs out of this present life, but the king of the world shall raise vs vp, who haue died for his lawes, vnto euerlasting life.

10 After him was the third made a mocking stocke, and when he was required, he put out his tongue, and that right soone, holding forth his hands manfully,

11 And said couragiously, These I had from heauen, and for his lawes I despise them, and from him I hope to receiue them againe.

12 Insomuch that the king, and

they that were with him marueiled at the yong mans courage,
for that he nothing regarded the paines.
13 Now when this man was dead also, they tormented and
mangled the fourth in like maner.
14 So when he was ready to die, he said thus, It is good,
being put to death by men, to looke for hope from God to
be raised vp againe by him: as for thee thou shalt haue no
resurrection to life.
15 Afterward they brought the fift also, and mangled him.
16 Then looked hee vnto the king and said, Thou hast
power ouer men, thou art corruptible, thou doest what thou
wilt, yet thinke not that our nation is forsaken of God.
17 But abide a while, and behold his great power, how he
will torment thee, and thy seed.
18 After him also they brought the sixt, who being ready
to die, said, Be not deceiued without cause: for we suffer
these things for our selues, hauing sinned against our God.
Therefore marueilous things are done (vnto vs.)
19 But thinke not thou that takest in hand to striue against
God, that thou shalt escape vnpunished.
20 But the mother was marueilous aboue all, and worthy
of honorable memorie: for when shee sawe her seuen sonnes
slaine within the space of one day, she bare it with a good
courage, because of the hope that she had in ẏ Lord
21 Yea she exhorted euery one of them in her owne
language, filled with couragious spirits, and stirring vp her
womanish thoughts, with a manly stomacke, she said vnto
them,
22 I cannot tell how you came into my wombe: for I
neither gaue you breath, nor life, neither was it I that
formed the mēbers of euery one of you.
23 But doubtlesse the Creator of the world, who formed the
generation of man, and found out the beginning of all things,
wil also of his owne mercy giue you breath, and life againe,
as you now regard not your owne selues for his Lawes sake.
24 Now Antiochus thinking himselfe despised, and suspecting
it to be a reprochfull speach, whiles the yongest was yet aliue,
did not onely exhort him by wordes, but also assured him
with oathes, that he would make him both a rich, and a
happy man, if hee would
turne

turne from the Lawes of his fathers, and that also he would take him for his friend, and trust him with affaires.

25 But when the yong man would in no case hearken vnto him, the king called his mother, and exhorted her, that she would counsell the yong man to saue his life.

26 And when hee had exhorted her with many words, she promised him that she would counsell her sonne.

27 But shee bowing her selfe towards him, laughing the cruell tyrant to scorne, spake in her countrey language on this maner; O my sonne, haue pitie vpon mee that bare thee nine moneths in my wombe, and gaue thee sucke three yeeres, and nourished thee, and brought thee vp vnto this age, and endured the troubles of education.

28 I beseech thee, my sonne, looke vpon the heauen, and the earth, and all that is therein, and consider that God made them of things that were not, and so was mankinde made likewise;

29 Feare not this tormentour, but being worthy of thy brethren, take thy death, that I may receiue thee againe in mercy, with thy brethren.

30 Whiles she was yet speaking these words, the yong man said, Whom wait ye for? I will not obey the kings commandement: but I will obey the commandement of the Law that was giuen vnto our fathers, by Moses.

31 And thou that hast bene the authour of all mischiefe against the Hebrewes, shalt not escape the handes of God.

32 For wee suffer because of our sinnes.

33 And though the liuing Lord bee angrie with vs a little while for our chastening and correction, yet shall hee be at one againe, with his seruants.

34 But thou, O godlesse man, and of all other most wicked, be not lifted vp without a cause, nor puffed vp with vncertaine hopes, lifting vp thy hand against the seruants of God:

35 For thou hast not yet escaped the iudgement of Almightie God, who seeth all things.

36 For our brethren who now haue suffered a short paine, are dead vnder Gods Couenant of euerlasting life: but thou through the iudgement of God, shalt receiue iust punishment for thy pride.

37 But I, as my brethren, offer vp my body, and life for
the Lawes of our fathers, beseeching God that he would
speedily bee mercifull vnto our nation, and that thou by
torments & plagues mayest confesse, that he alone is God;
38 And that in me, and my brethren, the wrath of the
Almighty, which is iustly brought vpon all our nation, may
cease.
39 Then the King being in a rage, handled him worse then
all the rest, and took it grieuously that he was mocked.
40 So this man died vndefiled, and put his whole trust in
the Lord.
41 Last of all after the sonnes, the mother died.
42 Let this be ynough now to haue spoken cōcerning the
idolatrous feasts, and the extreme tortures.

CHAP. VIII.

1 Iudas gathereth an hoste. 9 Nicanor is sent against him: who presumeth to make much money of his prisoners. 16 Iudas encourageth his men, and putteth Nicanor to flight, 28 and diuideth the spoiles. 30 Other enemies are also defeated, 35 And Nicanor fleeth with griefe to Antioch.

THen Iudas Maccabeus and they that were with him,
went priuily into the townes, and called their kinse-
folkes together, and tooke vnto them all such as continued in
the Iewes religion, and assembled about sixe thousand men.
2 And they called vpon the Lord, that hee would looke
vpon the people that was troden downe of all, and also pitie
the Temple, prophaned of vngodly men,
3 And that he would haue compassion vpon the city sore
defaced and ready to be made euen with the ground, and
heare the blood that cried vnto him,
4 And remember the wicked slaughter of harmelesse infants,
and the blasphemies committed against his Name, and that
hee would shew his hatred against the wicked.
5 Now when Maccabeus had his company about him, hee
could not be withstood by the heathen: for the wrath of the
Lord was turned into mercy.
6 Therefore he came at vnawares, and burnt vp townes and
cities, and got into his hands the most commodious

ous places, and ouercame & put to flight no small number of
his enemies.
7 But specially tooke he aduantage of the night, for such
priuie attempts, insomuch that the bruite of his manlinesse
was spread euery where.
8 So when Philip sawe that this man encreased by little and
little, & that things prospered with him still more and more,
hee wrote vnto Ptolemeus, the gouernour of Coelosyria &
Phenice, to yeeld more aide to the kings affaires.
9 Then forthwith choosing Nicanor the son of Patroclus,
one of his speciall friends, he sent him with no fewer then
twentie thousand of all nations vnder him, to root out the
whole generation of the Iewes; and with him he ioyned also
Gorgias a captaine, who in matters of warre had great experience.
10 So Nicanor vndertooke to make so much money of the
captiue Iewes, as should defray the tribute of two thousand
talents, which the king was to pay to the Romanes.
11 Wherefore immediatly he sent to the cities vpon the sea
coast, proclaiming a sale of the captiue Iewes, and promising
that they should haue fourescore and ten bodies for one
talent, not expecting the vengeance that was to follow vpon
him from the Almighty God.
12 Now when word was brought vnto Iudas of Nicanors
cōming, and he had imparted vnto those that were with him,
that the army was at hand,
13 They that were fearefull, and distrusted the iustice of
God, fled, and conueyed themselues away.
14 Others sold all that they had left, and withall besought
the Lord to deliuer them, being solde by the wicked Nicanor
before they met together:
15 And if not for their owne sakes, yet for ẏͤ couenants he
had made with their fathers, and for his holy and glorious
Names sake, by which they were called
16 So Maccabeus called his men together vnto the number
of sixe thousand, and exhorted them not to be stricken with
terrour of the enemie, nor to feare the great multitude of the
heathen who came wrongfully against them, but to fight
manfully,
17 And to set before their eyes, the iniury that they had
vniustly done to the holy place, and the cruell handling of
the city, whereof they made a mockery, and also the taking
away of the gouernment of their forefathers:

18 For they, said he, trust in their weapons and boldnesse,
but our confidence is in the Almightie God, who at a becke
can cast downe both them that come against vs, and also all
the world.
19 Moreouer, hee recounted vnto them what helps their
forefathers had found, and how they were deliuered, when
vnder Sennacherib an hundred fourescore and fiue thousand
perished.
20 And he told them of ye battel that they had in Babylon
with the Galatians, how they came but eight thousand in all
to ye busines, with foure thousand Macedonians, and that the
Macedonians being perplexed, the eight thousand destroyed
an hundred and twenty thousand, because of the helpe that
they had from heauen, & so receiued a great booty.
21 Thus when hee had made them bold with these words,
and ready to die for the Lawes, and the countrey, he diuided
his army into foure parts:
22 And ioyned with himselfe his owne brethren, leaders of
each band, to wit, Simon, and Ioseph, & Ionathan, giuing
each one fifteene hundred men.
23 Also (hee appointed) Eleazar to reade the holy booke:
and when he had giuen them this watchword, The help of
God; himselfe leading the first band, he ioyned battell with
Nicanor:
24 And by the helpe of the Almightie, they slew aboue
nine thousand of their enemies, and wounded and maimed
the most part of Nicanors hoste, and so put all to flight:
25 And tooke their money that came to buy them, and
pursued them farre: but lacking time, they returned.
26 For it was the day before the Sabbath, and therefore
they would no longer pursue them.
27 So when they had gathered their ||armour together, and
spoiled their enemies, they occupied themselues about the
Sabbath, yeelding exceeding praise, & thanks to the Lord,
who had preserued them vnto yt day, which was the beginning of mercy, distilling vpon them.
28 And after the Sabbath, when they had giuen part of the
spoiles to the ||maimed, and the widdowes, and Orphanes, the
residue they diuided among themselues, and their seruants.
29 When this was done, and they had made a common
supplication, they besought the mercifull Lord to be reconciled with his seruants for euer.

|| *That is, the enemies armour.*

|| *Or, lamed with tortures.*

30 Moreouer of those that were with Timotheus & Bacchides, who fought against them, they slewe aboue twentie
thousand, and very easily got high and strong holds, &
diuided amongst them selues many spoiles more, and made
|| Or, lamed. the ||maimed, orphanes, widowes, yea, & the aged also, equal
in spoiles wͭ themselues

31 And when they had gathered their armour together, they
laid them vp all carefully in couenient places, and the remnant of the spoiles they brought to Ierusalem.

32 They slew also Philarches that wicked persõ who was wͭ
Timotheus, & had annoied the Iewes many waies.

33 Furthermore at such time as they kept the feast for the
victorie in their coũtry, they burnt Calisthenes that had set
fire vpon the holy gates, who was fled into a litle house, and
so he receiued a reward meet for his wickednesse.

34 As for that most vngracious Nicanor, who had brought
a thousand merchants to buy the Iewes,

35 He was through the helpe of the Lord brought downe
by them, of whõ he made least account, & putting off his
glorious apparell, and discharging his company, he came like
a fugitiue seruant through the mid land vnto Antioch, hauing very great dishonour for that his hoste was destroyed.

36 Thus he that tooke vpon him to make good to the
Romanes, their tribute by meanes of the captiues in Ierusalem, told abroad, that the Iewes had God to fight for them,
and therfore they could not be hurt, because they followed
the lawes that he gaue them.

CHAP. IX.

1 Antiochus is chased from Persepolis. 5 Hee is striken with a sore disease, 14 and promiseth to become a Iew. 28 He dieth miserably.

|| Or, disorderly. ABout that time came Antiochus with ||dishonor out of the
countrey of Persia.

2 For he had entred the citie called Persepolis, and went
about to rob the Temple, and to hold the citie, whereupon the
multitude running to defend thẽselues with their weapons,
put them to flight, & so it happened yͭ Antiochus being put
to flight of the inhabitants, returned with shame.

3 Now when he came to Ecbatana, newes was brought him
what had happened vnto Nicanor & Timotheus.

4 Then swelling with anger, hee

thought to auenge vpon the Iewes the disgrace done vnto
him by those that made him flie. Therfore commanded he
his chariot man to driue without ceasing, and to dispatch
the iourney, the iudgement of God now following him.
For he had spoken proudly in this sort, ẏ[t] he would come to
Ierusalem, & make it a common burying place of ẏ[e] Iewes.
5 But the Lord almightie, the God of Israel smote him
with an incurable and inuisible plague: for assoone as hee
had spoken these words, a paine of the bowels that was
remediles, came vpon him, & sore torments of the inner parts.
6 And that most iustly: for hee had tormented other mens
bowels with many and strange torments.
7 Howbeit hee nothing at all ceased from his bragging, but
still was filled with pride, breathing out fire in his rage
against the Iewes, and commanding to haste the iourney:
but it came to passe that he fel downe frō his chariot, caried
violently, so that hauing a sore fal, al the mēbers of his body
were much pained.
8 And thus hee that a little afore thought he might command the waues of the sea (so proud was hee beyond the
condition of man) and weigh the high mountaines in a
ballance, was now cast on the ground, and carried in an horse-
litter, shewing foorth vnto all, the manifest power of God.
9 So that the wormes rose vp out of the body of this wicked
man, and whiles hee liued in sorrow and paine, his flesh fell
away, and the filthinesse of his smell was noysome to all his
army.
10 And the man that thought a little afore he could reach
to the starres of heauen, no man could endure to carry for
his intollerable stinke.
11 Here therefore being plagued, hee began to leaue off his
great pride, and to come to the knowledge [of himselfe] by
the scourge of God, his paine encreasing euery moment.
12 And when hee himselfe could not abide his owne smell,
hee saide these wordes: It is meete to bee subiect vnto God,
and that a man that is mortall, should not proudly thinke of
himselfe, as if he were God.
13 This wicked person vowedalso vnto the Lord, (who
now no more would haue mercy vpon him) saying thus:
14 That the holy citie (to the which hee was going in haste
to lay it euen
with

with the ground, & to make it a common burying place) he
would set at liberty.
15 And as touching the Iewes, whom hee had iudged not
worthy so much as to be buried, but to be cast out with
their children to be deuoured of the foules, and wild beasts,
he would make them al equals to ye citizens of ‖Athens,
16 And the holy Temple, which before he had spoiled, hee
would garnish with goodly gifts, and restore all the holy
vessels with many more, and out of his owne reuenew defray
the charges belonging to the sacrifices:
17 Yea, and that also hee would become a Iew himselfe,
and goe through all the world that was inhabited, and declare
the power of God.
18 But for all this his paines would not cease: for the iust
iudgement of God was come vpō him: therfore despairing of
his health, he wrote vnto the Iewes the letter vnderwritten,
containing the forme of a supplicatiō, after this maner.
19 Antiochus king and gouernour, to the good Iewes his
Citizens, wisheth much ioy, health, and prosperity.
20 If ye, and your children fare well, and your affaires be
to your contentment, I giue very great thankes to God, hauing my hope in heauen.
21 As for mee I was weake, or else I would haue remembred kindly your honour, and good will. Returning out of
Persia, and being taken with a grieuous disease, I thought it
necessary to care for the common safety of all:
22 Not distrusting mine health, but hauing great hope to
escape this sicknes
23 But considering that euen my father, at what time he
led an armie into the hie countries, appointed a successor,
24 To the end, that if any thing fell out contrary to expectation, or if any tidings were brought that were grieuous,
they of the land knowing to whom ‖the state was left, might
not be troubled.
25 Againe considering, how that the princes that are border-
ers, and neighbors vnto my kingdome, waite for opportunities,
and expect what shalbe the euent, I haue appointed my sonne
Antiochus king, whom I often cōmitted, and cōmended vnto
many of you, when I went vp into the high prouinces, to
whom I haue written as followeth.
26 Therefore I pray, and request you to remember the
benefits that I

‖ *Or, Antioch.*

‖ *Or, common affaires.*

haue done vnto you generally, and in speciall, and that euery
man will be still faithfull to me, and my sonne.
27 For I am perswaded that hee ||vnderstanding my minde, || *Or, following.*
will fauourably & graciously yeeld to your desires.
28 Thus the murtherer, and blasphemer hauing suffered
most grieuously, as he entreated other men, so died he a
miserable death in a strange countrey in the mountaines.
29 And Philip that was brought vp with him, caried away
his body, who also fearing the son of Antiochus, went into
Egypt to Ptolomeus Philometor.

CHAP. X.

1 Iudas recouereth the Citie, and purifieth the Temple. 14 Gorgias vexeth the Iewes. 16 Iudas winneth their holds. 29 Timotheus and his men are discomfited. 35 Gazara is taken, and Timotheus slaine.

NOw Maccabeus, and his company, the Lord guiding
them, recouered the Temple, and the citie.
2 But the altars, which the heathen had built in the open
street, & also the Chappels they pulled downe.
3 And hauing cleansed the Temple, they made another
Altar, and striking stones, they tooke fire out of them, and
offered a sacrifice after two yeeres, & set forth incense, &
lights, and Shewbread.
4 When that was done, they fell flat downe, and besought
the Lord that they might come no more into such troubles:
but if they sinned any more against him, that he himselfe
would chasten them with mercie, and that they might not
bee deliuered vnto the blasphemous, and barbarous nations.
5 Now vpon the same day that the strangers prophaned the
Temple, on the very same day it was cleansed againe, euen
the fiue and twentieth day of the same moneth, which is
Casleu.
6 And they kept eight dayes with gladnes as in the feast of
the Tabernacles, remembring that not long afore they had
helde the feast of the Tabernacles, when as they wandered
in the mountaines, and dennes, like beasts.
7 Therefore they bare branches, and faire boughes and
palmes also, and sang Psalmes vnto him, that had giuen
them good successe in clensing his place.
8 They ordeined also by a common statute, and decree,
That euery yeere

those dayes should be kept of the whole nation of the Iewes.
9 And this was the ende of Antiochus called Epiphanes.
10 Now will wee declare the acts of Antiochus Eupator,
who was the sonne of this wicked man, gathering briefly the
calamities of the warres.
11 So when he was come to yͤ crowne, he set one Lysias
ouer the affaires of his Realme, and [appointed him] chiefe
gouernour of Coelosyria and Phenice.
12 For Ptolomeus that was called Macron, chosing rather
to doe iustice vnto the Iewes, for the wrong that had bene
done vnto them, endeuoured to continue peace with them.
13 Whereupon being accused of [the kings] friends, before
Eupator, & called traitor at euery word, because he had left
Cyprus that Philometor had cōmitted vnto him, & departed
to Antiochus Epiphanes; ||and seeing that hee was in no
honorable place, he was so discouraged, that he poysoned
himselfe and died.
14 But when Gorgias was gouernour of the ||holds, hee
hired souldiers, and nourished warre continually with the
Iewes:

|| Or, and not bearing his authoritie as it becommeth a noble man.

|| Or, strong places.

15 And therewithall the Idumeans hauing gotten into their
handes the most commodious holdes, kept the Iewes occupied, and receiuing those that were banished from Ierusalem,
they went about to nourish warre.
16 Then they that were wich Maccabeus made supplication,
& besought God, that he would be their helper, and so they
ranne with violence vpon the strong holds of the Idumeans,
17 And assaulting them strongly, they wanne the holds, and
kept off all that fought vpon the wall, and slew all that fell
into their hands, and killed no fewer then twentie thousand.
18 And because certaine (who were no lesse then nine thousand) were fled together into two very strong castles, hauing
all maner of things conuenient to sustaine the siege,
19 Maccabeus left Simon, & Ioseph, and Zaccheus also, and
them that were with him, who were enow to besiege them,
and departed himselfe vnto those places, which more needed
his helpe.
20 Now ||they that were with Simon, being led with coue-
tousnes, were perswaded for money (through certaine of those
that were in the castle) and

|| Or, Simon.

tooke seuentie thousand drachmes, and let some of them
escape.
21 But when it was told Maccabeus what was done, hee
called the gouernours of the people together, and accused
those men, that they had sold their brethren for money, &
set their enemies free to fight against them.
22 So he slew those that were found traitors, and immediatly tooke the two castles.
23 And hauing good successe with his weapons in all things
hee tooke in hand, hee slew in the two holdes, more then
twentie thousand.
24 Now Timotheus whom the Iewes had ouercome before,
when he had gathered a great multitude of forraine forces,
and horses out of Asia not a few, came as though hee would
take Iewrie by force of armes.
25 But when hee drew neere, ||they that were with Macca-
beus, turned themselues to pray vnto God, and sprinckled
earth vpon their heads, and girded their loynes with sackcloth,
26 And fell downe at the foot of the Altar, and besought
him to be mercifull to them, and to be an *enemie to their
enemies, and an aduersarie to their aduersaries, as the Law
declareth.

|| *Or, Maccabeus, and they that were with him.*

* Deut. 28.

27 So after the prayer, they tooke their weapons, & went
on further from the city: and when they drew neere to their
enemies, they kept by themselues.
28 Now the Sunne being newly risen, they ioyned both together; the one part hauing, together with their vertue, their
refuge also vnto the Lord, for a ||pledge of their successe and
victorie: the other side making their rage leader of their
battell.

|| *Or, warrant, or suretie.*

29 But when the battaile waxed strong, there appeared vnto
the enemies from heauen, fiue comely men vpon horses, with
bridles of golde, and two of them ledde the Iewes,
30 And tooke Maccabeus betwixt them, and couered him
on euery side with their weapons, and kept him safe, but shot
arrowes & lightenings against the enemies: so that being
confounded with blindnesse, and full of trouble, they were
killed.
31 And there were slaine [of footemen] twentie thousand
and fiue hundred, and sixe hundred horsemen.
32 As for Timotheus himselfe, hee fled into a very strong
holde, called Ga-
zara,

zara, where Chereas was gouernour.
33 But they that were with Maccabeus, laid siege against
the fortresse couragiously foure dayes.
34 And they ꝧ were within, trusting to the strength of the
place, blasphemed exceedingly, & vttered wicked words.
35 Neuerthelesse, vpon the fifth day early, twentie yong
men of Maccabeus company, inflamed with anger because of
the blasphemies, assaulted the wall manly, and with a fierce
courage killed all that they met withall.
36 Others likewise ascending after them, whiles they were
busied with them that were within, burnt the towres, and
kindling fires, burnt the blasphemers aliue, and others broke
open the gates, and hauing receiued in the rest of the army,
tooke the city,
37 And killed Timotheus that was hidde in a certaine pit,
and Chereas his brother, with Apollophanes.
38 When this was done, they praised the Lord with Psalmes
and thankesgiuing, who had done so great things for Israel, and
giuen them the victory.

CHAP. XI.

3 Lysias thinking to get Ierusalem, 8 Is put to flight. 16 The letters of Lysias to the Iewes; 22 Of the king vnto Lysias: 27 and to the Iewes: 34 Of the Romanes to the Iewes.

† *Gr. tutour.*

NOt long after this, Lysias the kings †protectour &
cousin, who also managed the affaires, tooke sore displeasure for the things that were done.
2 And when he had gathered about fourescore thousand,
with all the horsemen, he came against the Iewes, thinking
to make the citie an habitation of the ||Gentiles,

|| *Or, Grecians.*

3 And to make a gaine of the Temple, as of the other
Chappels of the heathen, and to set the high Priesthood to
sale euery yeere:
4 Not at all considering the power of God, but puffed vp
with his ten thousand footmen, and his thousand horsemen,
and his fourescore Elephants.
5 So he came to Iudea, & drew neere to Bethsura, which
was a strong town, but distant from Ierusalem about fiue
furlongs, and he laid sore siege vnto it.

|| *Maccabeus and his company.*

6 Now when ||they that were with Maccabeus heard that
he besieged the holdes, they and all the people with lamentation and teares besought the

Lord, that he would send a good Angel to deliuer Israel.
7 Then Maccabeus himselfe first of all tooke weapons,
exhorting the other, that they would ieopard themselues together with him, to helpe their brethren: so they went forth
together with a willing minde.
8 And as they were at Ierusalem, there appeared before
them on horsebacke, one in white clothing, shaking his
armour of gold.
9 Then they praised the mercifull God altogether, and
tooke heart, insomuch that they were ready not onely to
fight with men, but with most cruell beasts, & to pierce
through wals of yron.
10 Thus they marched forward in their armour, hauing an
helper from heauen: for the Lord was mercifull vnto them.
11 And giuing a charge vpō their enemies like lions, they
slew eleuen thousand footmen, & sixteene hundred horsemen,
and put all the other to flight.
12 Many of them also being wounded, escaped naked, and
Lysias himselfe fled away shamefully, and so escaped.
13 Who as hee was a man of vnderstanding, casting with
himselfe what losse he had had, and considering that the
Hebrewes could not be ouercome, because the Almighty
God helped them, he sent vnto them,
14 And perswaded them to agree to all reasonable con-
ditions, & [promised] that hee would perswade the king,
that he must needs be a friend vnto them.
15 Then Maccabeus consented to all that Lysias desired,
being carefull of the common good; and whatsoeuer Maccabeus wrote vnto Lysias concerning the Iewes, the king
granted it.
16 For there were letters written vnto the Iewes from
Lysias, to this effect: Lysias vnto the people of the Iewes,
sendeth greeting.
17 Iohn and Absalon, who were sent from you, deliuered
me the petition subscribed, and made request for the performance of the contents thereof.
18 Therefore what things soeuer were meet to be reported
to the king, I haue declared them, and he hath granted as
much as might be.
19 If then you wil keepe your selues loyall to the state,
hereafter also will I endeuour to be a meanes of your good.
20 But of the particulars I haue gi-

uen order, both to these, & the other that came from me, to
commune with you.
21 Fare ye wel. The hundred & eight and fortie yeere,
the foure and twentie day of the moneth Dioscorinthius.

‖ *Or, Dioscoros.*

22 Now the kings letter conteined these words, King Antiochus vnto his brother Lysias sendeth greeting.
23 Since our father is translated vnto yͤ gods, our will is,
that they that are in our realme liue quietly, that euery one
may attend vpon his own affaires.
24 Wee vnderstand also that the Iewes would not consent
to our father for to bee brought vnto the custome of the
Gentiles, but had rather keepe their owne manner of liuing:
for the which cause they require of vs that we should suffer
thē to liue after their own lawes.
25 Wherefore our mind is, that this nation shall be in rest,
and we haue determined to restore them their Temple, that
they may liue according to the customes of their forefathers.
26 Thou shalt doe well therefore to send vnto them, and
‖grant them peace, that whē they are certified of our mind,
they may be of good comfort, & euer goe cheerefully about
their owne affaires.

‖ *Or, giue them assurance.*

27 And the letter of yͤ king vnto the nation of the Iewes
was after this maner: king Antiochus sendeth greeting vnto
the counsel, & the rest of the Iewes
28 If ye fare well, we haue our desire, we are also in good
health.
29 Menelaus declared vnto vs, that your desire was to returne home, and to follow your owne businesse.
30 Wherefore they that will depart shall haue safe conduct,
till the thirtieth day of Xanthicus with securitie.
31 And the Iewes shal vse their owne kind of meats, and
lawes, as before, and none of them any maner of wayes shal
be molested for things ignorantly done.
32 I haue sent also Menelaus, that he may comfort you.
33 Fare ye wel. In the hundred, forty and eight yeere,
and the fifteenth day of the moneth ‖Xanthicus.

‖ *Or, Aprill.*

34 The Romanes also sent vnto them a letter containing
these wordes: Quintus Memmius, & Titus Manlius ‖em-
bassadours of yͤ Romanes, send greeting vnto the people of
the Iewes.

‖ *Or, consuls*

35 Whatsoeuer Lysias the kings cousin hath granted, therewith we also are well pleased.
36 But touching such things as hee

iudged to be referred to the king: after you haue aduised
therof, send one forthwith, that we may declare as it is conuenient for you: for we are now going to Antioch.
37 Therefore send some with speed, that we may know
what is your mind.
38 Farewell, this hundred and eight and fortie yeere, the
fifteenth day of the moneth Xanthicus.

CHAP. XII.

1 The Kings lieutenants vexe the Iewes. 3 They of Ioppe drowne
two hundred Iewes. 6 Iudas is auenged vpon them. 11 Hee maketh
peace with the Arabians, 16 and taketh Caspis. 22 Timotheus
armies ouerthrowen.

WHen these Couenants were made, Lysias went vnto the
king, and the Iewes were about their husbandrie.
2 But of the gouernours of seueral places, Timotheus, and
Apollonius the sonne of Genneus, also Hieronymus, and
Demophon, and besides them Nicanor ye gouernor of Cyprus
would not suffer them to be quiet, and liue in peace.
3 The men of Ioppe also did such an vngodly deed: they
prayed the Iewes that dwelt among them, to goe with their
wiues, and children into the boats which they had prepared,
as though they had meant them no hurt.
4 Who accepted of it according to the common decree of
the citie, as being desirous to liue in peace, and suspecting
nothing: but when they were gone forth into the deepe,
they drowned no lesse then two hundred of them.
5 When Iudas heard of this crueltie done vnto his countrey
men, he commanded those that were with him [to make
them ready.]
6 And calling vpon God the righteous iudge, he came a-
gainst those murtherers of his brethren, & burnt the hauen
by night, and set the boats on fire, and those that fled thither,
he slew.
7 And when the towne was shut vp, he went backward, ||as
if he would returne to root out all them of the citie of Ioppe.
8 But when he heard that ye Iamnites were minded to doe
in like maner vnto the Iewes yt dwelt among them,
9 He came vpon the Iamnites also by night, and set fire on
the hauen, & the nauy, so that the light of the fire was seene
at Ierusalem, two hundred and fortie furlongs off. 10 Now

|| *Or, with a purpose to returne.*

10 Now when they were gone from thence nine furlongs
in their iourney toward Timotheus, no fewer then fiue
thousand men on foote, & fiue hundred horse men of the
Arabians, set vpon him.
11 Whereupon there was a very sore battell; but Iudas side
by the helpe of God got the victory, so that the Nomades of
Arabia being ouercome, besought Iudas for peace, promising
both to giue him cattell, and to pleasure him otherwise.
12 Then Iudas thinking indeede that they would be profitable in many things, granted them peace, wherupon they
shooke hands, and so they ||departed to their tents.
13 Hee went also about to make a bridge to a certaine
strong citie, which was fenced about with walles, and inhabited by people of diuers countries, and the name of it was
Caspis.

|| Or, went from place to place, with their families and cattell.

14 But they that were within it put such trust in the
strength of the walles, and prouision of victuals, that they
behaued themselues rudely towards them that were with
Iudas, railing, and blaspheming, and vttering such words, as
were not to be spoken.
15 Wherefore Iudas with his company, calling vpon the
great Lord of the world (who without any rammes, or engines
of warre did cast downe Iericho in the time of Iosua) gaue a
fierce assault against the walles,
16 And tooke the citie by the will of God, and made vn-
speakeable slaughters, insomuch that a lake two furlongs
broad, neere adioining thereunto, being filled ful, was seen
running with blood.
17 Then departed they from thence seuen hundred and
fifty furlongs, and came to Characa vnto the Iewes that are
called Tubieni.
18 But as for Timotheus they found him not in the places,
for before hee had dispatched any thing, he departed from
thence, hauing left a very strong garrison in a certaine hold:
19 Howbeit, Dositheus, and Sosipater, who were of Maccabeus captaines, went forth, and slew those that Timotheus
had left in the fortresse, aboue tenne thousand men.
20 And Maccabeus ranged his armie by bands, & set ||them
ouer the bands, and went against Timotheus, who had about
him & hundred and twentie

|| Dositheus, and Sosipater.

thousand men of foote, and two thousand, and fiue hundred
horsemen.
21 Nowe when Timotheus had knowledge of Iudas comming, he sent the women and children, and the other baggage
vnto a fortresse called Carnion (for the towne was hard to
besiege and vneasie to come vnto, by reason of the straitnesse
of all the places.)
22 But when Iudas his first band came in sight, the enemies
(being smitten with feare, and terrour through the appearing
of him that seeth all things) fled amaine, one running this
way, another that way, so as that they were often hurt of
their owne men, and wounded with ye points of their owne
swords
23 Iudas also was very earnest in pursuing them, killing
those wicked wretches, of whom he slew about thirtie thousand men.
24 Moreouer, Timotheus himselfe fell into the hands of
Dositheus, & Sosipater, whom he besought with much craft
to let him goe with his life, because hee had many of the
Iewes parents, and the brethren of some of them, who, if
they put him to death, should not be regarded.
25 So when hee had assured them with many words, that
hee would restore them without hurt according to the agreement, they let him goe for the sauing of their brethren.
26 Then Maccabeus marched forth to Carnion, & to the
Temple of ||Atargatis, and there he slew fiue and twenty || *i. Venus.*
thousand persons.
27 And after he had put to flight, and destroyed them,
Iudas remooued the hoste towards Ephron, a strong citie,
wherin Lysias abode, and a great multitude of diuers nations,
and the strong yong men kept the wals, and defended them
mightily: wherin also was great prouision of engines, and darts.
28 But when Iudas and his company had called vpon Almighty God (who with his power breaketh the strength of
his enemies) they wanne the citie, and slew twentie and fiue
thousand of them that were within.
29 From thence they departed to Scythopolis, which lieth
sixe hundreth furlongs from Ierusalem.
30 But when the Iewes that dwelt there had testified that
the Scythopolitans dealt louingly with them, and entreated
them kindely in the time of their aduersitie: 13 They

31 They gaue them thankes, desiring them to be friendly
stil vnto them, and so they came to Ierusalem, the feast of
the weekes approching.
32 And after the feast called Pentecost, they went foorth
against Gorgias the gouernour of Idumea,
33 Who came out wt three thousand men of foot, & foure
hundred horsemen.
34 And it happened that in their fighting together, a few of
the Iewes were slaine.
35 At which time Dositheus one of Bacenors company, who
was on horsbacke, and a strong man, was still vpon Gorgias,
and taking hold of his coate, drew him by force, and when
he would haue taken that cursed man aliue, a horseman of
Thracia comming vpon him, smote off his ||shoulder, so that
Gorgias fled vnto Marisa.
36 Now when they that were with Gorgias had fought long
& were wearie, Iudas called vpon the Lord that he would
shew himselfe to be their helper, and leader of the battell.
37 And with that he beganne in his owne language, & sung
Psalmes with a lowd voyce, & rushing vnawares vpon Gorgias men, he put them to flight.
38 So Iudas gathered his host, and came into the city of
Odollam. And when the seuenth day came, they purified
themselues (as the custome was) and kept the Sabbath in the
same place.
39 And vpon the day following ||as the vse had bene, Iudas
and his company came to take vp the bodies of them that
were slaine, and to bury them with their kinsmen, in their
fathers graues.
40 Now vnder the coats of euery one that was slaine, they
found things consecrated to the idoles of the Iamnites, which
is forbidden the Iewes by *the Law. Then euery man saw
that this was ye cause wherefore they were slaine.
41 All men therefore praising the Lord the righteous Iudge,
who had opened the things that were hid,
42 Betooke themselues vnto praier, and besought him that
the sinne committed, might wholy bee put out of remembrance. Besides, that noble Iudas exhorted the people to
keep themselues from sinne, forsomuch as they saw before
their eyes the things that came to passe, for the sinne of
those yt were slaine.
43 And when he had made a gathering throughout the
company, to the

|| *Put by his armie: wounded him in the shoulder: or stroke him in the shoulder.*

|| *Or, at such time, &c.*

* Deut. 26. ver. 7.

sum of two thousand drachmes of siluer, hee sent it to Ierusalem to offer a sinne offering, doing therein very well, and honestly, in that he was mindfull of the resurrection.
44 (For if he had not hoped that they that were slaine should haue risen againe, it had bin superfluous and vaine, to pray for the dead.)
45 And also in that he perceiued that there was great fauour layed vp for those that died godly. (It was an holy, and good thought) wherupon he made a reconciliation for the dead, that they might be deliuered from sinne.

CHAP. XIII.

1 Eupator inuadeth Iudea. 15 Iudas by night slayeth many. 18 Eupators purpose is defeated. 23 He maketh peace with Iudas.

IN the hundreth forty and ninth yere it was told Iudas that Antiochus Eupator was cōming with a great power into Iudea;
2 And with him Lysias his protector, and ruler of his affaires, hauing either of them a Grecian power of footemen, an hundred and ten thousand, and horsmen fiue thousand, & three hundred, and Elephants two & twenty, and three hundred charets armed wt hooks.
3 Menelaus also ioyned himself with them, and with great dissimulation encouraged Antiochus, not for the safegard of the countrey, but because hee thought to haue bin made gouernour.
4 But the King of kings mooued Antiochus minde against this wicked wretch, and Lysias enformed the king, that this man was the cause of all mischiefe, so that the king commanded to bring him vnto Berea, and to put him to death, as the maner is in that place.
5 Now there was in that place a towre of fifty cubites high full of ashes, and it had a round instrumēt which on euery side hanged down into the ashes.
6 And whosoeuer was condemned of sacriledge, or had committed any other grieuous crime, there did all men thrust him vnto death.
7 Such a death it happened that wicked man to die, not hauing so much as buriall in the earth, & that most iustly.
8 For inasmuch as he had committed many sinnes about the altar whose fire and ashes were holy, hee receiued his death in ashes.

9 Now

9 Now yͤ king came with a barbarous & hautie mind, to do far worse to yͤ Iewes then had beene done in his fathers time.

10 Which things when Iudas perceiued, hee commanded the multitude to call vpon the Lord night & day, that if euer at any other time, he would now also helpe them, being at the point to be put from their Law, from their country, and from the holy Temple:

|| *Or, had had a litle respite.*

11 And that hee would not suffer the people, that ||had euen now been but a little refreshed, to be in subiection to the blasphemous nations.

12 So when they had all done this together, and besought the mercifull Lord with weeping, and fasting, and lying flat vpon the ground three daies long, Iudas hauing exhorted them, commanded they should be in a readinesse.

13 And Iudas being apart with the Elders, determined before the kings host should enter into Iudea and get the city, to goe foorth and try the matter [in fight] by the helpe of the Lord.

|| *Or, Lord*

14 So when he had committed [all] to the ||Creator of the world, & exhorted his souldiers to fight manfully, euen vnto death, for the Lawes, the Temple, the city, the country, and the common-wealth, he camped by Modin.

15 And hauing giuen the watchword to them that were about him, Victory is of God; with the most valiant and choice yong men, he went in into the kings tent by night, & slewe in the campe about foure thousand men, and the chiefest of the Elephants, with all that were vpon him.

16 And at last they filled the campe with feare and tumult, and departed with good successe.

17 This was done in the breake of the day, because the protection of the Lord did helpe him.

18 Now when the king had taken a taste of the manlinesse of the Iewes, hee went about to take the holds by policie,

19 And marched towards Bethsura, which was a strōg hold of yͤ Iews, but he was put to flight, failed, & lost of his men.

20 For Iudas had conueyed vnto them yͭ were in it, such things as were necessary.

21 But Rhodocus who was in yͤ Iewes hoste, disclosed the secrets to the enemies, therefore he was sought out, & when they had gotten him, they put him in prison.

22 The king treated with them in Bethsura the second time, gaue his hand, tooke theirs, departed, fought with Iudas, was ouercome:

23 Heard that Philip who was left ouer the affaires in
Antioch ||was desperately bent, confounded, intreated the
Iewes, submitted himselfe, and sware to all equal con-
ditions, agreed with them, and offred sacrifice, honoured
the Temple, and dealt kindly with the place,
24 And accepted well of Maccabeus, made him principall
gouernor from Ptolemais vnto the Gerrhenians,
25 Came to Ptolemais, the people there were grieued for
the couenants: for they stormed because they would make
their couenants voide.
26 Lysias went vp to the iudgement seat, said as much as
could be in defence of the cause, perswaded, pacified, made
them well affected, returned to Antioch. Thus it went
touching the kings comming and departing.

|| *Or, rebelled.*

CHAP. XIIII.

6 Alcimus accuseth Iudas. 18 Nicanor maketh peace with Iudas. 39 He seeketh to take Rhasis, 46 who to escape his hands, killeth himselfe.

AFter three yeres was Iudas enformed that Demetrius the
sonne of Seleucus hauing entred by the hauen of
Tripolis with a great power and nauie,
2 Had taken the countrey, and killed Antiochus, and Lysias
his protectour.
3 Now one Alcimus who had beene hie Priest, and had
defiled himselfe wilfully in the times of their mingling (with
the Gentiles) seeing that by no meanes hee could saue himselfe, nor haue any more accesse to the holy Altar,
4 Came to king Demetrius in the hundreth and one and
fiftieth yeere, presenting vnto him a crowne of golde, and a
palme, and also of the boughes which were ||vsed solemnly
in the Temple: and so that day he helde his peace.
5 Howbeit hauing gotten opportunity to further his foolish
enterprise, [and] being called into counsel by Demetrius, &
asked how the Iewes stood affected, and what they intẽded,
he answered therunto;
6 Those of the Iewes that bee called Asideans (whose captaine is Iudas Maccabeus) nourish warre, and are seditious,
and will not let the realme be in peace.
7 Therfore I being depriued of mine ancestors honor (I
meane the hie Priesthood) am now come hither.
8 First verily for the vnfained care I haue of things pertaining
to the king, and secondly, euen for that I intend the good
of

|| *Or, thought to be of the Temple.*

of mine owne countrey men: for all our nation is in no small
misery, through the vnaduised dealing of them aforesaid.
9 Wherefore, O king, seeing thou knowest all these things,
bee carefull for the countrey, and our nation, which is pressed
on euery side, according to the clemency that thou readily
shewest vnto all.
10 For as long as Iudas liueth, it is not possible that the
state should be quiet.
11 This was no sooner spoken of him, but others of the
kings friends being malitiously set against Iudas, did more
incense Demetrius.
12 And foorthwith calling Nicanor, who had bene master
of the Elephants, and making him gouernour ouer Iudea, he
sent him forth,
13 Cōmanding him to slay Iudas, & to scatter them that were
wt him, & to make Alcimus high priest of the great Temple.
14 Then the heathen that had fled out of Iudea from Iudas,
came to Nicanor by flocks, thinking the harme and calamities
of the Iewes, to be their well-fare.
15 Now when the Iewes heard of Nicanors comming, and
that the heathen ‖ were vp against them, they cast earth vpon
their heads, and made supplication to him that had stablished
his people for euer, and who alwayes helpeth his portion with
manifestation of his presence.

‖ *Or, were ioyned to them.*

16 So at the commandement of the captaine, they remooued
straightwayes from thence, and came neere vnto them, at the
towne of Dessaro.
17 Now Simon, Iudas brother, had ioyned battell with
Nicanor, but was somewhat discomfited, through the suddaine silence of his enemies.
18 Neuerthelesse Nicanor hearing of the manlinesse of them
that were with Iudas, and the courageousnes that they had
to fight for their countrey, durst not try the matter by the sword.
19 Wherefore he sent Posidonius, and Theodotus, &
Mattathias to make peace.
20 So when they had taken long aduisement thereupon,
and the captaine had made ye multitude acquainted therewith, and it appeared that they were all of one minde, they
consented to the couenants,
21 And appointed a day to meet in together by themselues, &
when the day came, and stooles were set for either of them,
22 Iudas placed armed men ready in conuenient places, lest
some treachery should bee suddenly practised by the enemies;
so they made a peaceable cōference.

23 Now Nicanor abode in Ierusalem, and did no hurt, but
sent away the people that came flocking vnto him.
24 And hee would not willingly haue Iudas out of his sight:
for hee loued the man from his heart.
25 He praied him also to take a wife, and to beget children:
so he maried, was quiet, and ‖tooke part of this life. ‖ *Or, liued together with him.*
26 But Alcimus perceiuing the loue that was betwixt
them, and considering the couenants that were made, came
to Demetrius, and tolde him that Nicanor was not well
affected towards the state, for that he had ordained Iudas,
a traitor to his realme, to be the kings successour.
27 Then the king being in a rage, and prouoked with the
accusations of the most wicked man, wrote to Nicanor,
signifying that he was much displeased with the couenants,
and commaunding him that hee should send Maccabeus
prisoner in all haste vnto Antioch.
28 When this came to Nicanors hearing, he was much
cōfounded in himselfe, and tooke it grieuously, that hee
should make voyd the articles which were agreed vpon,
the man being in no fault.
29 But because there was no dealing against the king, hee
watched his time to accomplish this thing by pollicie.
30 Notwithstāding when Maccabeus saw that Nicanor
began to bee churlish vnto him, and that he entreated him
more roughly then he was wont, perceiuing ỳ such sowre
behauiour came not of good, hee gathered together not a
few of his men, and withdrew himselfe frō Nicanor.
31 But the other knowing that he was notably preuented
by Iudas policie, came into the great and holy Temple, and
commanded the Priestes that were offering their vsual sacrifices, to deliuer him ỳ man.
32 And whē they sware that they could not tel where ỳ
man was, whō he sought,
33 Hee stretched out his right hand toward the Temple, &
made an oath in this maner: If you wil not deliuer me Iudas
as a †prisoner, I will lay this Temple of God euen with the † *Greeke, bound.*
ground, and I will breake downe the Altar, and erect a notable
temple vnto Bacchus.
34 After these words he departed; then the Priests lift vp
their handes towards heauen, & besought him ỳ was euer a
defēder of their nation, saying in this maner:
35 Thou, O Lord of all things, who hast neede of nothing,
wast pleased that the Temple of thine habitation should be
among vs. 36 There-

36 Therefore now, O holy Lord of all holinesse, keepe this
house euer vndefiled, which lately was cleansed, and stop
euery vnrighteous mouth.
37 Now was there accused vnto Nicanor, one Razis, one of
the Elders of Ierusalem, a louer of his countrey men, and a
man of very good report, who for his kindnesse was called
a father of yͤ Iewes.
38 For in the former times, when they mingled not themselues with the Gentiles, he had bin accused of Iudaisme,
and did boldly ieopard his body and life with al vehemency
for the religion of yͤ Iewes.
39 So Nicanor willing to declare the hate that he bare vnto
the Iewes, sent aboue fiue hũdred men of war to take him.
40 For he thought by taking him to do [the Iewes] much
hurt.
41 Now when the multitude would haue taken the towre,
and violently broken into the vtter doore, and bade that fire
should be brought to burne it, he being ready to be taken on
euery side, fell vpon his sword,
42 Chusing rather to die manfully, then to come into the
hands of the wicked to be abused otherwise then beseemed
his noble birth.
43 But missing his stroke through haste, the multitude also
rushing within the doores, he ran boldly vp to the wall, and
cast himselfe downe manfully among the thickest of them.
44 But they quickly giuing backe, and a space being made,
he fell downe into the midst of the void place.
45 Neuerthelesse while there was yet breath within him,
being inflamed with anger, he rose vp, and though his blood
gushed out like spouts of water, and his wounds were grieuous,
yet hee ranne through the midst of the throng, and standing
vpon a steepe rocke,
46 When as his blood was now quite gone, hee pluckt out
his bowels, & taking them in both his hands, hee cast them
vpon the throng, and calling vpon the Lord of life and spirit
to restore him those againe, he thus died.

CHAP. XV.

5 Nicanors blasphemie. 8 Iudas incourageth his men by his dreame
28 Nicanor is slaine.

BVt Nicanor hearing that Iudas and his company were in
the strong places about Samaria, resolued without any
danger to set vpon them on yͤ sabbath day.

2 Neuertheles, the Iewes that were compelled to go with
him, said, O destroy not so cruelly and barbarously, but
giue honour to that day, which he that seeth all things,
hath honoured with holinesse aboue [other dayes.]
3 Then this most vngracious wretch demanded, if there
were a mightie one in heauen that had commanded the
Sabbath day to be kept.
4 And when they said, There is in heauen a liuing Lord,
and mightie, who commanded the seuenth day to be kept,
5 Then said the other, And I also am mightie vpon earth,
& I cōmand to take armes, and to do the kings busines: yet
he obteined not to haue his wicked wil done.
6 So Nicanor in exceeding pride and haughtinesse, determined to set vp a publike moument of his victorie ouer
Iudas, and them that were with him.
7 But Maccabeus had euer sure confidence that the Lord
would helpe him.
8 Wherfore he exhorted his people not to feare the comming
of the heathen against them, but to remember the helpe which
in former times they had receiued from heauen, and now to
expect the victory, and aid which should come vnto them
from the Almightie.
9 And so comforting them out of the law, and the prophets,
and withall putting them in mind of the battels that they won
afore, he made them more cheerefull.
10 And when he had stirred vp their minds, he gaue them
their charge, shewing them therewithall the falshood of the
heathen, and the breach of othes.
11 Thus he armed euery one of them not so much with
defence of shields and speares, as with comfortable and good
words: and besides that, he tolde them a dreame worthy to
be beleeued, as if it had bin so indeed, which did not a litle
reioyce them.
12 And this was his vision: that Onias, who had bin high
Priest, a vertuous, and a good man, reuerend in conuersation,
gentle in condition, well spoken also, and exercised from a
child in all points of vertue, holding vp his hands, prayed
for the whole bodie of the Iewes.
13 This done, in like maner there appeared a man with
gray haires, & exceeding glorious, who was of a wonderfull
and excellent maiestie.
14 Then Onias answered, saying, This is a louer of the
brethren, who prayeth much for the people, and for the holy
citie,

citie, (to wit) Ieremias ye prophet of God.
15 Whereupon Ieremias, holding forth his right hand, gaue
to Iudas a sword of gold, and in giuing it spake thus:
16 Take this holy sword a gift from God, with the which
thou shalt wound the aduersaries.
17 Thus being well comforted by the words of Iudas, which
were very good, and able to stirre them vp to valour, and to
encourage the hearts of the yong men, they determined not
to pitch campe, but couragiously to set vpon them, and manfully to trie the matter by conflict, because the citie, and the
Sanctuarie, and the Temple were in danger.
18 For the care that they tooke for their wiues, and their
children, their brethren, and kinsfolkes, was in least account
with them: but the greatest, and principall feare, was for the
holy Temple.
19 Also they that were in the citie, tooke not the least care,
being troubled for the conflict abroad.
20 And now when as all looked what should bee ye triall,
& the enemies were already come neere, and the armie was
set in aray, and the beasts conueniently placed, and the
horsemen set in wings:
21 Maccabeus seeing the comming of the multitude, and
the diuers preparations of armour, and the fiercenesse of the
beasts, stretched out his hands towards heauen, and called
vpon the Lord, that worketh wonders, knowing that victorie
commeth not by armes, but euen as it seemeth good to him,
he giueth it to such as are worthy:
22 Therefore in his prayer he said after this maner: O Lord,
thou diddest send thine Angel in the time of Ezekias king of
Iudea, and diddest slay in the host of Sennacherib, an hundred,
fourescore, and fiue thousand.
23 Wherfore now also O Lord of heauen, send a good Angel
before vs, for a feare, and dread vnto them.
24 And through the might of thine arme, let those bee
stricken with terror, that come against thy holy people to
blaspheme. And he ended thus.
25 Then Nicanor, and they that were with him came
forward with trumpets, and songs.
26 But Iudas, and his company encountred the enemies
with inuocation, and prayer.
27 So that fighting with their hands,

The end of

and praying vnto God with their hearts, they slew no lesse then thirty and fiue thousand men: for through the appearance of God, they were greatly cheered.

28 Now when the battell was done, returning againe with ioy, they knew that Nicanor lay dead in his harnesse.

29 Then they made a great shout, and a noise, praising the Almighty in their owne language:

30 And Iudas, who was euer the chiefe defender of the citizens both in body, and minde, and who continued his loue towards his countrymen all his life, commanded to strike off Nicanors head, and his hand, with his shoulder, & bring them to Ierusalem.

31 So when he was there, and had called them of his nation together, and set the priests before the altar, he sent for them that were of the Towre,

32 And shewed them vile Nicanors head, and the hand of that blasphemer, which with proud brags he had stretched out against the holy Temple of the Almightie.

33 And when he had cut out the tongue of that vngodly Nicanor, he commanded that they should giue it by pieces vnto the foules, and hang vp the reward of his madnesse before the Temple.

34 So euery man praised towards the heauen the glorious Lord, saying, Blessed be hee that hath kept his owne place vndefiled.

35 He hanged also Nicanors head vpon the Towre, an euident, and manifest signe vnto all, of the helpe of the Lord.

36 And they ordained all with a common decree, in no case to let that day passe without solemnitie: but to celebrate the thirteenth day of the twelfth moneth, which in the Syrian tongue is called Adar, the day before Mardocheus day.

37 Thus went it with Nicanor, and from that time forth, the Hebrewes had the citie in their power: and heere will I make an end.

38 And if I haue done well, and as is fitting the story, it is that which I desired: but if slenderly, and meanly, it is that which I could attaine vnto.

39 For as it is hurtfull to drinke wine, or water alone; & as wine mingled with water is pleasant, and delighteth the tast: euen so speech finely framed, delighteth the eares of them that read the storie. And heere shall be an end.

END OF VOLUME IV

Cambridge:
PRINTED BY JOHN CLAY, M.A.
AT THE UNIVERSITY PRESS.

Lightning Source UK Ltd.
Milton Keynes UK
UKHW021524121219
355262UK00005B/1167/P